HADFIELD'S BRITISH CANALS

THE INLAND WATERWAYS OF BRITAIN AND IRELAND

EIGHTH EDITION

FULLY REVISED BY

JOSEPH BOUGHEY

SUTTON PUBLISHING

First edition published in 1950 by Phoenix House

First published in this revised edition in the United Kingdom in 1994 by Alan Sutton Publishing Limited, an imprint of Sutton Publishing Limited
Phoenix Mill · Thrupp · Stroud · Gloucestershire GL5 2BU

This edition reprinted with corrections in 1998

British Library Cataloguing-in-Publication Data

A catalogue record for this book is available from the British Library.

ISBN 0-7509-1840-3

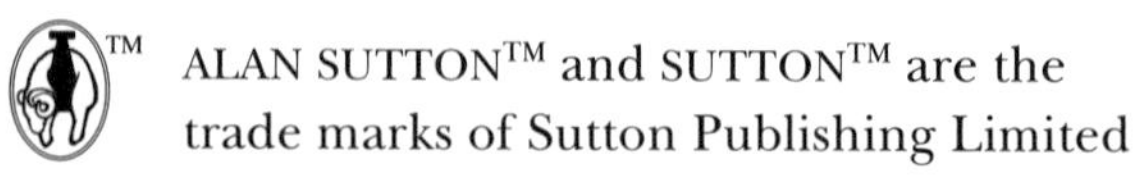

Typeset in Baskerville 10/13 pt.
Typesetting and origination by
Sutton Publishing Limited.
Printed in Great Britain by
WBC Limited, Bridgend, Mid-Glamorgan.

Contents

List of Maps

Preface to the Eighth Edition

In my Preface to the seventh edition, published in 1984, I wrote:

> Half a mile from my Devon school there ran the Grand Western Canal. Occasionally a boat laden with stone passed along it, but its main use was for fishing and bathing and for walks along its towpath for courting couples. One day in 1925 I mentioned the canal to a local solicitor, and was told of a box of old papers in his office. There were annual accounts, engineers' reports, Acts of Parliament and shareholders' registers of a hundred or more years before.
>
> So I became interested in the history of one canal, and from the Grand Western set myself to find others. I experienced the delight of discovering for myself a piece of the past and its life, in old documents and maps, and by tramping, clutching an Ordnance map, along towpaths, down lanes and through fields in search of some long disused wharf, lock or inclined plane.
>
> I produced my first article on canal history in 1942, my first (shared) canal book in 1945, and in 1950 the first edition of *British Canals*. Twice rewritten and reset since then, it now appears once more, corrected here and there, its final chapter and that on the Manchester Ship Canal brought up to late 1983, and with a rewritten bibliography. My thanks, going back to 1950, are due to so many who have helped and taught me over the years, that most cannot possibly be named here. I must, however, mention the late David Higham, the literary agent who (with some difficulty) placed the original manuscript, and whose firm still looks after my books, the late John Baker of Phoenix House who published the first two editions, and David Thomas of my old firm of David & Charles who has brought out five more editions as well as a range of my other books . . .
>
> Happily, I have been blessed with a sense that history is continuous, that what is past, what is happening now, and what is likely (or can be influenced) to happen in the future form one pattern. I have therefore been fortunate in being from the 1940s actively associated not only with archivists, librarians, historians, authors and industrial archaeologists, but with very many of those, then and later, active in the

British waterways world, whether policy-makers, administrators, canal staff or enthusiasts. . . . happy is the man who writes history while also living it.

I owe three special debts. One to my wife who, standing at the gas-stove in 1948, approved the first-drafted paragraphs of *British Canals*, and who, unwearied, has encouraged me to produce this seventh edition. One to canals themselves, at first in the British Isles, more recently throughout the Old and New Worlds, which have since 1925 been my companions. Lastly, one to the book itself, once a risk obstinately undertaken, continuingly a friend, a responsibility and a chore, now a milestone in my seventy-fifth year. I owe it affection for the absorption in research and the discipline of writing it has brought me, the waterways it has shown me, the friends I have made and the readers I gave gained during our long relationship.

I was proud of those seven editions, and grateful to those who bought and read them, but I then decided *British Canals* needed to be completely and radically revised by a fresh mind and younger head. I was fortunate to find Joseph Boughey to whom to transfer my old friend. He is therefore, with my best wishes, entirely responsible for this eighth edition. May good fortune attend it.

Charles Hadfield

My interest in inland waterways began in the summer of 1963, when my father hired *Kingfisher* from Ernest Thomas at Gailey, in Staffordshire, for a slow fortnight's journey to Ellesmere and back. Even to a small boy it soon became clear that the waterways that we were exploring were rapidly changing, and indeed might disappear altogether. I soon became interested in finding out about waterways in the past as well as in the present, and acquired a copy of *British Canals*; I still have a somewhat battered copy of the 1962 edition.

The mid-1960s was a good time to begin a lifelong interest in waterways history; most of the volumes in the 'Canals of the British Isles' series were appearing, and many histories of individual waterways and various aspects of waterways history followed. There must have been many others whose curiosity was aroused by this growing literature, much of it inspired by Charles Hadfield's work, and who would go on to explore further details in the field, in archives and in the collection of oral reminiscences. No history is ever finally complete, however, and there remains a great deal of material (some now rapidly disappearing) for students, whether professional or amateur, to record, collate, interpret and present.

I should explain why *Hadfield's British Canals* differs from the editions of *British Canals* authored by Charles Hadfield. My general brief was both to reduce the length of the earlier text and to enlarge the coverage of the twentieth century, as well as to incorporate further details about the waterways of Ireland, so that this book now introduces the history of all the waterways of the British Isles. The earlier editions involved extensive written coverage of waterways in southern England, and I have attempted to alter the balance by the inclusion of most of the new illustrations from outside that area.

The coverage of the postwar period was achieved in a series of stages after the first edition, and I have almost entirely rewritten this account in two new chapters. For the remainder, new material has been inserted and older material reduced, while some sections have been amended to reflect new developments in history; in the case of Thomas Telford, these new perspectives were initiated by Charles Hadfield himself. I should stress that all amendments, rewriting and new material are my own responsibility, and that only I can be blamed for any errors that may have crept in!

While many have assisted me, I would detail five specific and diverse debts here. My mother, Joan, and my late father, Joseph, encouraged me to explore waterways and their history, although they had many other interests. Dr Peter Morgan, now Director of the School of the Built Environment, first encouraged me to engage in research into the built environment, and more recently ensured the backing of university resources for this book. Charles Hadfield placed enough confidence in me to request that I should take over his first major book and rewrite it without preconditions, and he has constantly encouraged progress. My wife, Brenda, has borne 'canal widowhood' and over a decade of marriage to a workaholic; her love and support cannot be overstated. Finally, no historians could operate without the assistance of archivists and librarians, those public servants whose commitment and patience so often goes unrecorded.

Joseph Boughey

Note and Acknowledgements

Some waterways have been through so many changes of ownership and name that it has been difficult to describe them exactly. I have, therefore, tended to retain within the *text* the contemporary names used at each historical period, while deferring towards more modern names in the *illustrations*. I have diverged from names recognizable in modern times only in the case of the entirely unhistorical 'Montgomery Canal'.

In the later chapters I have tended towards abbreviations for recurring titles and names: 'BTC' is much more readable than 'Docks and Inland Waterways Board of Management of the British Transport Commission', which was the controlling body for many British waterways between 1953 and 1955!

I have converted pre-1971 British currency to post-1971 equivalents; of course, inflation has removed any real comparability from these. I have resisted the temptation to metricate measurements, since this is largely a work of history; the only exception to this is the reproduction of statistics of tonnages which are now recorded in metric tonnes. In the interests of uniformity, I have used converted statistics which do not treat a multiple chambered lock in Ireland as a single lock; thus the 41 locks on the Grand Canal represent thirty-six sites with changes of level.

Beyond the diverse people mentioned in the preface, many others have assisted in the process of re-writing this book. Mr Paul Hodgkinson redrew many of the original maps at unconscionably short notice, while Mr Richard Dean provided a new one and updated ones provided for earlier editions.

Most of the historical photographs come from four sources. Exceptional assistance was provided by Mr Terence Reeves-Smyth, of the Department of the Environment for Northern Ireland, which holds the McCutcheon Collection; Mr Roy Jamieson of British Waterways at Gloucester, who allowed me to examine the entire photographic collection there; Mr Lynn Doylerush and Mr Tony Hirst of the Boat Museum at Ellesmere Port (as ever); and Ms Leonie Brennan of the Guinness Museum, who traced some obscure items.

For permission to use illustrations (and their supply in most cases) I must thank Mr L.A. Edwards, Dr Ian Bath, the National Library of Ireland, and the Office of Public Works. I have been unable to trace K.C. Ward, whose photographs are included in the Ware Collection.

Many people have helped with information and comment, and while these are too many to list, it would be invidious not to acknowledge the exceptional assistance of Mrs Ruth Heard (who writes as Ruth Delany, Ireland's principal canal historian). She has forwarded literature and photographs, answered numerous queries and provided much helpful advice; the enlarged coverage of Irish waterways would not have been possible without her assistance.

CHAPTER ONE

The Old Days

On a summer day the motor cruisers rise in Boulter's lock on the surge of water from the gates, till they are released to explore Cliveden Reach and the approach to Cookham. The pleasure craft, and the holiday-makers in them, seem to suit the river, as if it had been dredged and given locks for ease of holidaying. To our forefathers the River Thames, as seen sixty years ago from the Prospect of Whitby at Wapping or the Grapes at Limehouse, would have seemed more natural. The public houses were sandwiched between warehouses, while all around craft unloaded. Up and down the river moved ships, sailing barges or tugs with trains of lighters, seeking at wharves or moorings a place to feed the land with their cargoes.

In medieval times rivers were the veins of the body politic as well as economic. Serving as boundaries between states or shires, they were crossed by fords, which became the sites of towns, or by bridges, which were often points of battle. The people of that time depended on rivers for food, power and transport.

In our day fish are caught in the sea and brought to us by road; only the angler still thinks freshwater fish are important. But in earlier times, when sea fish were eaten only by those who lived on the sea coast, and when meat was obtainable only for part of the year, river fish played an important part in national life. Every abbey and great house had its fish pond, and across most rivers stretched fish weirs, usually made of stakes and nets or basketwork. A continuous war was fought between the owners of the fisheries and the barge masters, who needed an unimpeded passage, until the importance of freshwater fish lessened as meat became available all the year round, and as the transport of sea fish inland became practicable.

Rivers were also the most important source of power. Every stream had its mills, not only for grinding corn, but also for all of the other industrial processes of the time, such as fulling cloth or driving the hammers of ironworks. Placed down the bank wherever a head of water could be obtained, these mills were to be found on the tiny stream that ran through a village, or on the bigger river that was also used for navigation. An artificial cut was made from the river to bring the water at proper height to the waterwheel, and, in order to secure a supply of water in all seasons, the mill owner usually built a weir across the river to hold back the water and so form an artificial reservoir. If the river was navigable the centre of such a weir was made of planks held upright by cross-beams, or dropped into vertical slots, so that they could be removed when it was necessary to pass a barge, or it was fitted with a pair of swinging gates, or a single gate rising vertically. Different types of these weir openings were called staunches, flash-locks, watergates or half-locks. They did not disappear from the bigger rivers until the 1930s, one of the last in use being that at Cropthorne, on the Lower Avon Navigation. Their remains may be found on Bottisham Lode, a tributary of the River Cam, and elsewhere.

There was seldom a towing-path in those days, and the sailing barges that were common craft on rivers were towed by gangs of men, called bow hauliers, able to ford the side streams and scramble through obstructions better than horses whenever the sails could not be used. It was not unknown for them to damage the property of gentlemen or farmers on their way, or to steal 'Hennes, Geese, Duckes, Piggs, Swannes, Eggs, Woode and all other such Commodytyes'.[1] Going upstream on a river that was rarely dredged, and the waters of which were held back, since each miller needed to protect the supplies to his mill, if a barge went aground it was necessary to bargain with the owner of the next mill upstream for a flash – enough water to be released from the weir to raise the water level and so free the barge. Then when the barge reached the weir there was more bargaining before the miller would consent to open it, and so allow the levels of the river above and below to be equalized sufficiently for the barge to be hauled up against the flow by a winch. Alternatively, going downstream, the miller would be asked to provide a flash to carry the barge over the shallows below. It was reported of the river Lea in 1760 that

> the natural inconveniences of the River [are] made much worse by the practice of those who own the Mills, for tho Flashes from the Mill be in some places necessary, for which the Bargemen pay . . . for the most part the Millers by deepening and enlarging their bye streams that bring water to the Mill, draw off from the main River very much more than they need, that so they may sell the same water to the bargemen again and help those for money whom they have first themselves disabled. It is certain that some of the Mills do so command the streams, that they can lay a whole fleet of Barges on ground upon the adjoining sharps and help them off again upon Composition, and one Turnpike there is that lays the whole River dry.[2]

It was written later, but pertinently, that this practice 'brings on a considerable charge to the Barge-Owner, renders his Arrival at any given Place uncertain, and gives the Land Carriage the greatest Advantage over that of the River Navigation.'[3]

The records are full of quarrels between the two interests, over excessive charges, refusals to give a flash, fights and stratagems. In medieval times, but dying away later, are records of similar efforts to do away with the fish weirs.

Transport and power are essentials in any expanding economy. Progress in agriculture and industry soon exert pressure on sources of power and transport for similar improvements, and, if they are not forthcoming, progress is inhibited. Similarly, innovations in power or transport give opportunities to industry and agriculture, which may consolidate progress if they are taken; if they are not, the new development may prove to be unsuccessful. It is to the gradual correlation of improving transport with expanding industry that we can attribute the slow forward movement that became perceptible in Elizabeth I's reign, and which later gathered speed and, allied to improved means of power generation, became what was characterized as the Industrial Revolution. From a total of 4 million people in 1600 the population of England increased to over 7 million by 1750. Industry and mining slowly grew in output and variety, but their products could be moved in only three ways, by land, sea or river.

Land transport has always existed, of course, but, before the days of the road engineers of the later eighteenth century, roads were often so bad that waggons could not always be used, and much was carried on the backs of horses and mules. For instance, in the early eighteenth century the clay, coal and flints supplied to the Staffordshire Potteries, together with the distribution of finished goods, relied on packhorses. The cost of road transport was prohibitively expensive: one horse could draw around 2 tons on a level road and from 50 to 100 tons on a good waterway, depending on its size. Road transport was therefore often limited to short-distance carriage, for instance the transport of coal for a few miles around a colliery, or of goods to and from a river or the sea. Only where perishable or valuable goods were involved, where water transport would cause damage, or the cost and unreliability of water transit were increased by monopolies or delays, was road transport used over long distances. Waggon services in England and Wales eventually grew with the expansion of trade in the canal age, with many roads being turnpiked between 1750 and 1770.

Around the coasts, especially those of England and Wales, the ships of the coastal trade carried many of the goods that would nowadays be

A packhorse train. Over the terrain depicted, of course, only horses could be used prior to the development of motorized road transport. This and other drawings from Samuel Smiles's Lives of the Engineers *tend to overemphasize the advances made by civil engineers in the Industrial Revolution, but they are nevertheless reasonably accurate*

moved by road or rail. Vessels went up the estuaries in England to minor inland ports on the smaller rivers of, for example, East Anglia, or to the greater seaports like London, on the Thames, Bristol, on the Avon, and King's Lynn, on the Great Ouse. There goods were transhipped to smaller craft – keels, trows or Western barges – to be taken up river to smaller ports, such as the inland port of Bewdley on the Severn. From its warehouses the goods landed from Severn trows were distributed by packhorse and waggon to the countryside of Worcestershire, Staffordshire and Shropshire, and a returning flow was sent down river to the seaports and the West of England. The town was particularly helped in that its own boats were free of the tolls levied by other towns on the river, as a result of a grant of Edward IV after the Battle of Tewkesbury to the people of Bewdley.

Other natural waterways were adapted for navigation merely by the construction of landing-places. In some cases small boats were used to land the goods carried in larger craft directly on the waterside. Estuaries and lakes often represented a barrier that had to be crossed by ferries

Sand dredged from the estuary of the River Taw at Crow Point being landed on the Yeo at Barnstaple in summer 1993. This traffic has been continuous since at least the sixteenth century, before the canal age. The wharf buildings, somewhat ironically, date from the railway age, serving the Lynton & Barnstaple Railway, which closed in 1935. Small creeks like the Yeo (which once served Rawle Gammon & Baker, in the background) carried large quantities of local and seagoing traffic before, and indeed during, the canal age

where there were no bridges or fords. For lakes such as Windermere and Coniston in the Lake District, Llyn Padarn in North Wales and Lough Corrib in the west of Ireland, the water was not viewed as a barrier to trade but used as a means of transport. Estuarial or tidal waterways were navigated without recourse to the sea; for example, barges carried lead up the River Dee from the Flintshire mines to the leadworks at Chester. In other cases the river itself was the source of raw materials, such as sand and gravel dredged from its bed, which was then landed nearby.

The River Severn was the main water carrier in England. Apart from traffic upstream from the port of Bristol, and that originating from the industries and crafts carried on along its length, such as the saltworks of Droitwich, it transported great quantities of coal from the collieries of Broseley, Benthall and Barr in Shropshire. Of the two to three hundred thousand tons of coal carried on English rivers at the end of the seventeenth century, one hundred thousand were borne on the Severn to Shrewsbury, Bridgnorth, Bewdley, Worcester, Tewkesbury and Gloucester.

The Thames, too, was a distributing and trading river, spreading along its banks the goods and coal that flowed in to the port of London, and connecting towns such as Windsor, Reading and Oxford. Other notable waterways were the Lea, Trent, Tyne and Tees. In Scotland, Wales and coastal Ireland, where rivers tended to be fast-flowing, the sea was extensively used for navigation and few rivers could be used far inland, although in Scotland the Clyde played its part in the growth of Glasgow.

On the other side of England, Cambridge had from the earliest times been a centre for the distribution of goods brought by water from King's Lynn, sending corn and other produce downstream. The great Stourbridge Fair was maintained largely by waterway trade.

The waterways of the Fens were in a special position. They were, indeed, the highways of their country, carrying goods from overseas and from coastal ports up the Great Ouse, Nene, Welland and Witham, and sending back the produce of the countryside; bringing into the Fens from the Barnack Quarries in Northamptonshire the stone to build the abbeys of Ramsey and Crowland, and the cathedrals of Peterborough, Ely and Lincoln; and carrying passengers and goods on their daily journeys about the fenland. The fourteenth-century records of Ely:

> show the sacrist and his fellows using the fenland waterways as their normal means of transport; whether it was to synods at Barnwell, or to buy cloth, wax, tallow, lead and other necessaries at Lynn and Boston, or merely to conduct their ordinary day-to-day business at Shippea, Quaveney, Littleport and elsewhere among the fens.[4]

The period before the reign of Elizabeth I was one in which much legislation was passed mainly to preserve or restore the navigation of rivers already naturally navigable; the period after her reign was taken up much more with attempts to make new navigable rivers. Beginning with the Lea in 1424, the Thames, Yorkshire Ouse, Kentish Stour and other rivers had been put under the care of corporations or other bodies charged with maintaining the navigation. Meanwhile Acts of Parliament had been passed to authorize the removal of fisheries and other obstructions from the biggest rivers, such as the Medway and Wye, the former without success. Any attempts to improve the navigation had to be made by bodies with powers to invade the rights of private property. Usually they were the corporations of cities like London, Gloucester and York, or Commissions of Sewers. The latter, set up by an Act of Henry VIII, comprised local landowners with rating powers who were concerned primarily with drainage and flood prevention rather than with navigation.

When emphasis fell on making navigable rivers that had not formerly been so, the usual practice was to grant letters patent to one or more people who undertook to make the navigation. For instance, in 1634 such authority was granted to Thomas Skipwith to make the River Soar navigable. In other cases trustees were appointed or powers were given to a company. Those involved were given powers to collect tolls from all who used the improved navigation, and sometimes the exclusive right to carry goods on it.

In Elizabeth I's reign the pound-lock, already in use on the Continent, was introduced into England. This invention made possible the improvement of river navigation far beyond the level achieved simply by dredging and the removal of obstructions. It created so great an economy in the use of water compared with the old flash-lock that sometimes a compromise with the millers became possible. The pound-lock, used on rivers and canals to alter the level of navigable water, was described by a Victorian civil engineer as

> a chamber, placed at the junction of two reaches, in which the water can be raised or lowered so as to be on a level with either the upper or lower reach. The lock-chamber is usually closed by a pair of gates at each end; it is filled by letting in water from the upper pool through sluices in the upper gates or side walls, and emptied by letting it out through similar sluices at the lower end. A vessel . . . can thus be easily raised or lowered to the level of the adjoining reach.[5]

If pound-locks were used to pass boats from one level of a river to another, weirs no longer needed to contain a central moveable portion, but could be made continuous. At the same time much water was saved, for only a lockful of water was used to pass a boat through a pound-lock, whereas a flash given to a barge might have meant lowering the whole stretch of river up to the next weir.

The first known examples of such pound-locks in Britain were not on a river, but on a canal born before its time. John Trew of Glamorgan, an otherwise unknown engineer, built three on the Exeter Canal between 1564 and 1566. They began also to be built on rivers – seemingly one on the River Lea and another on the River Trent in Elizabeth I's reign. Then in the seventeenth century they were constructed on the Thames between Iffley and Abingdon, the Warwickshire Avon, the Wey and elsewhere. Pound-locks were now included in improvement schemes, as with the six 'sluices' built on the Great Ouse between 1618 and 1625, along with the older 'staunches' (flash-locks), which continued to be used at lower toll charges.

Opposition to navigation improvements came from many quarters: those interested in road transport naturally disliked a cheaper competitor; landowners along the banks of rivers objected to the introduction of pound-locks because of the danger that their land might be flooded as a result of raising the water level, or that their water-meadows would not be flooded because of better flood control; farmers feared that the wider areas of trade opened up by improved transport would cause prices to fall, since, in times of scarcity, corn could be obtained from farther away by water. But the most sustained opposition to particular schemes came from those towns that acted as distributing centres for goods, and which saw themselves being supplanted. For example, Nottingham, high up on the navigation of the Trent, bitterly opposed the efforts of Derby to make the Derwent navigable, and so cause goods coming up the Trent for Derby to pass by Nottingham without transhipment; Reading opposed the making navigable of the Kennet to Newbury; Liverpool the passage by Mersey and Irwell to Manchester; while York feared that, if the rivers Aire and Calder were made navigable to Leeds and Wakefield, the textile workers of those parts would be given facilities to compete with the citizens of York. Lawyers were therefore engaged, petitions from interested groups sought and Members of Parliament approached for their support as battles took place over Parliamentary Bills on navigation.

The first serious attempts to drain the Fens were made in the first decades of the seventeenth century. Towns like Cambridge were afraid that the navigation of their rivers might be damaged. In 1630 an agreement, the Lynn Law, was made with the Duke of Bedford, the chief promoter of the drainage, to preserve the navigation of the 'Ouse, Grant, Nean, Welland and Glean'[6], and the port of King's Lynn.

Although successive regulations, to keep a minimum depth in the watercourses for navigation purposes, often conflicted with the drainage engineers' wishes to have as little water as practicable in them before possible floods, the rights of navigation were preserved in all legislation for the better drainage of the Fens, in spite of many disputes. There were major arguments over Denver Sluice, which was considered to cause the silting up of the channel below it, until it collapsed early in the eighteenth century.

Thereafter there were three main periods of activity in making rivers navigable. Before the first, from 1662 to 1665, following the restoration of Charles II, England had about 685 miles of river navigation, including the Thames, Severn, Trent, Yorkshire Ouse and Great Ouse. Of the Acts passed between 1662 and 1665, those covering the Worcestershire Stour and Salwarpe, the Wye and Lugg, Medway, Hampshire Avon and Itchen are important. On 2 March 1665 the Speaker of the House of Commons told the Lords:

> Cosmographers do agree that this Island is incomparably furnished with pleasant Rivers, like Veins in the Natural Body . . . Therefore we have prepared some Bills for making small Rivers navigable; a Thing that in other Countries hath been more experienced, and hath been found very advantageous; it easeth the People of the great Charge of Land Carriages; preserves the Highways, which are daily worn out with Waggons carrying excessive Burdens; it breeds up a Nursery of Watermen, which, upon Occasion, will prove good Seamen; and with much Facility maintain Intercourse and Communion between Cities and Countries.[7]

During this Restoration period some canal Bills were introduced, for instance to join the Thames to the Severn, which failed to pass. An interest in canals was expressed by Sir Robert Southwell when he read a paper to the newly formed Royal Society on the advantages of digging canals from the Midlands to supply London with coal.

In the second period of activity, after the peace of Ryswick and before the War of the Spanish Succession, from 1697 to 1700, Acts were passed for the Tone, Aire & Calder, upper Trent, Lark, Yorkshire Derwent and other rivers. In the third, from 1719 to 1721, river navigation was caught up in the boom associated with the South Sea Bubble, resulting in Acts for the Derbyshire Derwent, Douglas, Weaver, Mersey & Irwell, Bristol Avon and others. The 685 miles of navigation before 1660 had by 1724 reached 1,160 miles, although some navigation works were short-lived or ineffective. Apart from the mountainous areas, most of England was by then within 15 miles of a navigable river, and goods moved more freely, at less cost and often in new patterns. Before the Aire & Calder was made navigable, wool finished its journey to the Yorkshire manufacturers from east coast ports, or from Lincolnshire or Leicestershire, by road, while cloth from the Leeds and Wakefield markets also went by road to the nearest points on navigable rivers, Knottingley or Rawcliffe on the Aire, Selby on the Ouse or Tadcaster on the Wharfe. York, again, received much of its coal not from the West Riding mines only 20 miles from the city – from where it was brought by road transport – but from Newcastle, by keel down the Tyne, ship to the Humber and then up the Ouse in lighters – a distance of 200 miles. Sometimes difficult cargoes were handled, as when at Leominster,

> in 1756, the seven Bells were removed from the Tower, and taken to the Wharf on the Lugg . . . where they were placed on board a barge

The main navigable rivers of England and Wales, indicating navigation improvements up to 1727. The main coasting ports are also shown. Earlier editions of British Canals *reproduced two maps from T.S. Willan's* River Navigation in England, *indicating districts which were more than 15 miles from navigable waterway. This map attempts to replace the earlier maps, indicating a much more modest advance than the Willan maps suggested. Some navigations were short lived (such as the Lugg), while others varied in their condition and usefulness. It is noteworthy that it was the industrial centres in the English Midlands which were not served by water transport*

> and taken down the Lugg and Wye to Chepstow to be recast. The voyage was an adventurous one, for the Lugg Navigation Scheme carried out about that time (by erecting Flood Gates at intervals at a cost of several thousand pounds, instead of building proper Locks) was something of a failure . . . The Bells were brought back again, with some little difficulty, by water.[8]

Failures were frequent, and often three or four groups of undertakers would at different times attempt to make the same river navigable. Many were defeated by opposition from one interest or another, some by the rivers themselves: the Worcestershire Stour, through flooding, destroyed the work done between 1665 and 1667 to make it navigable to Stourbridge; and the newly built locks of the Calder & Hebble were ruined by floods in 1767 and 1768. Many plans failed also because of the lack of engineering knowledge at that time. As described in Chapter 2, it was the building of canals that largely created the profession of civil engineering by producing a demand sufficient to encourage the development of specialists, and levels of capital investment that necessitated the reliable and accurate estimating of costs, design and supervision of works. However, even after well-known engineers with much practical experience were available, the making navigable of rivers was always more difficult than the building of canals because there were more factors not under the control of the engineer. Such rivers as the Severn and the Trent were not made properly navigable until the canal age was over; others, like the Swale, never were.

Among the rivers that had successfully been made navigable were the Mersey and the Irwell. From Liverpool the River Mersey ran past Runcorn to Warrington and on to a point near Irlam, where it was joined by the River Irwell, on which Manchester stands. Before 1697 the Mersey had been made navigable as far as Warrington by clearing away the fish weirs, but it was in 1721 that an Act was passed to authorize a company of undertakers to make the river navigable as far as Manchester, which

> will be very beneficial to Trade, advantageous to the Poor, and convenient for the Carriage of Coals, Cannel, Stone, Timber, and other Goods, Wares and Merchandizes, to and from the Towns and Parts adjacent, and will very much tend to the Imploying and Increase of Watermen and Seamen, and be a Means to preserve the Highways.[9]

By 1734 the navigation was open, with eight locks between Manchester and Warrington taking flats, sailed if possible, otherwise towed. However, Manchester needed not only trade with Liverpool, but also a supply of coal, and in 1737 the company obtained an Act to make navigable the Worsley Brook, to carry coals from mines near Worsley down to the Irwell and so to Manchester. Although this scheme was never carried out, it was to have important consequences.

The Romans used the Fossdyke from the Witham at Lincoln to the Trent at Torksey as a navigation, but not, it is now thought, the Caerdyke onwards from the Witham to the Nene at Peterborough. Later the Fossdyke was dredged by Bishop Atwater in the reign of Henry I and was thenceforward used by boats. It is the oldest canal in the British Isles. In the twelfth or thirteenth century two short canals were built to carry the stone for building Rievaulx Abbey in Yorkshire, while in around 1490 Sir Andrew Wood is thought to have constructed a short private canal at Largo in Fife.

The Exeter Canal was built between 1564 and 1566, then considerably enlarged between 1698 and 1701. In about 1696 Sir Humphrey Mackworth built a short canal from the River Neath to the Melyn lead and copper works. The Wey Navigation of 1651–3 included some 9 miles of artificial cuts in its 15 mile length. The upper course of the Welland was bypassed by a 9½ mile cut, with 12 locks, known as the Stamford Canal, between Stamford and Market Deeping. While this was authorized in 1623, work did not begin before 1664 but was completed by 1673. This navigation would not prove a major success and traffic ceased in 1863. The first true canal in the British Isles, since the Exeter Canal had been reconstructed in 1701, was to be built in the north of Ireland, to link Lough Neagh and the port of Newry.

Ireland's lakes, linked to rivers such as the Bann, Erne and Shannon, were used for transport by small boats in the medieval period. Navigation along Lough Corrib was improved as early as 1178 by the construction of Friars' Cut, at the south end of the lake, by the friars of Claregalway Abbey. This improved access to the port of Galway, and in 1498 there was an unsuccessful attempt to link the lake westwards to the sea through Lough Athalia.

While there were schemes to link the main rivers in Ireland from the early seventeenth century, this had to await the end of fighting between William III and James II, after which there were moves to build inland navigations as a means of Irish economic development. Several proposals and Bills were considered by the Irish Parliament between 1697 and 1709 for improving the Shannon, Barrow, Boyne and Suir, and for building a canal from Newry to Lough Neagh. None was authorized. In 1715, however, an Act was passed to develop the midland counties of Ireland by drainage works and by making 'navigable and communicable passages for vessels of burthen to pass through'.[10] More far-sighted than practical, this

Act (and those of 1721 and 1729, which supplemented it) provided for local commissioners to appoint undertakers for the different works and to levy tolls. It also foreshadowed the later Grand Canal from Dublin to the Shannon.

Nothing resulted except for some work on the River Maigue and a disastrous attempt to canalize the Liffey. Work here concentrated on a length between Leixlip and Lucan. By 1723 the company involved had collapsed, despite an appeal for assistance from the Irish Parliament. The latter recognized that the failure of the Liffey scheme was stifling private investment in navigation schemes, and in 1729 it replaced the small local bodies of commissioners with four new ones, one for each province.

Dublin was expanding rapidly at that time, but it relied on coal imported from Britain, and Dublin merchants were interested in developing coalfields in east Tyrone, which could be served by way of Lough Neagh, a new canal to Newry and then the coastal route to Dublin. This interest, and the more centralized approach brought by the 1729 Act, combined to initiate work in 1731 on the Newry Canal. A third influence was Richard Castle, a French refugee who had studied Continental waterway engineering. He came to Ireland in 1728 to work for Edward Pearce, a Dublin architect, who, appointed Surveyor General in 1730, was much concerned in executing the 1729 Act.

Engineered at first by Pearce, then by Castle, and after his dismissal in 1736 by Thomas Steers of Liverpool, the Newry Canal was opened in March 1742, when it was reported from Dublin that 'the Cope of Loughneaghe, William Semple (commander), came into this harbour laden with coals and being the first vessel that has come through the new canal, she had a flag at her topmost head and fired guns as she came up the channel'.[10]

The Newry Canal was 18 miles long, some 45 ft wide and over 5 ft deep, with 14 short, wide locks, with stone chambers, timber floors and sizeable falls of 12 ft to 13½ ft. These locks rose to a summit level at Lough Shark, from which the canal drew its water supply. From the River Blackwater, across Lough Neagh from the Newry, work began in 1733 on another canal towards Coalisland, from where coal was to be brought by road from the Tyrone pits. However, sand, bog and silt held up work, and this 4⅜ mile long canal was not finished for nearly fifty years. This limited the traffic of the Newry Canal, as coal was brought to Lough Neagh by road rather than down the Coalisland Canal.

At first the new canal was used by sailing craft, which sailed across Lough Neagh, were horse-drawn along the canal and then hoisted sails to travel by sea to Dublin in the summer months. The latter practice was soon replaced by transhipment into lighters at Newry. Engineering

Lock 11 at Poyntzpass on the Newry Canal in the mid-1960s. While many of the structures on this canal were rebuilt after 1810, this gives an impression of the earliest major canal in the British Isles (McCutcheon collection)

problems on the Newry Canal soon became manifest, while the condition of the river approaching Newry was such that a new ship canal to bypass the existing route was authorized in 1755. After it was completed in 1769, seaborne traffic to Newry was more significant than that on the inland canal. Another waterway, the Lagan Navigation, was begun under an Act of 1753, also to reach Lough Neagh, so that Belfast could share in the hoped for development. Partly river, partly canal, the line, engineered by Thomas Omer, reached Sprucefield near Lisburn in 1765, when work stopped. It was not to be completed until 1794.

Thomas Steers, the Newry's main engineer, had been born as long ago as 1672 and had built Liverpool's first dock in 1715. He then engineered the Mersey & Irwell Navigation and part of the Douglas, and was also concerned with the Weaver, before taking on and completing the Newry Canal. While engaged in this project he began the Salthouse Dock at Liverpool in 1738, and in the following year became the town's mayor. Britain's first great navigation engineer, he died in 1750.

Steers's pupil, Henry Berry, built the first modern canal in England, the Sankey Brook, later called the St Helens Canal. The authorizing Act was passed in 1755, nominally to make navigable the little Sankey Brook from the Mersey near Sankey Bridges to St Helens. Berry, however, had probably already decided to build a canal instead. He agreed with the principal shareholder, John Ashton of Liverpool, that 'the work should commence on 5 September 1755, but the project was carefully concealed from the other proprietors, it being apprehended that so novel an undertaking would have met with their opposition.' [12] Most of the canal was opened in 1757, a further portion in 1759 and the whole original line into St Helens in 1772.

Henry Berry and John Ashton must receive their tribute, yet the credit for creating the heavy transport basis of the Industrial Revolution must go to the third Duke of Bridgewater, for it was his work that brought time and place and need together.

Water and coal underlay that revolution. The cotton mills that had been built to exploit the new inventions were driven by water power, and as the mills increased so they spread up the river valleys into the hills of Lancashire and Derbyshire. Industrial towns began to grow in the west, but the sea coal of the Tyne, which was carried to all of the rivers and creeks of the east coast, to London and the south coast, was not available to the west coast. The hearths of Manchester had to be warmed by coal carried on horseback or road waggon from local collieries, and was therefore expensive and scarce. Wood, the fuel of the village, was not available to the town. In these circumstances the Duke, who had travelled on the Continent and seen canals there (which must have long been known to engineers and travellers), and who must have been aware of the Sankey Brook already open not far away, decided to build a waterway to carry coal from his collieries. He obtained an Act in 1759 for a canal from Worsley to Salford, opposite Manchester, and from Worsley to Hollin Ferry on the Mersey below the Irwell junction.

It was probably then that the Duke was introduced by his land agent, John Gilbert, to James Brindley, then forty-three years old. The son of a crofter of the High Peak of Derbyshire, Brindley had been apprenticed to a millwright, a trade that covered many crafts other than the building and repair of mill machinery. Through the care he took to understand each piece of machinery he saw, he became more efficient than his master. He received a little education, and set himself up as a millwright at Leek in Staffordshire. There he gained a wide local reputation and, shortly before the Duke employed him, he had been experimenting with steam engines. Because of his knowledge of mills, including the water power that drove them, he had obtained employment in 1758 to survey a possible line for a canal from the Potteries to the Trent. This was being promoted by Lord Anson, Thomas Broade and Earl Gower, the Duke's brother-in-law, whose agent was John Gilbert's brother. It was in this way

Worsley on the Duke of Bridgewater's Canal, showing entrances to the underground colliery canals, which operated until about 1887. The boats are 'starvationers'. This drawing from Smiles is generally accurate, and the site can be recognized today

that the Duke met Brindley. He took to the careful, solid millwright and engaged him to help to build his canal under John Gilbert's supervision. Brindley made what he described as an 'ochilor survey or a ricconitoring', and it was decided to abandon the Salford line and to carry the canal over the Irwell on an aqueduct, and so into Manchester, probably to make a link with Cheshire easier than it would have been via the Worsley–Hollin Ferry Canal. A new Act was then obtained to vary the line. In spite of active opposition from the Mersey & Irwell Company, which now realized that the Duke's real object was to obtain access to

Liverpool in competition with themselves, Gilbert and Brindley were told to go ahead.

While the canal was being built it was a wonder to all. One writer said that, when finished, it 'will be the most extraordinary thing in the kingdom, if not in Europe. The boats in some places are to go underground, and in another place over a navigable river, without communicating with its waters . . .[13] A year later, in 1761, the canal was open to the outskirts of Manchester, and barges were passing over the 200 yd long aqueduct 38 ft above the Irwell. At Worsley a basin was built at the foot of a sandstone cliff, and from this tunnels ran into the mine so that coal could be loaded directly into small boats, ancestors of the later narrow boat. Eventually 46 miles of canal on four different levels were tunnelled through the mines, as the Duke's prosperity increased.

Coal and water had been brought together and had been fruitful. The lesson was to be quickly learned. Before moving on, however, let us share the memories of an old man looking back to his boyhood:

> I remember the delight with which I entered the Duke of Bridgewater's canal boat . . . I remember his dark brown coat with old buttons, the handsome rose of black ribbon which ornamented the tie of his hair, his placid but cheerful countenance, his manly and dignified form and carriage – they will never be forgotten . . . I can almost fancy I can still see the Duke, Lord Gower . . . and Mr Bradshaw [the canal superintendent], standing on the fore end of the vessel on a fine summer evening, enjoying the refreshing breezes excited by quick sailing.[14]

CHAPTER TWO

Building the Canals

The Duke's canal created the canal age that ended with the railway mania of the 1840s. When it began George II was on the throne, and only thirteen years had passed since Prince Charles had been beaten on Culloden Moor. When it ended Victoria was queen. In those eighty years what was termed the Industrial Revolution took place in Britain.

Before beginning the story of the development in transport that permitted the revolution, this and the following chapter will try to give a composite picture of the birth, growth and adult life of the canals in their prime, and of their circumstances.

The beginnings of canals in Britain (but not Ireland) were essentially local. They were usually projected by manufacturers or mine owners, like the pottery manufacturers led by Josiah Wedgwood who pushed the Trent & Mersey Canal idea past objectors and pessimists to its successful end, the ironmasters who promoted the Glamorganshire Canal, the copper mine owners of Devonshire who built the Tavistock Canal and the coalmasters behind the Barnsley Canal or the Dearne & Dove Canal. Sometimes those living and working in a town to which coal would be brought were the leading promoters, in association with the colliery owners. This was the case with the Shrewsbury, Coventry, Birmingham and many other canals. Sometimes the merchants of a small port hoped that canal development in the hinterland would not only develop their town, but also expand its export and import trade. These motives lay behind the Chester and Swansea canals. The arguments put forward in favour of a canal were basically that a waterway would bring raw materials to the factory, carry away the finished products and supply the people with coal more cheaply than land carriage. Thomas Telford listed the most useful purposes for canals:

> 1st, For conveying the produce of Mines to the Sea-shore. 2d, Conveying Fuel and Raw Materials to some Manufacturing Towns and Districts, and exporting the Manufactured Goods. 3d, Conveying Groceries and Merchant-goods for the Consumption of the District through which the Canal passes. 4th, Conveying Fuel for Domestic Purposes; Manure for the purposes of Agriculture; transporting the

produce of the Districts through which the Canal passes, to the different Markets; and promoting Agricultural Purposes in general.[1]

In those times each inland county in the British Isles was almost self-contained. Industrial works were built where raw materials were found, and sold their finished products in the near neighbourhood. Only along the banks of rivers and around the sea coast was it possible to move products in bulk. Therefore the idea of a canal that would allow trade to be opened up to a different part of the country, or even to a seaport, brought visions of prosperity to manufacturers. The cheapening of raw materials and the opportunities for the mass production of finished goods given by a widening of the market filled them with enthusiasm. This prospective improved market also tended to receive support from the ordinary consumer, since it tended to equalize supplies of coal and foodstuffs. The dangers of famine and the inconveniences of dearth were reduced, while almost every account of the opening of a canal refers to the reduction in the price of coal and the consequent benefit to the poor.

Since canals in Britain were local projects they had mostly to be financed locally. Only if solid advantages were promised could money be obtained for a canal that might take many years to build, during which time there would be no return unless interest was paid out of capital, and which locked money up in such a static and inconvertible asset as a waterway. It was local doggedness that finished canals like the Leeds & Liverpool, which took forty-six years to complete, and many others that took ten years or more.

Local capital was supplemented by regional funds, as in Wales, where ironmasters, merchants, bankers and landed gentry held shares in a number of companies. When Walter Jeffreys of Brecon died in 1815 he held a promissory note (convertible into shares) and seven shares in the Brecknock & Abergavenny Canal, three shares in the Glamorganshire, five in the Swansea, and ten in the Aberdare Canal, as well as shares in the Hay and Llanvihangel tramroads, both of which were connected to a canal. Birmingham and London investors spread their money widely but seldom thickly, and there are occasional oddities of investment such as the group of Leicester people who, during the canal mania, took shares in the Ellesmere Canal and even the Crinan Canal in Scotland.

As one would expect much capital came from colliery and works owners and merchants, and a good deal from noblemen, landed gentry and the wealthier clergy. Some came from tradesmen and professional people such as doctors and lawyers, while during the canal mania people who were involved in quite small businesses tried to get rich quick, like the four grocers, two coopers, the innholder, mealman, joiner, mercer and perukemaker of Stratford, all of whom subscribed to the Stratford-upon-Avon Canal.

It would be interesting to study the part that the unreformed municipal corporations played in the development of canals. They were concerned earlier with river development. Though they seldom took the principal part, as did Exeter in building the Exeter Canal, or Beverley in making Beverley Beck navigable, they sometimes helped to finance surveys, as Liverpool did for the Leeds & Liverpool Canal, and often subscribed for shares, as corporations in Nottingham, Chester, Carlisle and Swansea did for their local canals. In such cases the mayor or other representative of the corporation would sit on the committee.

The joint-stock company – one financed by the proceeds of shares sold to the public – goes back to before the South Sea Bubble of 1720. It was, however, the frenzy of financial speculation in the Bubble companies of the time that caused Parliament to pass an Act that made it necessary for anyone who intended to act as a corporation to be set up by Act of Parliament. The trouble and expense involved in getting a private Act each time that a company was formed meant that few came into existence in order to make rivers navigable.

When canals began to be built, however, their cost was clearly beyond the resources of all but a few wealthy men and partnerships, and thus joint-stock companies were necessary. Compulsory powers to buy land, divert streams, cross highways and so on also required an Act. The number of canal corporations therefore grew rapidly.

Many short branches were built privately without an Act but few bigger waterways were constructed because of the difficulty of buying land and getting water without compulsory powers. A notable branch built by a canal company without an Act was the Hatherton branch of the Staffordshire & Worcestershire Canal. Among private canals were included the Donnington Wood (Duke of Sutherland's) Canal in Shropshire, the Tennant Canal in Wales and the Torrington Canal in Devon.

The formation of a canal company followed a common sequence of events. First there was an advertisement in the local newspaper, which ran like the following example for the Leeds & Liverpool Canal:

> whereas such a navigation would be of great utility to trade, especially in time of war, and more particularly to the counties of York and Lancaster, a meeting would be held at the house of Mr John Day, known by the Sign of the Sun in Bradford aforesaid, on Wednesday, the 2nd day of July, 1766, at 10 of the clock in the forenoon, to consider of the proper ways and means to effect such navigation, at which meeting

> the nobility, gentry, and clergy of the said several counties, and all others who think it their duty to interest themselves in a matter of so great importance are requested to attend.[2]

Then followed the public meeting (often in the assembly room of an inn), which involved the election of a provisional committee; the subscription for preliminary expenses; the appointment of an engineer to survey and report on a route and give an estimate of the cost and probable receipts; the further meeting to receive the report; the resolution to apply to Parliament for an Act; the opening of a subscription book for shares and the payment of deposits; the organization of petitions to Parliament in favour of the project; the despatch by river interests, other canal companies, turnpike trustees, landowners, land carriers and anyone else aggrieved of counter petitions; the expensive battle before the Parliamentary committees of Lords and Commons, with a full array of counsel and witnesses, including eminent engineers; the various compromises such as clauses to pay compensation tolls, to limit dividends (on the Derby Canal dividends were limited to 8 per cent, after which money had to go to a reserve balance to reduce tolls), guarantees of another company's dividends (as of the Droitwich and Stourbridge canals by the Worcester & Birmingham), or of turnpike trustees against loss, as the Leicester Navigation had to do, and finally the Act, whereupon,

> on receiving the agreeable news that His Majesty had been at the House of Peers and signed the Bill for making the Navigable Canal from this Town (Birmingham) to Wolverhampton, the Bells were set to ringing, which were continued the whole Day.[3]

All of this cost a great deal of money and promotion expenses were a serious drain on capital.

Opposition to canals came from many sources. Landowners feared lest the waterway should be carried through their fertile low-lying lands and should drain their water-meadows. They also sought compensation for the inconvenience caused by a canal that might prevent them from enlarging a park, or which divided part of their property from the rest, and brought with it boatmen who did not always respect the game laws.

The local population, while understanding that canals could bring to them cheaply the fuel and goods that they needed, sometimes feared that local produce would be taken away. Cobbett spoke for this kind of opposition when he wrote of the canal at Cricklade:

> while the poor creatures that raise the wheat and the barley and the cheese and the mutton and the beef are living upon potatoes, an accursed *canal* comes kindly through the parish to convey away the wheat and all the good food to the tax-eaters and their attendants.[4]

Rural millowners feared loss of water from their streams to the canals and were supported by farmers who depended on the mills for the grinding of corn, while owners of industrial mills, driven, for instance, by the Pennine streams, fought bitterly against possible deprivation of their power resources. Road turnpike trustees thought that canals would reduce the tolls on their roads. Road carriers anticipated a loss of livelihood, an argument that they backed up with the accusation that a transport monopoly was being created, and that the reduced demand for horses would lessen the demand for oats and so hit the farmer. The coasting trade suspected a reduction in the amount of coal and goods carried by sea and the diversion of these goods to the more direct inland navigations. The existing river and canal interests did all they could to make sure that, if they were affected, they did not suffer. On the one hand they demanded compensation payments for loss of tolls, or the erection of physical bars to conserve their water; on the other they insisted on positive inducements, as when the Monmouthshire Canal offered the Brecknock & Abergavenny company £3,000 and ample water if the latter would join its line to the Monmouthshire, rather than build an independent outlet to the River Usk.

All in all there were some bitter arguments before the parliamentary committees. The following is a specimen, from the speech of the counsel for the Thames Commissioners opposing a proposed canal (the Hants & Berks Junction) to join the Kennet & Avon Canal at Newbury to the Basingstoke Canal near Old Basing, so as to avoid the passage of the Thames below Reading:

> Yet even if, which is impossible, water could be procured; and if, which is equally impossible, the repairs [to the Basingstoke Canal] required to an extent little short of beginning *de novo*, could be effected for the sum of ten thousand pounds, instead of ten times ten thousand, where is the money to come from? And what prospect is there of any return for it? Might it just as well be thrown into the sea; and much better thrown *literally* into the Basingstoke Canal, as in all probability there would not be water enough there to cover it? And what guarantee has this Committee that it ever will be forthcoming? The concern has long been bankrupt; its dividends are, as they have always been, naught. There is but one last lingering trader upon it, and he is on the point of

> flitting, lest his ruin should be consummated. From what quarter can a single ray of hope be expected to break in upon a scene of such utter desolation? This is not a rational project for improving an eligible line of Canal navigation, but is rather like many of those New World schemes, with unpronounceable names, which are so rife these days, distinguished by such a fatuous and headlong rage for speculation that, if any one were to start a Mining Company in Utopia, he could presently dispose of the shares at a profit.[5]

Sometimes the opposition was overwhelmed; sometimes it was persuaded, by conversion of the heart, lining of the pocket or the allotment of shares likely to appreciate quickly in value. For instance, a Bristol newspaper remarks of the opponents of the Kennet & Avon Bill:

> Those who went up to London to petition against it, are returned, and now are most laudably employed in pointing out its beneficial effects, and soliciting the assent of all their late demurring neighbours.[6]

Opposition overcome and the Act obtained, a first general assembly of the shareholders was held. At this a committee and officers were appointed: a clerk, who was probably the local solicitor, to take the minutes, write the important letters and do the legal work, with a full-time assistant paid by the company; an accountant, a treasurer, very likely a banking firm; a principal and a resident engineer; and usually also one or two assistants and a clerk of works. Land was bought and workmen engaged, and then with junketings the first sod was cut. On 26 July 1766, for instance, the population of Burslem and its neighbourhood took the day off to celebrate the beginning of work on the Trent & Mersey Canal. Everyone, from Lord Gower the Shropshire coal owner to the newest worker, put on their best clothes and gathered beneath the Brownhills. The leaders of the project made speeches. Mr Wedgwood cut the first sod and Mr Brindley, the engineer of the canal, wheeled it away in a barrow. Then

> a barrel of old Staffordshire ale was broached on the spot; the healths of Earl Gower, Lord Anson, Lord Gray, the county members, the Committee, and other officers were drunk; and Mr Wedgwood was specially thanked, in the name of the whole assembly, for his indefatigable services in this good cause. Succeeding to this were luncheons and dinners at the Leopard and other inns . . . A sheep was roasted whole for the benefit of the poorer potters, and at sunset bonfires were lighted in various parts of the town.[7]

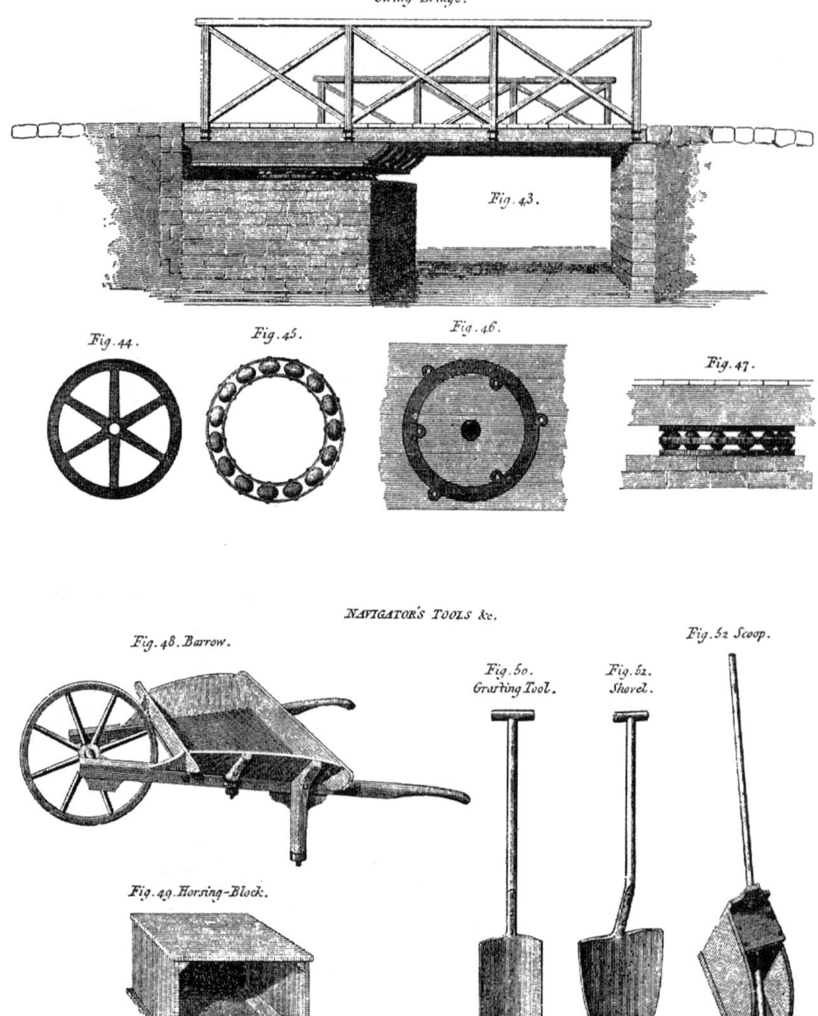

Some examples, from Rees' Cyclopedia *of 1819, depicting the construction process: designs for a swing bridge, and examples of the simple tools used to build the canals. Horsing-blocks were used to support the planks of barrow runs*

Then work began. Local brickworks were set up if suitable clay could be found, stone was brought from the quarries and timber was bought. Gangs of men began to dig with picks, shovels and barrows, occasionally with mechanical help such as that provided by John Carne's cutting

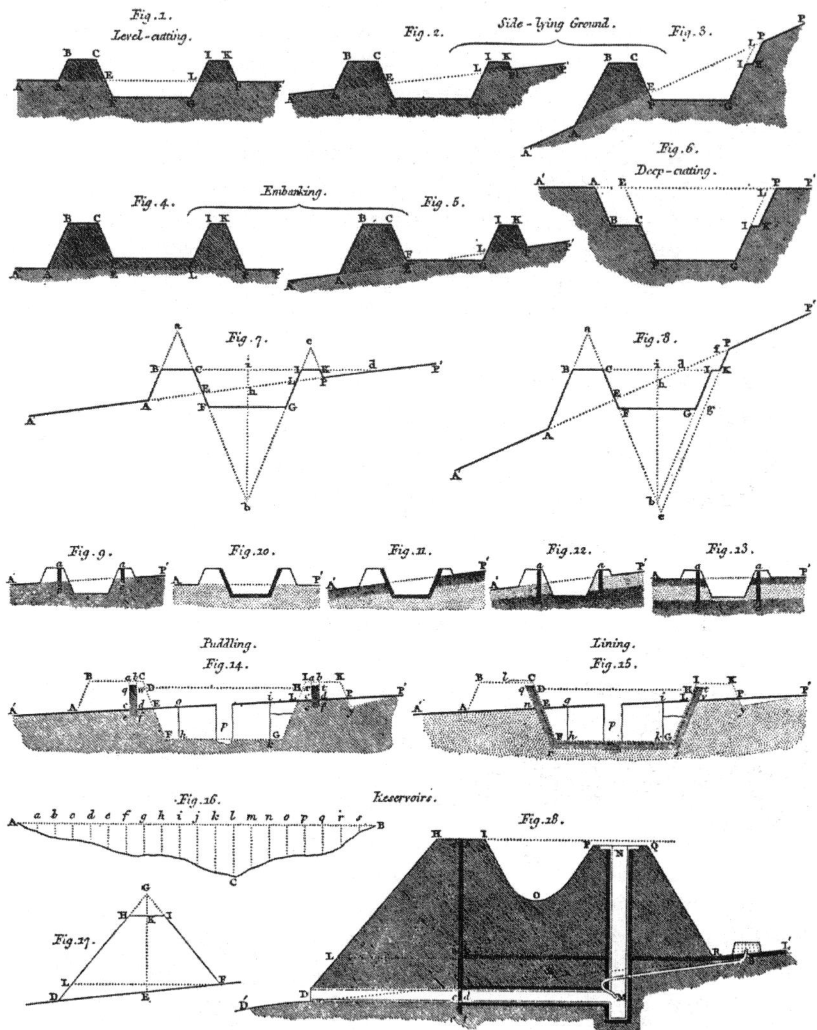

Varied profiles of canal construction from Rees' Cyclopedia. *The canal towpath is on the left in all of these examples*

machine on canals like the Herefordshire & Gloucestershire. Masons worked on the locks, shafts for the tunnels were sunk to the right depth from the ground above and the tunnels were dug inwards and outwards. This work was often carried out by miners, who set their charges of gunpowder by the light of candles. Water that percolated into the workings was drained off or removed by steam pumps. Ventilation was provided by lighting a fire under a shaft to provide an up draught, which in turn caused a down draught at other shafts.

The skilled workmen who dug the canal navigations – to use the older term – were called cutters or bankers, the unskilled being labourers. The word 'navigator' appeared in the 1770s with two meanings: 'canal boatman' and 'canal cutter'. Both meanings persisted, the first only used occasionally and the second common by the 1790s, though not until 1832, according to *The Shorter Oxford English Dictionary*, was it first shortened to 'navvy'. In England some of these cutters were labourers who had probably left the land because of the enclosure Acts; some were fenmen, used to digging and embanking drains; some were drawn from the vagrants who had been a Poor Law problem since the days of Elizabeth; and many were Scottish or Irish. As the construction gangs moved through the countryside they must have brought consternation to villagers who had not seen such uproar since the days of the English Civil War. They were rough men, and local newspapers and books carry stories of robbery and even murder. The following account records how the navvies working on the improvement of the River Witham under the Act of 1812 were caught up in a dispute with a local baker:

> the riot began on the west side of the river, at a public house with the sign of 'The Plough' – they drove the landlord away from the house, took out his barrels, and drank the beer; having taken his sign down, they also took the baker's basket and bread, and, crossing the river, proceeded up to the village of Bardney . . . They pelted the baker with his bread, and hung his basket on the top of a tree in the village; they then attacked the 'Bottle and Glass' public house – fetched the barrels of beer out of the house, knocked the ends out and drank the ale; Mr Benson, a person who was then the landlord of the 'Angel' Inn, to prevent them entering his premises, brought or rolled out his barrels of beer himself, and by this means saved himself and his house.
>
> During the time they invested the houses in Bardney, the people were so frightened that they gave them anything they asked for; the navvies went about to the inhabitants of the village demanding money and different articles from them, and proclaiming their own prices for provisions for the future . . .
>
> The constable of the village was called out, but he alone was of no use . . . thirteen constables were sent for from Horncastle, they also were useless, and had to go home again – one of them so much injured

that he died from the effects afterwards; the cavalry were then sent for, and came as soon as possible.[8]

The Riot Act was read, the cavalry restored order, and the rioters were taken off in three carts and a waggon for trial and imprisonment.

They had some excuse, for often they were not even paid their 2s. (10p) to 3s. (15p) a day in cash each week. Those working on the Kennet & Avon Canal in 1797, for instance, were paid in twenty-one-day notes, which they then had to have cashed at a discount, while in 1804 the tunnellers and cutters working directly for the canal company on the Grand Junction at Blisworth were paid monthly. A doctor was occasionally retained to look after them when they were injured or ill, as on the Liskeard & Looe Union Canal. More often, however, the men paid into a fund, as on the Peak Forest, to which the company also subscribed, and from which sickness payments were made.

There were more intellectual moments in their lives, such as that recorded by the Committee of the Gloucester & Berkeley Canal: 'Ordered, That Mr Wheeler pay the workmen who found the Coins £1-1-0 and that he count them over and deliver them to Mr Cheston, who has kindly offered to decypher them, and give his opinion of their value.'[9]

However, many references to them by the engineers ran as the following example, which refers to work on the Sapperton Tunnel: 'Rich[d] Jones . . . not in the work at 2 o'clock P.M. nor had been in the work this day. All his men a Drinking except 3 men in the Big Tunnel.'[10]

Now and then a few lines appeared in the local newspaper: 'Early on Saturday morning last, a little beyond Winson Green, in the Birmingham Canal Navigation, the Earth fell suddenly in and killed John Lester, one of the workmen, occasioned, it is thought, by the heavy Rains on Friday evening.'[11]

Just as later most of the railways were built by large contractors like Brassey, so were some of the canals. The extensive Pinkerton family worked on canals and navigations as widely spread as the Selby, Driffield, Barnsley, Erewash, Birmingham & Fazeley, Gloucester & Berkeley, Kidwelly & Llanelly and Basingstoke canals. Edward (later Sir Edward) Banks, himself or through the firm of Joliffe & Banks, built parts of the Leeds & Liverpool, Lancaster, Ulverston, Ashton-under-Lyne and Huddersfield canals, and also the Goole Canal of the Aire & Calder. Hugh McIntosh worked on the Croydon and Grand Western extension, and rebuilt much of the Aire & Calder. Most of the earlier canals, however, were built by local contractors, many of them leading groups of workmen formed for this purpose and often undertaking quite small sections. A few were built by direct labour, or finished by this means after the contractors had withdrawn.

Token issued by John Pinkerton to the workmen on the Basingstoke Canal. There was a serious shortage of coinage in the 1790s, and contractors had to issue their own. Some tokens, based on the truck system, could only be exchanged for goods supplied by the contractors, but those on the Basingstoke could be exchanged at a number of public houses, including the George at Odiham

A clerk of works or resident engineer, with his subordinates, was in charge of construction, while over him was the principal engineer who had laid out the line and was generally responsible for the work, though he might have had charge of building half a dozen major canals at the same time. The resident engineer in turn employed overlookers, for, as Robert Whitworth told the Ashby Canal shareholders in 1794, 'neither puddlers or masons ought to be left to themselves, even one Day, in some particular situations'.[12] He also hired checkers to count the men employed by the contractors, in order that 'subsist' money could be advanced by the company to the contractors until the work was periodically measured up and a progress payment made. Cutting went on to the accompaniment of bickering with the contractors over payment on account and accusations of bad work, and with the men over demands for a rise in pay or the loss of tools.

It was in the canal age that the profession of civil engineering came into being. John Smeaton (1724–92), the son of an attorney who began as a maker of scientific instruments, designed the Eddystone Lighthouse and supervised its construction up until 1759, prior to his involvement with waterways. One of the founders of the Society of Civil Engineers in 1771, he was probably the first to adopt what is recognized today as a professional approach to engineering work.

Other great names in engineering came from many origins and, because of their ability, these people had become expert in the new problems: Brindley learned his trade as a millwright; Rennie was a mechanically minded farmer's son; Telford a working mason; Jessop the son of a foreman shipwright; Outram the son of a 'gentleman'. Others learned from these men. Robert Whitworth senior and Thomas Dadford senior had been Brindley's assistants and in turn fathered engineers, while Hugh Henshall was Brindley's brother-in-law. Jessop had been Smeaton's pupil. Others again, such as Thomas Sheasby, began life as contractors.

It should be realized that in the period when most of the canals were surveyed the first Ordnance Survey map had not been issued – that did not appear until 1 January 1801, and it was not till 1844 that all of England south of a line from Hull to Preston had been mapped. No previous detailed survey of England had ever been made, so the engineer was dependent on local maps, which were probably inaccurate, and the special survey he carried out himself, which was later published for the encouragement of prospective subscribers. The engineers found themselves in greatest difficulty with geology. Even a careful survey, including trials of the ground over which the canal was to pass or through which tunnels were to be made, often failed to detect formations that were difficult to cope with; and not all surveys were careful. Many were sketchy, with the result that the engineer encountered construction difficulties that ran up the expenses. One of the founders of the study of geology, William Smith, surveyed the line of the Somersetshire Coal Canal.

Some engineers took on too much. Brindley early on found himself with half a dozen big schemes on his hands at once. He handled them by delegating as much responsibility as possible to his assistants, whom he installed as resident engineers on the Birmingham, Staffordshire & Worcestershire, Coventry and Oxford canals, while he gave most of his own time to the Duke's canal and the Trent & Mersey Canal. This view of his responsibilities did not commend itself to the businessmen of the Birmingham Canal, who observed 'that Mr Brindley hath frequently passed by, and sometimes come into town, without giving them an opportunity of meeting to confer with him upon the progress of the undertaking'. They expressed 'their dissatisfaction at not being able to see him at such times'.[13] A few months later the Coventry proprietors summarily dismissed him. All the same he probably died of overwork, combined with his diabetes and the nephritis he contracted at Ipstones while surveying for the Caldon branch of the Trent & Mersey Canal.

Brindley was primarily involved with narrow-boat canals. Of all those he worked on only the Bridgewater and Droitwich canals took barges, in

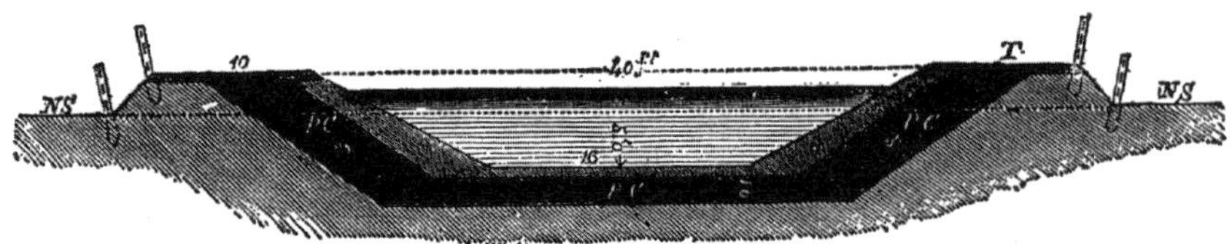

Puddling a canal, from Tomlinson's Cyclopedia of Useful Arts *of 1866. In porous ground the bed is given 18 in of puddle below, and 3 ft at the sides; in retentive soil, puddle is only needed at each side to prevent lateral leakage, which would weaken the banks*

A more modern canal profile, using metal piling to protect the banks. This length of canal is part of the Whitchurch Branch of the Shropshire Union canal, which was filled in during the early 1950s but re-excavated in 1993 in the first phase of a restoration programme

each case from a neighbouring river. Of his assistants, trained by having responsibility thrust on them, Thomas Dadford senior (and later his sons) and Samuel Simcock of the Oxford and Birmingham canals were also mainly narrow canal builders. A third, Robert Whitworth, did much of his best work on broad canals: the Thames & Severn, Leeds & Liverpool summit level, Forth & Clyde and Ashby de la Zouch.

Two other groups were more in the European tradition of bigger waterways. One was headed by John Smeaton, who had travelled abroad before basing himself in Yorkshire. He built much of the Calder & Hebble and the Forth & Clyde canals, and had as a pupil William Jessop,

England's greatest builder of broad waterways. Among these were much of the Aire & Calder of that time; the Barnsley, Rochdale, Trent Navigation, Nottingham, Cromford and Grand Junction canals. He only built one narrow canal, the Ellesmere, and then by accident, for when he was engaged the promoters intended it to be broad. Smeaton's and Jessop's school can justifiably claim John Rennie, builder of two great broad canals, the Lancaster and the Kennet & Avon; the two William Crosleys, first-class working engineers; and later George Leather, who made the Goole Canal and created the modern Aire & Calder. Telford, too, owed much to the Smeaton tradition. His first major canal work was as Jessop's resident engineer for many years on the Ellesmere; his second with Jessop to create, and alone to execute, the great Caledonian; and finally, paralleling in the Midlands what Leather was doing in Yorkshire, to build the new Birmingham main line and the Birmingham & Liverpool Junction Canal.

An Irish group of engineers also drew on experience in continental Europe. English engineers worked in Ireland, notably Steers, Jessop, Rennie and Chapman, but Ireland also had its own school: Richard Castle of French, Davis Ducart of Italian and Thomas Omer of Dutch descent; John Killaly, greatest of them all, John Brownrigg and Richard Evans.

One is struck by the engineering skill and resourcefulness that built Britain's canals. No tunnel of any size, other than mining tunnels, had ever been built in Britain before the building of the Harecastle and Norwood tunnels, each one over 1½ miles long. Aqueducts, embankments, cuttings, locks, inclined planes and canal lifts were designed and built as the need for them arose. To us they may seem small enough feats compared with the achievements of modern engineering, but to contemporaries they were a source of wonder. Josiah Wedgwood wrote of the flight of locks on the Duke of Bridgewater's Canal at Runcorn:

> I was quite astonish'd at the vastness of the plan and the greatness of stile in the execution. The Walls of the Locks are truly admirable, both for strength and beauty of workmanship. The front Lock next the sea (for such it seems when the Tide is in) in particular, whose walls are compos'd of vast stones from 1 to 12 Tons weight, & yet by the excellent machinery made use of, some of which is still left standing, they had as perfect command of these huge masses of Rock as a common bricklayer of the brick in his hands. In short, to behold Ten of these Locks all at a view . . . the whole seems to be the work of the Titans, rather than the production of our Pigmy race of beings . . .[14]

The engineer would ride from one end of the line under construction to the other, living in inns, working out problems by candlelight, and now and then getting involved in unpleasantness: when the engineer on the Leeds & Liverpool had to dismiss a contractor, the committee assured him that 'you will be supported in every proper measure, and that no sinister, envious or ilnatural insinuations will be listened to.'[15]

The general meeting of proprietors met once or twice a year to hear reports on progress, and sometimes to dine at the company's expense. Usually the Act provided that a certain number of shares had to be present in person or by proxy if a valid meeting was to be held, and meetings that had to be adjourned for lack of attendance were not uncommon. Affairs were managed by an executive committee, under which there might be one or two working committees to superintend construction: the Oxford Canal had three such district committees.

On the executive committee the chairman or some other moving spirit would keep an eye on the engineer and the spending of money, and would handle the negotiations for the purchase of land. Land acquisition was always a difficult procedure. The land was first valued by valuers employed by the company. If the landowner did not agree with this valuation the chairman or someone from the company tried to reach an agreement. If this failed the dispute was referred to a body of commissioners named in the Act, who were usually all of the landowners of the county over a certain landed income per annum, a quorum of whom had power to judge. Since landowners tended to favour their own kind, the scales were weighted against the canal companies and the obstructive usually got their price. It was therefore often the case that the land for a canal cost more than the estimates allowed for. A further right of appeal, from the commissioners to a jury, was seldom exercised, although in one case on the Leeds & Liverpool in Yorkshire the jury did reduce values put on land by the commissioners. Most rural land was bought at about thirty years' purchase, with special compensation when the line of canal cut house from farm or farm from road. This sum was increased when a great estate was affected. For example the Grand Junction paid £5,000 to Lord Clarendon for the right to pass through Grove Park, and another large sum to Lord Essex to pass through Cassiobury Park. Sometimes the severance of land was partly compensated for by the provision of accommodation bridges, often constructed in ornamental fashion where these cut through aristocratic estates.

Canal shares were usually in denominations of £100. A deposit was payable when the shares were first subscribed and then, as the canal was built, calls of so many pounds a share were made on the shareholders

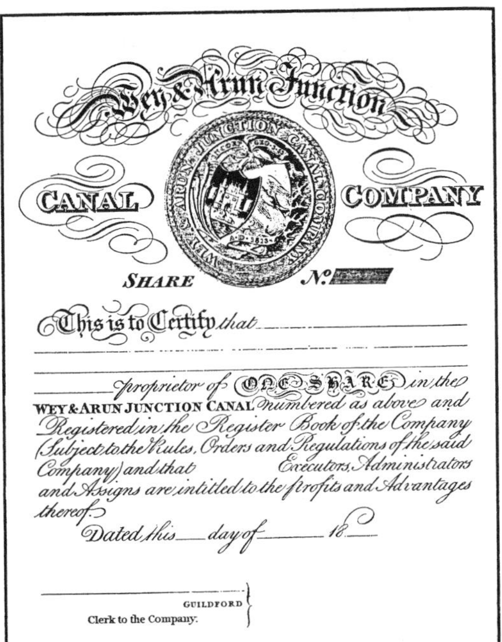

Wey & Arun Junction
CANAL COMPANY
SHARE No.
This is to Certify that ______
______ proprietor of ONE SHARE in the WEY & ARUN JUNCTION CANAL numbered as above and Registered in the Register Book of the Company (Subject to the Rules, Orders and Regulations of the said Company) and that ______ Executors, Administrators and Assigns are intitled to the profits and Advantages thereof.
Dated this ___ day of ______ 18__

______
GUILDFORD
Clerk to the Company.

A blank share certificate for the Wey & Arun Junction canal, authorized in 1815. This illustration was printed from original blocks discovered by Charles Hadfield before the first edition of British Canals

until the full amount had been paid. Procuring the money for these calls was not always easy. Even if everything was going well the shareholder always liked to hold on to his money for as long as possible in order to earn interest. For this reason payment of interest out of capital was usually made on the calls paid up while work was in progress. If the canal was in difficulties, and it was clear that it would cost more and therefore earn less on its capital than had been intended, the shareholder was even more reluctant to pay the calls, often preferring to forfeit his shares or risk litigation rather than put more money into a hopeless enterprise. On the other hand canal committees in such cases did everything they could to wheedle extra money out of their shareholders, for instance by sending their clerk to call personally on nervous proprietors. Many canals got into difficulties because of a clause in their Acts authorizing them to pay interest on capital during construction. If this was paid in cash it drained away the resources needed for building; if paid in bonds it created a debt that hampered the company afterwards.

Canal committees naturally turned for temporary accommodation to their banks and found, as have others, that bankers took a more gloomy view of the future than they did themselves. In April 1797 the Kennet & Avon's bankers refused to advance more money against unpaid calls 'on account of the pressure of the times',[16] but relented after making conditions which included slowing down expenditure on construction to the tempo of the calls made. In 1796 the Peak Forest committee, faced with an overdraft of £4,000, themselves guaranteed £1,000 of this sum and £4,000 more to complete the summit level and the tramroad at Marple that preceded the locks. In 1803 there was the curious case of the Glamorganshire Bank, which made the Swansea Canal a loan on condition of being appointed its treasurers. Finally there was always the danger of bank failure or embarrassment, which was awkward if partners in the bank were also members of the canal committee. For example in 1816 the Shrewsbury Canal switched from a failing Shrewsbury bank to one in Wellington; committee members were involved in both.

The original Act of Parliament always provided for the raising of an additional amount – usually a third as much again – should the original capital prove insufficient to finish the canal. This amount could be found in a number of different ways. On the one hand calls beyond the nominal amount of each share could be made on the original shares, or fresh shares could be issued, the latter perhaps at a discount, or auctioned. On the other hand some form of preference could be given to those who came to the rescue, either by the issue of preference shares or by bonds, convertible or not, annuities, promissory notes or mortgages, either of the tolls of the canal or of the waterway and tolls together. If the canal was later a success the interest payments and later repayments of capital on these prior charges only delayed the dividends on the ordinary shares. In some cases, however, the existence of the prior charges extinguished all hope for the ordinary shareholders, for these canals never succeeded in paying off their debts.

An instance of the removal of prior charges involved the Thames & Severn Canal. By 1808 this concern had accumulated a debt of £193,892, including a principal debt of £117,125 and arrears of interest. Since the company was not earning enough to pay the current interest on the debt, financial reconstruction was essential, and eventually the debt-holders agreed to a scheme (detailed in earlier editions of this book) by which the old shareholders gained a hope – and later the actuality – of dividends.

Government aid to industry has a long history. In 1784 the government lent £50,000 to the Forth & Clyde Canal Company and in 1799 it lent £25,000 to the Crinan Canal proprietors out of the repayments. In 1817 the Poor Employment Act set up Exchequer Bill Loan Commissioners with power to lend money to concerns that would employ the poor, especially unskilled labourers, to relieve the unemployment that had followed the end of the Napoleonic Wars. A number of canals were helped in this way. Some, like the Gloucester & Berkeley and the Regent's canals, were successes, and the money essential to finish the waterway was repaid. Some, like the Portsmouth & Arundel canal, were not. This company was unable to repay any of the £40,000 it had been lent, though fortunately the sum had been guaranteed by the Earl of Egremont.

In Ireland most inland waterways were financed and constructed with government support. Even those that were built by private companies, like the Royal Canal, depended on government loans, and this canal was only completed after the Directors General of Inland Navigation took over in 1813.

At last the canal would be completed (unless, like the Salisbury & Southampton and the Dorset & Somerset canals, the money that could possibly be raised was not enough to overcome all of the difficulties of finishing the line). Financial troubles would be forgotten, the water would be let in, boats bought, toll and lock-keepers and accounting staff appointed, security bonds arranged and plans made for the opening day.

The opening of a canal was an occasion for considerable jollification. Sometimes verse contributed to the event, as when Elizabeth Davies, who kept a lollipop shop in Wind Street, Neath, wrote a song of nineteen verses, of which two are given below, to commemorate the opening of the Neath & Swansea Junction (usually called the Tennant) Canal:

> O! could I make verses with humour and wit,
> George Tennant, Esquire's great genius to fit;
> From morn until even, I would sit down and tell;
> And sing in the praise of Neath Junction Canal.
>
> I hope when he's dead and laid in his grave,
> His soul will in heaven be eternally saved;
> It will then be recorded for ages to tell,
> Who was the great founder of Neath Junction Canal.[17]

The following extract from a contemporary newspaper account describes the opening in 1814 of the Thames & Medway Canal. This ill-fated venture was built to connect the Thames at Gravesend with the Medway at Strood opposite Rochester. Its tunnel, 2¼ miles long and the second longest canal tunnel built in Britain, is now used by railway passengers travelling from Strood to Higham:

> There were four barges occupied by the company, and there was a fifth barge, preceding such four barges, occupied with musicians . . . Previously to starting, Sir C. Flower stood up by the flag-staff, and

> exclaimed Success and prosperity to the Thames and Medway canal, with three times three. These were given with considerable effect. The most gratifying part of the view, however, was the entrance into the tunnel.
>
> Above the Higham entrance immense crowds of persons were assembled, Ladies, Naval and Military Officers; and Sir Charles Flower again gave the signal for huzzas, which were answered by the surrounding spectators. At the entrance of the Tunnel, the light of Frindsbury Arch at the end could be distinctly seen; and the effect was very curious. The towing-path was thronged with spectators, and the Canal-workers carried lighted torches . . .
>
> The barges, which occasionally paused in the tunnel, were about forty minutes in passing through it. On passing through Frindsbury outlet, there is a capacious basin, which forms the terminations of this canal. Around this basin there were great crowds of persons and several of His Majesty's boats, with Officers on board . . . The Officers greeted the company on their coming out of the tunnel most cordially, giving the signal for huzzas, and the band struck up 'Rule Britannia'. The Officers and others joined the procession on the landing, and proceeded to the Crown Inn, Rochester . . .

At the Crown Inn a dinner was provided for more than a hundred persons, with entertainment and a series of toasts. Among the latter the chairman

> spoke of the magnitude of the work which had been accomplished. There had been united two of the most valuable rivers in the kingdom, and two of the richest rivers of the world, and the importance of the work, he thought, could not well be too highly appreciated. The value of the works they could all understand. If any person's property or comforts had been disturbed, it was the subject of lamentation; and he could state that, if ample remuneration had not already been made, the Company would be happy to make the completest compensation.

Several other toasts followed at this celebration, and 'After the procession the workmen, to the amount of between two and three hundred, had a dinner at the Canal Tavern, &c.'[18]

CHAPTER THREE

Life on the Canals

The opening of a canal often had an astonishing effect on the development of the towns with which it was associated. Stourport was indeed created by the trade that followed the cutting of the Staffordshire & Worcestershire Canal. Again, the Lancaster Canal ended its northerly course at Kendal, and a local historian stresses that

> the spirit of improvement fully manifested itself in 1818 and 1819. The date of the new town may, we conceive, truly be placed here, at the time of the opening of the Lancaster and Kendal canal. This event gave an impulse to the public spirit of the inhabitants, and formed the commencement of a new era in the history of Kendal . . . The old Miller's Close Bridge, which had stood since 1743, and was very narrow, and ill adapted to be the general medium of intercourse with the canal, was now thrown down, and wholly rebuilt on a wider scale. The large warehouses and other buildings at the canal harbour, were all erected at this time; Kent Lane (which before was very steep, and so narrow that two carts could scarcely pass) was thrown open, and the ascent considerably diminished . . . in a very short time, the town assumed a new and modern appearance – so very different that any person having been absent a few years, could scarcely have identified it.[1]

In some places the canal company owned much land, and, when trade caused this to be developed, a large income accrued from rents, as with the Grand Junction Canal's property in Paddington.

Along the lines of the canal and at the basins great changes took place. Factories were built and wharves provided for them, often on side cuts. At the basins warehouses were built, and coal-wharves, sheds, cranes and weigh-houses provided. In Coventry the coal-wharves lay below the boats so that coal could be unloaded directly into carts. Offices were provided for the clerks, often in a specially built eighteenth-century house that still stands to remind us of those days. Along the line of the waterway and at the basins public houses were called the Canal, the Navigation Inn or the Wharf, as earlier they had been called the Pack Horse or the Row Barge.

More closely related to a particular canal were the Grand Junction Arms in Praed Street, Paddington; the Calder & Hebble at Salterhebble, near Halifax; and the Grosvenor Basin, which stood at the side of Victoria Station in London when this book was first published.

The administration of a canal was never easy in the days before telephones and telegrams, or even the penny post. In the canal office, usually in a main town, were the agent or superintendent; the accountant and chief toll-collector; and the resident clerk, each with a staff, while the engineer often had his own house. Strung out along the line were toll-collectors, who usually had to give security bonds for their honesty; wharfingers; lock-keepers; on the bigger canals assistant engineers in charge of portions of the route; lengthsmen or bank rangers; maintenance craftsmen such as carpenters and masons; and the mole catcher. When the company did its own carrying, and employed craft and crews, there was also a carrying manager to seek traffic and supervise the boatmen.

The shareholders would usually meet twice a year to hear a financial statement and declare a dividend which, unlike today, was usually only paid through a bank on application and was therefore advertised in the local press. At the earlier of these two meetings in the year the managing committee was elected.

This committee was the real governing body of the canal and met as often as needed – probably monthly on a big canal, three or four times a year on a small one. It had about fifteen members, who were drawn from the more influential shareholders. Occasionally it was constituted regionally, as on the Kennet & Avon Canal, where a number of seats were allotted to each of the three districts into which the canal was divided. The Swansea Canal committee comprised all of the shareholders with five or more shares, which, surprisingly, did not lead to inefficiency. The quorum for committee meetings was low – three on the Peak Forest, five on the Glamorganshire – for attendances were often poor. The members therefore usually received an attendance payment to compensate for the distances they had to travel, and sometimes a free meal as well, 'Beer and a genteel Dessert to be included'.[2] Meetings were either at the company's office or at the local inn, while once a year many committees made a boat trip to inspect their property.

When the canal was a big concern and could afford to pay permanent officials well, business was carried on efficiently. Trouble occurred with concerns too small to pay salaries. Much of the administrative responsibility then fell on the managing committee, which often consisted of country gentlemen and professional men without the time or inciination to undertake the necessary duties. The company's fortunes then depended on the chairman and still more on the clerk. The latter was usually a solicitor from a local and established firm, who might put much more work into the canal company than his salary justified in order to please his clients among the shareholders. If both men were energetic, business went well; if not, it went badly. Energy in chairmen was often helped by their large shareholdings, and often by annual honoraria from the shareholders, or occasional gifts of silver plate. One or two were paid regular salaries, and gave much of their time to the work. For instance the Grand Junction Canal had for many years a paid chairman on its managing committee.

In the bigger concerns the difficulties of the committee were of other kinds. Their administration was good but their policies, being of such great importance to the economic life of their area, were targets for constant criticism both from inside and outside their number. An example of an inside criticism, which reads with a modern air, comes from the Birmingham Canal in 1769:

> That upon examining into the Particulars of a Misunderstanding which happened in the Committee between Messrs. Garbett and Bentley, it appeared, that Mr Garbett did not intend to insinuate Mr Bentley's having wilfully mispent any of the Company's Money, but always thought he did his best; and (taking the whole of Mr Bentley's Conduct into Consideration) that the Public were under Obligations to him. It likewise appeared that Mr Garbett did frequently *request for the Poor* to be supplied with Coal, *in Preference to any Person whatsoever*, and that there is no Reason to say, he ever did make a Point for the Brass Work to receive the constant Supply of Three Tons per Day . . .[3]

The size of canals varied greatly, owing to the essentially local characteristics of each project. In width they can be grouped roughly into ship, broad, narrow and tub-boat canals, although no definite line can be drawn between one class and another.

The early ship canals such as the Caledonian, the Gloucester & Berkeley and the Exeter were, of course, small compared with the later Manchester Ship Canal. The size of locks at the time of opening were 170 ft × 38 ft on the Caledonian, 163 ft × 38 ft on the Gloucester & Berkeley and 128 ft × 26 ft 8 in. on the Exeter Canal. On the Manchester Ship Canal the large locks are 600 ft × 65 ft.

The broad canals such as the Kennet & Avon, Leeds & Liverpool, Rochdale, Bridgewater and Forth & Clyde could take vessels from 55 ft to some 80 ft long, and from 12 ft to 21 ft wide, carrying between about 50 and 100 tons. Many of them, like the Droitwich, Sir John Ramsden's,

The Gauxholme Locks on the Rochdale Canal, one of the two broad routes across the Pennines

Stroudwater, Erewash and the lower part of the Chesterfield Canal, were branches of river navigations and were built broad to take river craft.

Three main routes in Britain were built broad: from Forth to Clyde; from Liverpool across the Pennines by the Leeds & Liverpool or the Rochdale to Hull; and from Bristol to London by the Thames & Severn or the Kennet & Avon. Two others failed. In 1793 and 1794 the Grand Junction company decided to build a broad canal from London to Braunston near Rugby, and the Ashby followed suit. Pressure from the Grand Junction was put on the Oxford, Coventry and Trent & Mersey canals to widen also so that, by building a short link from the Ashby Canal across the Trent to the Trent & Mersey, a broad canal would be obtained from London to Manchester and Liverpool. The Coventry and the Oxford stalled, while the Trent & Mersey opposed. In 1796 the Ashby and the Chester (broad) canal shareholders, helped by Sir Nigel Gresley (a colliery owner of Newcastle under Lyme) and some dissident pottery manufacturers, promoted a new broad canal, the Commercial. This was to join the Ashby to the Chester canals by way of Uttoxeter, Hanley and Newcastle, to achieve the same object once the Coventry and Oxford had widened from Braunston to Marston. This scheme also failed, and no further serious attempt was ever made to build a broad line from London to Manchester and Liverpool. Future development was thereby stultified.

There was also a vision of a broad canal from Exeter to London: first by way of the Grand Western to Taunton, the proposed Bristol & Taunton and Bristol–Cirencester Canals, the Thames & Severn, the Thames Navigation, the broadened Oxford to Hampton Gay, and the proposed London & Western or Hampton Gay Canal to London; later from Bristol by the Kennet & Avon. The former route is shown on a map issued in about 1792 by the supporters of the Hampton Gay Canal. Of the latter scheme a pamphleteer of 1811 stated that

> it is proposed to make the Canal from Bristol to Taunton of the same dimensions as the Kennet & Avon Canal and the Grand Western Canal: so that barges of fifty tons burthen may be laden at Exeter, and proceed to London (a distance of upwards of 200 miles) without shifting their cargoes.[4]

However, the cohesive forces necessary to carry out such coordinated plans were not strong enough.

Most English Midland canals were built to narrow dimensions, to take narrow boats 70–2 ft long and about 6 ft 10 in wide, carrying some 25–30 tons. In Wales the important canals took boats 60–5 ft long and about 9 ft wide. No true narrow-boat canals were built in Ireland, though one, the far from successful Ulster Canal, could only take craft 11 ft 6 in. wide. Brindley and his assistants surveyed and engineered the early narrow canals of the Midlands, and experience in Yorkshire and Lancashire was bypassed when the size of boat was chosen. This was probably based on the Worsley coal-carrying mine boats, or possibly influenced by the challenge of constructing barge-sized bores for the long tunnels at Harecastle and Norwood, for which there was no precedent. Such canals were cheaper (though not much cheaper) to build and economical of water. However, the Industrial Revolution was quickly to catch up with what they could do and then leave them aside.

The tub-boat canals had very small boats carrying about 5 tons and often had inclined planes – that is, railways up and down which boats were drawn by one method or another – instead of locks. There were two groups of these canals, which were suited to hilly country – one in west Somerset, Devon and Cornwall, the other in Shropshire – and also a single canal, the Kidwelly & Llanelly, in Wales.

The boats that were used varied as greatly. On the river navigations sailing boats were the most common: trows and barges on the Severn, flats on the Mersey and the Weaver, keels on the Tyne and in Yorkshire, wherries in Norfolk, lighters in the Fens, Western barges on the Thames and Medway barges on the River Medway. These all differed in size and build, but the following will serve as examples: the trow was nearly flat-bottomed, 16–20 ft wide and some 100 ft long, carried 40–80 or more tons according to the depth of the river, with a main mast and topmast perhaps 80 ft high, sometimes a mizzen mast, and square sails; the barge (sometimes called a frigate) was a good deal smaller and carried 20–40 tons; the Tyne keels were some 42 ft long and 19 ft broad, while those of Yorkshire were about 54 ft long and 14 ft broad, and carried upwards of 80 tons. Horse-drawn barges were also used on river navigations. Those of the Kennet were 100 ft long and 17 ft wide.

On the broad canals horse-drawn barges and river sailing barges were used. On the narrow canals monkey boats were common, each of which was of an appropriate size to fit the locks on the canal where it was used. Most long-distance haulage on the midland canals within the Manchester–Stourport–London–Nottingham cross was done on narrow boats, since they could be worked singly through narrow locks and in pairs through broad locks. Tub-boat canals had small boats carrying a few tons, often operated in trains. Those on the Bude Canal were fitted with wheels on the bottom so that they could run on the rails of the inclined planes.

The first barge made of iron, *The Trial*, was built by John Wilkinson the ironmaster and launched on the River Severn at Coalbrookdale on 9 July 1787. 'It answers all my expectations,' he wrote, and 'it has convinced the unbelievers, who were 999 in a thousand.' Some iron narrow boats were built: Eric Svedenstierna saw several at Wilkinson's Bilston works in 1803. However, wood remained the usual building material until much later.

Experiments were made with steamboats on inland waterways before the end of the eighteenth century. From 1818, however, passenger and goods-carrying steam packets multiplied, especially on the Yorkshire Ouse, Trent, Mersey and Thames. In 1826 a steam tug began to work regularly through Islington Tunnel on the Regent's Canal, and experimental cargo carriers began to appear on the canals, like the stern paddle-wheeler that arrived at Birmingham from London in 1826 carrying 20 tons. In 1831 the Aire & Calder put a steam paddle tug on their Goole–Leeds run, and thereafter extended steam working rapidly. Tugs followed on other waterways, like the Caledonian and the Norwich & Lowestoft, but not until after the middle of the century were steam canal boats much developed for cargo carrying. Never, indeed, did they replace the horse. That had to wait for diesels.

The canal company usually provided public wharves in the charge of a wharfinger. The crane, weighing machine, warehouses and stables were enclosed by a wall and gates. Other warehouses built by the company might be let to permanent tenants – either local traders or one or more carrying concerns like Pickfords – and specialized buildings like salt houses, and warehouses for iron, flour and cheese, were put up when they were needed. A company would also maintain wharves on waterways other than its own, from which goods intended for its line would be collected. Private wharves and warehouses, either on the line of the waterway or on private branches, were built by other users.

Towing on the river navigations was usually carried out by gangs of men, a practice that continued well into the nineteenth century. Thomas Telford, writing about the Severn in 1797, condemned the 'barbarous and expensive custom of performing this slave-like office by men'.[5]

A witness for the Severn Towing Path Bill of 1803 said that about 150 men were employed in this work on the 24 miles from Bewdley to Coalbrookdale. The cost of towing this distance was put at 3s. (15p) per man, each of whom was reckoned to pull 3 tons, while one horse could do the work of six men, at a third less cost. Within the next ten years a horse towing-path was made northwards to Shrewsbury and southwards to Gloucester. On the upper Medway, however, this bow-hauling (said to be so called from the bows of rope attached to the towing line on which the men pulled) continued till about 1838. Sometimes these river towpaths were made by separate towing-path companies, as on the Severn or the Wye, or by a separate public body, as on the Great Ouse from Denver Sluice to King's Lynn, or privately, with access allowed on payment to the landowner, as on the Stour, where haling rents, as they were called, were paid for many years to Abram Constable, the brother of the painter.

In Yorkshire, East Anglia (where many rivers had no towing-paths), on the Medway, the Weaver and the Severn, sailing was commonly employed as an alternative to towing when it was practicable. Nowadays, of course, motor barges and tugs are used on rivers, often to tow or push other craft.

On canals, also, towing by men was an occasional practice in the early days, for instance on the Trent & Mersey and the Stroudwater. Usually, however, horse towing was used from the beginning. When boats going in opposite directions met, the empty boat dropped its towline under the laden boat or, if both were laden, the outer under the inner. Overtaking of one moving boat by another was usually prohibited by by-laws, with the maximum speed laid down as 2–3 mph. A few later and improved canals, such as Telford's reconstruction of part of the Birmingham Canal, had towpaths on both sides.

Horses usually drew a single boat but, when steam and, later, diesel craft were introduced, one boat often towed another. A narrow-boat motor, for instance, towed a butty. In such cases the butty or towed boat had to be worked through a single lock by its crew. Until recent times the push-towed barges of the Sheffield and South Yorkshire canals were still being bow-hauled by men through the small locks above Doncaster.

In order to save expense in their construction, tunnels seldom had a towpath. Therefore the boats had to be legged through by the boatmen or by special leggers lying on their backs on boards projecting from the boats, and pushing with their feet against the sides or roof. They were recommended to 'strap themselves to a short Cord affix'd to the Boat to prevent their being drown'd'.[6] The following is a description from 1858 of a night passage through Islington Tunnel in the narrow boat *Stourport*:

> A couple of strong thick boards . . . are hooked on to places formed on each side of the barge, near the head . . . On these two narrow, insecure platforms, the two venturesome boatmen lie on their backs, holding on by grasping the board underneath, and with their legs, up to the waist, hanging over the water . . . the operation consists in moving the *Stourport* through the black tunnel, by a measured side-step against the slimy, glistening walls; the right foot is first planted in a half-slanting direction, and the left foot is constantly brought over with a sweep to take the vacated place, until the right can recover its footing . . . the four stout legs, and its four heavily hobnailed boots . . . make a full echoing sound upon the walls like the measured clapping of hands.[7]

On the Grand Junction in 1825 there was a complaint of 'the nuisance arising from the notoriously bad characters of the persons who frequent the neighbourhood of the Tunnels upon the plea of assisting Boats through them'.[8] It seems that later, at Blisworth at any rate, leggers were licensed and carried an identifying armplate. Occasionally also boats were shafted or poled through, or a fixed or power-driven endless chain was used.

Probably the first tunnel to be built with a towpath through it was either Armitage (opened out in 1970-1) on the Trent & Mersey Canal or Cookley on the Staffordshire & Worcestershire. Later, longer tunnels were built with towpaths, such as Berwick on the Shrewsbury Canal, which had a path on wooden bearers over the water, or the second Harecastle. Some tunnels built still later had a path on each side, like Newbold on the Oxford Canal or Netherton on the Birmingham Canal. Where a tunnel had no path through it a horse path ran over the top. Beside Sapperton Tunnel on the Thames & Severn there stands Tunnel House, a public house where the men in charge of the horses paused while the leggers did their work.

An example of a horse which was not *ill-treated. Horse towing of narrow boats has continued to the present with trip boats like the* Maria, *here seen on a somewhat wet day crossing Marple Aqueduct on the Peak Forest Canal. This craft is perhaps the oldest narrow boat afloat, having originally been constructed in 1854. Based at Guide Bridge on the Ashton Canal, it engages in regular trips to Marple, on the waterways for which it was built. Many towing-paths are no longer fit for use by horses*

Where bridges had no towpath through their arches the towrope had to be cast off at each bridge and the horse and trailing line taken across the road. On the Stratford-upon-Avon Canal and part of the Staffordshire & Worcestershire Canal the bridges, instead of having towpaths beneath them, had a slot in the centre of the arch to take the towrope. On the Lagan Navigation some bridges had separate arches for the horses.

The most common means of towing was the horse, although donkeys were used in pairs on some canals, and mules were also occasionally employed. A writer on the Birmingham Canal in 1783 shows that the occupant of the towpath did not always enjoy the work:

> The boats . . . are each drawn by something like the skeleton of a horse, covered with skin: whether he subsists upon the scent of the water, is a doubt; but whether his life is a scene of affliction, is not; for the unfeeling driver has no employment but to whip him from one end of the canal to the other. While the teams practised the turnpike road,

> the lash was divided among five unfortunate animals, but now the whole wrath of the driver falls upon one.[9]

This was, of course, long before the date of the first Act to prevent cruelty to horses (1823), or the foundation of the Royal Society for the Prevention of Cruelty to Animals (1824).

When a towpath changed sides on a canal a bridge, for this reason called a turnover bridge, was provided to carry the path across, often designed so that the towline did not have to be cast off while the horse changed sides. On rivers, however, there was often nothing so convenient. Horses might be ferried over by a special boat or by the boat they were towing, as on the River Stour in Suffolk, on which short piers were provided for the horse to use to and from the boat carrying it over.

The towing was usually done by the animals belonging to the carrier who owned the boat. Sometimes, however, as on the Tennant Canal and, from 1847, on the Regent's Canal, towing was the responsibility of the canal owners, who provided their own horses and added a charge for the service to the toll. On waterways taking coastal or seagoing craft towing was often carried out by independents – in Yorkshire called horse marines, elsewhere trackers – who waited at places like Goole, Weston Point and Sharpness for incoming craft and then bargained with the captains for the services of themselves and their animals. In the Midlands steering firms existed that would hire boats, horses and men as required.

Stables were provided at wharves by canal companies and carriers, these latter also providing them at their own depots. Canalside pubs, too, had stable accommodation, for boats tended to moor at night where stables could be found. In England animals were never stabled on the boats, as on American canals.

Stoppages or delays caused by floods, ice, repairs or a shortage of water were recurrent hindrances to the passage of boats. The effects could be considerable when canal traffic had to compete with the regularity, even more than the speed, of delivery offered by the railways. Little could be done about floods unless the canal was built above the flood meadows or, on river navigations, special flood-locks or floodgates controlled the water levels inside the lock cuts.

Ice boats, usually short, wide and built of iron, with a high rail down the centre that men could hold, helped to keep traffic moving during frosts, unless the broken ice blocked the locks. When ice formed thickly a team of farm horses was hired to pull such a boat, and men to rock the vessel as it crashed its way forward. In London the ice-cream maker Carlo Gatti had a contract with the Regent's company to buy their ice, which was stored in a special ice-well near Hampstead Road lock. An ice-well nearby, used until about 1906, was later re-excavated within the London Canal Museum, which opened in 1992.

Stoppages for repairs to lock gates, or the puddling of the bed, always took a week or two each year. If different canals on a through route closed their waterways at different times, delays to goods could be very serious, so neighbouring groups of canals usually arranged to stop at the same time.

Maintenance consisted mainly of tunnel, lock and bridge repairs, and dredging, the latter laboriously done by manual labour using a spoon dredger or similar device until the power of steam could be harnessed. In 1808 the Grand Junction's engineer, having seen 'a Steam Engine invented by Mr Trevethick on a very simple construction',[10] ordered a 4 hp engine from Bridgnorth, which was to be put on a boat and used to drive a pump. The Stroudwater had a steam dredger in 1815, and by the 1820s they were becoming usual.

Water shortages became more and more serious as the traffic carried during the canal age continued to increase, and as the concurrent expansion of large towns caused competition for water supplies. To counteract the effects of leakage, evaporation and the transfer of water from the higher to the lower levels as the locks were worked, a constant accession of supply to the higher levels was needed. This came either from side streams entering the canal or from some big source of supply such as a reservoir, itself fed by streams.

The Acts under which canals were built specified exactly the streams that could be tapped and the other water that could be taken. At a time when so much of industry depended on water power, mill owners naturally opposed the building of canals that might draw off their water during times of drought, and only gave way if their supplies were protected by the provision of special reservoirs, if they were compensated for water taken or even if their mills were bought by the canal company. The supply of the summit or top level was often difficult, especially when the canal crossed a watershed and was therefore, by definition, out of reach of large supplies. Reservoirs, like those at Tring on the Grand Junction, were built wherever possible, or the summit level was deepened to provide an additional supply, as on the Cromford Canal. In other cases water was pumped to the summit level. The Worcester & Birmingham Canal was so strongly opposed by the mill owners that the Bill was twice thrown out, until the company agreed to pump water up 425 ft from the Severn. Luckily for the proprietors, however, it was found practicable to build reservoirs at the summit level. The enabling Act for this canal specifically reserved the water from any springs in the bed of the canal and such rainwater as fell on its surface! The Wisbech Canal was entirely dependent for its water on supplies that could enter from the River Nene at spring tides, and it was sometimes hardly navigable just before this water was admitted. Water that needed in any case to be pumped from collieries was sometimes an important source of supply, as in the Birmingham area.

Measures were also taken to economize on the use of water at the locks by making boats pass the locks alternately up and down, thus making one lockful do for two boats, by using locks with more than one set of gates or pairs of locks of different sizes, thereby using the minimum of water necessary to pass small craft, or by building side ponds. A side pond was a basin alongside the lock, into which was run not quite half of the water from an emptying lock, instead of into the lower pound of the canal. When the lock had next to be filled the first part of its contents came from the side pond and not from the upper pound. Thus one lockful of water passed two boats. Such ponds can often be seen, as on the Atherstone flight of the Coventry Canal, although many later fell into disuse. A variation on this practice, said to have been first introduced by James Morgan, the engineer of the Regent's Canal, was to build pairs of locks, one for up and one for down traffic, so that as far as possible one could act as a side pond for the other. Another practice was to build stop gates where two canals joined, such as where the Dearne & Dove Canal joined the Barnsley Canal, or even a physical bar, like that at Worcester Bar where the Worcester & Birmingham joined the Birmingham, to prevent loss of water from the better supplied waterway to the other. Lastly, water was sometimes pumped back from a lower to a higher level, as on the Birmingham Canal Navigations or the Tinsley flight of the Sheffield Canal.

The design of locks remained more or less the same from the early days to the twentieth century. Today there are power-worked paddles and gates on the bigger canals in Britain, with a single hydraulic pattern on many of the smaller ones. There were some early experiments with alternatives to hand-operated paddle gear, such as the compressed-air type that the Peak Forest company seems to have tried. Early locks, however, did not have the usual iron or masonry protection to the sill, nor did boats carry a stem fender, for many by-laws enjoin the boatman to use a piece of timber to prevent the boat striking the sill. Damage to locks was the reason given for prohibiting the double-ended boat, with a detachable rudder hung on projecting eyes at each end.

Not all early locks had a railed walkway over the gates, or a bridge, to enable the boatman to get quickly from one side to the other. When keel captains asked the Driffield Navigation commissioners to provide a safer passage over the gates, they minuted in 1841 that

> it was ordered that some little repairs to the tops of the Gates should be made without putting up a Rail which would make the passage over too much of a thoroughfare for persons not concerned on the Navigation, which the Commissioners think they ought not to do.[11]

Many of the most bitter quarrels and lasting enmities between canal companies arose from water questions. The Staffordshire & Worcestershire company was continually preoccupied with efforts to buy cheaply from the Birmingham company the water coming down the Wolverhampton locks, with buying further supplies from the Wyrley & Essington, which was blessed with a superfluity, and with selling dearly what was needed by the Birmingham & Liverpool Junction.

In very hilly country the inclined plane and the canal lift were both used to save water by making the building of locks unnecessary. Since the Trench plane closed in 1921 there has been no boat-carrying canal inclined plane working in Britain, but at one time there were over twenty – on the Bude, Torrington, Chard, Grand Western, Kidwelly & Llanelly, Shrewsbury, Shropshire, Donnington Wood, Grand Junction and Monkland Canals. The first in the British Isles, three built in the north of Ireland by Davis Ducart on the Tyrone (Ducart's) Canal, worked intermittently between 1777 and 1787. These three were the only ones constructed in Ireland. England's first was built in 1788 by William Reynolds on the private Ketley Canal in Shropshire, and a contemporary description is representative:

> Instead of descending in the usual way, by locks, [he] continued to bring the canal forward to an abrupt part of the bank, the skirts of which terminated on a level with the iron-works. At the top of this bank he built a small lock, and from the bottom of the lock, and down the face of the bank, he constructed an inclined plane with a double iron railway. He then erected an upright frame of timber, in which, across the lock, was fixed a large wooden barrel; round this barrel a rope was passed, and was fixed to a movable frame; this last frame was formed of a size sufficient to receive a canal boat, and the bottom upon which the boat rested, was preserved in nearly an horizontal position, by having two large wheels before and two small ones behind, varying as much in the diameters as the inclined plane varied from an horizontal plane. This frame was placed in the lock, the loaded boat was also brought from the upper canal into the lock, the lock gates were shut, and on the water being drawn from the lock into a side pond, the boat settled upon the horizontal wooden frame, and as the bottom of the lock was formed with nearly the same declivity as the inclined plane, upon the

The inclined plane at Ketley, shown on a token

> lower gates being opened, the frame with the boat passed down the iron railway, on the inclined plane, into the lower canal, which had been formed on a level with the Ketley iron-works, being a fall of 73 feet . . . A double railway having been laid upon the inclined plane, the loaded boat in passing down, brought up another boat containing a load nearly equal to one-third part of that which passed down. The velocities of the boats were regulated by brake acting upon a large wheel placed upon the axis on which the ropes connected with the carriage, were coiled.[12]

This plane was counterbalanced, the loaded boat bringing up an empty or partly loaded one, a system only practicable when the predominant traffic carried was downwards. Otherwise a steam engine was used if coal was cheap, and hydraulic power if it was not. Most of the West Country planes had waterwheels fed by a stream, but another and somewhat unreliable hydraulic method was used on the Hobbacott Down plane of the Bude Canal, the biggest of all, with a vertical rise of 225 ft. A Victorian civil engineer, Vernon-Harcourt, described the method:

> The barges are drawn up in trains, and are to some extent counterpoised by the descending trains of barges . . . The water power

> is supplied . . . by two large tubs ascending and descending alternately in two wells, the tub at the top of its well being filled with water, and in its descent drawing the barges up the incline. When the tub full of water reaches the bottom of the well, the water is emptied through a flap-door in the bottom of the tub; and the empty tub in the other well, having been drawn up its well by the descending tub, is at the top ready to be filled with water in its turn.[13]

The canal lift, or balance lock as it was sometimes called, though invented in Britain, was not successfully used until James Green installed seven of them on the Grand Western Canal's Taunton extension, which opened in 1838. Previously two inventors, Edward Rowland and Exuperius Pickering, had built in 1796, probably near Ruabon, an experimental lift for use on the Ellesmere Canal. It used the float principle, whereby a caisson holding the boat rode up and down on a float in a well, which could be filled with water or emptied as necessary. It was never used, but the principle is that of some modern Continental lifts like that at Henrichenburg. Others were later built on the Somersetshire Coal Canal, the unfinished Dorset & Somerset Canal, at Tardebigge on the Worcester & Birmingham Canal and on the Regent's Canal, but none was put to regular use.

A lift usually consisted of a caisson or tank, into which the canal boat was floated, and cables that ran over wheels at the top of the lift, either to counterbalance weights or to another caisson. Chains under each caisson, which coiled or uncoiled as they moved in relation to each other, kept the caissons in balance. In order to raise a boat from one level to another, water was added to the upper caisson, either until the caisson to be lifted began to move upwards, in which case the movement was controlled by a brake, or nearly to that point, the final impetus being given by manual or mechanical power. A lift could have one or two independently operated caissons, or two that balanced each other. The seven lifts on the Grand Western Canal, with rises varying from 12½ ft to 42 ft, were counterbalanced, one 8 ton boat being raised while another was lowered. These worked successfully for thirty years. Subsequently, in 1875, the Anderton lift connecting the Weaver Navigation with the Trent & Mersey Canal, and capable of lifting two full-sized narrow boats, was built. This still exists, although it has been out of use, awaiting repair, since 1983. Its caissons, once counterbalanced, are now independently operated. The Anderton was the prototype of canal lifts later used on the Continent and in Canada. The earlier of these was built by its designer, Edwin Clark.

After all precautions had been taken, however, shortage of water, especially in the summer, was a perennial problem on canals and river navigations. It meant that smaller cargoes were carried than were possible, thereby increasing overhead costs, and that boats ran aground unnecessarily and had to be lightened, to everyone's annoyance and loss. This state of things became increasingly serious. Some industrial canals, especially those around Birmingham, had the advantage that they could draw most of their water from supplies pumped from colliery workings. Others built more and larger reservoirs, or installed machinery to pump upwards from streams or from their own lower levels.

Water was often sold to canalside works, but in the early days of steam engines, when it seems to have been considered that they consumed no water, the following clause was inserted in the Birmingham Canal's Act of 1783:

> And whereas sundry Improvements have lately been made upon Steam or Fire Engines . . . And Whereas such Engines will consume considerable Quantities of Coal, and by the tonnage thereupon promote the Interest of the Navigation, as well as that of the Manufactories of Birmingham, if erected in its Neighbourhood; but as such Machines can only be erected where cold Water can be obtained to condense the Steam which is necessary to the working of them; and as such Water can be taken from the Navigation without Prejudice thereto, because such Machines, when properly constructed, do not waste or destroy any Water, but may be made to return to the Navigation a Quantity of warm Water equal to the cold Water which they drew from it . . . be it therefore enacted . . . That it may be lawful . . . to draw from the said Canal such Quantities of Water as shall be sufficient to supply the said Engines . . .[14]

Today canals supply water for industrial or agricultural purposes, much of it being returned for re-use. The resulting revenue helps to meet maintenance costs. During the Second World War canals were, in many English towns, the principal source of emergency water supply for the National Fire Service, and they still form an emergency reserve.

The revenue of canal companies chiefly arose from tolls charged at the rate of so many pence per ton per mile carried, as distinct from the freight charges of the carriers. Milestones were set up along the towpaths so that these point-to-point tolls could be accurately calculated. Charges were lowest for bulk commodities such as coal, culm (slack for lime burning) and limestone, higher for more valuable bulk cargoes such as iron ore, and higher still for finished goods like iron castings, and for groceries and general merchandise. In the case of coal it was the usual practice to allow 21 cwt or more to the ton (a ton is 20 cwt) to cover transfer losses and theft.

The maximum tolls that could be charged on each class of goods were laid down in the company Act and could not be increased without further Parliamentary authority. The tendency was, however, in the opposite direction, as increasing trade, together with the competition of road transport, the coasting trade and later railways, worked to reduce tolls. In addition there was always pressure from the industrialists on one canal to get tolls lowered so that they might compete better with factories or mines served by other canals. Small transport concerns, often very dependent on a few businesses for their livelihood, found it difficult to resist such pressures.

Companies were not allowed to discriminate between users by giving special tolls, nor to charge more on one part of the line than another, until the Canal Tolls Act of 1845 gave power to vary tolls. Trade was encouraged by granting long credit: three months was usual, and, with railway competition, it tended to become longer.

Often drawbacks, subsidies in the form of a partial refund of tolls, were paid to those who shipped goods for long distances. They were usually given to encourage the development of markets for coal on other canals than that of the company granting them. The Ashby Canal, for instance, gave a drawback on all Moira, Gresley and Swadlincote coal carried the length of the canal and on to the Coventry Canal. This enabled these collieries, especially Moira, to build up good distant sales, among them to Oxford colleges. Canal companies often competed briskly with one another in this way on the fringes of their territories, sometimes also carrying out raids far into each other's heartlands.

In order to meet opposition to their Acts, canal companies often had to hamper themselves with clauses allowing certain goods to move without payment of tolls. This was detrimental when they came to compete with railways, which were not similarly handicapped. For instance, on the Chesterfield Canal hay and corn in the straw going to be stacked had to be carried toll-free for five miles; materials for the repair of parish roads, and manures for lands which had been cut by the canal, were carried toll-free provided no locks were passed. On the Derby Canal up to 5,000 tons of coal a year had to be carried toll-free to Derby for the use of the poor, thus relieving the poor rates of the town at the expense of the company. Apart from tolls, some companies reaped a harvest from compensation payments. These arose when a new canal was projected that might cause trade to be diverted from existing navigations. In such cases the opposition of the old proprietors was only withdrawn when the new company had agreed to compensate them for any loss of trade. These payments became a widespread and restrictive network over the waterway system. For example, the Act for the Ashby de la Zouch Canal

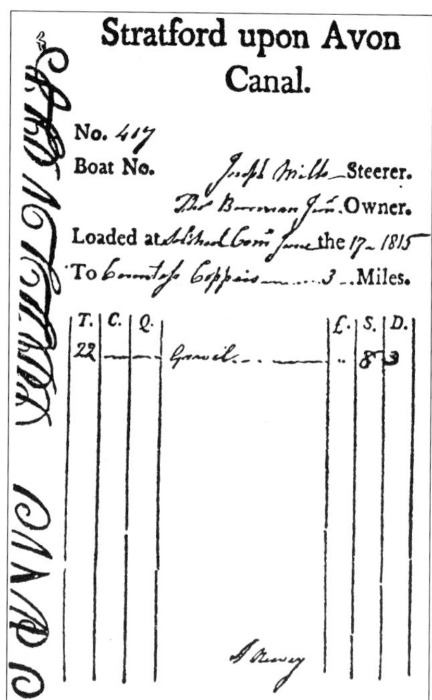
Stratford upon Avon Canal.

No. 417

Boat No. ... Steerer.

... Owner.

Loaded at ... the 17 1815

To ... 3 Miles.

T.	C.	Q.		£.	S.	D.
22	—	—	Gravel	..	8	3

A toll ticket from 1815 for a boat belonging to Thomas Bowman, showing the distance involved, the tonnage of 22 tons of gravel and the toll of 8s. 3d. (now 41p)

(1794) provided that the Coventry Canal should collect 5d. (2p) a ton on all goods, with certain exceptions, passing between the Ashby Canal and the Coventry, Oxford or Grand Junction canals, and should have power to place its own toll-houses, stop bars and collectors on the Ashby Canal in order to collect the payments.

The tolls payable were calculated on a written note declaring the type, weight, origin and destination of the cargo, presented by the carrier and endorsed by the toll-collector. Often the latter would suspect the accuracy of the declaration and could make his own check of the tonnage the boat was carrying. This was found out by gauging. When it first came into use on a canal each boat was taken to a dock, where its draught, both empty and when carrying various loads, was found. Figures were then marked on the boat's side in four or six places, being either cut into the wood or cast on a metal plate.

Some canals had weighing machines instead of docks. These substantial structures had a cradle onto which a boat was floated. The water was then let out and the boat weighed empty for record purposes. Once that figure was known it was simple to detect an overweight cargo by sending the boat to be weighed. Indeed, the machine's existence was usually deterrent enough. Weighing machines were installed on a number of waterways, among them at Midford on the Somersetshire Coal Canal, Brimscombe on the Thames & Severn, and North Road lock, Cardiff, on the Glamorganshire Canal. The latter was later re-erected at the Canal Museum, Stoke Bruerne.

An improved method of gauging was introduced in about 1810. Instead of the figures showing different immersion depths for different loads being marked on the boat's side, they were entered in books, which were kept at the toll-houses. The actual depth at which a boat was floating at any given time was found by using a hollow tube, with a rest to fit on the gunwale, which was put into the water beside the boat at four or six places. Inside the tube was a rod marked in feet and inches that rose as the tube sank and showed the freeboard in inches. The average of the readings was then compared with the figures in the company's book for the boat concerned, and the tonnage could be read off.

Most waterway concerns insisted that boats coming onto their water from another canal should be gauged by their officers, a rule less onerous in fact than it appeared since most boats worked along well-defined routes. In about 1798, however, eight canal and river companies in the Trent area joined in common gauging arrangements, the printed record books of which now provide researchers with an exact picture of the boats used at the time in that area.

River and canal companies were hardly ever either empowered to put, or prohibited from putting, boats on their own or neighbouring waterways and carrying goods, so long as there was fair competition with other carriers. Many did carry from the beginning, like the Aire & Calder or the Mersey & Irwell. Others did intermittently, usually buying barges and running them until independent traders appeared, and then selling them. Yet others organized carrying firms, nominally separate by being run by groups of canal shareholders, as the Trent & Mersey company originally did with its carrying counterpart, Hugh Henshall & Co.

It is probable that, as competition increased after the Napoleonic Wars had ended, canal companies that also ran carrying craft realized that they could, in practice, vary tolls in their own favour by adjusting freight charges, and that this led to complaints. The Ellesmere & Chester company at that time sought special authority to carry, an authority made general in 1845 by the Canal Carriers Act. Many companies, however, remained only toll-takers to the end on waterways that were open to all users. Until 1987 this system remained, the British Waterways Board's fleets operating side by side with private carriers.

Many canal and navigation companies ran businesses in some of the commodities they carried. The Upper Medway Company traded in coal

A scene on the Regent's Canal, showing a pair of Pickfords boats passing through City Road Locks, with Islington Tunnel beyond. Note the side paddle, which enabled water from a full lock to be partly transferred to the empty parallel lock

so successfully that it had a virtual monopoly for a century, and it was also involved for a time in timber and iron. The Brecknock & Abergavenny company went in for trading in coal and thought of acquiring a colliery. Later it transferred its trading interests to the nominally independent Brecon Boat Company. Some companies actually ran or leased collieries, including the Grand Canal Company in Ireland. Many owned limekilns, but the Peak Forest Company was exceptional. This company owned a number of kilns, rented others and also worked large limestone quarries. They used modern ways of encouraging the greater use of limestone: paying part of the cost of new kilns built within a time limit if only their limestone was used; subsidising publications on the uses of lime; making bulk contracts for sales that included toll, freight and the cost of the stone in one price; and offering loads at special rates to let turnpike trustees experiment with limestone for road building.

Much canal carrying was done by private carrying companies or partnerships. These could be of any size, some running two or three boats, some twenty or more. They paid their men by the ton carried rather than a weekly wage. Some men worked part-time as boatmen and others full-time, but for different employers. The best-known firm during the canal age was Pickfords, originally road waggon proprietors. The company's activities were widespread in the 1790s: they leased warehouses and wharves, and owned many boats, 'which travel night and day, and arrive in London whith as much punctuality from the midland and some of the most distant parts of the kingdom, as the waggons do.'[15] The canals felt the loss severely when, in the 1840s, Pickfords ceased to carry by canal and transferred to the railways.

There were, of course, many other firms, some general carriers and some specializing in fly-boat (express) work. There were, again, trading firms owning their own boats, or hiring them, and carrying their own raw materials or finished products, as on the Swansea Canal, where there were hardly any independent traders. Lastly, there were the small men, each owning a boat or two, and plying for hire like a tramp steamer. There were never many of them on the narrow canals, but a few of the 'Number Ones' survived to the 1950s. There were probably more in Yorkshire, where the individually owned keel fitted well into the way that carrying was organized on such navigations as the Don and the Calder & Hebble. Here the navigation company accepted goods even though it did not possess its own boats: instead, it contracted carriers, individual owners and partnerships alike, to do the work for them.

If one should ask what manner of men these were, part of the answer is on a blue printed earthenware plate that was made between 1800 and 1820. Round the edge are the names on ribbons, and in the centre is a canalside scene with the following verse below:

> Pickford, Beach, and Snell's, are jolly Lads, & true ones:
> Kenworthy, & Worthington's, You'll likewise find true blue ones:
> Wakeman, Green & Ames, amiss you'll never find Sirs,
> Holt's, Crocket & Salkeld's, will sail fast as the wind Sirs.
> True harted & jolly ones you'll find with Heath & Crawley,
> Sturland's Henshall's, Alkin's too, can likewise use their mauley
> So likewise can the Boatmen all, & drink their can of flip Sirs,
> Thay'll drink there grog, & toast their lass, & then thay'll
> Crack their whip Sirs.[16]

Those who work on the waterways today are inheritors of a craft with detailed and interesting traditions. It has sometimes been suggested that the canal boatmen and boatwomen had a special origin, for example that they were gypsies. It is much more likely that many early boatmen had been small farmers, men with horses and carts who found good employment carting for local contractors building the canal, who then probably took to the boats because they already possessed horses and were losing their traditional road traffic. Many boatmen were recruited in the same ways as other workers were drawn to the new industrial areas of

A boatwoman carrying a baby and steering a narrow boat, as depicted, perhaps somewhat fancifully, in the tract against family boats, Rob Rat, *discussed in Chapter Eleven*

the late eighteenth and early nineteenth centuries. Some doubtless came from river and coastal craft to the canals; many had probably been locally employed navvies, who took to the waterways they had built; others came from canalside towns and villages, places where the building, loading and passing of boats was a familiar sight.

During the canal age boats seem in the main to have been worked by men and boys, the usual by-laws demanding two men to each boat, or at least a man and a stout boy, the latter to lead the horse. A Stourbridge Canal by-law of 1789, however, demanded two men and a boy for any boat passing a lock. Let us not forget the boys: they were numerous and hard-worked. Wages were relatively good, the profits of carrying were reasonable and boatmen earned enough money to keep their families in cottages ashore. ('Men' here does refer directly to males; women were rarely employed, and never in Ireland).

It used to be thought there were few family boats in Britain before railway competition, but it is now known that family narrow boats were quite common by the 1810s. This use of family instead of paid help was the result of several factors: competition between different carriers and different routes; the housing shortage after the Napoleonic Wars; and the increase in length of canal journeys with the system's growth, making it less likely that boatmen would see much of a family ashore. The coming of railways encouraged what was already taking place, until, by the time of George Smith, the canal reformer of the 1870s, the family boat was common on narrow canals, though fly-boats were always worked by men only. Under quite different circumstances many of the sailing keels that traded along the Yorkshire navigations were also family boats, certainly from early in the nineteenth century.

In Scotland, Ireland and in the South Wales valleys the family boat was unknown, although employment on boats was often passed down through generations.

Time's pressure on the boatmen, toll-keepers and lock-keepers slowly increased through the canal age. It was a consequence of the increased development of the transport system that took place more especially after the end of the Napoleonic Wars, though symptoms of it had appeared earlier. For instance some fly-boats began running in the 1790s. The process can be seen at work on the Staffordshire & Worcestershire Canal, which moved over the years from a near monopoly to a very competitive transport position. Before 1816 the normal hours for boats to pass the locks were 5.00 a.m.–9.00 p.m. on moonlit nights and 6.00 a.m.–8.00 p.m. otherwise. In that year express or fly-boats were put on, which paid an annual licence fee to be allowed to pass the locks at any time. In 1820 the hours were extended to 4.00 a.m.–10.00 p.m. during the summer, and soon afterwards boats were allowed to pass at any hour if they paid a small extra charge for each trip. Finally from 1830 the locks were open day and night for all boats, the lock-keepers being paid a little extra. For example in February 1832 the man at Stourport lock got 14s. (70p) a week and 4s. (20p) night wages. One sympathizes with William Bagnall when the committee minuted in the same year 'That the Bed in the Nighthouse at Heywood be taken away and that our Clerk do warn William Bagnall to be more vigilant in his Duty and not permit any Boat to pass without his knowledge.'[17] Separate day and night men were later employed at the busy points on the canal.

A sign of the increasing pressure of business was the passing in 1840 of the Constables Act, empowering canal and river authorities to appoint their own police, though it does not seem that many companies did so.

Early boats had no cabins – these began to appear in the 1790s. However, as journeys lengthened, crews often slept ashore in canalside inns, while their horses occupied the inn stables, or in friends' houses.

While in the early days boat people were recruited from outside, there soon grew up a largely self-perpetuating boating community, increasingly separated from the population it served. Then slowly the situation reversed: as carrying reduced, younger people left the boats to begin a different life with better prospects.

The life of the waterways has always had its hazards. Men, women and children have now and then fallen into a lock, been crushed by a boat or slipped into the canal in the darkness. Boat horses have been drowned or burned in their stables. Of accidents to the boats themselves, two examples follow – one normal enough, the other fortunately exceptional.

The Basingstoke company reported in 1802 that

> one of the Company's Barges, the *Baxter*, encountered a sudden and violent Storm, about the Nine Elms, as she was going up the Thames, loaded with Grocery and Merchandize, which rendered her totally unmanageable, and she must have sunk in the Middle of the River, but for the assistance of a large Sailing Vessel which kept her floating till she gat near the Shore, when she went to the Bottom and was soon filled with Water . . . At the same Time another loaded Barge, the Property of a Mr Jones, also going up the River, sunk, after she had been hauled close to the Shore; and Three other Vessels, of different Descriptions, were seen to go down about the same Time . . .[18]

This accident was not the result of the boatmen's negligence. Neither was the famous Regent's Park explosion, which was reported in 1874 by the *Illustrated London News*:

> An extraordinary accident, which happened yesterday week at five o'clock in the morning, cost the loss of several lives, much damage to houses and furniture, and a vast alarm to the north-western suburbs of London. This was the blowing up of a barge laden with petroleum and gunpowder for blasting, which was one of a train drawn by a steam-tug along the Regent's Canal . . . The train of six light barges, of which the first was a steamer, left the wharf in the City-road about three o'clock that morning. Next after the steamer, the Ready, was the fly-boat Jane, whose steerer or captain was named Boswell. Next to her was the Dee, the steerer Edwards; and next came the unfortunate Tilbury, whose steerer was Charles Baxton, of Loughborough, in Leicestershire. The Jane 'had a little gunpowder on board'. The Tilbury's lading is thus described by the official report: 'The cargo consisted chiefly of sugar and other miscellaneous articles, such as nuts, straw-boards, coffee, and some two or three barrels of petroleum, and about five tons of gunpowder.' . . . Three or four minutes before five o'clock, this train of barges was passing under the bridge at North Gate, Regent's Park . . . The Tilbury was directly under the bridge when by some means yet unexplained, the powder caught fire and the whole was blown up. The men on board this barge were killed, and the barge was shattered to

> pieces, while one of the other barges was sunk. A column of thick smoke and a great blaze of fire followed the explosion. The bridge was entirely destroyed; several of the neighbouring houses were half-ruined, their roofs and walls being greatly injured; and in hundreds of other houses, a mile east or west of the place, the windows were broken . . . The noise and shock were perceived in every quarter of London, and in many instances ten or twelve miles away, both on the north and the south side of the Thames . . . People soon hastened up from every quarter of town. The police, the Fire Brigade, and a detachment of Horse Guards (Blue) from Albany Barracks, presently arrived and kept order, while the task of saving what remained and searching for the lost was actively begun.[19]

The boat people in the past had few friends and many enemies. This perpetually moving population was not welcome to those who lived near waterways, and new canal projects were sometimes opposed for fear of the damage that might be done by them to property or the poaching that might result. The owners of boats also complained of them pilfering, bartering coal from cargoes for food and drink, dumping coal in rivers to lighten barges (and, incidentally, to warm the riverside villagers who dredged it) and spending money in public houses that had been given them to pay tolls. Their good service and hard, laborious work remained unrecorded.

Another hard-working group of people deserves to be mentioned – the lock-keepers and toll-keepers. On the canals lock-keepers were given a house as well as their wages, and often a coal allowance (to remove temptation) and perhaps one for candles too. They were sometimes asked to do some gauging and toll-collecting on traffic loading near their locks, inspect tonnage bills, help pass the boats and trim hedges or break ice. They were expected not to leave their posts, unlike Eynon Bowen on the Swansea Canal, who was fined in 1818 because 'A great part of his time is taken up in farming and other concerns'.[20] Some companies, like the Peak Forest, provided 'an upper Waistcoat and a Badge thereupon to distinguish them from other persons . . .'[21] The toll-keepers had, of course, to be honest in accounting for receipts (they were usually covered by security bonds), for making sure that boats were properly gauged and that their waybills were in order. They also had to refrain from trading with the boatmen or borrowing money from them.

When these men were old they were usually given a small pension. In 1823 the Staffordshire & Worcestershire committee, whose records reveal a long tradition of good works, minuted:

John Buttery . . . being incapable of attending to his Situation owing to Old Age. Ordered that he be replaced, and that an annual pension be allowed him . . . and until a Successor be appointed, Ordered that our Clerk write to Crowley and Company requiring them to give notice to their Boatmen not to molest or insult John Buttery in his passing their Boats along the Canal.[22]

They had to be strong characters, for their work was lonely and responsible. Here, to end this chapter, are three examples of the life they led. The first concerns a Thames lock-keeper.

Tedding^n Lock 28/3/1818

It has been always Customary with me to rise at dawn of day because in general ye Barges move from Richmond then & often do before if the Moon shines till day & this was the Case on ye 20th early. I rose at just past 4 & was Employed in the Office arranging some small matters before ye Craft came when I heard a Man's Voice calling. I open'd one of the Shutters & saw a Man standing about ½ Way between my Window & the lower Gate, and he Pointed with his hand and said here's a Trow coming. I had no doubt in my own mind but that the Trow was very near, & as the Wind blew hard & right into the Pound it was highly necessary the Gates should be opened & ready. I now took my hat & was going out but the Ins^t I open'd the Door a Stout Fellow rushed in & seized me by the throat. While we were struggling in came 2 More & one of them had something in his hand resembling ½ a Sack. I was thrown with Violence over a Chair and we both came rolling to ye Ground & I then felt one of them cover my head & press it so close down that I really began to fear they meant to suffocate me . . . They then took my Keys from my Coat pocket by rolling me over, and having broke every Lock and Emtied every small Box of Mrs S in the next room they all ran out leaving me locked in & in darkness. By their bad discourse I must (think) them Bargemen of lowest Class. I had about 11 or 12 Single Pound Notes & full six Pounds Silver and ye most part Sm^l Silver & 4 or 5 shillings in Copper. I do indeed much fear that this is only ye beginning, for which ever Lock Receives much value it will be a Temptation to such Villains to make an attempt at ye end of ye Week . . .

. . . Richd Savory.[23]

On the Regent's Canal in London in 1830 the

Eastern division of the Canal, was almost constantly the scene of the most disgraceful Riots. Such were the lawless set that frequented the

FELONY
AND
Reward.

WHEREAS on the Night of *Tuesday* the 13th instant, the Hatches of a Boat lying in the Docks at MULLINGAR were forced open, and the TOOLS belonging to four Ship Carpenters taken away; and on the Night of *Wednesday* the 25th instant, Boat No. 49, lying in the Docks upon the BROADSTONE LEVEL, DUBLIN, was attacked by a number of Persons, when they tied the Men belonging thereto, and carried away the TOOLS of six Ship Carpenters that had been working at said Boat. They also made use of expressions threatening destruction to any Carpenter that would work under certain Wages; and that they would destroy the Property of any individual that would not give the prescribed Wages for the Repairs of their Boats. A WRITTEN NOTICE to the foregoing effect was left in the Boat at Mullingar.

NOW the COURT OF DIRECTORS of the NEW ROYAL CANAL COMPANY, for the purpose of preventing the continuance of such an illegal Combination, do hereby offer

A REWARD OF
Fifty Pounds

for the discovery, and prosecution to conviction, of the Person or Persons who were concerned in the carrying away the said Tools, or in the writing or publishing of the Felonious Threats aforesaid, or

A Reward of Ten Pounds

shall be given to any Person giving private Information, which may lead to the conviction of such Offender, or Offenders, as aforesaid, or of any Person who shall, in consequence of said Notice, conspire to carry into effect the Threats therein contained, or commit any Outrage on the Person or Property of any Trader on the Royal Canal, or any Person in his Employment.

By Order of the Court of Directors,

SAMUEL DRAPER,
Secretary.

ROYAL CANAL HOUSE,
***30th July*, 1821.**

A notice issued by the Royal Canal Company (Ruth Heard)

> Canal (to hunt Ducks, Swim Dogs, etc.) that a party of the Police were in constant pay, and absolutely necessary to protect the Lock-keepers from personal harm; but this did not always succeed, for on several occasions, Lock-keepers have been so severely treated, in defending the Company's property from damage, that in some cases they were several months in recovering from the Injuries they received.[24]

Quite different hazards to canal workers and boatmen were experienced in Ireland. The condition of the Irish people in the hard economic environment of the early nineteenth century affected the working of the Grand and Royal canals. Both during and after construction, banks were often breached by local people who hoped to be employed in their repair, while the workers who completed the western part of the Royal Canal between 1813 and 1817 were attacked by armed bands. Military protection was needed to prevent the plunder of goods carried on the Grand Canal, while there was a war between smaller and larger traders in turf on that canal, which included the burning of boats and threats to destroy the canal works. In the 1820s and 1830s armed gangs backed the demands of combinations of horse-drivers on the Royal. Finally, during the Famine of the 1840s, pillaging of boats on both canals led to the re-introduction of convoys of craft under military protection.

CHAPTER FOUR

The Arteries of the Revolution

So immediate was the success of the Duke of Bridgewater's canal from Worsley towards Manchester, which had been opened in 1761, that he went back to Parliament during the following year for authority to continue to the Mersey near Runcorn, so that his coal might go to Liverpool without using the Mersey & Irwell.

This was a much more ambitious plan. The significance of its promotion by the Duke after his experience with the Worsley canal, and the prominent involvement of James Brindley, was not lost on businessmen, among them Josiah Wedgwood of the Potteries and his partner Thomas Bentley, and the salt manufacturers of Cheshire dependent upon the River Weaver.

People were used to rivers being navigable, and it was a logical development, though a startling one when it came, that rivers could be joined together so that goods could travel from the sea at either end to any intermediate point, and from any point to either river mouth. Many such schemes had been proposed in the past – such as between the Thames and Severn rivers by way of the Bristol Avon proposed by Mathew in the seventeenth century – but now they suddenly seemed practicable. Such an arrangement to link the Trent and Mersey would greatly suit Wedgwood, whose raw material came mostly by sea from Cornwall and Devon to the Mersey, by barge up the Weaver to Winsford Bridge and then by packhorse to the Potteries. It could now be brought from the Mersey to his doorstep, while products could be carried away in either direction as far as Liverpool or Hull.

The upper section of the Trent had already been made navigable to Burton on Trent by an Act of 1699. When, therefore, Wedgwood and his associates supported proposals for a canal, at first called the Grand Trunk and later the Trent & Mersey, from Wilden Ferry below Burton to the Mersey, there was heavy opposition from river interests. The Burton (upper Trent) Navigation maintained that the canal should end at Burton rather than 14 miles lower down at Wilden Ferry, while the Weaver Navigation, which had so far carried all of the salt and part of the pottery trade, tried to get the western end of the proposed canal connected to its own river. The promoters of the new scheme were anxious to obtain efficient transport, by avoiding any commitments to join their canal to unimproved waterways or to be charged monopoly rates. The opposition of the rivers was so active that, at one stage, the Cheshire gentlemen who supported the case of the River Weaver surveyed the route for an alternative canal to the Trent by way of Stafford, and fought the Trent & Mersey Canal Bill right to the parliamentary committee. The owners of the Burton Navigation continued their opposition until their activity ended in 1805.

To get the Duke's support an agreement was reached by which he would build the Trent to Mersey line between Preston Brook and Runcorn, altering his own line from Manchester to Runcorn to join the new canal. This led to further plans to connect the Trent & Mersey Canal with the River Severn at what is now Stourport, then a hamlet. Both groups of promoters obtained their Acts on the same day of the same year, 1766.

These great projects, the Trent & Mersey, 93⅜ miles long and with an authorized capital of £150,000, and the Staffordshire & Worcestershire, 46⅛ miles long and with £100,000 of capital, involved major engineering works. The Bridgewater Canal had been built level from Worsley to Manchester and was being continued on the same level to Runcorn, where it would fall to the Mersey via a flight of ten locks. The locks had not yet been built, and the experience of Brindley and Gilbert was limited to the construction of level line, to the embankments and aqueduct at Barton and the tunnels at Worsley. Yet 4 aqueducts, 43 locks and 2 short tunnels on the Staffordshire & Worcestershire, and 75 locks, the 2,880 yd long Harecastle tunnel and several shorter tunnels on the Trent & Mersey, were planned. In spite of many difficulties the Staffordshire & Worcestershire Canal was completed in 1772 (the year of Brindley's death) and the Trent & Mersey Canal in 1777.

Once the line of the Trent & Mersey had been decided the effort to join it to the Thames began in 1768 with the Act for the Coventry Canal. This Act aimed to supply Coventry with coal from mines along the line, and also to join the Trent & Mersey near Lichfield. Brindley surveyed the line, and was engineer for a time before his dismissal by the Coventry Company for inattention. The initial capital of £50,000 only sufficed to complete half of the line, from Coventry to Atherstone, and for ten years the completed portion remained isolated. Meanwhile, in 1769, a canal was authorized between the Thames at Oxford and the Coventry Canal at Longford near Coventry, also to be surveyed and engineered by Brindley. By 1778 the 63¾ miles of canal between Longford and Banbury were open, and it was therefore important to the Oxford Canal proprietors that they should induce the Coventry company to complete its line.

A romantic picture of Harecastle Tunnel, published in 1785 in John Phillips' A Treatise on Inland Navigation, *one of the earliest canal books. This says more for the author's enthusiasm than for attention to detail; nothing shown is remotely accurate*

In the same year as the Coventry Act, two tributary canals were authorized. The Droitwich Canal was an artificial tributary to a natural river, linking the Severn to Droitwich. It was made large, in order to take river craft, whereas the other canals from this period had all been planned with narrow locks. The first canal to be built as a tributary to one of the new artificial rivers, which became the prototype of many more industrial canals, was the Birmingham Canal, which ran off the Staffordshire & Worcestershire Canal at Autherley. This was completed in 1772. It was to form the heart of the Industrial Revolution canals, from which the arteries to the main river estuaries and ports would radiate.

The Birmingham Canal not only brought coal to Birmingham from pits along its line, together with goods from the Staffordshire & Worcestershire, and so from the whole completed canal system, it also carried coal away from the fields around Wednesbury and sent it towards the Severn to compete with that from Shropshire. Before the canal was built a historian of Birmingham, Hutton, says that coal brought by land cost 13s. (65p) a ton and that it was common to see a train of waggons for miles, to the great destruction of the road and the annoyance of travellers. Its construction brought the price down to 7s. (35p), while its profits raised the value of its £140 shares to £420 by 1782, when a dividend of 15 per cent was paid.

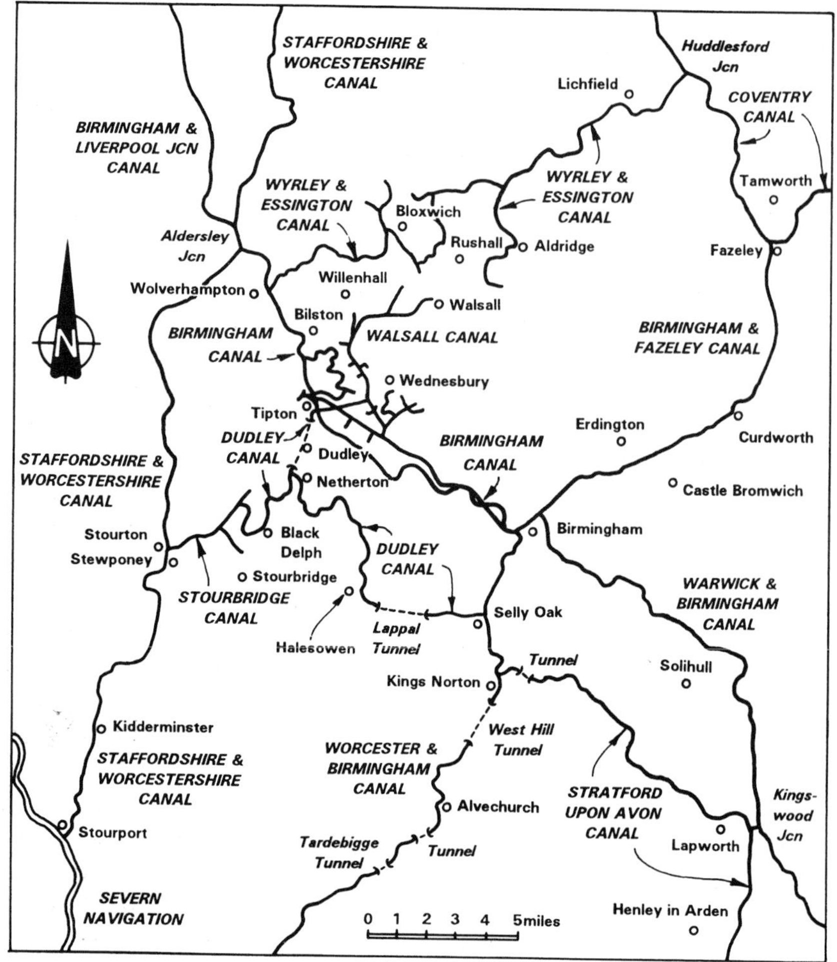

The canals of the Birmingham area as completed by the end of the canal age, before the completion of final links

In 1776 there began the process that ended in giving Birmingham its present network of canals. Two new companies obtained their Acts on the same day. One, the Stourbridge Canal Company, was to spend £38,000 on making a cut from Stourbridge to the Staffs & Worcs Canal at Stourton, together with two branches, one being to Black Delph in the direction of Dudley. The other, the Dudley Canal Company, was to spend £9,700 to build a line from Dudley to join the Stourbridge Canal at Black Delph. The combined navigations enabled coal to be carried from the mining district around Dudley to the Severn, in competition with that taken on the Birmingham Canal to Autherley (later called Aldersley) Junction and sent down the Staffs & Worcs Canal.

In 1785 the Dudley Canal proprietors obtained an Act to connect their canal with the Birmingham at Tipton by means of the proposed Dudley Tunnel. In this way a shorter line was made possible between Birmingham and the Severn than that by Autherley. However, the tunnel was not completed before a new navigation was promoted, also to connect the Black Country with the Severn.

To complete this account it is necessary to discuss canals promoted during the canal mania of the 1790s (see Chapter Five). These included the Worcester & Birmingham Canal, which provided a direct line from Birmingham to the Severn at Worcester. This line gave the new company a decided advantage over the Staffs & Worcs for Birmingham traffic, including egress to a more easily navigable part of the Severn, and tended to divert Birmingham–Severn trade away from the Birmingham Canal. Both companies strongly opposed the Bill, which was, however, carried in 1791, albeit with a clause that no physical junction was to be made between the new canal and the Birmingham Canal. Ostensibly to conserve water, this ruling meant that traffic originating on the Birmingham would have to go by way of Autherley to the Severn, or at least by Tipton, if it was not to be transhipped. This Worcester Bar, as it was called, between the two canals at Birmingham was not pierced until 1815.

The Dudley proprietors at once saw their opportunity to gain traffic from the Birmingham as a result of the physical bar. They thus sought an Act to join their canal to the Worcester & Birmingham at Selly Oak. The Birmingham Canal proprietors realized that traffic for the south would be able to pass from Tipton down the Dudley and along the new branch to Selly Oak, thus avoiding the Birmingham altogether, while coal from Netherton, instead of passing through the Dudley Tunnel to the Birmingham Canal, would pass along the new branch. Their opposition to the Dudley Canal plan was defeated in spite of their cry that

> A parallel Canal, as this [to Selly Oak] certainly is, goes to the almost total Destruction of the Coal Trade on the present Birmingham Canal, and the Coals which ought from their Locality to be brought to the Birmingham Market, may be conveyed into Worcestershire, Gloucestershire, &c. without any equivalent Advantage or Prospect of any of the Inhabitants of Birmingham.[1]

The Dudley extension to Selly Oak through the Lapal Tunnel, at 3,795 yd the fourth longest in Britain, was opened in 1798. Later, in 1802, the first

Galton Bridge spanning the cutting, 71 ft deep, on the improved line of the Birmingham Canal. This was one of the few lengths of canal with double towpaths. The boat appears to be a horse-drawn spoon dredger. By the date of this photograph, the majority of traffic on the Birmingham Canal Navigations was local (Ware Collection/Boat Museum)

part of the Stratford-upon-Avon Canal was opened, from a junction with the Worcester & Birmingham at King's Norton to join the recently built Warwick & Birmingham at Kingswood. This gave water access to London for coal and iron traffic from the Stourbridge, Dudley and Netherton districts, and also from Coalbrookdale on the Severn and from Stourport and other places on the Staffs & Worcs, without using the Birmingham Canal.

During the rivalry with the Dudley Canal, the Birmingham Canal proprietors increased the capacity of their original line by lowering the old summit level at Smethwick, eliminating three locks at each end, duplicating those that remained, and making a cutting that was 46 ft deep at one point. Later, in 1827, the old summit was completely removed by substituting a cutting running up to 71 ft deep. There was indeed trade for everyone then, though in time the character of the traffic changed as the coal areas around Wednesbury and Bilston became exhausted. The Birmingham system of canals continued to grow and throw out branches, until in 1898 the waterways then included in the group had a total length of 159 miles with 216 locks. This network formed the heart of the canal system into the twentieth century.

In 1781 and 1782 the Oxford, Coventry and Trent & Mersey companies supported a project for a canal from the coalmines around Wednesbury to join the Coventry Canal near Fazeley, from where the coal could be taken north or south. The promoters and their supporters met at Coleshill in 1782 and agreed to complete the Oxford Canal from Banbury to Oxford, and the Coventry Canal from Atherstone to Fazeley, while the Trent & Mersey and the Birmingham & Fazeley, as it was called, would each finish half of the Fradley–Fazeley section. The Birmingham Canal Company became very worried lest it should lose its monopoly position in the coal-carrying trade of the Birmingham area, and its consequent prosperity. It organized a nominally separate company (amalgamated with its parent in 1784) to build from its canal at Farmer's Bridge, Birmingham, to Fazeley, so that Wednesbury coal would not bypass its line. After a terrific parliamentary battle the Birmingham Canal group won with an Act of 1783. It took over the Coleshill agreement and began construction. In 1790, after some recalcitrance by the rather faint-hearted Coventry Company, the whole Birmingham–Fazeley–Fradley–Coventry–Oxford line was finished. Thus the last link in the interconnection of the four great rivers of Trent, Mersey, Severn and Thames was completed.

That the traffic had only been waiting for the communication is shown by the tolls and weighing charges taken by the Oxford company:

Years	£
1789–90	10,697
1792–3	17,970
1795–6	25,880

In the same year of 1766 that saw the authorization of the Trent & Mersey and the Staffordshire & Worcestershire canals, the Forth & Clyde Canal was projected with John Smeaton as engineer, and two years later its tributary, the Monkland Canal, followed. Since the Forth & Clyde was, in concept, a sea-to-sea canal it will be described in Chapter Six.

Two chains still waited to be thrown across England from river to river: in the north a connection between the Mersey on the west and the Aire & Calder Navigation in Yorkshire that gave access to the Humber; in the south a junction between the Bristol Channel and the Thames by way of the Severn or the Bristol Avon.

The first Act to make navigable the Aire to Leeds, and its tributary, the Calder to Wakefield, had been passed in 1699 as a result of efforts by the mayor and several aldermen of Leeds, and some Wakefield gentlemen. Under the Act, locks were built and a depth of 3½ ft was obtained. The northern link between the Aire at Leeds and the Mersey at Liverpool was

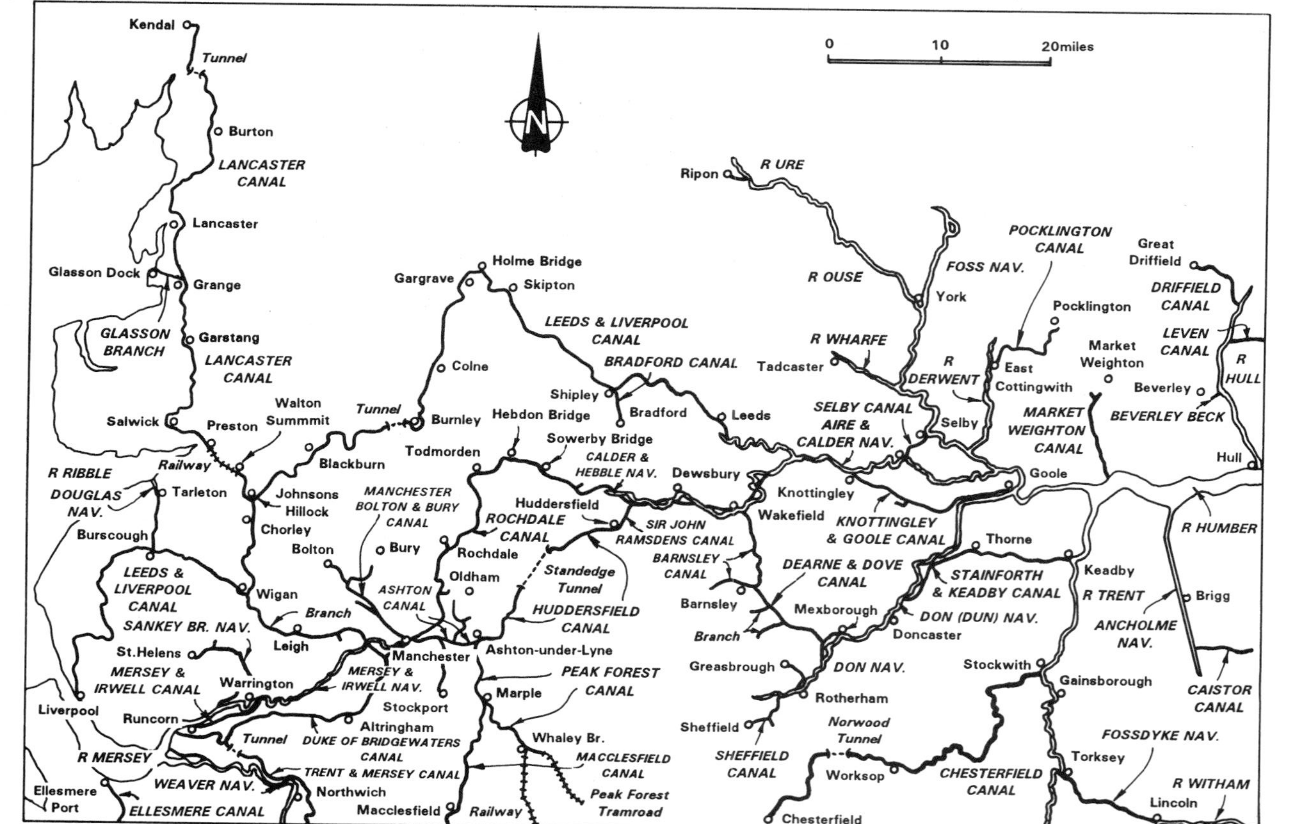

The main inland waterways of Lancashire and Yorkshire, prior to the replacement of much of the Mersey & Irwell Navigation by

first planned and in 1766 surveyed by the Yorkshire engineer John Longbothom. This survey was checked by Brindley and his assistant Robert Whitworth, and in 1770 an Act was obtained, the authorized capital being £260,000. The planned line of this Leeds & Liverpool Canal was 108¾ miles long. The Yorkshire side was built as planned, but on the Lancashire side it ran north of the present line by Whalley and the Ribble Valley, then south of Preston and by Leyland to Newburgh and the present line to Liverpool.

The coal of the Wigan neighbourhood had in the past been distributed via the River Douglas, finally made navigable to Tarleton on the Ribble in 1742, from where it was carried by coasting vessels to the Mersey or farther, especially to Ireland. The new Leeds & Liverpool company soon bought a controlling interest in the Douglas Navigation, and later the two concerns were amalgamated.

Before building began there had been controversy between the promoters in Yorkshire, whose interest was in a direct and cheap communication with Liverpool, and those in Lancashire, who wanted a less direct line that would include more Lancashire towns. The Yorkshire promoters, led by the appropriately named John Hustler, carried the day and the Act was obtained for the shorter line.

John Longbothom began construction. By 1774 28 miles on the Lancashire side had been opened from Liverpool to Newburgh, from where there was access to Wigan via the Douglas. Three years later 30 miles on the Yorkshire side had been completed from the Aire & Calder Navigation at Leeds to Gargrave. While the Lancashire part was under construction, however, a group of dissident Lancashire promoters, who had withdrawn from the Leeds & Liverpool company, had promoted a canal from Wigan to Liverpool, saying that the route by the Douglas to Newburgh, and from there by the Leeds & Liverpool, was too roundabout and uncertain. Their Bill was defeated in 1772 and by 1779 an all-canal line had been opened from Wigan to Liverpool. Two years later the Rufford branch from Burscough to the Ribble, to bypass most of the Douglas, was completed.

Meanwhile a moment for choosing life or death had come to the Aire & Calder, for in 1772 a newly promoted company, supported unofficially by many concerned with the Leeds & Liverpool Canal, had introduced a Bill to build a canal from Leeds to Selby on the Ouse, thus bypassing the Aire & Calder completely. The latter defeated the Bill and then built a shorter canal from the Aire at Haddlesey to Selby, the present Selby Canal, avoiding the difficult passage of the lower Aire. Other side cuts to improve the river passage were also begun as part of a modernization programme.

The Bingley five-rise staircase on one of the earliest lengths of the Leeds & Liverpool Canal in Yorkshire. There were several staircase locks on this length, one of the earliest to be completed

Work had stopped, however, on the Leeds & Liverpool as a result of a lack of money, and for thirteen years nothing was done. The completed portions were of value, however, for that in Yorkshire joined Bradford (by the Bradford Canal) and Gargrave above Skipton to Leeds and the Aire & Calder Navigation, while that in Lancashire carried rapidly increasing quantities of coal from Wigan. By 1785 nearly 4 per cent was being earned on the capital expended to that date.

In 1790 work began again at the Gargrave end, with Robert Whitworth as engineer, though his estimate of the money needed to finish the canal sufficed for only 14 miles to Barrowford, including Foulridge Tunnel. Meanwhile the growth of new manufacturing districts had made the company decide that a short route between east and west was less important than a route that passed through these areas. The line was therefore altered to run by Burnley, Church and Blackburn to Johnson's Hillock, and work proceeded as the debts of the company grew. The branch canal from Newburgh to Wigan became part of the main line, while the Lancaster Canal, authorized in 1792, was used for 11 miles of the route in Lancashire, from Johnson's Hillock to Wigan top lock. At last, in 1816, forty-six years after the canal had been authorized, it was completed by making the last portion below Blackburn. It had cost some £800,000 and had grown in length to 127¼ miles. Though designed for through carriage, its revenue came primarily from the separate trade of the two ends: from Burnley, Blackburn and the other cotton towns, and from Wigan down to Liverpool, and from the highlands of Yorkshire to Leeds and the Aire & Calder. In 1820 the Leeds & Liverpool Canal was linked by the Leigh branch to the Bridgewater Canal, and so to Manchester. However, though it ran to Liverpool it had no physical connection with the Mersey until 1846. Ironically, although the Leeds & Liverpool was by over twenty years the first trans-Pennine canal to be begun, it was the last of three to be finished: another broad canal, the Rochdale, from the Bridgewater at Manchester to the Calder & Hebble at Sowerby Bridge, was authorized in 1794 and opened in 1804; the narrow Huddersfield Canal, also authorized in 1794, was finished in 1811 through the then 5,456 yd long Standedge Tunnel. The Leeds & Liverpool was to outlast the Rochdale and Huddersfield canals as a through route.

The idea of joining the Severn to the Thames is at least as old as the reign of Elizabeth I. The first practical step was taken in 1730 with an Act to make navigable the River Stroudwater from the Severn to the town of Stroud. The owners of the many mills on the river were so strong in opposition, however (they even inserted a clause that no boat was to pass between 14 August and 15 October without their majority consent), that nothing was done. A second Act, in 1759, is of interest because of the extraordinary scheme it produced. In order to overcome the objections of the millowners it was proposed to make the river navigable without locks. Below each mill a cut was to be made towards the river above the mill, the two waterways being separated by a 12 ft bank on which a double crane was to be fitted. The boats themselves were to carry six to eight boxes of cargo, each holding 1 ton of goods, which were then to be lifted from one boat to another by the crane at each bank. A crane with two jibs was provided so that the boxes could be interchanged without setting them down. John Kemmett and the other projectors did about half of the work (and offered also to make the Calder and the upper Don navigable in the same way) and then gave up, apparently due to a lack of capital.

From 1774 the promoters attempted to build a canal under powers given in former Acts to improve the river. After some work had been done they were stopped by an injunction, and a new Act had to be obtained in 1776. The canal opened in 1779 and was big enough to take Severn trows. It was 8 miles long with twelve locks.

The building of the Stroudwater Canal encouraged action to join the Severn to the Thames. An Act was passed in 1783, Whitworth was

Thames & Severn Canal tokens, showing a Severn trow and the Coates entrance to Sapperton Tunnel

engaged as engineer with Josiah Clowes under him, and the Thames & Severn Canal opened in 1789. The canal was 30¼ miles long, including the branch to Cirencester, and ran from the Stroudwater at Wallbridge (Stroud) to the Thames at Inglesham, above Lechlade. Its length included Sapperton Tunnel, over two miles long, the third longest canal tunnel in Britain.

The Thames & Severn started life with three handicaps: disordered finance as a result of loose administration while it was being built; chronic water supply problems worsened by a summit level through the Great Oolite that throughout its long life lost up to 3 million gallons of water a day in leakage; and the bad state of the navigation of the upper River Thames. These causes persisted, though the finances were reorganized. The canal was never more than partly successful and proved a failure for most of its life.

It was a different story with the second of the three canals built to join the Bristol Channel to the Thames. The proposal to link the Kennet at Newbury with the Avon at Bath grew from a 1788 plan to extend the Kennet Navigation from Newbury by a canal to Hungerford, but got its impetus from the canal mania of 1792, and was authorized as the Kennet & Avon Canal in 1794.

The project was on a grand scale: a broad canal 57 miles long, to include a great flight of 29 locks at Devizes. John Rennie was the engineer. The first part of the line, from Newbury to Hungerford, was opened in 1798 with 'a barge freighted with a wrought Portland stone staircase, for J. Pearce, esq., of Chilton Lodge, a large quantity of deals, and nine chaldron of sea coal, in the whole amounting to 40 tons'.[2]

Troubles were many, and as early as 1800 450 of the 3,500 issued shares of £120 had been forfeited for non-payment of calls on them, owing to the nervousness of shareholders. The lack of a proper survey before work began caused much extra expense, and it was not until 1810 that the line was completed, at a cost of £980,000. Yet the shareholders, already with a controlling interest in the Avon, went on to buy the Kennet Navigation, followed by plans for expansion and through routes. Some Kennet & Avon proprietors took up shares in the Grand Western Canal of Devon, seeing it as part of a through route from Exeter to London.

The Kennet & Avon was a successful canal. Its dividends were small, for the cost of upkeep was high, but in its prime it carried 341,878 tons of goods in a year (1838–9), against 60,894 on the Thames & Severn for the same year. Sold to the Great Western Railway while still a going concern, it survived attempts at closure in 1926 and in the 1950s, and is now open for pleasure craft use. Its two competitors remain largely derelict.

The Wilts & Berks was a narrow canal, planned not as a through waterway from Bristol to London but as a carrier of coal to the agricultural areas of the Vale of the White Horse. It was built under an Act of 1795 from Semington on the Kennet & Avon to Abingdon on the Thames, by way of Swindon (not then, of course, a large town), and with branches to Calne, Chippenham and Wantage. Its history was that of many agricultural canals, although its high cost of £255,000 was not. It declined after railway competition but had a few years of exciting life.

The promoters of the Wilts & Berks Canal regarded it as a competitor for both the Kennet & Avon and the Thames & Severn, although they forgot that the Wilts & Berks was a narrow and shallow canal, longer than the Kennet & Avon, and they made a bid for the through traffic between Bristol, London and the Midlands. First they planned a short connecting link to the Thames & Severn, to take traffic from that canal to Latton and carry it by Swindon and the Wilts & Berks to Abingdon, so bypassing the upper Thames. This link was built as the North Wilts Canal and opened in 1819. To avoid the navigation difficulties of the lower Thames, second only to those of the upper river, they then proposed a cut from Abingdon across country to join the Grand Junction. Another was planned from Wootton Bassett, direct to Bristol, to cut out the Kennet & Avon west of Semington and also the Avon, and yet another canal was planned from Abingdon to the Stratford-upon-Avon Canal to attract the Birmingham and Midlands trade. It was a gloriously grandiose plan, but narrow boats and a winding line were not serious competitors for a broad canal on a through route like the Kennet & Avon.

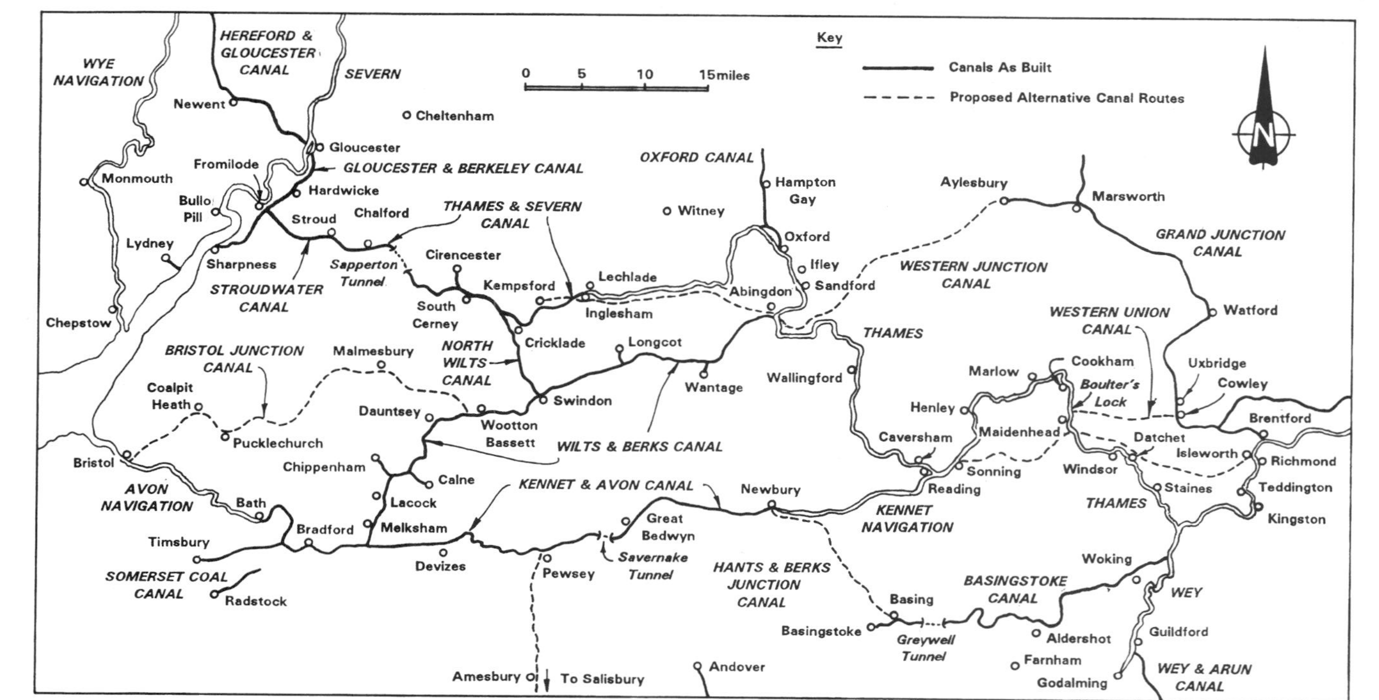

The waterways of southern England, including the Basingstoke Canal, showing a number of proposed connections

The Broadwater on the extension of the Lagan Navigation, on a length of the summit level which opened in 1792 (McCutcheon Collection)

These three canals completed the circuit of Britain, by the Mersey, Trent, Thames, Severn and Mersey again. In time, however, they fall outside the first period of canal building to which the others belong.

Meanwhile two arteries were being built in Ireland to supplement Steers's old Newry Canal, which Thomas Omer, an engineer of Dutch descent, had by 1769 extended via a small ship canal taking craft of 120 tons.

The first, the Lagan Navigation from Belfast to Lough Neagh, was begun by Thomas Omer in 1756. While the river section to Lisburn was completed by 1765, there work stopped, partly because of doubts as to whether it was sensible to continue a river navigation so liable to floods as the Lagan. After Robert Whitworth had put up alternative ideas for continuing by canal, a company took over from the old commissioners, Richard Owen from the Leeds & Liverpool was engaged as engineer and work resumed in 1782. The whole line was opened to Lough Neagh on the first day of 1794, 25¾ miles long with 27 locks, each 62 ft by 14 ft 6 in, very similar in size to those of Owen's former canal. Owen's work included the four-arched Spencer's Bridge aqueduct and the Union Locks triple staircase at Sprucefield above Lisburn, both now demolished.

The second artery was the Grand Canal, the line from Dublin to the

The Grand Canal crossing the Bog of Allen, 35 miles from Dublin, pictured in the 1960s. The height of the embankment here is shown by the houses on either side of the canal. Blundell's Aqueduct is just beyond the moored boat; this and the embankment took ten years to build, owing to the nature of the ground, making the construction of the embankment a major engineering achievement (Ruth Heard)

Shannon, and its major branch the Barrow. The idea of opening up the centre of Ireland had lain behind the Act of 1715. In 1751 the Corporation for Promoting and Carrying on an Inland Navigation in Ireland was set up by the Irish Parliament to amalgamate the four bodies of provincial commissioners established in 1729. The corporation put impetus behind waterway building but was dissolved in 1787, having spent some £850,000, and separate bodies of commissioners for different waterways were substituted. It had initiated work on the Shannon in 1755, the Grand Canal in 1756 and the Barrow and Boyne in 1759.

The Grand Canal was to be 79 miles long without branches, reaching the Shannon at Shannon Harbour above Banagher. The chosen line was surveyed by Thomas Omer and work began on a large scale, Omer's first lock being 136 ft long and able to take a 175 ton barge. Not long afterwards the city of Dublin decided to draw water for town use from the canal, now to serve a double purpose. Canal work proceeded very slowly, however, until, after about 20 miles had been built, it stopped in 1768, with a series of inquiries as to why so much had been spent and so little achieved.

Eventually a company was formed to take over and complete the work on a reduced scale. John Smeaton brought over his pupil William Jessop in 1773. The latter spent some time with John Trail, who had worked mainly as Dublin's water supply engineer, and, supported by Smeaton, recommended that the canal should continue on this smaller scale. This was agreed and construction went on with Trail, William Chapman and other engineers as residents, and Jessop as consultant. The first 12 miles opened to traffic in 1779, the Bog of Allen was crossed in the 1790s and at last, in 1805, after John Killaly had been engineer since 1798, the whole canal, with its 41 locks of 70 ft by 13 ft 7½ in, was finished, two months after Jessop's Grand Junction Canal in England.

Its major offshoot – mainly river navigation, partly canal – the Barrow, had been started by Thomas Omer in 1759, but work went on very slowly indeed until, in 1790, a company was formed. Under this William Chapman rebuilt some of the old work and created some new. Early in the new century, with Government help, the navigation was finished, nearly 42 miles long from the Grand's Barrow branch to Athy (itself 28½ miles long, and opened in 1791) to the tideway of the Barrow at St Mullins.

In 1759 Omer also began work on the lower Boyne from Drogheda to Slane, mostly by building a lateral canal. Though £75,000 had been spent, the section to Slane was seemingly unfinished and semi-derelict when the corporation was abolished in 1787. A River Boyne Company took over in 1790, and by 1800 had extended the line to Navan, 19 miles from Drogheda with 20 broad locks.

Back in England, after the authorization of the Leeds & Liverpool Canal in 1770, three tributary canals were built: the little Bradford to link Bradford with the Leeds & Liverpool; the Chester from the Dee at Chester through to Nantwich; and the great Chesterfield Canal to run from Chesterfield through the nearby coalfield to the River Trent at Stockwith.

Then followed a long period of consolidation, lasting from 1774 to 1788. Capital and labour were being fully employed on the great routes that crossed the British Isles, the War of American Independence was being fought and lost, and investors and government were watching to see if this new method of transport would be a financial success, when speculators could take a hand. How successful it was can be seen from the takings on the Duke of Bridgewater's Canal, which in 1791 amounted to £61,143.

The first period of canal development in England saw the authorization of waterways linking the Mersey with the Severn and the Trent, and also with the Aire & Calder, together with some tributaries.

Some sixteen years elapsed between the Act for the Chester Canal in 1772 and those for the Andover and Cromford canals in 1789 – the harbingers of canal mania. In this period the few canals that were authorized included the Erewash, a tributary of the Trent, a number of small privately owned and privately built navigations from Cornwall to Yorkshire and the Basingstoke Canal, the first of the agricultural canals.

While the great expansion of canal building was taking place in the growing industrial area around Birmingham, the prosperous landowners of the south had been considering a canal that was not to carry fuel, raw materials or finished goods to or from factories or large towns, but was to open up the countryside and enable the latest agricultural methods to be used on poor land. Suggested as early as 1769, the Basingstoke Canal obtained its Act in 1778, although work did not start until the War of American Independence was over.

This line, 37½ miles long as constructed, ran from Basingstoke to the River Wey near its mouth at Weybridge. It was partly intended to form a route for goods to pass to and from Salisbury, Bristol and the west by road transport, rather than by the existing route via the Thames and Kennet to Newbury. This hoped for change of through route to the west was, however, not the principal reason for promoting the canal; this was the improvement of agricultural land en route by the carriage of lime and manure.

The Basingstoke Canal was a financial failure, partly owing to the requirement to pay interest on capital during construction, which meant that costs escalated. After it opened in 1794 the estimated revenues were never achieved, the highest being realized in 1838–9, and to the end of its days the company continued to pay off bonds without ever being able to pay any dividend on its original share capital. While it was of local benefit, any hopes of carrying through traffic destined for the west were ended by the Kennet & Avon Canal, and vessels slowly disappeared through railway competition. Several attempts were made to revive the canal – some distinctly ludicrous, some definitely fraudulent – until its acquisition by local authorities in the 1970s began its restoration and revival for pleasure boating.

CHAPTER FIVE

The Canal Mania and the Wars

The first period of canal expansion had ended in 1778, with the opening of the Selby Canal from the old Aire & Calder line to the Yorkshire Ouse. A year earlier the Trent & Mersey had been completed, and the year before that the Bridgewater to the Mersey at Runcorn. However, the effects of existing canals and those under construction on the British economy were delayed. At the time when results might have been looked for, the difficulties of the American War and the period of national gloom that followed did not encourage enterprise. Gradually trade improved, and even the French Revolution could not disguise the prosperity that was resulting from the cheap transport of coal and commodities. The possibilities of expansion were encouraged by the owners of capital, who saw in the solid prosperity of the older canals a means to tempt money out of the pockets of the incautious, and by engineers, who, like John Longbothom, put advertisements in newspapers for

> The survey of canals by the piece, or examining them by the day. His terms by day are Three Guineas per day, exclusive of expenses. He has men, good surveyors and levellers, very capable of taking the survey of canals, which he charges as common surveyors, and staff-holders, exclusive of expenses.[1]

The boom began in 1790 and was dead by 1797. It reached its peak in Britain in late 1792 and early 1793, which was reflected in legislation of 1793 and 1794. The following table shows its legislative progress:

Year	*No. of new canals authorized*	*Capital authorized* £
1789	2	131,000
1790	1	90,000
1791	7	743,000
1792	7	1,056,000
1793	20	2,824,700
1794	10	2,037,900
1795	4	395,000
1796	3	585,000
1797	1	18,000

The waterways system of lowland England, as completed in 1789, just before the canal mania

The first cause of the boom was the prosperity of the earlier waterways. Everyone thought that they knew how profitable the Duke of Bridgewater's Canal was, but the Birmingham Canal paid over 23 per cent for 1789, and others like the Trent & Mersey and the Staffordshire & Worcestershire were very solid businesses. The second was, perhaps, the opening of the Thames & Severn in 1789, which gave a water route of a sort between the Midlands and London, and between Bristol and

London, together with the completion, in 1790, of a shorter line from Birmingham to London via Fazeley and Oxford. The last cause was, perhaps, the interest taken by industrialists who backed local canal promotions, including the Darbys and Reynolds of Coalbrookdale with the Shropshire Canal, Sir Richard Arkwright and the Cromford Canal, Richard Crawshay of Cyfartha and other ironmasters with the Glamorganshire Canal.

All over Britain the canal mania took hold and raged, so much so that at Leicester and Birmingham special 'Navigation Share Offices' were set up. Because they wanted to keep a good thing to themselves, promoters tended to hold subscription meetings quietly. Thus, whenever a meeting was held, hopeful speculators rushed to the place seeking to put down deposits on shares that they could immediately sell at a profit, in one case only to find that the supposed canal meeting was really a hunt dinner.

Let us follow the mania in the columns of a single rural newspaper, the *British Chronicle* of Hereford, far from Britain's industrial heart. In 1789 there was to the north of Hereford no canal at all; none of any size in South Wales; none to the west; and in the direction of England nothing nearer than Droitwich. Small barges carrying about 20 tons each brought coal and other goods up the Wye to the city, when there was enough water in the river. There were no locks and no horse towing-path.

In 1790 the Glamorganshire Canal had been authorized, not very far away, and in 1791 two nearer home, from Hereford to Gloucester with £105,000 of capital, and from Kington and Leominster to Stourport with £190,000, both promoted to bring coal to the towns and villages, and to carry away their goods and produce. These two appeared often in the paper's columns, but soon news from farther away was featured. In May 1791 it was reported that £60,000 had been subscribed in an hour for a canal from Manchester to Rochdale; in June that the Forth & Clyde Canal was open; in September that a meeting had been held at Ellesmere to consider a canal from the Severn to the Dee; in November that the capital of £40,000 for the Grantham Canal had been raised at a single meeting; in December, nearer home, that £51,000 had been subscribed for the Monmouthshire Canal from Newport to Pontypool and Crumlin.

By early 1792 the columns were filling up with canal news; the Gloucester & Berkeley ship canal project was going ahead; so were the Leominster, the Monmouthshire and the Lancaster canals, to the last of which £170,000 had been subscribed at one meeting; and a canal from Birmingham to London was planned. In July, appositely for author and publisher, John Phillips' *General History of Inland Navigation* was published, the first book about British canals as a whole, which must have opened many eyes to the possibilities of water transport. By August an

The Herefordshire & Gloucestershire Canal at Monkhide. Although this section of the canal was authorized during the canal mania, it was not completed until 1845, when the canal age was over. The exceptionally skewed bridge carries only a minor road; the earliest canal skew bridge, on the Rochdale Canal, was constructed only fifty years earlier. This section was disused after 1881, but the length into Monkhide, one of the few in water, has been restored, with ambitious plans for the restoration (or rebuilding) of the whole line from the Severn to Hereford

extension of the Monmouthshire Canal was being considered – the Brecknock & Abergavenny – and in September the newspaper published a list of canal shares that were standing at a premium. These were headed by the Birmingham Canal, which was open, and projected canals such as the Grand Junction.

On 19 September the paper reported that 'last Saturday's Gazette gives notice of applications . . . for no fewer than twenty-five navigable Cuts and Canals, many of them of immense extent . . .'. By November and December the paper was full of canal news, which died away before the onset of the wave of merchant and banking bankruptcies of early 1793. For instance, on 13 March 1793 the newspaper recorded that, 'In consequence of the temporary suspension of business of the Monmouthshire bank at Chepstow, the premium on Monmouthshire Canal shares has dropped from near 100 per cent by 25 per cent in the course of last week.' Many who had borrowed to cover their liabilities for shares must have been caught.

Three local canal schemes had been born during the mania and were wound up in 1793. A canal from Brecon to Hay and Whitney quietly died, and one from Abergavenny to Hereford was turned down by a meeting of landowners. (Horse tramroads were built over the general routes of both twenty years later.) A third, from the Leominster Canal to the Montgomeryshire Canal via Ludlow and Bishop's Castle, was seen to be too expensive and was dropped.

So much for Hereford. The following extract from an account of what happened around Bristol helps to bring the canal mania to life:

> The 'canal mania' of 1792, though productive of less important results than the railway mania of 1845, was in many respects a counterpart of that memorable delirium. On the 20th November a meeting to promote the construction of a canal from Bristol to Gloucester was held in the Guildhall, when the scheme was enthusiastically supported by influential persons, and a very large sum was subscribed by those present, who struggled violently with each other in their rush to the subscription book. A few days later, a Somerset paper announced that a meeting would be held at Wells to promote a canal from Bristol to Taunton. The design had been formed in this city [Bristol], but the promoters strove to keep it a secret, and bought up all the newspapers containing the advertisement. The news nevertheless leaked out on the evening before the intended gathering, and a host of speculators set off to secure shares in the undertaking, some arriving only to find that the subscription list was full. The third meeting was at Devizes, on the 12th December. Only one day's notice was given of this movement, which was to promote a canal from Bristol to Southampton and London, but the news rapidly spread, and thousands of intending subscribers rushed to the little town, where the proposed capital was offered several times over. The 'race to Devizes' on the part of Bristolians, who had hired or bought up at absurd prices all the old hacks that could be found, and plunged along the miry roads through a long wintry night, was attended with many comic incidents. A legion of schemes followed, Bristol being the proposed terminus of canals to all parts of the country.[2]

All over Britain waterways had been projected and sufficient money raised to pay an engineer for a survey, however hurried. Many were never embodied in a Bill, and fewer still were authorized by an Act. Those that passed the sieve were mostly solid schemes that, though they probably cost much more than their projectors had foreseen and took much longer to build, were successes in the end. Such were the Neath and Manchester, Bolton & Bury canals authorized in 1791, the Lancaster, Nottingham, Monmouthshire and Ashton in 1792, the Grand Junction, Shrewsbury, Barnsley and Dearne & Dove in 1793, and the Swansea and Rochdale canals in 1794. More of them, while useful, were only moderately profitable: the Worcester & Birmingham (1791), Wyrley & Essington (1792), Stratford, Ellesmere (1793), Peak Forest, Huddersfield and Ashby (1794). Six were failures: the Herefordshire & Gloucestershire took from 1791 to 1845 to reach Hereford from Gloucester; the Grand Western, the Leominster and the Foss never completed their lines; and the Salisbury & Southampton and Dorset & Somerset were abandoned during construction. None of these, except for the Foss, ever paid a dividend during their working lives.

The immediate consequence of the mania was that a great deal of canal building started at the same time, many companies sharing engineers and competing for cutters. In September 1793 Denys Rolle wrote:

> From the Immense Numbers of Canals now coming on and the not only absence of a Multitude of the Labouring Class abroad in the War but the vast suppos'd Diminution that there will arise from the destruction in it, a great scarcity of Hands for the Cultivation will be found at the End . . .[3]

He went on to propose that more Irish labourers should be encouraged to come over. This scarcity of hands must have led the Peak Forest committee to decide in July 1794 to start cutting 'so soon as the Corn Harvest shall be got in'.[4]

Out of the mania came a harvest of useful hard-working waterways, essential to the continued growth of the Industrial Revolution, of which the Barnsley and the Dearne & Dove may serve as examples. Promoted as rivals, the Barnsley, a client of the Aire & Calder, and the Dearne & Dove of the Don met at a junction stoplock outside Barnsley, from where the Barnsley Canal's line extended upwards to the edge of the especially valuable Silkstone coalfield. Their Acts were passed on the same day in 1793 and both opened in 1804. Within fifteen years each was carrying over 100,000 tons of coal, besides stone and timber for building houses and mills, iron and corn. The latter, coming from the fields of Lincolnshire and East Anglia by sea or by the Trent, was carried along the canals in the opposite direction to the coal to feed the Barnsley area and the coalfield.

A somewhat romanticized view of Pontcysyllte Aqueduct on the Ellesmere (later Llangollen) Canal, with the older pack-horse bridge over the Dee in the foreground

It is worth examining here one of the less successful canals authorized in the mania, but one that produced one of the biggest engineering achievements of the Industrial Revolution. What the Forth Bridge is to the railway enthusiast, or the Holyhead road to the road historian, Pontcysyllte is to the canal lover. Opened in 1805, this great aqueduct, created by William Jessop and Thomas Telford, is 1,007 ft long with nineteen arches, and carries the Ellesmere Canal (now known as the Llangollen) 121 ft above the River Dee. The piers were built solid for 70 ft and then hollow, and on them was laid a cast-iron trough 11 ft 10 in wide, with a towpath carried over part of it on iron pillars. Pontcysyllte was a monument to canal engineering and to the use of cast iron pioneered at Longdon on the Shrewsbury Canal and The Holmes on the Derby Canal. It also commemorates a complete change of mind on the part of a canal company.

The story of the Chester and Ellesmere canals, which later became part of the Shropshire Union system, begins with the 1772 Act for the Chester Canal to run from the Dee at Chester to Nantwich, and to Middlewich to join the Trent & Mersey. This project was the first thoroughly unsuccessful canal. It reached Nantwich by 1779, but the Middlewich connection was not made for fifty years, owing to opposition from the Trent & Mersey Company. So unsuccessful was the canal that it became semi-derelict.

In the 1790s two schemes were promoted to link Chester on the Dee with Shrewsbury on the Severn. The chosen line was from Netherpool on the Mersey (now called Ellesmere Port) across the Wirral peninsula to Chester, and then by way of Wrexham, Ellesmere, Frankton and Weston to Shrewsbury on the Severn. Among the proposed branches was one to Llanymynech to join the proposed Montgomeryshire Canal to Welshpool and Newtown. The intention was to serve the North Wales industrial area near Wrexham and distribute its products, and to open up the county by bringing in fuel and manure, as well as commodities carried up the three rivers from farther afield.

The proprietors started with the broad Wirral line, which opened in 1795, and also began cutting in the middle of their line, from Chirk to Weston, along with the Llanymynech line, while putting in hand the expensive Chirk and Pontcysyllte aqueducts. It was planned that coal from the Ruabon collieries, near Pontcysyllte, would be carried south towards Montgomeryshire.

A new line for the canal between Pontcysyllte and Chester was authorized by an Act of 1796, but by 1800 the opening of new collieries offered Chester cheaper coal than the canal could bring. A less expensive way for the sections already built or under construction to reach Chester was therefore decided on. The line was taken from Frankton to the Chester Canal at Hurleston near Nantwich, with short branches to Whitchurch, Ellesmere and towards Prees. This work, accomplished in 1805, provided a waterway from the Mersey and Dee to Weston quite different from that originally intended.

Though the original main line by way of Wrexham had been abandoned, the aqueducts at Chirk and Pontcysyllte were proceeded with, even though they lay on what had become a branch. It was evidently thought that the coal to be carried from the Ruabon collieries made the works worthwhile, and when the great aqueduct was finished a basin and lines of tramroad were built at its far end to handle the coal and other products of Ruabon. The water supply feeder from Llantysilio past Llangollen was also made navigable to provide additional traffic.

The aqueduct was opened with ceremony. On one of its piers it still carries the cast-iron plate commemorating the laying of the first stone on 25 July 1795.

By 1805 over £450,000 had been spent and the company had come to the end of its resources. In 1813 an Act was passed to amalgamate the Chester and Ellesmere companies, and in 1826 a new canal, the Birmingham & Liverpool Junction, was authorized to shorten the distance and reduce the lockage between the Mersey and Autherley to 66½ miles and 45 locks instead of 80¾ miles and 75 locks by way of the Trent & Mersey.

Because so much Irish canal money came from public funds, the canal mania hardly touched Ireland, except perhaps with the Royal Canal from Dublin to the upper Shannon. Even with a government grant of £96,856, the Royal Canal company could not complete its line, and in 1813, with nearly a million spent, the Directors General of Inland Navigation took over. They finished the line in 1817 and then handed the canal to a New Royal Canal Company, in which shareholders got £40 stock for each £100 they held in the old company. The Royal had cost over £1.4 million for its 90 miles from Dublin to Cloondara on the Shannon. With its written-down capital the company could pay dividends of up to 2 per cent until the railways came. In 1836 88,334 tons were carried, and in 1837 46,450 passengers.

Another factor in transport began to affect projected canals at this time. With the financial crisis having dried up, available capital and the rise in prices had caused many canals under construction to cost more than had been estimated, and engineers began to find many proposed branches or extensions unnecessary. Instead they proposed tramroads.

The use of waggons running on rails dates back to the reign of Queen Elizabeth I. The earliest known were those serving Wollaton Colliery, near Nottingham, which were completed in 1603 or 1604, shortly before two in East Shropshire carrying coal to the Severn. Later they were employed to bring coal from the collieries of the north-east to the staithes of the Tyne, and from the Shropshire collieries to the Severn. It was natural therefore that horse tramroads, which for two hundred years had been used as feeders to rivers, should be used as feeders to canals.

Tramroads, which here include all kinds of horse-drawn line, initially had wooden rails; later the wood was covered with a strip of iron and the waggon wheels were flanged; later still iron edge-rails were used. Then

Lock 12 at Blanchardstown, on the Royal Canal, the main example of the canal mania in Ireland. This was part of the first length to be completed, in 1796. The photograph was taken on the occasion of the reopening of Lock 12 in 1990; it had been closed since 1961. The section above this lock was the first to be restored, after 1974 (Dr Ian Bath)

John Curr, followed by Benjamin Outram, introduced the plateway. Instead of rails, this used L-shaped iron plates about 3 ft long. The sleeper was a rough cube of granite with a hole in the centre, which was filled with an oak plug, into which a spike to hold the plate was driven. The waggon wheels were flangeless, being held in position by the flanges on the inner sides of the plates. These plateways became very popular and Outram, his assistant and successor John Hodgkinson, and other engineers laid several hundred miles of them. They also converted many of the older railways to plateways between the early 1790s and about 1830, after which these tramroads began to give way to the conventional railway as we know it today, with edge-rails and the flange on the wheel. Some plateways continued in use well into the present century, including that serving the Peak Forest Canal at Whaley Bridge, which only ceased work in 1920.

These horse tramroads constituted an adjunct to canals, the importance of which has not perhaps been fully understood, since they

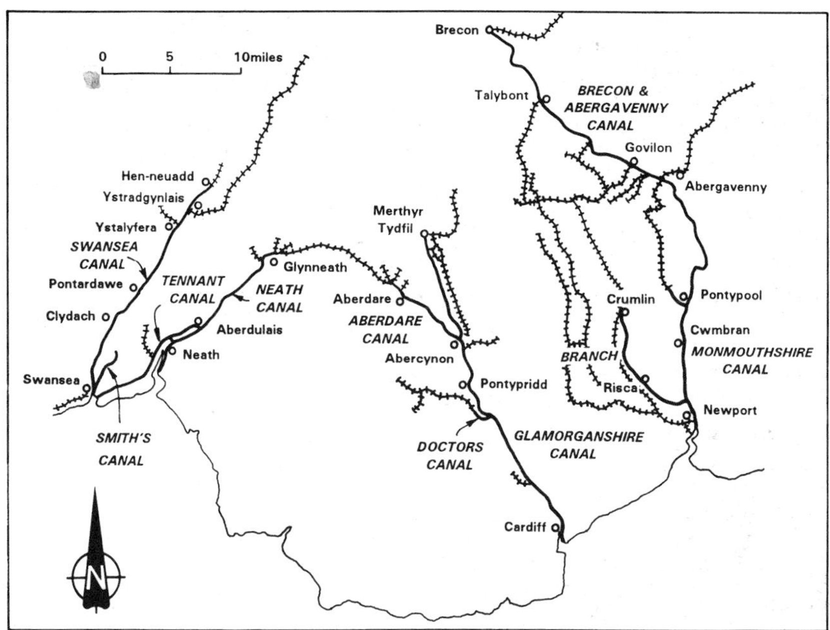

The canals of the South Wales valleys, showing some of their tramroad connections

enabled canal branches to be built that as waterways would have been uneconomic. For instance in 1794 the Ashby de la Zouch Canal was authorized from a junction with the Coventry Canal to Ashby, with branches to limeworks at Ticknall and Cloudhill, a total of 43 miles with a great deal of lockage. In fact the canal was only cut for 30 miles to Moira, the branches being built by Outram as plateways.

The tramroads extending from the two arms of the Monmouthshire Canal were an outstanding example of such development. In the 1830s a considerable mileage of tramroads ran up the valleys, much of it owned by the canal company. Some of these in turn connected to another tramroad system, depending on the Brecknock & Abergavenny Canal and extending as far as Hereford. Tramroads were also developed elsewhere in South Wales, near Coalbrookdale in connection with the local tub-boat canals, in Derbyshire (notably plateways owned by the Peak Forest and Derby Canal companies), and in the north, especially near the Tyne and Wear rivers.

In 1800 Telford advocated the use of iron railways:

> in countries whose surfaces are rugged, or where it is difficult to obtain water for lockage, where the weight of the articles of produce is great

> in comparison with their bulk, and when they are mostly to be conveyed from a higher to a lower level . . . Upon the whole, this useful contrivance may be varied so as to suit the surface of many different countries, at a comparatively modest expense. It may be constructed in a much more expeditious manner than navigable canals; it may be introduced into many districts where canals are wholly inapplicable; and in case of any change in the working of the mines or manufactures, the rails may be taken up and put down again, in a new situation, at a moderate expense.[5]

Tramroads could be double-track or single with passing places. The usual load for the four-wheeled waggons was 2 tons, a number – called a gang or train – being pulled by each horse. When the lines could be worked by gravity, as often happened on the Tyne, in Wales or in the Somerset coalfield, a train of half a dozen or more waggons was run by its own weight to the canalside, a boy applying the brake and a horse being tied to the last waggon or riding in it to pull back the empty train.

Outram tried to put rafts on the Somersetshire Coal Canal, which would take such tramroad waggons without it being necessary to shift their contents, but the difficulties on the one hand of getting the waggons onto the rafts, and on the other of navigating the rafts when a wind was blowing, were too great. Waggon-boats were, however, later used successfully on the Don Navigation in Yorkshire and on the Forth & Clyde Canal to carry waggons from the Monkland & Kirkintilloch Railroad.

Tramroads were also used to connect portions of canal. The flight of sixteen locks at Marple on the Peak Forest Canal, and the tunnel at Blisworth on the Grand Junction Canal, took so long to construct that temporary tramroads were built to enable through trade to begin. In the case of the Lancaster Canal the difficulties of fulfilling the original intention of carrying the waterway over the Ribble Estuary were so great that the two parts of the canal were permanently connected by a tramroad.

Sometimes these tramroads were built and owned by canal companies: the Brecknock & Abergavenny, remarkable for having completed and worked a tramroad before having cut a yard of canal, the Monmouthshire, Peak Forest, Trent & Mersey and others were important tramroad owners. Sometimes they were built by independent companies, such as the Surrey Iron Railway or the Oystermouth, or by companies having many common shareholders with a neighbouring canal, such as the Hay Railway. Often these were privately owned by the proprietors of the collieries or works they served; thus the Hills of Blaenavon or Crawshay Bailey of Nantyglo owned lines from their works to the canals.

In Ireland the only significant tramroad to be constructed served one canal, the Coalisland, and superseded another, the Ducarts Canal. John Smeaton had suggested that the latter should be replaced by a tramroad, and one was built between the Drumglass Colliery and the basin at Coalisland in about 1790. It was still operating in around 1830.

Many canal Acts gave companies the power to make tramroad branches, usually to a distance of 4–8 miles from the canal. If the owner of a mine or works within the specified distance applied and the canal company refused to build a tramroad, the powers of construction were transferred to the applicant. Some canal companies, like the Swansea, steadfastly refused to make tramroads and left them to the businessmen; others like the Monmouthshire built many. These powers were included to avoid the system of wayleaves in force on the Tyne and Wear, where railway owners had to make a payment to the landowner for everything that passed over his land. In the Chesterfield Canal Act, instead of tramroads, power was given to make toll-free roads up to a mile long, and in other Acts the power to make 'stone-roads' was alternative to that for making tramroads. Many roads were general purpose feeders to canals throughout the country, and canal companies spent much time complaining to the town and country local authorities that such feeder roads were inadequate or badly maintained.

When the canals were built the takings of turnpike trustees of the roads that ran parallel with canals fell sharply. For example those of the Loughborough to Leicester road fell from £1,800 in 1792 to £1,162 in 1802, after the Leicester Navigation had opened in 1794. Not until 1830 did the takings again equal the earlier figure, and then only because of the increase of passenger traffic. On the other hand, roads that from their situation were natural feeders to canals gained in revenue. Thus the tolls of the Hinckley road in Leicestershire rose from £602 in 1792 to £888 in 1802. Roads that suffered from canal competition had two consolations: the removal of heavy traffic reduced upkeep costs; and the waterway was useful for carrying roadstone, usually toll-free unless water was short. In some cases, such as the impecunious Chester Canal, the parallel road competed successfully and contributed to the canal's failure.

The outbreak of the French Revolution in 1793, and the accompanying financial crisis and inflation, put a brake on developments at a time when industrial and transport expansion was taking place. A number of canals begun during the mania soon found themselves with lines uncompleted and capital exhausted owing to rising prices, at a time when money was difficult to borrow.

In 1797 the Kennet & Avon Company said 'the distress of the times during the last year . . . has increased the pressure on your committee for money to carry on the work', and in 1798 'not only the rise of labour and the increased price of almost every article employed on the Works, have occasioned a considerable excess beyond the original estimate', while in 1800 450 of the company's shares were forfeited because the owners either would not or could not pay further calls on them. In the north the Huddersfield Canal's shareholders were being told that, 'from the bankruptcy of several of the proprietors of shares . . . the deaths of other proprietors insolvent, and . . . several of the proprietors having left the kingdom, it is become impossible to procure payment of the whole of the money subscribed'.[7]

Five problems raised by the war especially affected the canals. French privateers lay in wait around the coasts, reducing the reliability of the coasting trade. The diversion of coasting trade to inland navigations was investigated in 1800 by a House of Commons Committee on the Coal Trade. This considered whether coal could be brought to London in adequate quantities by inland waterway or road transport, should the Tyne colliers be unable to make the sea passage. There was support for schemes to provide alternative routes to those by sea, such as plans for a canal from London to Portsmouth, and for a connection between the Basingstoke, now acting as a carrier of Portsmouth and Southampton trade, and the River Itchen. Schemes for a canal across Somerset and Devon were pursued to enable traffic to get to the south coast from Wales without having to pass around Land's End, thereby risking the privateers who waited there and along the south coast. Projects between the Tyne and Solway Firth to move troops more quickly should the French attack Ireland or the east coast were also considered. The great state enterprise of the Caledonian Canal began partly to enable warships to cross quickly from one side of Scotland to the other.

The second problem was that of possible invasion. The government built the Royal Military Canal from Shorncliffe to Winchelsea along the south-east coast. It was designed originally both as a barrier to an invading army and to move troops and stores quickly along the stretch of coast most threatened by the enemy.

Some canal companies, or their workers, thought that they might be affected. In July 1797 the Grand Junction Committee received the following letter from their employees:

> We, the underwritten, being the Engineer, Inspectors, Foremen, Hagmasters, and Workingmen, employed on the works of the Grand Junction Canal, highly sensible of the blessings of our free Constitution, and truly loyal to our King, think ourselves called upon,

> as Englishmen, to stand forth in support of our Laws and Property, and that of our Honourable Employers; and do therefore associate, under the following Rules and Articles . . . with our firmest assurances that we will spill the last drop of our blood, in the cause of Old England, against all Foreign and Domestic Enemies.[8]

Later, in October 1803, the Basingstoke Committee recorded the following:

> Several of the London Proprietors having called upon the Committee, recommending, that after the Example of other corporate Bodies, the Company should offer such Assistance, as they may be able to give to Government, towards transporting Baggage, or Stores up or down the Canal, and the consent of Mr George Smith and the Rest of the Bargemasters, having been obtained, a Letter was written . . . to Lord Hobart, offering Ten of the Basingstoke Canal Barges, in Case of Invasion, or the Appearance of the Enemy on the Coast, to transport Stores, free of Expence, from London to any Part of the Canal.[9]

In 1803 Pickfords, at that time both canal and road carriers, also offered the government the use of 400 horses, 50 waggons and 28 boats.

The third problem was that of obtaining quicker transport around the country for troops and stores, and for the first time the usefulness of canals to speed up movement became clear to the authorities. On 18 June 1798 the Grand Junction Company issued a notice to its men that a considerable body of troops was to embark at Blisworth for Liverpool, and that the locks and canal were to be kept clear for the urgent movement of fifteen boats on each of two days. Another example, from *The Times* of 19 December 1806, announces that the first troop division

> for Liverpool, and thence by transports for Dublin, will leave Paddington to-day, and will be followed by others to-morrow and Sunday. By this mode of conveyance the men will be only seven days in reaching Liverpool, and with comparatively little fatigue, as it would take them above fourteen days to march that distance. Relays of fresh horses for the canal boats have been ordered to be in readiness at all the stages.

Indeed, when invasion threatened, a central fortified citadel was built at Weedon, to which king and cabinet could be moved, served by a short branch from the Grand Junction Canal, with portcullises against water penetration of the defences.

An early illustration of the Grand Junction Canal at Paddington Basin. On this occasion, a passenger packet boat is leaving; a more familiar sight than the carriage of troops

The fourth problem was inflation, especially of food prices. While this led in time to a rise in wages, the time-lag caused distress. For instance, on 1 September 1800 the town clerk of Nottingham drafted a letter to the home secretary, in which he said 'riot has been occasioned by the Difficulty of obtaining Flour & the Price at which the small Quantity that could be procured was obtained . . . They seemed Disposed to plunder the Warehouses & some Boats laden with Corn'.[10]

Nervousness of what the working class might do, if it ceased to 'stand forth in support of our Laws and Property, and that of our Honourable Employers', also showed itself. The Grand Junction employees' loyal sentiments of 1797 did not extend to the men working on the Wolverton Embankment in 1801, who faced the engineer with a strike for higher wages. The Grand Junction Committee told him

> to discharge at all risque these offenders, and to use his utmost endeavours to bring them to Justice, and to call on the Magistracy and Yeomanry of this County to repress and punish all acts of Outrage and Violence and an illegal conspiracy or combination for increase of wages.[11]

The fifth problem was that of increasing output from the homeland. This was achieved under the inducement that rising prices gave to producers and led to many kinds of new enterprises. The story of the Tavistock Canal is one such enterprise.

Today Britain produces hardly any copper, but in the early part of the nineteenth century Devonshire and Cornwall mined 25 per cent of the world's supply. The war brought steeply rising prices for the ore, but the output from Wheal Crowndale near Tavistock in Devon was limited by the difficulty of getting the copper to the River Tamar, from where it could be taken to Devonport to be put on board the coasting ships. In 1803, therefore, a meeting was held on 16 March in the Tavistock Guildhall to consider connecting Tavistock to the navigable portion of the River Tamar at Morwellham Quay by

> a CANAL to be taken up from the *River Tavy*, near the *Abbey Bridge*, in *Tavistock*, and carried from thence to *Lumburn Valley*, from thence by an *Embankment* across that Valley, and a TUNNEL through MORWELL-DOWN, and a BRANCH or SIDE-CUT to the *Slate-Quarries*, at MILL HILL.[12]

The proprietors were men of enterprise and imagination, for their canal swam with oddities. Though only 4 miles long, 1½ miles lay through a tunnel. At the far end of this tunnel was a drop of 237 ft to the level of the Tamar, and

> after duly weighing the merits of various plans . . . the Committee . . . adopted that of an inclined Plane, furnished with iron railways, on which carriages fitted to transport boxes which may contain ores, coals, lime, etc., are made to ascend and descend by the application of a machine driven by water supplied from the canal.[13]

The water in the canal was deliberately given a current flowing downwards to the plane from the intake on the River Tavy at Tavistock. On its way it drove the mining machinery, carried the boats filled with ore down through the tunnel and finally worked the wheel of the inclined plane.

The canal company obtained from the Duke of Bedford, owner of the surrounding land, the right to mine any copper or other mineral found in the course of making the canal, and copper was indeed struck soon after the tunnel was begun. This lode became Wheal Crebor, and until 1828 the mine was managed in conjunction with the canal.

It took thirteen years to cut the tunnel. One may indeed agree with the report of the canal committee for 1816, which says:

> The Tavistock Tunnel will be a lasting monument of the patience of those who executed and of the spirit and enterprise of the Proprietors

> who supported the work and who have so steadily pursued their object through the disheartening circumstances which have of late attended all mining pursuits.[14]

The canal was opened on 24 June 1817, but the boom in copper caused by the war had given way to a depressed state of trade that never fully passed away, and which led in the third quarter of the century to the disappearance of the Devonshire copper industry. The canal had cost some £62,000, but it seldom returned to its owners more than £600 a year in net profit. Yet for forty years it carried about 17,000 tons of goods a year in its 8 ton boats (it was only 16 ft wide at the top and 3 ft deep): merchandise for the town of Tavistock up against the stream, and copper ore, limestone, slate and granite downwards to the Tamar.

At last the competition of the South Devon & Tavistock Railway and the decline of the mines proved too much for the little enterprise, which was sold to the Duke of Bedford for £3,200. Yet today it is not useless, for the water that once drove the engines of Wheal Crowndale and Wheal Crebor now provides the power for a hydroelectric plant beside Morwellham Quay. The tunnel, still in use, is 'a lasting monument of the patience of those who executed and of the spirit and enterprise of the Proprietors who supported the work.'[15] It now forms one feature within the Morwellham Quay open-air museum.

Meanwhile the Act of Union with Ireland of 1800 had made the new United Kingdom responsible for most Irish waterways expenditure, which was undertaken to further development or provide employment. Just before, Directors General of Inland Navigation had been appointed, with powers to take over all Irish waterways not under private companies, whether administered by local commissioners (now abolished) under the 1787 Act or not, and to make grants to enable company-owned canals to be finished.

Except for the great Caledonian Canal, nearly all of the new waterways authorized between 1800 and the end of the war in 1815 were near London, or were connected to the Grand Junction line, which joined the Midlands to London by a more direct route – from Braunston on the Oxford Canal – than the old one by way of Oxford and the Thames.

The Grand Junction Canal had been authorized in 1793 with a capital of £600,000. The Duke of Grafton, the Earl of Clarendon, the Earl of Essex and Earl Spencer were on its board, with the Marquis of Buckingham a strong supporter. Later, when the Commons became more important in relation to private Bills, there were fewer peers and more members of parliament on its managing committee. This political influence, supported as it was by the considerable connections the

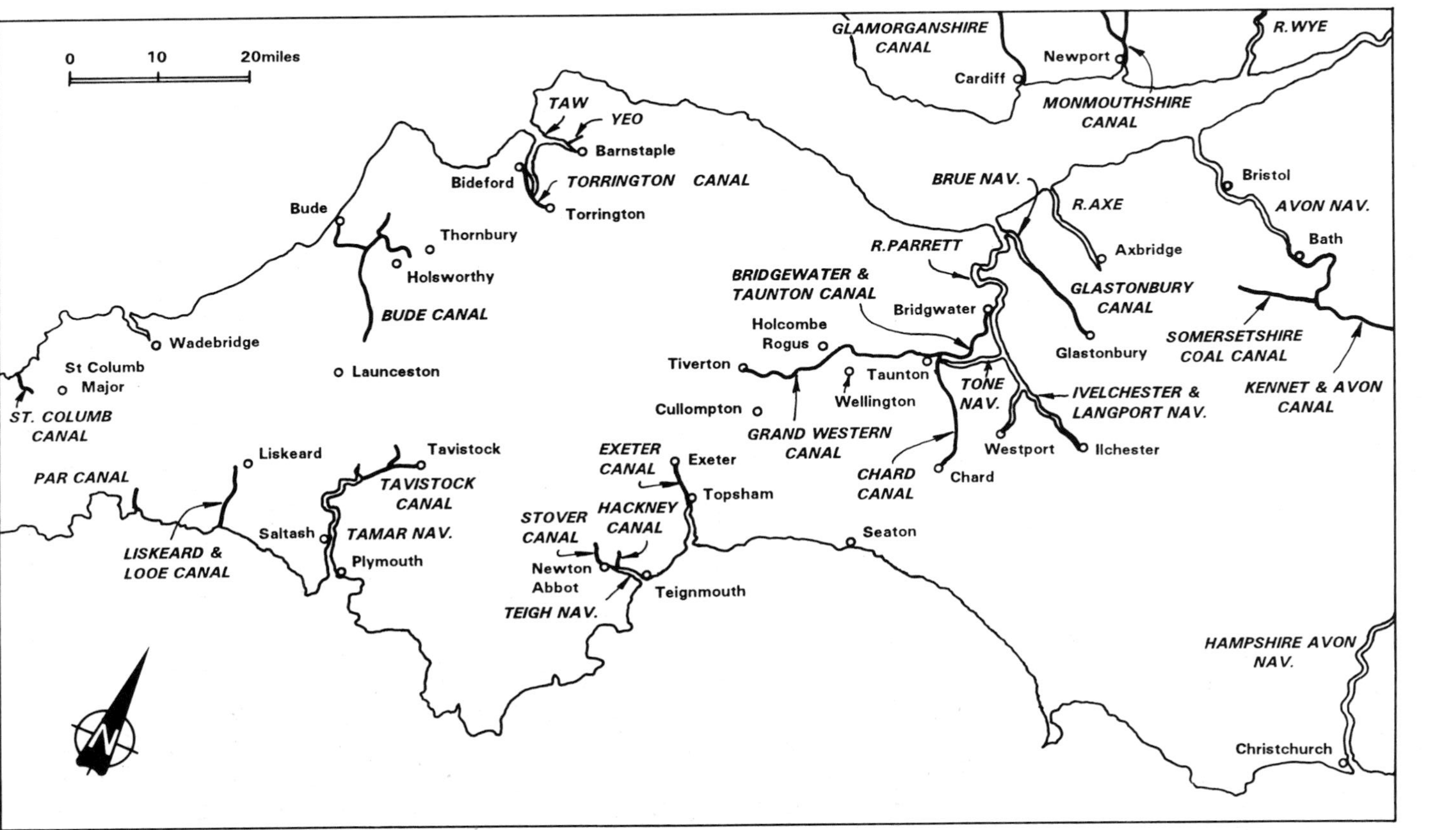

The main waterways of south-west England

committee members had with shareholders in other canal companies, was a grievance to those who got in the way of the Grand Junction company.

The chairman was William Praed, who, after having been a partner in the Cornish Bank at Truro, had in 1803 started Praed & Co. in London. William Jessop was chief and James Barnes resident engineer. The canal, 93½ miles long, ran from the Oxford Canal at Braunston by way of Braunston and Blisworth tunnels to Wolverton, Leighton Buzzard, Tring and King's Langley to the Thames at Brentford. It was finished in 1800, except for the 1¾ mile long tunnel at Blisworth. The first attempt at this tunnel failed. Outram then built a double-track tramroad over the hill to make a temporary link between the two parts of the canal and to enable it to carry through traffic. The second tunnel was then begun and was opened on 25 March 1805. Branches were built before that date to Stony Stratford and on to Buckingham; to the military depot at Weedon; to Wendover; and to Newport Pagnell by an independent company. Later, further branches were made to Aylesbury and Northampton.

The opening of the Grand Junction Canal gave the Birmingham–London waterway route its final form. This line, say from Newhall Basin, Birmingham, to Brentford, was originally completed in 1789 by way of the Birmingham, the Staffs & Worcs, the Severn, the Stroudwater and Thames & Severn canals and the Thames. This roundabout route of 269½ miles was superseded within a few months, in 1790, by that via Fazeley and Oxford to the Thames, which reduced the distance to 227½ miles. This was itself spectacularly reduced to 138½ miles in 1800, on the one hand by the opening of the Grand Junction and on the other by the substitution of the Warwick & Birmingham and Warwick & Napton canals for the line by way of Fazeley and Hawkesbury. The Oxford Canal, now reduced to a 5 mile link in this through line from Napton to Braunston, was compensated for its loss of tonnage and did not suffer, but the Coventry temporarily lost some of its trade and its share prices fell from £400 to £350. By 1825, however, these losses had been far more than recouped by its rapidly growing coal trade, and its shares in that year stood at £1,230. Finally, in 1801, a branch from Bull's Bridge on the main Grand Junction line was opened to Paddington Basin, and the last river section in what was then an all-canal route into London disappeared. In turn this branch was in 1820 connected by the Regent's Canal, authorized in 1812, to the Thames at Limehouse.

Other developments were taking place around the upper end of the Grand Junction. In the time of the mania the Leicestershire & Northamptonshire Union Canal had been projected to link Leicester, itself connected to the Trent through the Loughborough and Leicester navigations, with the Nene at Northampton. Building began from the Leicester end, and in 1797 was completed to Debdale Wharf, 17 out of the proposed 44 miles. There the project rested for a time, apart from the building of a branch to Market Harborough in 1809. The construction of the Grand Junction Canal re-animated the project, and eventually it was decided to join the uncompleted Leicestershire & Northamptonshire to the Grand Junction at Buckby Wharf (Norton Junction) by means of a new company's line. Known as the Grand Union (not to be confused with the later amalgamation of the same name), this was authorized in 1810, promoted partly by Leicester interests and partly by the Grand Junction. The canal opened in 1814, thereby making a connection between London and the Trent, although its two flights of narrow locks at Foxton and Watford prevented the development of through wide-boat services.

A plateway from the Grand Junction to Northampton was built in 1805 and, when this was replaced in 1815 by a canal branch, the Nene was joined to the other two and the original object of the canal line from Leicester was partly (albeit through narrow locks) attained.

Around London several canals were authorized: the Grand Surrey (1801), planned to run from the Thames at Rotherhithe to Mitcham, but which got no farther than Camberwell; the Croydon, from Rotherhithe to Croydon; the Thames & Medway, from Gravesend to Frindsbury opposite Rochester; the Isle of Dogs Canal, built by the City of London and designed to shorten the passage around the Isle of Dogs from Limehouse to Blackwall; and the Wey & Arun Junction, to create a through communication from the Thames to the south coast at Littlehampton. In addition to these canals the Surrey Iron Railway from Wandsworth to Croydon and its extension, the Croydon, Merstham & Godstone, which was only partly built, were parts of the same development of communications around the rapidly growing city of London.

One last enterprise falls within the scope of this chapter. Although the main rivers of England had by this time been joined together, the only connection of the canal system to the network of Fenland waterways that served the combined purposes of drainage and navigation was the tramroad, later the canal, that joined the Grand Junction to Northampton. One suggestion for a link was the Stamford Junction Canal, proposed by J. Jepson Oddy (who fought a local election on it and published a book in 1810) to link the Nene and the Witham to the Welland at Stamford, and the Welland to the Oakham Canal. This agricultural canal had been opened in about 1803, an extension of the Melton Mowbray or Wreak Navigation, itself a branch of the Leicester Navigation. A second suggestion of about the same time proposed a Market Harborough–Stamford link.

However, it was another scheme that got as far as an Act of Parliament. As early as 1778 Whitworth, acting on the orders of the Common Council of the City of London, surveyed a line of junction between the River Stort, which through the Lea was joined with the Thames at Bow Creek near Blackwall, and the Cam, near Cambridge. The plan was revived during the war and an Act obtained in 1812 for a canal, the London & Cambridge Junction, to run from the Stort near Bishop's Stortford to the Cam near Clayhithe Sluice, with a branch to Whaddon. The line was to be 28½ miles long. The authorized capital was £870,000, but it was enacted that £425,250 should be raised before work began. For this the times were not propitious, and in 1814 permission was granted for only part of the line to be built, from the Cam to Saffron Walden, with the branch to Whaddon. This also failed to materialize, and the last of the great river connections, between the Thames and Great Ouse by way of the Cam, was never made.

CHAPTER SIX

Canals, Ports and Seas

Sea transport continued to be important during the canal age, both in supplying the ports that provided traffic, often transhipped between ships and canal craft, and in the promotion of canals to link the seas.

Two notable areas in Britain where canals to link the seas were proposed were Scotland and the Somerset and Devon area. In the first area canals were built; in the second no plan succeeded.

Among the consequences of the '45 rebellion in Scotland were that the British government sought to break up a clan system that had given strength to rebellion, and also to create a network of good roads through the Highlands to make them less inaccessible. Landowners were replacing cattle farms with large sheep farms, with no place for the old peasant economy. At the same time the building of the new roads gave Highlanders news of easier lives to be led to the south or over the seas in America, as well as the means to get there.

Many were dismayed by this trend and sought to develop the Highlands to relieve the distress and slow emigration. Among them was John Knox, a Scotsman who had made his money in England and who, when retired, used it to further the prosperity of the north. He saw that the promotion of fisheries and manufacturing, which he and others had suggested, depended on improved transport. Writing in 1784 about the proposed establishment of Highland fisheries, he advocated the construction of three new lines of canal – from Fort William to Inverness, from Loch Fyne to the Atlantic and from the Forth to the Clyde – which would 'open up a circumnavigation within the heart of the kingdom to the unspeakable benefit of commerce and the fisheries'.[1]

All three canals had been suggested, and in fact surveyed, before he wrote. One, the Forth & Clyde, had been partly built. However, he had much influence on events, which in time provided all three of the sea-to-sea canals he advocated. They are now called the Caledonian, the Crinan and the Forth & Clyde canals.

A glance at the map of the Highlands shows the Great Glen, that astonishing rift across Scotland from Loch Linnhe north-east to Inverness. With a sea loch at either end and with four lochs in its length, the Great Glen seemed made for a canal that would save ships from the great dangers of passing round the north of Scotland. The natural difficulties of a passage in the days of sail from one side of Great Britain to the other, both for merchant ships and fishing vessels, provided a good argument for a canal, as did the Napoleonic Wars, which drove ships everywhere to keep close to the land. Yet the high cost and uncertain returns involved in the project did not make it commercially attractive. For this reason, and also because the government saw the providing of public works as a means for preventing wholesale emigration from the Highlands, Telford was sent by the Treasury to report on the cost and practicability of such a canal, along with other works such as roads and bridges.

Telford reported in 1802 in favour of a ship canal. The government agreed and appointed commissioners. Jessop was called in, and the two engineers then re-surveyed the line, Jessop alone signing the final estimate. Soon afterwards the proposed dimensions were enlarged to take thirty-two-gun frigates. Jessop did working drawings, and cutting began as a canal 20 ft deep with 23 locks to run from sea to sea through the Great Glen, connecting lochs Lochy, Oich, Ness and Dochfour. It was to cost over £500,000. Jessop, as senior engineer, worked on the project with Telford until 1812, not long before the former's death.

Hopes were great. An excitable contemporary chronicler of canals, writing in 1804 and recalling what water transport had done for Wales, asserted that:

> Undoubtedly in digging this canal veins of minerals will be found that will incite artists and manufacturers to flock to a place where land can be had at a cheap rate, and will induce the land owners to give pecuniary assistance where wanted to forward undertakings, by which the riches of the bowels of the mountains may produce ten or twenty-fold returns, eight or ten times a year. The mountains in Wales continued unexplored, barren, and useless for ages, but are now found to contain lead, iron, copper, coals, marble, &c. &c. in the greatest plenty, and some hundreds of people are employed, and whole villages built to accommodate them on a spot which a very few years ago was an uninhabited waste.[2]

The Caledonian Canal was unlucky. For Telford it was a comparative failure; for the State a perpetual drain of money; for the inhabitants of the Highlands something of a white elephant. When it opened in 1822 it was unfinished, and would not take the bigger ships from which Telford had expected much of the canal's trade; when it re-opened in 1847, deepened and reconstructed, though even then not to the planned depth of 20 ft, the age of steam had come, and the best argument for the existence of the canal had ceased to be valid.

During 1804 an organization was built up, staff recruited, the line laid out, materials ordered and work begun inwards from the sea locks. Given the problems posed by size, terrain and climate, progress was bound to be slow. The canal cost over £900,000 before, unfinished, it was opened at the insistence of a government annoyed by continuing expense and public criticism. Estimating had indeed been good, but war had caused a heavy rise in the prices of labour and supplies. There were also construction troubles, the worst in the middle district – Fort Augustus to Loch Lochy – the last to be built. By the time work seriously started there in 1817, John Simpson, who had been in charge of construction, had died, and Matthew Davidson, another of the engineers, had only a year to live. Deprived of these two highly experienced men from Pontcysyllte days, and with heavy pressure from above to open as soon as possible, work went on too fast: there were slips in the Laggan cutting and the side wall of the bottom lock at Fort Augustus fell in.

On 24 October 1822, two years after Telford ceased to be engineer, the canal was opened, with 12 ft of water in the cuts and 15 ft in the locks – enough only for fishing boats and small ships. However, this did not spoil the opening ceremony. Vessels passed through the canal carrying the commissioners and local notables, and the *Inverness Courier* reported that:

> The termination of the voyage was marked by a grand salute from the Fort, whilst the Inhabitants of Fort William demonstrated their joy by kindling a large bonfire. A plentiful supply of whisky, given by the gentlemen of Fort William, did not in the least tend to damp the ardour of the populace. At half past seven o'clock 67 gentlemen, the guests of Mr Grant sat down, in the hall of the Mason Lodge, to a handsome and plentiful dinner.

It was. The reporter tells with decreasing accuracy of the thirty-nine toasts that were drunk and the more than thirty-nine speeches that were made (including one of which he frankly says: 'Corrimony returned thanks in a speech of considerable length, of which we regret we cannot give even an outline'), and ends: 'At 12 o'clock the party broke up; but some of the gentlemen still remained, and, with genuine Highland spirit, prolonged the festivities of this memorable evening.'[3]

Apart from a lack of water and a number of mishaps and accidents, partly the result of the premature opening, the working of sailing ships through the lochs turned out to be difficult. There was no towing-path along their sides, and the Great Glen acted as a funnel for wind which, when it was adverse, could and did hold ships up for weeks, thus preventing a saving in time over the route through the Pentland Firth. On the canal sections there was a horse towage service charged at 5s. (25p) a day, Corpach to Loch Lochy and Clachnaharry to Loch Ness each being reckoned one day's towage.

After nearly twenty years of inefficient operation the commissioners asked James Walker to report on the canal. In 1839 he pointed out that the traffic passing was probably only about 2½ per cent of that rounding the north of Scotland, and recommended that the canal should be completed, deepened to 17 ft and provided with steam tugs to assist sailing ships. After three years of reports and select committees, the government decided it was better to complete than to abandon the canal. Work therefore started in 1843, and the canal re-opened in 1847 to take craft of up to 500 tons, at an additional cost of £228,000. Since then it has continued in use: in earlier years its toll receipts usually balanced its maintenance costs but seldom provided anything towards major repairs; more recently even its maintenance has required subsidy.

During the First World War there was a time, in 1918, when traffic on the canal was really heavy, and when those who foresaw its value in war were justified. Mines and sinkers were brought from America to Corpach at the western end of the canal, transhipped into 100 ton lighters and passed through the canal to Muirtown basin near Inverness. Here, at US Naval Base 18, they were assembled before being taken out into the North Sea to form part of the Northern Barrage, the minefield planned to stretch from the Orkneys to the coast of Norway and to cut off German submarines from the Atlantic.

In 1920 the long and onerous task of the commissioners came to an end, and the management of the canal passed to the Ministry of Transport. Discussions went on about the possibility of constructing a much larger ship canal with a lower summit level, which would avoid most of the lockage on the old canal, including the eight locks at Banavie known as Neptune's Staircase, which acted as a bottleneck to traffic. During a time of economy, however, such a proposal had no chance of success. During the Second World War the canal again found a period of activity. With nationalization it passed to the British Transport Commission and later to the British Waterways Board. It still takes small ships (larger ones at the Corpach or western end) and fishing craft, but also now an increasing number of yachts in transit and locally based motor cruisers.

The second of John Knox's proposals was for a canal from Loch Fyne to the Atlantic. The Crinan Canal was to cut through the great peninsula

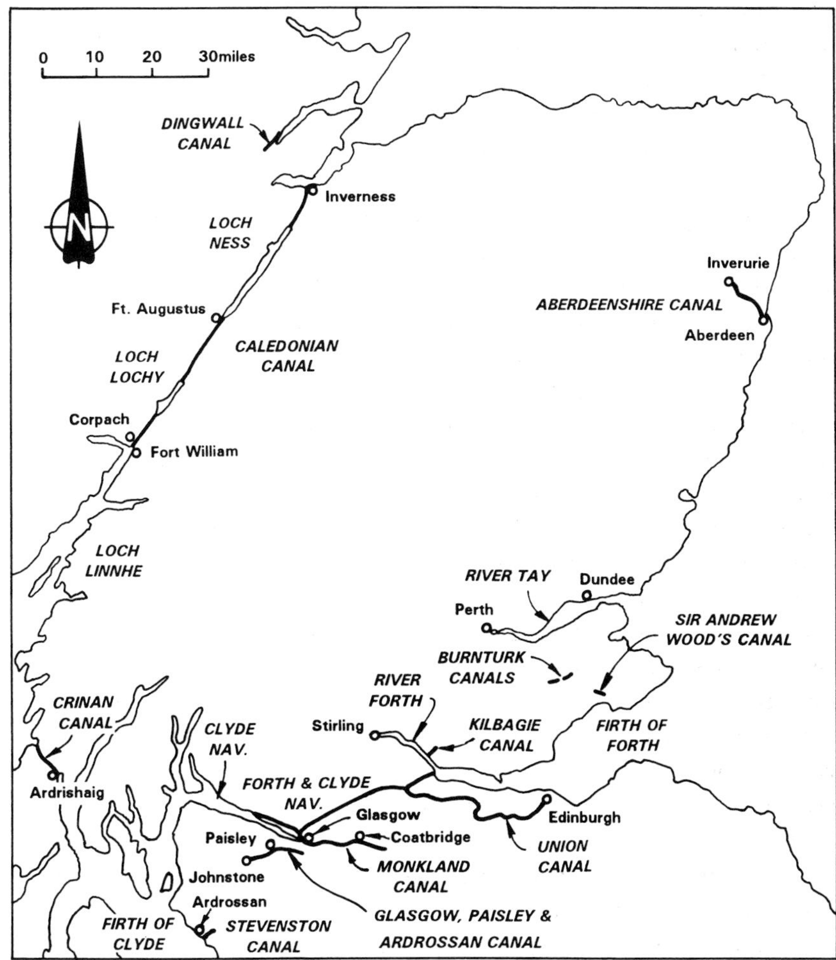

The main waterways of Scotland. The Glasgow, Paisley & Ardrossan Canal was only completed to Johnstone. There were some smaller waterways elsewhere in Scotland

of Kintyre, which blocks off the direct route to the north, thus saving vessels 85 miles of voyage and the passage of the Mull of Kintyre. It was considered partly as a continuation of the Forth & Clyde Canal, so that vessels proceeding from the west coast of Scotland to the east coast, or vice versa, could use both navigations, but also partly to help the prosperity of the western coasts and isles by making them more accessible to the Glasgow market.

The Crinan projectors put out their prospectus ten years before the state had agreed to build the Caledonian Canal. Their scheme was much smaller – the estimate was £63,628 – and it is clear that the promoters had philanthropic rather than commercial motives in mind:

> While the extensive prospects of the present existing trade of the kingdom, passing through the Crinan canal, and the natural increase which may be expected from a greater facility of communication, hold out a probable return for the money to be expended in making and maintaining it, the inestimable benefit which must arise therefrom to the inhabitants of the Western Coasts and Islands of Scotland, are extremely interesting to a benevolent mind, and may alone be an inducement to many to subscribe without an anxious regard to future profit.[4]

Rennie, the engineer, revised the estimate to £107,512 for a canal now to be 15 ft and not 12 ft deep. An Act was obtained in 1793 and a capital of £150,000 was authorized. Philanthropy in fact raised £98,000, and to complete the canal the proprietors had to borrow £25,000 from the Treasury, to whom the canal was mortgaged. It opened in 1801, but owing to a shortage of money it remained unfinished at the western end, where a shallow and awkward channel remained to damage and discourage ships. Because the canal was built as economically as possible it also had inadequate depth (10 ft) and a very short summit level (1,114 yd), approached by four locks on one side and five on the other. The expense of cutting through this short summit would have simplified the navigation of the canal.

The waterway was always in financial difficulties. Money was lent by the Treasury on several occasions to pay for repairs and in 1817 the management was vested in the commissioners of the Caledonian Canal. In 1848 it was formally transferred into state ownership. The commissioners retained control until superseded by the Ministry of Transport in 1920, and later by the British Transport Commission and the British Waterways Board. Yachts, motor cruisers and fishing boats are now the principal users.

The third of the sea-to-sea canals of Scotland, and the most successful in its time, was the Forth & Clyde Canal. To join the seas with a waterway across the narrow isthmus between the two firths was so obvious a proposal that it had many times been made, for instance by Defoe in his *Tour* (1724–6), when he wrote:

> it would take up a Volume by itself, to lay down the several advantages to the Trade of Scotland, that would immediately occur by such a Navigation, and then to give a true Survey of the Ground, the Easiness

> of its being perform'd, and the probable Charge of it, all which might be done. But it is too much to undertake here, it must lye till Posterity, by the rising Greatness of their Commerce, shall not only feel the Want of it, but find themselves able for the Performance.[5]

Some forty years later, commerce felt the need for such a waterway. Posterity, however, divided itself into two groups. On the one hand there were those interested in the general prosperity of Scotland, including Edinburgh interests. They wanted a sea-to-sea canal that would link the trade of the western and eastern coasts and would be able to take coasting vessels. On the other hand there were the merchants of Glasgow, who did not want trade to pass through their city but to be centred in it. They therefore supported a barge canal to bring east coast and European trade to their city.

The trustees asked John Smeaton for a survey. He reported in 1764, offering two routes, the first roughly as the canal was later to be built, the second by way of Loch Lomond. The first, 5 ft deep, he estimated at £74,000. Glasgow interests then got Robert Mackell and James Watt (of steam kettle fame) to bring Smeaton's line nearer Glasgow and, with depth reduced to 4 ft, the plan reached Parliament in 1767. Meanwhile the supporters of a 'great canal' had been holding meetings as far away as Perth and Aberdeen, and succeeded in obtaining subscriptions of over £100,000. The original Bill was withdrawn, whereupon the disgusted Watt wrote to his wife: 'I think I shall not long to have anything to do with the House of Commons again – I never saw so many wrong-headed people on all sides gathered together . . . I believe *the Deevil* has possession of them.'[6]

Smeaton reported on a canal 7 ft deep and costing £147,337. Some supporters wanted a depth of 10 ft so as to take sloops, but the 7 ft proposal went through in 1768, the Act authorizing £200,000 of capital. Smeaton, with Mackell as resident engineer, began work that year. By 1775 the canal, built from the Forth end, had reached Stockingfield, 3 miles from Glasgow. Two years later most of the Glasgow branch was opened. Glasgow had got what its merchants wanted – a canal to the eastern coast – but the through sea-to-sea communication was still lacking. In 1784, however, £50,000 was advanced to the company by the government and work resumed, this time with Robert Whitworth as engineer. At last, in July 1790, the canal was fully opened. It was 35 miles long with 39 locks and Whitworth's four-arched Kelvin aqueduct. Thenceforward the company became more and more prosperous. Receipts rose from some £8,000 a year to £50,000. The construction of the Monkland and later the Edinburgh & Glasgow Union Canal to join it

The Anzac *unloading barrels on the Glasgow Branch of the Forth & Clyde Canal towards the end of its working life, in the 1950s. This illustrates the small seagoing craft able to pass through this canal, necessitating opening bridges throughout* (British Waterways)

brought additional traffic, and it flourished until the opening of the Newcastle & Carlisle Railway, and later the Edinburgh & Glasgow, reduced its receipts. The Forth & Clyde Canal was finally bought by the Caledonian Railway in 1867, largely to acquire its harbour at Grangemouth, and continued to decline in usefulness: the tonnage carried fell from 3,022,583 tons in 1868 through 817,836 tons in 1908 and 27,751 tons in 1942, to 14,839 tons in 1953. The canal was closed in 1963, although parts have since been restored for local amenity use and sea-to-sea restoration is a long-term possibility.

In its day, however, the Forth & Clyde Canal was a giant. It is memorable partly because, on its waters in 1789, Symington tried out the second of his steam paddle-boats, and, as he records, 'in presence of hundreds of spectators, who lined the banks of the canal, the boat glided along, propelled at the rate of five miles an hour'.

This experiment interested Lord Dundas, the governor of the canal company, and he later employed Symington to prepare a new engine to be fitted to a hull specially built as a tug, the *Charlotte Dundas,* and to drive a stern paddle-wheel. Trials were held from January 1801, and in March 1803 the boat pulled two laden barges from Lock 20 to Glasgow in 9¼ hours. Though the trials had been successful, the proprietors decided not to use the vessel owing to the damage that the wash might cause to the banks. So the *Charlotte Dundas* was beached in a creek off the canal, till the hull was broken up by the weather and souvenir hunters. It was not until 1856 that the first steam craft was introduced on the canal.

From time to time a mid-Scotland ship canal has been proposed, and after the First World War a special association actively promoted it. In 1930, and again in 1946, government committees reported on the project, in both cases adversely. On the latter occasion the committee estimated that the cost of a sea-level canal 32 ft deep might be some £109 million, excluding interest on construction, and was doubtful whether such a canal would cover its maintenance costs, while its strategic importance would be relatively small.

We could pause here to study the three trans-Pennine canals that were built, all variations on the Humber–Mersey route, and to consider the various proposals, up to the present, for a new route to link the Aire & Calder and the Manchester Ship Canal. A fourth line, from the Tyne to the Solway Firth and Maryport, was also proposed from the time of the canal mania for forty years, but built in small part only as the Carlisle Canal from the Firth to that city. Instead we will examine one less well-known sea-to-sea scheme, which formerly held the imagination of Englishmen.

Of all the capes in England, the crews of small sailing ships of the coasting trade, before the days of steam, feared Land's End the most, both for its rocks and for its contrary winds. So from the onset of the canal age plans were made to cut a waterway across Somerset, Devon or Cornwall to avoid the dangers and shorten the duration of the voyage. The coal exporters and merchants of South Wales wanted to sell more goods along the south coast of England and in London, while the landowners and merchants of south-west England stood to gain from cheap goods brought by waterway to their harbours and countryside.

Two ways of sending goods across the south-west peninsula were suggested: by barge canal, which would have meant their transhipment into ships at each end of the canal, and by ship canal.

There were many plans for a barge canal, from 1769 when Whitworth, under Brindley's supervision, first surveyed two routes. One was from the River Exe to Taunton, from where barges would use the Tone Navigation to Bridgwater, where they would enter another canal to go via Glastonbury and Axbridge to Uphill near Bristol; the other was from Seaton across Devon to the River Parrett at Langport. Two of the many that were planned were partially built. Both were products of the canal mania.

The Grand Western Canal was intended to run from Topsham to Taunton in Somerset, from where traffic could work to Bridgwater by way of the navigable rivers Tone and Parrett. It was to be 46 miles long, including branches to Cullompton and Tiverton, and its total cost was estimated at £166,724. The enabling Act was passed in 1796, but wartime inflation made the proprietors view the whole project as too risky, and so the plan was laid aside till better times.

In 1809 it was thought that these times had come, and plans for building the canal were revived. Several engineers – Robert Whitworth, John Longbothom and William Jessop among them – had made surveys, but John Rennie's had been the final one, and he was therefore engaged to superintend construction. The proprietors allowed for costs to exceed the original estimate by 50 per cent as a result of increased prices, and a start was made on the original plan for a barge canal.

Two disastrous mistakes were made at the outset. The proprietors decided, for the sake of the carriage in stone – overestimated at £10,000 a year from the Burlescombe quarries to Tiverton – to begin the work of cutting not at one end of the canal but in the middle. Work therefore started on the Tiverton branch and on part of the main line, a length of 11 miles. If construction had begun at the Taunton or the Topsham end, there would have been a trade in coal as soon as the first few miles of the canal were open, while the materials used in construction could have been carried easily and cheaply.

The second mistake was made by Rennie, who decided to improve on the original plan by lowering the summit level at Holcombe Rogus by 16 ft to save lockage on the main line and the Tiverton branch, and to save the cost of a reservoir by using the Lowdwells springs. He did save these costs, but only at the expense of much heavy and difficult cutting and embanking. The next three years were spent in happy optimism by the local committee, which represented the shareholders, and in a struggle against physical obstacles by the engineer. At last, in 1812, the short section was open to traffic. Without a lock it had cost £244,505 for 11 miles – more than the 1793 estimate for the whole 46 miles of the canal with its branches. Coal had to be brought by road from Taunton to the end of the canal at Holcombe Rogus, and from there to Tiverton by water, while the stone traffic for which the section had first been constructed never yielded £1,000 in any one year.

The proprietors of this self-contained section of a sea-to-sea canal that they could not afford to finish resisted the blandishments of engineers who wanted to complete the canal at trifling cost. Eventually James

Green, an Exeter engineer who had done competent work on the Exeter, Bude and Torrington canals, and had even been called over to Wales to advise on the Kidwelly & Llanelly Canal, made a proposal that sounded workable. He suggested that the canal should be completed to Taunton on a smaller scale, to obtain the benefits of connection with the newly built Bridgwater & Taunton Canal, and thus with a seaport. He estimated the cost at £61,324, a figure just within the remaining resources of the committee.

On the Bude Canal inclined planes had been successfully used instead of locks. Green therefore suggested that the new section should have no locks, but instead an inclined plane at Wellisford and seven vertical lifts. He convinced the management committee and work began. Unfortunately for his reputation, Green not only failed to make the inclined plane work using the hydraulic power for which it was designed, resulting in the installation of a steam engine, but he was so confident of the design of his lifts that he went ahead with construction before he had made the necessary practical experiments. Too late he found difficulty in equalizing the levels of water in the two pounds of the canal and the two caissons, so that the stop gates could be raised and the boats pass easily in and out of the lifts. Eventually he cured the trouble, and at his own expense, but the delay in opening the canal cost the proprietors their last capital. To get traffic started the committee was forced not only to raise an additional subscription among themselves, but also to borrow from their own superintendent.

The extension opened in 1838, and a modest prosperity set in for the Grand Western Canal, until the railway came a few years later. However, no further word was heard of extending it to Topsham to join the English and Bristol channels.

The second project begun but not completed was the Dorset & Somerset. This 49 mile long canal was planned from beside the Dorset Stour to join the Kennet & Avon Canal near Bath, from where traffic could work down the Avon to Bristol. Like the Grand Western the Dorset & Somerset obtained its Act in 1796 and, similarly, chose to begin work on a 9 mile long branch in the middle of the line in order to carry coal to Frome from the collieries at Nettlebridge. A lift was built near Mells and others were begun, but by 1803 the working capital was exhausted and 1¾ miles of the branch remained to be cut. Shareholders, frightened at rising costs, failed to pay further calls on the shares, no one would take up promissory notes and so work stopped. It never began again, and today few traces remain of this canal that never carried traffic.

The principal ship canal project was surveyed by Thomas Telford and James Green along the same general line as many previous proposals.

The canal was planned to carry ships of 200 tons along a line 44½ miles in length from Stolford near Bridgwater to Beer near Seaton. There were to be sixty locks, and harbours at each end of the line. It was estimated that 1,095,527 tons of goods would pass through the canal each year and that receipts, including harbour dues, would be £210,847 from the through traffic alone. Of the proposed capital of £1,750,000, the sum of £1,518,000 was actually promised, and an Act for the English & Bristol Channels Ship Canal was passed in 1825. Soon after, however, a slump set in, and in 1828 the committee reported sadly:

> The severe shock . . . which was given to public confidence shortly after the passing of the Act, and the consequent aversion to almost every speculative activity, have not failed to affect the Ship Canal, so as to render it highly improbable that so large a capital as £1,750,000 will now be raised for the accomplishment of this object.[7]

The idea of cutting a waterway through the peninsula has attracted enthusiasts into the twentieth century, and many proposals have been made. One of the most charmingly optimistic was that of Mr Hern of Cardiff in 1922. He suggested that a canal should be built to carry ships of 15,000 tons, costing £37 million. Among the arguments he used was that:

> A Feature of attraction, and I think a source of considerable profit to the canal whichever route it follows, will be the pleasure traffic which will pass through beautiful country having near its banks many places of historic and other interest, providing for tourists a pleasant and useful journey, appealing more to many people than trains and motor chars-a-banc or even motor cars, to places of rest and beauty in South Devon, such as Torquay, Teignmouth, etc., and to the delightful neighbourhood of Bournemouth, Southampton, and the Isle of Wight.[8]

In reality the project of a ship canal ceased to offer any viability as soon as steam replaced wind as a motive power. Whereas sailing ships could spend days or even weeks waiting for the wind to take them around Cape Wrath or Land's End, and often came to grief from the tides of the Pentland Firth or the rocks of Scilly, steam power made such voyages both regular and safe. The saving of time and insurance premiums was therefore not enough to make it worthwhile for shipowners to pay the dues of the Caledonian Canal or the proposed English & Bristol Channels Ship Canal. For that reason the first lost money and the second was never built.

Apart from the sea-to-sea canals, we can envisage the waterway system of Britain as a network of canals and rivers joining together the principal towns, and linking sources of raw materials with industrial areas. Some of the traffic was purely internal, originating at one point and being carried to another; much, however, had either arrived at a port via a coasting or foreign-trading vessel, or was destined for shipment from a port. This trade passed to and from the ports at the edges of the network, where the navigable waterways ended and tidal water began. Many of these ports, like Bristol on the Avon or London on the Thames, had been distribution centres where goods were transhipped either into river barges or road waggons, before the advent of the canals. The arrival of artificial waterways merely increased their commercial importance. While ports in Ireland played a somewhat different role, trade serving Belfast, Newry and Dublin was enhanced by the development of waterways upstream. Other ports, like Goole on the Aire & Calder and Ellesmere Port on the Shropshire Union, were creations of the canal age.

Some rivers, like the Severn, had always been difficult navigations in their tidal stretches. Some – the Thames, the Tyne, the Tees and the Wear – were quite suitable for small craft but had to be dredged and possibly embanked in places to take the larger ships that were coming into use, especially after the introduction of steamships. Others, especially in the fenlands, silted up so much that extensive training works had to be carried out, as on the Great Ouse to King's Lynn, or an artificial cut provided in place of an unusable river channel, as on the Nene below Wisbech. The object of training works was to narrow and straighten a river channel in order to increase the speed of the current and thus its scouring effect on the river bed. In one case, Bristol, William Jessop cut a new channel for the river, the old one being cut off by locks and turned into a floating harbour. In other cases nothing was done, and the little ports that once flourished, like Hedon on the Humber, became no longer accessible. It sometimes proved impossible to preserve or improve the navigation of a river channel. Therefore, to prevent trade deserting a port on that river, a canal, such as the Exeter Canal, was cut from the sea to the town to take the place of the river navigation. Now and then a town near the sea, but without a harbour, decided to turn itself into a port by building a canal to salt water, like the Ulverston Canal.

The Exeter and the Gloucester & Berkeley canals are similar in that both ports suffered from a difficult river; they differ in that the Exeter led only to the city, while the Gloucester & Berkeley made Gloucester not only a port of import for the country around it, but also a place of transhipment into river barges and canal boats, which then went up the Severn into the Midland inland waterway system, or by way of the

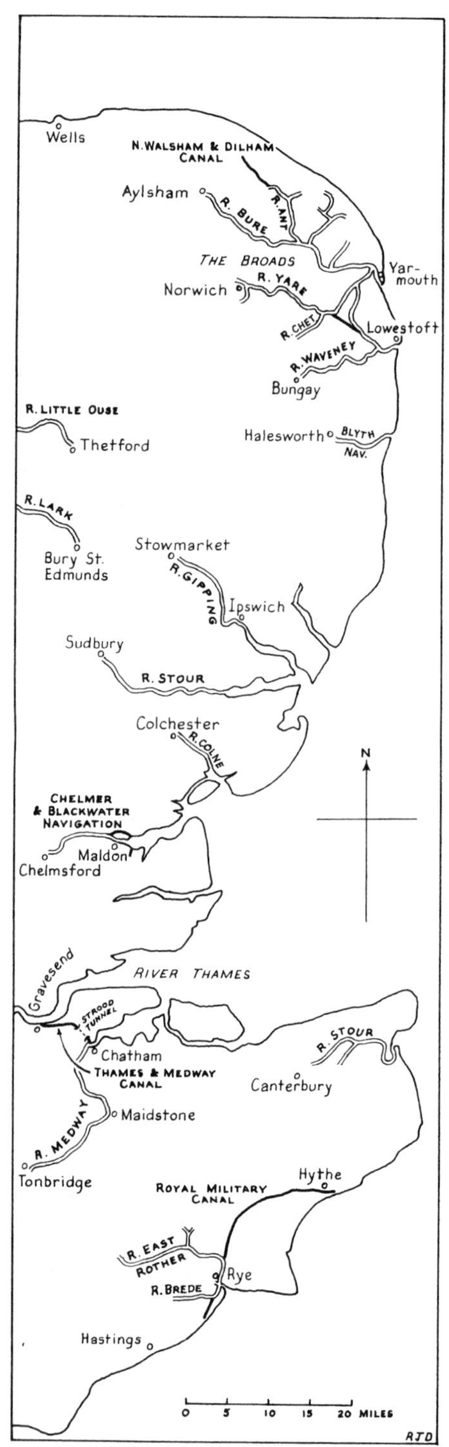

The waterways of Kent and East Anglia did not form a connected system and, apart from the Royal Military Canal in the south, were mostly river navigations which relied on ports and seaborne traffic

Stroudwater and Thames & Severn canals towards Oxford or the Vale of White Horse.

The story of the Exeter Canal goes back to the reign of Edward I in the thirteenth century. Until about that time the River Exe had been tidal as far as Exeter, and small craft used to ascend the river to the city. Then Isabella de Fortibus, Countess of Devon, built a weir across the river (Countess Wear is still well known). The earls of Devon followed her lead with other weirs, at the same time building a quay at Topsham, near the mouth of the Exe, where goods for Exeter had to be landed and had to pay the earl's dues. Though the citizens won lawsuits, the earls maintained the weirs.

In 1563 the citizens of Exeter, exasperated by three hundred years of obstructions in the river, engaged John Trew of Glamorgan as engineer of a barge canal to run from a point below Countess Wear alongside the Exe to the city, where it would rejoin the river. Here a wharf was to be built, fitted with a crane. The canal that Trew built was very small – only 3 ft deep, 16 ft wide and 1¾ miles long – but it had three locks on it, probably with vertically rising gates, which were the first pound-locks on any British navigation. It was, and remains, a municipal affair, and a tribute to the public spirit of the city.

Although Trew had promised to build a canal that was accessible at all states of the tide, he did not in fact do so. By 1677 the waterway had been carried farther down river to Topsham, and in 1701 it was enlarged to a depth of 10 ft and breadth of 50 ft, dimensions sufficient for coasting craft and small deep-sea ships.

After it became clear that the port of Exeter would not become, like Gloucester later, the focal point of canals running throughout the south-west, the corporation decided that its canal must be improved, both in the interests of the city itself and to attract capital to canals that might be connected with it.

James Green was called in, and between 1820 and 1827 he completely reconstructed the canal, making it 15 ft deep and carrying the entrance 2 miles farther down the estuary to Turf, where 12 ft of water was available at all tides. The canal could take vessels of 400 tons, but by now Exeter's most important business, the export of woollen goods, had ceased and nothing comparable had taken its place. However, the corporation supported an early railway Act of 1832 for a line from the canal basin at Exeter to Crediton, and, when action failed, agreed with the Bristol & Exeter Railway that its line should come to the basin.

Then two great changes took place. On the one hand the corporation changed its mind about the terminus of the railway, which in fact ended at Red Cow (St David's), and it was not until 1867 that the basin had

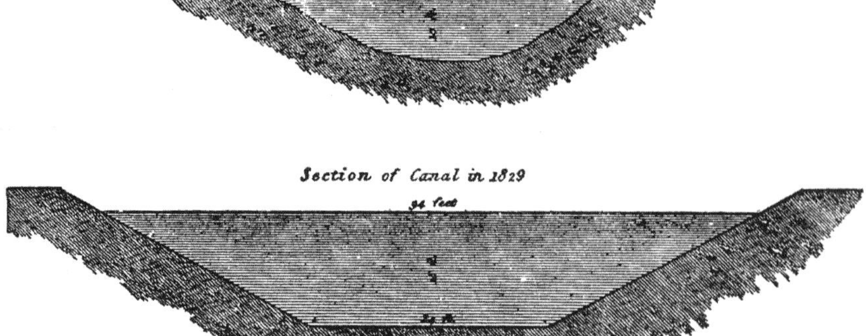

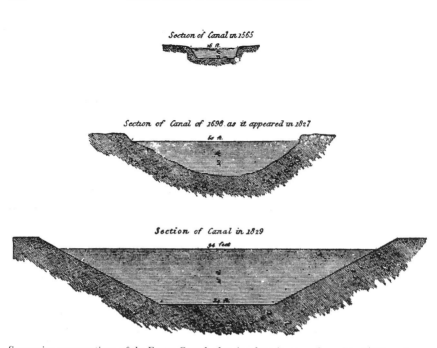

Successive cross-sections of the Exeter Canal, showing how it was enlarged in 1701 and 1827 from its original dimensions. Very little remains today of the original canal engineered by John Trew

railway communication via a branch line near St Thomas's. On the other hand the coming of steamships made the canal's dimensions inadequate. Competition from railways, instead of the cooperation that might have been possible, and the falling-off of traffic caused the tolls received to fall below the interest charges on the money that had been borrowed to reconstruct the canal. The creditors then took over the canal, and its ownership did not revert to the city until 1883. The canal is too small to make Exeter an important port, and its only traffic today is some 50,000 tons a year of sludge carried by the *Countess Wear*, which will cease before the end of the century. The basin, no longer commercially used, now displays part of the Exeter Maritime Museum's collection.

A ship canal from Berkeley Pill on the Severn to Gloucester was planned in order that shipping bound for Gloucester could avoid the difficult and dangerous passage of the river between those points, and that the transhipment of goods from ships to barges, or vice versa, should take place in the basin at Gloucester, into which craft could pass from the river by means of a lock. The Act for this canal was passed in

1793. Two years later John Phillips wrote in his *History of Inland Navigation*:

> This undertaking for its magnitude and accommodations, deserves to be considered as of the first importance; its magnitude is intended for the passage of vessels of more than three hundred tons burthen; and its accommodations to commerce, by uniting the city of Gloucester, by an easy and certain water carriage with the port of Bristol, and from thence with all the world, may justly be deemed an object of great magnitude to trade. The whole of this scheme evinces an extent of idea, known only in a free country; and an ardour of enterprise, which none but an industrious and commercial people could endure . . .[9]

When he wrote that last sentence John Phillips spoke more truthfully than he knew. The ardour of enterprise of the proprietors of the Gloucester & Berkeley Canal carried them to success through great difficulties. It was thirty-four years after they obtained their Act that the canal was opened, and, because they had needed to borrow heavily from the government and to mortgage their property in return, it was seventy-eight years before the descendants of those who first subscribed for shares were in full control of their property.

The threads of many happenings, made familiar in the stories of other canals under construction during the canal mania, meet in the history of this canal, the biggest promoted in Britain at the time. In the minute book are recorded the immediate attendance on the committee of a gentleman from Bristol to ask if they would discuss a plan to build a barge canal from Bristol to their own; the letter from Boulton & Watt saying that they could not have immediate delivery of a steam engine for pumping water out of the channel during cutting because of the great demand for steam engines; the agreement with the Herefordshire & Gloucestershire not to attract each other's workmen; the insistence by landowners on written authority for all surveyors coming on to their lands, and on compensation for all damage; and trouble with workmen, engineers, estimates, surveys and contractors.

Relations with the workmen started off well, the committee recording:

> It being understood, that it is customary, at the commencement of every Canal, to allow some liquor to the Workmen, and Mr Edson having reported that the number of Workmen now employed are fifty – Ordered, That he do give one shilling, to each of those men . . .[10]

Trouble with engineers was chronic until just before the canal was opened, when the family of Clegram moved in, the father as engineer and the son as clerk, and remained until, in 1885, the son, now engineer, retired and took a seat on the board. The usual practice was followed of appointing a 'Chief and Principal Engineer', in this case Robert Mylne, at a yearly retainer of £350 and travelling expenses, and a resident engineer. During the mania the few canal engineers who had reputations took on far more work than they could carefully deal with. Mylne was not, in fact, one of them, but rather, as engineer of London's New River Company, an expert on water provision and supply, as well as being an excellent architect. He was, however, as busy as the others and so, like most of them, he seldom visited the site unless a crisis occurred, depending on the reports of the resident engineer for the material on which to give advice. At the same time the number of canals simultaneously under construction made it difficult for canal committees to engage competent resident engineers. Yet if they were incompetent the damage was done before the chief engineer heard about it.

The first resident engineer on the Gloucester & Berkeley was Dennis Edson, engaged at 200 guineas a year, who lasted only nine months before he was dismissed. He had been dismissed twenty years earlier from the Chester Canal, and he was to suffer the same fate at the Grand Surrey seven years later. Already the committee were in difficulties as a result, for they took on the 26-year-old James Dadford, who at any rate came from a competent engineering family, and wrote anxiously to Mylne:

> and they are so very anxious to have doubts removed, that much embarrass them, and as they conceive very much affect their future operations, that they cannot be satisfied, but by your personal attendance, which they trust you will not defer longer than next week.[11]

Eventually the company's affairs reached such a state that a proprietor complained that he thought that Mylne was to oversee everything, the resident engineer merely carrying out instructions, instead of which:

> but a small quantity of his personal attendance has been *necessarily occupied* by the Works, and since our engagement with Mr Dadford, scarcely any . . . As for the Idea which in the Days of our ignorance was broached, with some success, that an Engineer may render us sufficient services, by *thinking* and *contriving* for us, while *sitting at his ease in London*: I will not suppose any member of the Committee is *now* amused by it.[12]

Mylne came down to face the committee and agreed in future to accept payment by the day, at four guineas plus travelling expenses.

From this it may be understood that the company was in trouble. The original plan had been for a canal 17¾ miles long, 70 ft broad at top (or water level) and 18 ft deep, estimated by Mylne to cost £121,330, to cover which the Act authorized £140,000 and a further £60,000, if necessary. Work began in 1794 at the Gloucester end in excavating the dock and cutting down towards Berkeley. By 1799 available cash had run out and the canal had only been cut to Hardwicke, about 5½ miles from Gloucester. Confidence had almost gone, and the efforts that the committee made to interest shareholders in putting up further money were in vain, either for a narrow canal to continue to the junction with the Stroudwater Canal, which would open trade through the Thames & Severn, or to change the final junction with the Severn from Berkeley Pill to Hock Crib, which was nearer but less convenient. The shareholders, like those of so many other canals of the mania who had been caught by the effects of the war and the results of inefficiency and over-optimism, refused to budge, and the partly finished canal lay useless. Dadford was given notice: there was nothing for him to do.

The committee spent the next twenty years alternating bursts of enthusiasm with long spells of inactivity, trying to decide where to end the canal (they finally chose Sharpness Point, rather than Berkeley Pill or Hock Crib) and to raise the necessary money, at one time even by a lottery scheme that was turned down personally by William Pitt.

The government in the end helped construction to resume. The Exchequer Bill Loan Commissioners were able to make loans for works that would employ the unemployed poor, and they lent part of the estimated money. Telford inspected the canal and pronounced it a good risk.

So work began again, and the Duke of Gloucester came down to lay the foundation stone of the docks at Sharpness, while three hogsheads of ale were drunk by the workmen. The sad history of the canal was compensated by the magniloquence of the inscription:

> To extend the advantages of commerce into the Interior of the Kingdom, and to facilitate the Intercourse with Foreign Countries, the Gloucester and Berkeley Canal Company projected this work. The approbation of the most illustrious and dignified Personages of the realm sanctioned the undertaking; and the countenance of His Royal Highness William Frederick Duke of Gloucester, assisted by the noble House of Berkeley, was particularly evinced in graciously condescending to lay the first stone of this Harbour, the fifteenth day of July, 1818.

> Long may it remain unmoved, a Monument of national enterprise, a benefit to the proprietors, and a secure Harbour for the commerce of the World.[13]

John Upton, who had been taken on as clerk and became engineer *de facto* in 1815, reverted to clerk six months after the resumption of work and soon afterwards resigned, when an inquiry brought to light that materials for the works had been supplied by him as seller to himself as engineer. John Woodhouse succeeded him and was in turn dismissed, only a year later, for the similar offence of allowing his son to supply unsuitable stone. There was further trouble with the contractors, one of whom went bankrupt, and at the end of 1820, with only the junction to the Stroudwater Canal finished and the rest of the works partly built, £120,000 was still needed. They could not pay the interest and repayments of principal due to the Exchequer Bill Loan Commissioners under their agreement and the commissioners were going to take over the canal as mortgagees, unless money was raised to pay them. Meanwhile all work had stopped.

A frantic search for money ended in the raising of capital in preference shares and further loans from the commissioners, who now administered the funds of the company jointly with the committee. Civil Service control in this case led to a great increase in efficiency. A new contractor was appointed, warehouses were built and the canal was finally completed.

In 1827 the canal opened in a flurry of settling debts to contractors, arranging for market passenger boats, dealing with the now numerous applications from traders to erect warehouses or wharves, looking for more water supplies and making terms with the organization of trackers, the men who hauled the sailing ships along the waterway until a regular service of tugs was introduced in about 1862. It was the greatest canal in Britain: at a depth of 18 ft, deeper than the Caledonian at that time, and taking ships carrying 600 tons of cargo. Trade increased – 2,360 vessels used the port in 1827, 4,272 in 1828, 5,199 in 1829 and 7,981 in 1830 – but an unpleasant letter arrived from the commissioners saying that they did not think it expedient any longer to control the affairs of the company and that they would therefore take steps to dispose of the concern for the recovery of the debt due to the public, unless the company could suggest an arrangement for its early liquidation.

Indeed, it was nearly twenty years later before the company was free from periodical threats to sell up, as a result of raising the money to repay the commissioners through the creation of first preference shares and by borrowing from an insurance company. The mortgage to the

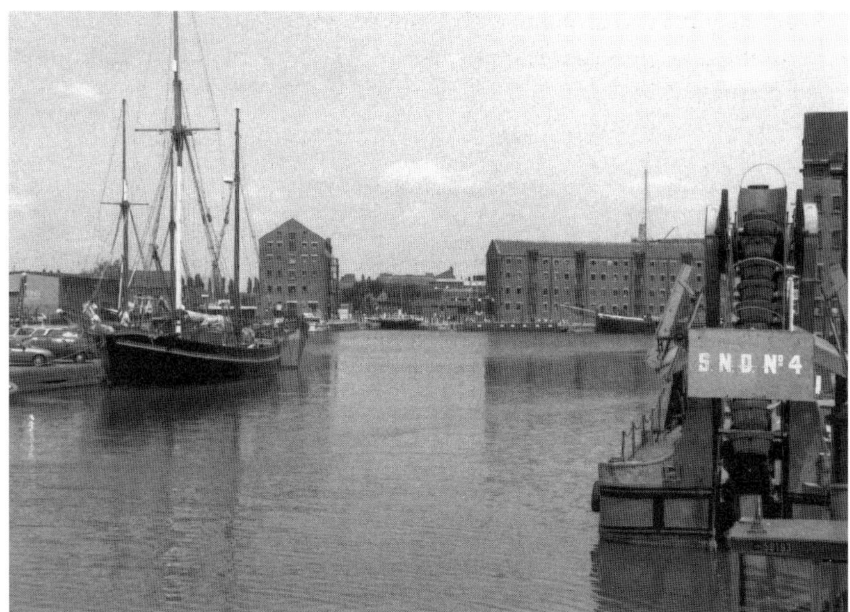

The docks at Gloucester, with Gloucester Lock, leading to the Severn in the distance. 'S.N.D. No. 4', on the dredger, signifies the Sharpness New Docks company. This is moored outside the National Waterways Museum, where it forms an exhibit

insurance company was not finally repaid until 1871, when the committee's report triumphantly read: 'this Company became free from the restrictions of the mortgages originally imposed by the Government, and received the whole of their title deeds into their own possession.'[14]

Thenceforward the policy of the company was made up of three strands, which met in the 1870s. The first was cooperation with railways.

It is so natural to think of railways as competitors of canals – as, indeed, they proved – that it is not at once realized that canals like the Gloucester & Berkeley, which were primarily ports, had much more to gain from good railway connections to their docks than to lose from rail competition along their route. This applied especially to ports having a foreign trade, for the general result of the coming of railways was to increase foreign and decrease coastal trade. As far back as 1806, three years before the Gloucester & Cheltenham Tramroad received its Act, the Gloucester & Berkeley agreed to have rails laid to its basin at Gloucester (where they remained until 1862). In 1843 it gave permission to the Birmingham & Gloucester Railway to lay its rails to the docks, and by 1862 the railway connections to the Gloucester basins were complete.

The company was also anxious to build up a coal export trade, at first from Gloucester and later from Sharpness Docks. Thus it gave every encouragement to a company formed to build a Severn Railway bridge near Sharpness, and so to bring Welsh and Forest of Dean coal. When the bridge company got into difficulties the Gloucester & Berkeley subscribed a considerable amount to its capital. The bridge was opened in 1879.

The second strand of policy was the promotion of inland waterways. It must be remembered that Gloucester was a terminal port with respect to the country around it. It was also a place of transhipment of cargoes from seagoing craft to river lighters going up the Severn to Worcester, to barges working through the Thames & Severn Canal to the Thames, and to narrow boats bound for the Wilts & Berks, by way of the Thames & Severn, for the Staffs & Worcs (from Stourport) and for the Worcester & Birmingham (from Worcester).

The Gloucester & Berkeley company opposed the improvement of the Severn by various proposed private navigation companies, nominally in the cause of a free river, but in fact because it feared that the improvement of the navigation would cost more in tolls to craft on the river than the added facilities were worth, thus discouraging traffic. When the Severn Commissioners were set up as a public body, however, the canal company supported them financially.

Its interest extended beyond the Severn. The Staffs & Worcs Canal was a prosperous concern that maintained its independence of railways without difficulty. The Worcester & Birmingham, however, was not, since it both had an expensive line to keep up and suffered severely from railway competition. As early as 1858 a proposal before Parliament for the lease of this canal to the Oxford, Worcester & Wolverhampton Railway was opposed and defeated. Thenceforward the Worcester & Birmingham was the prize for two sets of chess players: the railway interests on the one hand and the waterways on the other, on the whole led by the Gloucester & Berkeley. Though the Worcester & Birmingham passed into the hands of a receiver in 1868, the game lasted until 1874, when the Gloucester & Berkeley leased it, together with the Droitwich and the Droitwich Junction, both of these having formerly been leased to the Worcester & Birmingham. The canal company now possessed two separated waterways, one a ship canal and one a partly narrow, partly broad, canal, connected by the Severn in which they were financially interested, and which provided a through water route to Birmingham.

The Gloucester & Berkeley company started well by giving its new acquisitions a thorough overhaul and dredging. On the Droitwich 73,000 tons of mud were removed, according to the engineer 'the accumulation,

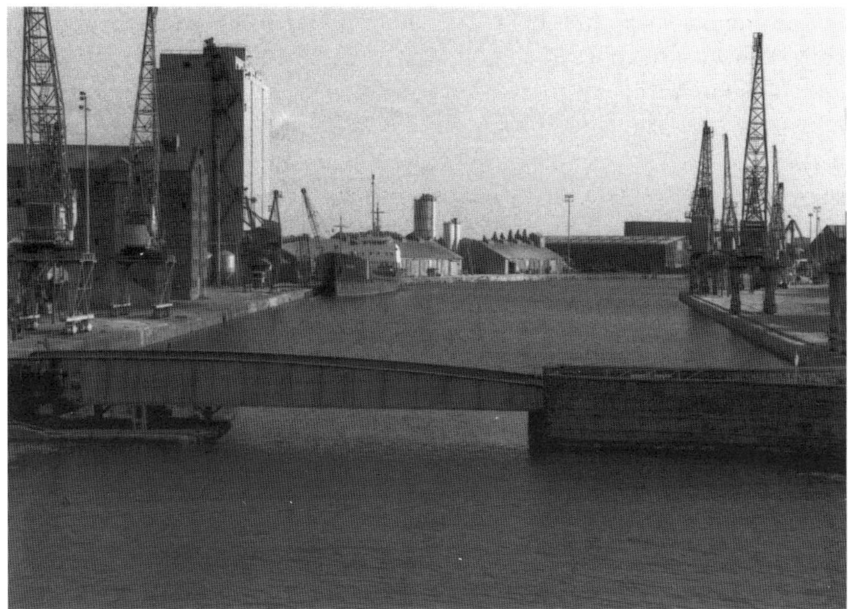

The docks at Sharpness, looking south. Only occasional shipping passes through the swing-bridge in the foreground, while the original terminal is used by pleasure craft alone

I should think, of the last half century'. Yet in no year did its new purchase earn enough to pay what it was costing the parent company in interest on the mortgage debt that had been taken over and in payments to shareholders guaranteed under the terms of the lease. By the end of the century the tolls received were hardly balancing the maintenance costs. Traffic had left both Droitwich lines by the 1920s and both closed in 1939.

The company also did its best to keep open the canals towards the Thames, successfully opposing in 1897 the abandonment of the Wilts & Berks by its owners. It became a stockholder in the Thames & Severn Canal Trust, which took over the waterway from the Great Western Railway, and ran it until funds gave out and it was passed to the Gloucestershire County Council.

The two threads of cooperation with the railways and encouragement of waterways were intertwined with a third, the improvement of the port at Gloucester and the harbour at Sharpness. New basins were built at the former, and many developments took place as warehouses and wharves were constructed. Sharpness, a port built for sailing ships, which could not take the bigger steamers, had been suffering heavy competition from the newer steamer docks in the Bristol Channel ports: a larger harbour and entrance lock were opened in 1874, and steamers carrying over 1,000 tons of cargo navigated the canal. A rate-cutting war with Avonmouth to attract the Bristol Channel trade was ended by agreement in 1882. From that time to the present the canal has continued to serve Gloucester, although by now traffic is rare.

Ulverston in Lancashire was a town from which the estuary of the River Leven had receded. In 1793, therefore, an Act was obtained to make a small ship canal of about 1¼ miles from the river to the town. On 23 August 1793 the inhabitants of Ulverston went in a procession headed by two fiddles and bagpipes to see the first sod cut by Lt.-Col. Sunderland, the company's chairman.

The canal was opened in November 1796. It was a substantial affair: 15 ft deep and 66 ft wide at water level, and provided with two large basins. It was used largely for the export of iron and copper ores and slate, and the import of coal, timber and the merchandise needed in the town and its district. At first its trade was small: in 1798 94 vessels entered the canal, the tonnage being 4,704 tons; by 1821 the number of vessels had risen to 259 and the tonnage was 13,960 tons; from 1829 to 1844 the number of vessels each year averaged 531 and the tonnage 35,009 tons. Then came two years of great activity as ships entered with materials for the building of the Furness Railway. When that line was opened in 1846 trade at once fell away: 388 ships and 25,220 tons in 1849. Thenceforward it declined, until in 1862 the Furness Railway Company bought it. Since the authorized capital was £7,000, to which must be added the cost of subsequent works such as the pier and a weir, and the railway paid £22,005 for it, the proprietors were probably not out of pocket. The last ship entered the canal in 1916. After the canal had been used for yacht storage and a very early restoration campaign (in 1938, to revive commercial traffic), it was abandoned in 1945.

This account of a short canal illustrates the economic importance to its neighbourhood even of such a minor work as the Ulverston Canal. Later in the nineteenth century a plan for a greater inland port was put forward and successfully carried out by a larger town than Ulverston. The story of the Manchester Ship Canal is told later.

Finally, one freak deserves a mention: the Grand Surrey Canal, which began as a canal and became an extended dock. The canal grew out of various proposals, among others one for a waterway from Deptford to Kingston, with branches to Epsom and Croydon. In 1801 a canal from the River Thames at Rotherhithe, through Peckham, Camberwell and Kennington to Mitcham, was authorized. The engineer, Ralph Dodd, got to work at once, and in 1801 cutting began on the Rotherhithe section.

In April 1802 Dodd was dismissed, and thereafter the company became less and less interested in extending the canal, which was slowly cut past the junction at New Cross with the Croydon Canal (opened in 1809) to Camberwell, together with a later branch to Peckham, while the entrance lock into the Thames opened in 1807. At Camberwell and Peckham the canal remained, while the company developed as a dock concern, though for a long time not a prosperous one, mainly owing to the competition of other docks.

The use of the Grand Surrey as an inland waterway really ended in 1836, when the through traffic from the Croydon Canal ceased. The Croydon was sold to a railway company, the earliest example of the use of a canal line to construct a railway. Thereafter the wharves that had sprung up along the Grand Surrey must be thought of as extensions to its docks. In 1855 the company became the Grand Surrey Docks & Canal Company and was authorized to build the Albion Dock. In 1864 it amalgamated with the Commercial Docks Company, which had bought the old Greenland and other docks, and the combined company became the owner of the Surrey Commercial docks system. Soon afterwards the canal was connected to the Greenland dock. In 1908 the canal, together with the docks, was transferred to the newly formed Port of London Authority, and in January 1971 the whole canal closed, a minor casualty in the ending of the long service to London of the whole Surrey Commercial docks system.

CHAPTER SEVEN

The Golden Years

The slump that followed the Napoleonic Wars affected all waterways, but especially those that had gained abnormal traffic during the war as a result of the danger from privateers that had faced the coastal trade. The Basingstoke committee welcomed the return of peace with the remark 'That from the facilities afforded in peace to the conveyance of goods by sea, some considerable injury must be sustained by the Canal . . .'[1]

The pattern of the waterways of the British Isles was now approaching its final complexity. We have examined in detail some of the groups of which it was made up, such as the arterial canals connecting the great rivers and the network around Birmingham. Other groups had been formed, and it is at these that we must now look to get a reasonable picture of the waterway system as a whole.

First, two in Lancashire and Yorkshire had grown up largely during the war, and were almost complete by its end. On the Lancashire side the great Leeds & Liverpool, not yet finished, curved through Blackburn, Burnley and Colne on its way to Yorkshire. Part of its route lay over the Lancaster. This broad canal began at Wigan and ran north through Preston and Lancaster, then over Rennie's great Lune aqueduct and through Hincaster Tunnel to Kendal in Westmorland. It was completed in 1819. The Lancaster was an oddity because it was broken in the middle by a 5 mile long tramroad that crossed the valley of the Ribble just south of Preston. This tramroad, which necessitated the double transhipment of goods, formed an obstacle to through traffic greater than its value. It was last used throughout in January 1862, after which the canal was divided into two separate sections.

From Manchester there ran out a spray of canals, climbing into the valleys where factories were still driven by water power. Even in 1831, possibly half of the cotton mills in Britain were on the banks of the Goyt or the Etherow. The Rochdale Canal left the Bridgewater Canal and climbed past Oldham to the valley of the River Roch. It gave a branch to Rochdale (and later one to Heywood) and then crossed from Lancashire into Yorkshire without a summit tunnel. It ended at Sowerby Bridge, where it joined the Calder & Hebble Navigation, which itself connected with the Aire & Calder system. To the south ran the narrow boat Ashton-under-Lyne Canal (connected to the Rochdale and so to the Bridgewater) to Ashton, where it joined the Huddersfield, also narrow, which once again climbed over the Pennines into Yorkshire, this time by way of the great Standedge Tunnel. This tunnel was the longest (then 5,456 yd, now 5,698 yd) and at the highest point (637 ft) of any artificial waterway in the British Isles. It ended at Huddersfield, where it was connected to the Calder & Hebble Navigation by the small but vital privately owned canal known as Sir John Ramsden's or the Huddersfield Broad Canal. It also connected at Dukinfield to the Peak Forest Canal, which passed over the great Marple aqueduct, and then climbed the valley of the Goyt to Whaley Bridge, where it joined the Cromford & High Peak Railway, which ran across the high lands to the Cromford Canal. This railway, with its many inclined planes, had been envisaged as part of a through canal–rail line from London via Leicester and the Cromford Canal to Manchester, but it never became so, though it served by its threat of competition to keep rates down between the Trent and Manchester on the competing Trent & Mersey and Macclesfield canal routes. Near Whaley Bridge was another terminus of the Peak Forest Canal at Bugsworth (now Buxworth), from where a tramroad owned by the canal company ran up to limestone quarries beyond Chapel-en-le-Frith. This tramroad worked until 1920, the last connected with a canal.

Although the Leeds & Liverpool was the first of the three Pennine canals begun, and although it was first over the summit, it was the last to be completed, in 1816. The Rochdale Canal provided the first through connection when it opened in 1804, followed by the Huddersfield, in 1811, after a long struggle to complete its great tunnel at Standedge. Of the three the Rochdale was the greatest carrier of trans-Pennine traffic. The Leeds and Liverpool flourished more on highly developed local traffic on each side of its summit, while the Huddersfield's traffic was far less than either.

North out of Manchester ran the Manchester, Bolton & Bury, to the west the Bridgewater Canal to Runcorn for Liverpool, to the north-west the Worsley branch, which was by then connected to the Leeds & Liverpool by the Leigh branch of that canal, while to Liverpool there was also available the old but efficient river route of the Mersey & Irwell Navigation. The Rochdale was connected to the Bridgewater Canal, but not to the Mersey & Irwell Navigation until, towards the end of the canal age, the Manchester & Salford Junction was built to join the two. From Marple on the Peak Forest was to run the Macclesfield Canal, not then built, down past Macclesfield to join the Trent & Mersey to the west of Harecastle Tunnel, and to shorten the distance between points on that canal and Manchester at the cost of additional lockage.

The southern portal of Standedge Tunnel, which was extended to this point when the adjacent railway was enlarged in 1892–3. The boat in front of the portal is an inspection craft, used in the recent comprehensive survey of the tunnel to discern its condition and the cost of repairs. At 648 ft above sea level, this is the highest summit level in the British Isles

Though rivers played a small part in the waterway system of Lancashire, in Yorkshire they were the basis of the network, canals or river cuts being used to improve the river navigations. The base line lay from west to east. From Leeds ran one branch of the Aire & Calder Navigation and from Wakefield another. The two joined at Castleford, and then used the Aire and the Selby canal to reach the Yorkshire Ouse at Selby, from where there was access to the Humber and Hull. This old but flourishing navigation had not yet been rebuilt, nor a new canal cut from Ferrybridge to Goole. From Selby there was access up the Ouse to York and, on suitable tides, up the Wharfe to Tadcaster. Beyond York lay the Linton Lock Navigation and then, on its continuation, the Ure, leading to the Ripon Canal, which terminated at Ripon. North of the Humber Estuary the navigable River Hull led to Beverley, Leven and Driffield, all on branch canals.

To the south the Stainforth & Keadby Canal ran from the Trent at Keadby into the busy River Don, passing by Doncaster and Rotherham to

In contrast to the Standedge Tunnel (opposite), the summit level of the Rochdale Canal reached 600 ft without any need for a tunnel, although the parallel railway line used a tunnel. Although this canal was closed in 1952, the lock in the far distance was restored in 1980, and the canal to the north was fully restored by 1990. This length had been polluted with toxic silt from a chemical works, formerly served by the canal

Tinsley, from where a canal climbing to Sheffield was opened in 1819. The older route for Don traffic by the Dutch River to Goole and the Ouse was now little used, most vessels going instead via Keadby. From Swinton on the Don the Dearne & Dove Canal ran past branches to Elsecar and Worsbrough (for iron and coal) to a junction with the Barnsley Canal, coming down from the Silkstone coalfield on its way to the Calder at Wakefield. On the Trent there was access via Stockwith to the Chesterfield Canal, and at Torksey passage could be made from the Trent through the Fossdyke to the Witham Navigation, and so to the Wash at Boston.

A third group to be considered are those canals cut especially to carry coal or iron to the nearest artery or to the sea. These waterways usually had no town at their inland end but instead terminated at an ironworks or a colliery. Their construction made a great contribution to the output of the two raw materials on which industrial development relied more and more heavily into the nineteenth century. There were isolated examples, such as the Monkland near Glasgow and the Somersetshire Coal Canal, which connected with the Kennet & Avon not far from Bath, but there were also three notable groups: the Welsh canals, the Derbyshire group and the Shropshire group.

A few small private canals existed in Wales before 1790, but all of the important canals of South Wales were built in the 1790s to transport coal, limestone, copper ore and other industrial raw materials up and down the valleys, and to carry away iron and industrial products to the ports. The Swansea Canal from above Ystradgynlais to Swansea, the Neath from Glynneath to Neath and on to Giant's Grave, the Glamorganshire from Merthyr Tydfil to Cardiff, the Monmouthshire with its two branches, one from Crumlin and one from above Pontypool to Newport, and the Brecknock & Abergavenny from the mines and ironworks near Gilwern to Brecon, were all open by 1800.

After 1800 three important additions were made to the existing Welsh canals: the Brecknock & Abergavenny was joined in 1812 to the Monmouthshire Canal at Pontymoile; the Aberdare Canal was completed in 1812 from near Aberdare to join the Glamorganshire; and the Tennant Canal, the biggest private canal next to the Duke of Bridgewater's, was finished.

The Tennant enterprise grew remarkably. It began as a small private canal that Edward Elton had built from a colliery at Glan-y-wern to the River Neath at Redjacket, which opened in 1790. It was leased in 1818 by George Tennant, who used part of it to make a canal joining the River Tawe below Swansea to the River Neath at Redjacket. While it aimed to offer coal coming down the Neath Canal a better shipping place on the Tawe than it had at Giant's Grave, it failed to serve this purpose. Tennant then extended it upwards past Neath Abbey and Neath itself to join the Neath Canal at Aberdulais, and at the Swansea end built new wharves at what was by then called Port Tennant. It was the opening of this canal that Elizabeth Davies so eloquently commemorated in her verses (see Chapter Two). It was completed in 1824.

There was one other canal that intended importance but did not achieve it. This was the Kidwelly & Llanelly, with a line to Pembrey New Harbour and Burry Port, and another up the Gwendraeth Valley to Cwmmawr, with three inclined planes built by James Green, only two of which were brought into use.

The main valley canals – the Swansea, Neath, Glamorganshire and Monmouthshire – were heavily locked: the Swansea fell 213 ft by 36 locks in 16 miles; the Neath 157 ft by 19 locks in 13 miles; the Glamorganshire 542 ft by 50 locks in 25 miles; and the Monmouthshire 337 ft by 31 locks in 9 miles from its Pontymoile branch, which connected with the Brecknock & Abergavenny Canal. Almost all loaded traffic was one-way, but there was less difficulty with water supply and almost no tunnelling.

These canals and the smaller private waterways that joined them, served by a network of horse tramroads, were profitable to their proprietors, as well as being of great industrial value, and helped to found their respective ports. Before they were built the products of the South Wales iron industry had been carried on horseback or muleback over the mountains to points where they could be loaded into waggons to be taken to the ports. How the waterways made possible the growth of the industry can be seen from the following figures of iron carried on two of the canals:

Year	*Glamorganshire tons*	*Monmouthshire tons*
1807	-	23,019
1817	39,497	43,407
1827	84,946	91,618
1837	124,810	144,277

Before the Glamorganshire was completed in 1798, Cardiff had a population of about a thousand. By 1841 its population was more than ten thousand, and its exports had increased many times. Representative figures for iron have been given. Those for coal are:

Year	*Glamorganshire tons*	*Monmouthshire tons*
1819	34,606	-
1829	83,729	471,675
1839	211,214	484,993

A second group of canals was in the Erewash Valley, running north from the Trent near Nottingham. These comprised the Erewash Canal and its continuation the Cromford, with the Nutbrook as a tributary of the Erewash. From this central line, offshoots led on the one side to Nottingham (the Nottingham Canal) and on the other to Derby (the Derby Canal), so that the coal, iron, limestone, paving-stones and other goods coming down the main line could be diverted to either of these towns or to places beyond them on other connecting navigations. Alternatively they could pass into the Trent to go down river as far as

The waterways of the West and East Midlands of England, with their connections into Wales and the north-west. These include the Shropshire group and those around the Erewash valley

Gainsborough (for shipping by sea) and Torksey (for Lincoln), or across it into the Loughborough Navigation and so to Leicester and the south. In 1808 269,456 tons of coal were carried on the Cromford, Erewash and Nottingham canals and this figure grew steadily until railway times.

The third group comprised the Shropshire tub-boat canals. The Shropshire coalfield was, as we saw, one of the first to use river transport and tramroads. Iron had been smelted in the district with charcoal since at least the first half of the seventeenth century, but, when Abraham Darby first learned to smelt iron with coke at Coalbrookdale, he laid the foundation of a tight little industrial pocket of collieries and ironworks. The country was so hilly, however, that to build ordinary canals was out of the question. William Reynolds of Ketley, one of the works in the Coalbrookdale group, provided the answer when he introduced the inclined plane at Ketley.

The earliest canal in the area, the Donnington Wood (or Duke of Sutherland's Tub-boat) Canal, had been built by 1767. It ran from collieries at Donnington Wood to Pave Lane near Newport, and was constructed by Earl Gower, the Duke of Bridgewater's brother-in-law, and the two Gilberts, Thomas and John. William Reynolds's little Ketley Canal led to the formation of the Shropshire Canal Company, which built 8 miles of canal from the Donnington Wood Canal past the Ketley Canal to the Severn at Coalport, with a branch to Coalbrookdale, and three inclined planes. This canal carried the industrial output of the area to the river, where it was transferred to river craft. Later the Shrewsbury Canal was built to carry coal more easily from Donnington to Shrewsbury. It also had an inclined plane, at Trench, which was to work until 1921 and was the last to operate in Britain. Lastly, a plane was built on a branch of the Donnington Wood Canal, which had previously had a vertical lift for the cargo, though not for the boats.

These canals were small in size and cheap to construct. Their small tub-boats holding 5–8 tons each were navigated in trains between the planes and the cost of operation was low. It was not until 1835 that this self-contained tub-boat system was connected to the main canal network by means of the Newport branch of the Birmingham & Liverpool Junction. The Shrewsbury Canal was then partly converted for narrow boat use. Cargoes from the rest of the system had to be transhipped to special 'Trench' narrow boats at Trench wharf below the plane there.

While it might be fascinating to trace in detail the new patterns of trade brought about by this wide and interlacing system of rivers and canals, it would demand a greater interest in economic history than can reasonably be expected in a book that is not written for specialists. However, a glance at the coal trade in England and Wales will give some

Coal being carried on the Bridgewater Canal over the Barton Swing Aqueduct, which crosses the Manchester Ship Canal. This unique structure replaced the earliest major aqueduct. This view was taken in the late 1940s, showing both wide and narrow boats. Traffic on this section, in coal to power stations, which ceased as late as 1973, was one of the last major traffics on the smaller canals (De Mare Collection/Boat Museum)

idea of what happened to every raw material and finished commodity, and of the repercussions on manufacturers, their employees and the towns where work was carried out.

Before the canals, coal went by sea from the north-east coast to those towns accessible to small coasting vessels. This sea coal came up the Thames to London and up the many rivers of the east coast into the heart of East Anglia, Lincolnshire and Yorkshire. Land coal was usually supplied by road transport only in the neighbourhood of the collieries, for the cost of carriage rose steeply as the distance increased, whether in waggons or on horseback. Only where there was a river to help the distribution, as with the Severn in Shropshire, was land coal transported far afield. There were therefore parts of Britain that found it difficult to get coal at all, except at a prohibitive price.

The motive of cheap coal was an important one in the history of canal development and, after the waterways were built, land or sea coal was transported by water everywhere south of Lancashire or Yorkshire, except to parts of North Wales. Yorkshire coal went east via the Aire & Calder or the Don, until it met the sea coal in from the Humber, although Yorkshire coal also went south along the coast; Wigan coal also crossed the Pennines, as well as going south to Liverpool and west on its old route down the Douglas Navigation on its way to Ireland; Welsh coal came down the valleys by canal and was then shipped to Bristol and the south-west; Forest of Dean coal went to Gloucester and Cheltenham, and through the Thames & Severn as far east as Oxford; Somerset coal, through the Kennet & Avon and the Wilts & Berks, also moved east, until at Reading it met the sea coal coming up the Thames, or at Abingdon or Oxford met Leicestershire or Warwickshire coal from the Oxford Canal. Coal within the Midlands competed freely – Leicestershire mainly against Derbyshire, Staffordshire against Warwickshire – and pressed down the Grand Junction towards London. Via main canals or their branches, such country places as Buckingham, Newport Pagnell, Oakham and Ledbury found themselves supplied with fuel for domestic and industrial use, while the great manufacturing towns had a constant supply, not dependent on the output of a single colliery and at a cheaper price, which naturally drew coal-using industries to the canal side.

In Scotland coal from the Monkland or the Forth & Clyde went by boat to Glasgow and then by ship from Bowling or Grangemouth up and down the coast: before long it was to be going by canal to Edinburgh too.

The coal trade played a much smaller part in Ireland, where turf (peat) was, and remains, a more significant indigenous fuel. Coal imported through Dublin did traverse the Grand and Royal canals. The first had opened to the Shannon in 1805, and the Barrow navigation to St Mullins fifteen years before. The Grand Canal Company leased a colliery near Athy and carried coal to Dublin for a time after 1805. The Royal from Dublin to the upper Shannon was almost finished as the war ended.

To the north, imported coal from Newry and Belfast was carried up the Newry Canal and the Lagan, the latter being completed to Lough Neagh in 1794. Coal from the Tyrone collieries was carried down the 4⅜ mile long Coalisland Canal, although by 1787, when it had opened, the earlier Ducart's tub-boat canal, with its three primitive inclines, had closed. On the north coast the Strabane Canal, 4 miles long from that town to the River Foyle, had been opened in 1796.

Such was the canal system at the end of the Napoleonic Wars. Peace brought a slump: both men and horses that had been used for the war returned and helped to compete with the navigations by taking to transport over the improving roads of the time. From then on road transport was a serious competitor for the trade in merchandise and groceries, which, while small in volume compared with that in raw materials, earned high tolls and was the support of the fly-boats. Prices fell as unemployment rose. The years from the peace of Waterloo, in 1815, to 1822, when the coming boom made investors willing to venture capital, were a time when little was done to expand the canal system and competition for the existing business was keen. In 1822 the Basingstoke Committee stated

> that one hundred weight of goods is conveyed from London to Farnham by land, for one shilling and sixpence, which by the Canal, the same quantity must cost one shilling and threepence, and where the difference is so slight, it may be readily imagined the land carriage will be preferred, for its rapidity.
>
> In ordinary times, the expense of conveyance on land was about three times as much as by water . . .[2]

Of the biggest projects of this period, the Aire & Calder's Ferrybridge and Goole Canal are described in Chapter 8. The Edinburgh & Glasgow Union was authorized in 1817, with a capital of £290,000 to connect Edinburgh with the Forth & Clyde Canal near Falkirk by a line 30 miles long, all on one level except for the flight of locks that brought the canal down 110 ft to the Forth & Clyde. However, this project only fell into the post-war period by accident. It had first been reported on in 1793, and from that time, with a pause during the mid-period of the war, pamphlets for or against one or another proposed course had poured out.

A second project, the Portsmouth & Arundel, was the unluckiest of all canals. In 1813 an Act had been obtained for the Wey & Arun Junction to bring goods from London up the Thames, through the Wey river and the Wey & Arun Junction Canal to the River Arun, and then to Arundel and Littlehampton. It was probably because this new means of communication with London was coming into existence that the Portsmouth & Arundel was planned to connect those towns, and so give a through water communication with London. It was proposed to make a canal from Ford on the Arun to Chichester harbour. Then a channel was to be dredged round Thorney and Hayling islands and across Langstone Harbour to Portsea Island, where a canal would be cut across the peninsula to Portsmouth.

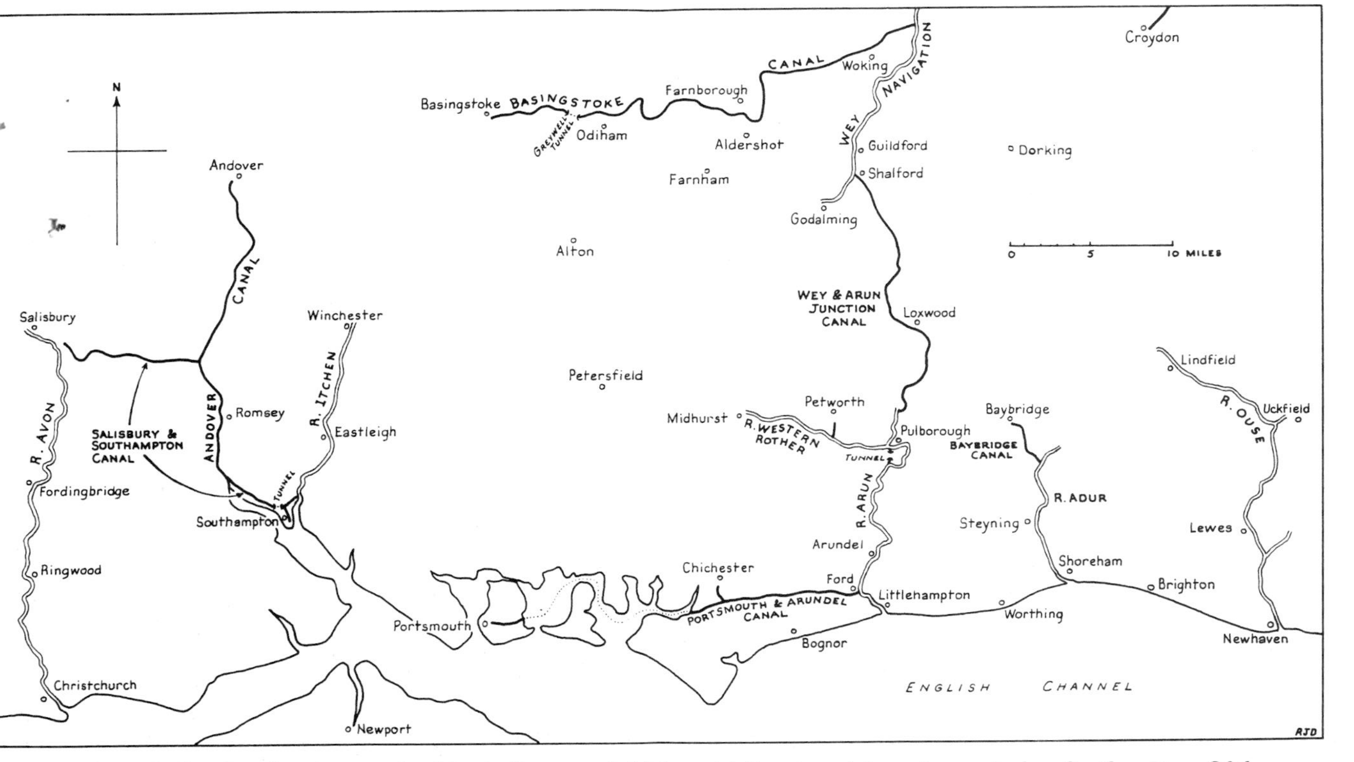

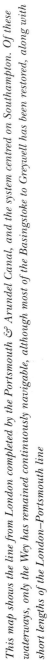

This map shows the line from London completed by the Portsmouth & Arundel Canal, and the system centred on Southampton. Of these waterways, only the Wey has remained continuously navigable, although most of the Basingstoke to Greywell has been restored, along with short lengths of the London–Portsmouth line

Before the canal was finished an agreement was made for tolls on traffic worked through the Portsmouth & Arundel, the Arun and the Wey & Arun Junction, and this last canal altered its waterway so that the same barges could be used for the through passage. The canal opened throughout in May 1823 and a certain amount of through traffic resulted. However, on 3 December 1824 an indignant meeting at the Beneficial Society's hall in Portsmouth called attention to the fact that seawater from the canal on the island was leaching into the springs and wells from which local inhabitants drew their drinking water. Three weeks later the proprietors at the meeting stated that, while compensation had been given in certain cases, and others were being considered, the company 'were not to be dictated to by any set of individuals, however respectable'.

The company survived but, despite efforts to build up the through trade, this languished and died, and the Portsmouth & Arundel Canal with it. The Portsea portion had hardly been used at all, and in about 1855 the rest of the canal followed, except for the short branch from Chichester to Chichester Harbour, which had been built on a larger scale. The company was finally wound up under an order of 1888.

The third of the new projects was the Bude Canal. Authorized in 1819 it was planned to run from Bude on the north coast of Cornwall to Thornbury, with a branch to Launceston, and various other branches, with a total length of almost 46 miles. The intention of the promoters was to build a tub-boat canal to carry sea-sand into the interior, to be used as a fertilizer. It was therefore planned on the model of the Shropshire Canal, without locks, except on the entrance section, and with six inclined planes, the biggest of which, at Hobbacott Down, was 225 ft high and 907 ft long. The boats, to carry some 4 tons each, had wheels permanently fixed beneath them so that they could run directly on to the rails of the inclined planes. Because coal was expensive in Cornwall the planes were worked hydraulically, five by waterwheel and that at Hobbacott Down by the bucket-in-the-well system, supplemented by a steam engine on the numerous occasions when one of the bucket-chains broke.

By 1826, 35 miles of the canal had been built at a cost of about £118,000. It carried some 50,000 tons of sea-sand a year for many years, but not until much later did it declare a dividend for its shareholders. In 1891 the whole canal, except for a length at Bude, was closed. The Bude-Stratton Urban District Council then took over the reservoir at Tamar Lake, together with part of the canal, as a means of water supply.

During the prosperity of 1824 three ship canal projects were presented to the public. The proposal for an English & Bristol Channels Ship Canal was sufficiently well thought of to obtain an Act of Parliament, but went no further. That for a waterway from the Dee Estuary to Manchester was speculative and not solidly supported, although it was the ancestor of the Manchester Ship Canal. The most ambitious scheme of all, for a ship canal from London to Portsmouth on a far bigger scale than the existing waterway and with a capital of £5 million, never seriously caught the public's imagination and was overwhelmed by the succeeding slump. A fourth scheme during this period, the Norwich & Lowestoft Ship Canal, was in fact a plan of river development and is described in the following chapter.

In 1825 the first public railway to be successfully operated by locomotive engines was opened between Stockton and Darlington. Originally a canal had been projected, but the proposal had then been changed to a railway. As we have seen, horse railways and tramroads were not a new idea in Britain. Starting as coal lines to feed the Tyne and the Severn, they had been extensively constructed to serve canals. Later, more ambitious lines were planned and built, notably the 33 mile long Cromford & High Peak Railway, which was authorized in 1825 (after the Stockton & Darlington was open) as a horse-operated line and opened in 1831, and the Stratford & Moreton, completed in 1826 as a branch of the Stratford-upon-Avon Canal. Extensive mineral lines such as the Sirhowy had existed for many years in the Welsh coal and iron districts.

In all some two dozen railways had been authorized by special Act of Parliament before 1824, along with many lines sanctioned in canal Acts or built privately. In the years 1824 and 1825, however, there was a tremendous outburst of speculative activity in railways, usually for locomotive routes. In those years most of the great lines of the next decade, such as the Great Western and the London & Birmingham, were first projected. In total, proposals for some sixty railways in the British Isles were put forward, and a number were authorized by Act of Parliament. A second outburst followed in 1830.

The use of locomotives on the Stockton & Darlington marks the virtual beginning of railway history. To contemporaries, however, this was an interesting development that increased the utility of railways but did not alter the general view: that railways were essentially feeders to waterways, useful in hilly country where the making of canals was impossibly expensive or over country where the expected traffic was light. Later public opinion was to swing to the other extreme: that waterways had no longer any part to play in the future of transport. This situation justified the legendary assertion of the old Duke of Bridgewater, that canals would last his time 'but I see mischief in those damned tramroads'.

The extension of the railway idea, and the faster operation of railways that followed the introduction of locomotives, was one cause of an increase in the efficiency and enterprise of the waterways.

The two tunnels at Harecastle, the older one, in which Brindley was involved, on the right. The drawing somewhat overemphasizes the more modern appearance of the second tunnel. The Brindley Tunnel was used until the First World War; the bore has now subsided to minimal headroom

One response was an effort at improvement. The Harecastle Tunnel on the Trent & Mersey Canal was doubled in 1827. The first tunnel – 12 ft high and 9¼ ft wide – had taken nine years, whereas the new tunnel – 16 ft high and 14 ft wide – took only three years to build, so greatly had engineering technique improved in the meantime. In other cases the distance between two points was reduced in order to save time and wages, since competition was becoming fiercer than that between water and road transport. Many early canals had adopted the principle of following as far as possible the contour of the ground, and had sacrificed shortness to ease and cheapness of construction and water conservation owing to the absence of locks. Later ones such as the Birmingham & Liverpool Junction were made as straight as possible, even at the expense of considerable cutting and embanking to maintain the level. A notable example of the straightening of a contour canal was the northern part of the Oxford, which between 1829 and 1834 was shortened from 91 to 77½ miles.

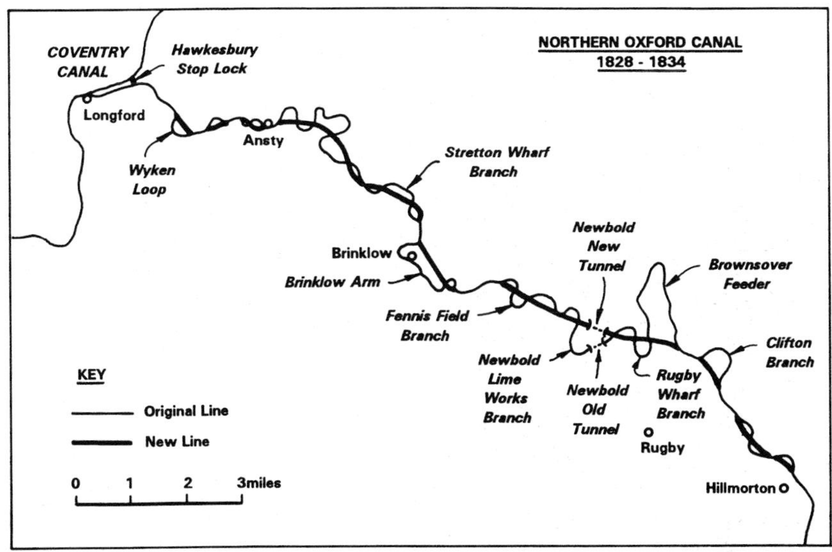

The shortening of part of the Oxford Canal. (Lengths further south, including a long loop near Braunston on the Grand Junction Canal, were also bypassed.) Some sections were retained as branches off the main line; only the Stretton Wharf Branch, in use for moorings, is now in regular use

The Birmingham & Liverpool Junction (now the Shropshire Union main line) was a 'modern' narrow canal. Authorized in 1826, opened in 1835 and engineered by Telford and Cubitt, it was intended both to shorten the distance between Birmingham and Ellesmere Port on the Mersey, and to provide a waterway less obstructed by tunnels and locks. It was expensive to build, for it completely deserted the contours and drove across country from the end of the old Chester Canal at Nantwich on embankments and through cuttings to a junction with the Staffs & Worcs at Autherley. After using ½ mile of that canal, boats from Ellesmere Port passed into the Birmingham Canal, itself having recently been reconstructed by Telford.

Efforts were then made to extend this new model right through to London by building a canal from a point on the Stratford-upon-Avon accessible from Birmingham to Highgate with a minimum of lockage. But by 1835, when the Birmingham & Liverpool Junction opened and the extension was being advocated, it was no longer possible to raise capital to build new canals: investment was going into new railways. Even the more modest Central Union proposal, to improve the London–Birmingham route by a cut from the Worcester & Birmingham to the

The Ulster Canal in Monaghan, where it passed under Old Cross Square by this short cut and cover tunnel. Since this photograph was taken in the 1960s, redevelopment has taken place in this area, forming a barrier to restoration, which was under serious consideration in the 1990s. Despite its name, the Ulster Canal now crosses the border between north and south at several points. This section is in the Republic (McCutcheon collection)

Warwick & Birmingham, and another from the Warwick & Birmingham Canal to the Coventry, was not seriously supported, though it would have reduced the number of locks between Birmingham and Braunston from 54 to 17 by avoiding the heavy lockage down to and up from the Avon valley at Warwick.

In Ireland, too, a great through canal line was projected to link Belfast and Newry with the Shannon. As these cities were already connected to Lough Neagh, the new line required a canal from the Blackwater river west of the lough to the River Finn, which led to upper Lough Erne, and another from Lough Erne to the Shannon at Leitrim, above Carrick-on-Shannon.

In 1825 the Ulster Canal Company was empowered to build the first of these links, from the Blackwater to the Finn. Much of the money was found not by shareholders but by the Exchequer Bill Loan Commissioners, whose engineer, Telford, worked with John Killaly on construction. Between them they made the serious mistake of building the locks to take craft of the same length as those on the Newry or the Lagan canals but 3 ft narrower – 11 ft 6 in against 14 ft 6 in, so that only specially built craft could navigate it. Finished in 1841 at a cost of £231,000, over half of it public money, and 45⅝ miles long with 26 locks, the Ulster was hardly being used twenty years later.

Meanwhile the second link in the through route, the Ballinamore & Ballyconnell Canal from upper Lough Erne to the Shannon, stimulated by the completion of the Ulster but with the additional aim of improving drainage, was begun in 1846. This time with 16 locks taking craft 82 ft by 16 ft 6 in, the new canal was built by the Board of Works and opened in 1858, the navigation works having cost some £229,000. Traffic was negligible, but nevertheless the board, now also the owners of the Ulster, closed the latter in 1865 and spent £22,000 on improving it, though without widening the locks. The Ulster was re-opened in 1873, by which time the Ballinamore & Ballyconnell was, in turn, almost impassable. The through line was therefore never achieved in practice. If it had been it is improbable that much traffic would have appeared on such an unlikely route.

There had also been a change in Irish waterway organization. The Directors General of Inland Navigation, who on the whole had done well, were replaced in 1831 by a new Board of Public Works to oversee all government works. In 1839, however, the Shannon was given its own commissioners, although in 1852 the navigation reverted to the board, whose successors still have charge of it.

We must now return to the period just before the railway age. At this time the running of fly-boats became important, although a certain number had run since the early days of canals. These express boats ran to a timetable using relays of horses and double crews, carrying merchandise and parcels, setting down and picking up at wharves along the line with priority over all other traffic and permission to work all through the night. They were usually light boats, carrying less cargo than their slower brethren. The following rules adopted by the Kennet & Avon Canal in 1840 for the operation of fly-boats show the conditions under which they worked and the surprisingly good service they gave:

> The following Resolutions relative to the passage of Fly Boats from Bath to Reading and vice versa are recommended for adoption:

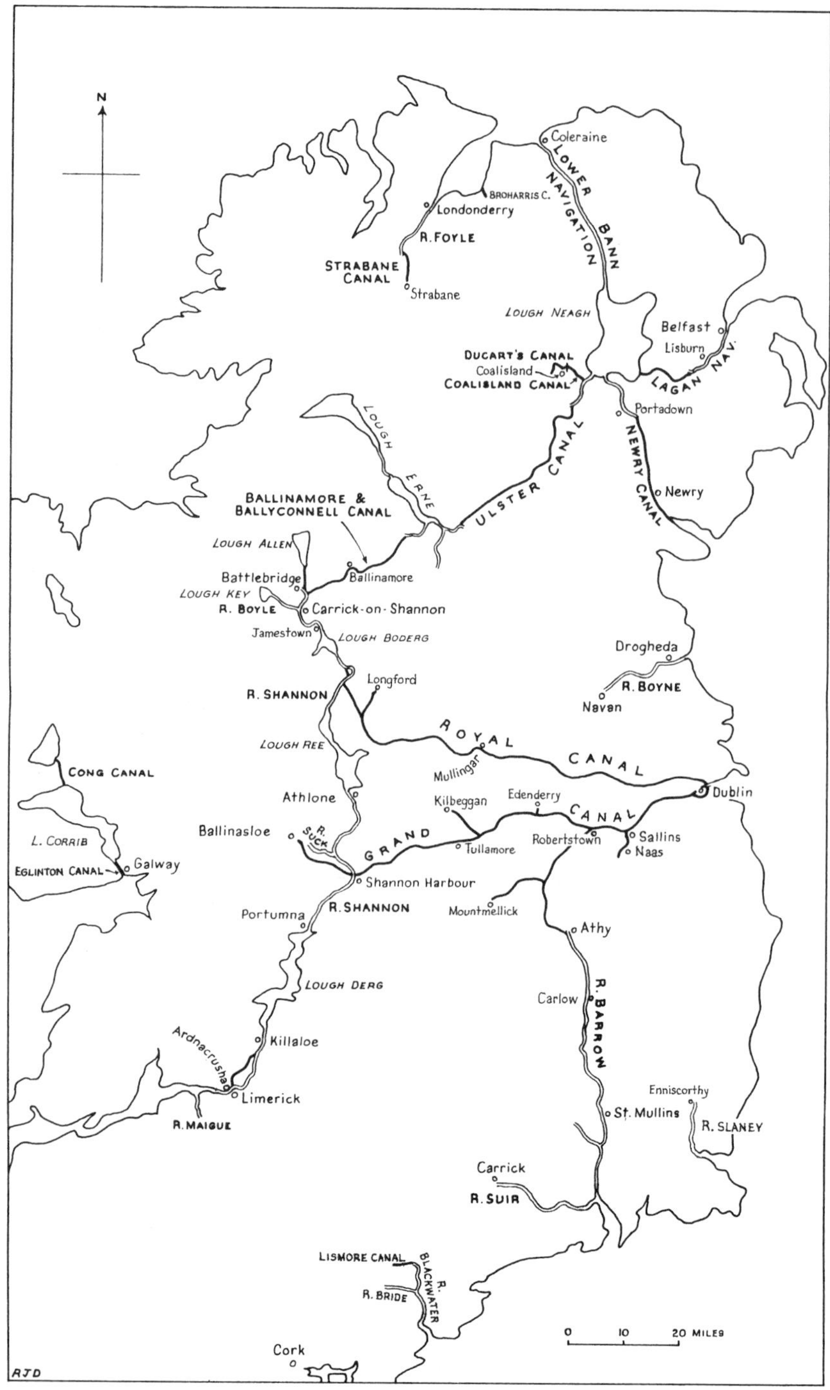

This map shows the waterway system in Ireland, as finally completed by the Ballinamore & Ballyconnell Canal. (Since restoration, this is known as the Shannon–Erne waterway.) One waterway which is not shown is the short Tralee Ship Canal, in the extreme south-west of the island

1st. That Boats not exceeding 15 Tons Tonnage will be allowed to trade on the Canal between Reading and Bath.
2nd. No Boat will be allowed to pass with the construction of which the Engineer shall not be satisfied.
3rd. Each single Boat shall be charged 3£ [sic] per day. When two Boats shall pass together each Boat will be charged £2-15-0 only.
4th. In case there shall be more than 15 Tons in one Boat, the same shall be liable to all the Charges and penalties imposed by the Company for false entries.
5th. In consideration of and to participate in the above terms, the parties must engage to start one Boat at least every day from Bath and from Reading whether having a complete Cargo or not, to deliver goods from Bristol to London and Vice Versa in 36 hours [36 hours from Bath to Reading], unavoidable stoppages excepted, the Boats to have every facility granted for their passage.[3]

At the same time experiments were tried with fly-boats to carry loaded carts and loaded tramroad waggons, put on the Forth & Clyde Canal in order to save transhipment costs.

It was during this period also that passenger-carrying on canals reached its peak. Few nowadays know that passenger services ever ran on British canals, until the modern trip and hotel boats revived for pleasure travel what was once provided as an ordinary means of transport. This had been a common practice even on the old river navigations. For instance the River Wey Act of 1651 laid down a maximum fare for passengers from Guildford to London. Soon after canals were first built passengers were carried on them, and this business grew until, in the 1820s and 1830s, it became very large on certain waterways. In 1773 Josiah Wedgwood wrote:

> From Warrington to Manchester the Duke has set up two passage boats, one carries passengers at a shilling each. The other is divided into three rooms, & the rates are 2/6 p head for the best room, 10d., and 12d., and it is the pleasantest and cheapest mode of travelling you can conceive . . .[4]

while a year later the Leeds & Liverpool Canal Company enacted

> That every person passing in any boat between Wigan and Liverpool, or any other part of the line, shall pay for every two miles or under, one half-penny; each passenger to be allowed fourteen pounds weight of luggage; and in case any boatman shall neglect to give a just account of the number of passengers he shall at any time carry on his boat, with

the distance each passenger shall have passed, he shall forfeit the sum of ten shillings.[5]

Again, in 1783, the Forth & Clyde Company put on its canal two track boats that carried both goods and passengers, described a few years later by a local poet, James Maxwell:

For here a cabin in each end is found,
That doth with all conveniences abound.
One in the head, for ladies nine of ten,
Another in the stern, for gentlemen,
With fires and tables, seats to sit at ease;
They may regale themselves with what they please.
For all utensils here are at command,
To eat and drink whate'er they have at hand.[6]

In Scotland passenger carrying reached a high degree of efficiency. On the Forth & Clyde itself, and later on the Edinburgh & Glasgow Union, which connected with it, regular services were provided both by the company's own boats and by others, although in England the usual practice was to allow private carriers to operate passenger services, the canal company merely taking tolls.

These mixed Forth & Clyde boats carried about five thousand passengers a year, and in 1809 the company put on a daily service for passengers only. Each boat had cabin and steerage accommodation, the cabin being provided with newspapers, books and games, with meals and drinks obtainable on board. These boats did the 25 miles between Glasgow and Lock 16 (Falkirk) in 5½ hours, later reduced to 3 hours. They were pulled by two horses, the second ridden, which were changed every 2 miles at the stables, many of which are still to be seen alongside the canal, now converted into houses.

Passengers found the boats cleaner and more comfortable than the stagecoaches, and the numbers carried on the Forth & Clyde Canal rose from 44,000 in 1812 to nearly 200,000 in 1836. In 1831 sleepers were put on between Glasgow and Edinburgh, which made the journey of 56 miles in under 11 hours, and a handbill of 1841 shows that four passenger boats a day were then leaving Glasgow, with through bookings by canal or canal and coach together to Edinburgh, Stirling, Alloa, Falkirk, Perth and Kirkcaldy.

The achievement of the Glasgow, Paisley & Ardrossan Canal is even more striking. This narrow waterway had originally been planned to run from Glasgow through Paisley to the sea at Ardrossan, and it obtained its

Various forms of carrying craft on the Forth & Clyde Canal, taken from a prospectus for the proposed Stirling Canal; these drawings indicated uses to which the proposed canal could be put. From top to bottom, these illustrate a boat to carry loaded carts; a boat to carry loaded tramroad waggons; a night mixed goods and passenger boat; and a swift passenger boat. The growth of railway transport halted the development of these imaginative uses of water transport.

Act in 1806. Funds ran out when it had reached Johnstone beyond Paisley in 1811, and eventually it was completed by a railway.

Before 1830 the passengers carried on it between Paisley and Glasgow, a distance of 8 miles, did not exceed 30,000 a year. William Houston, who had money in the company, determined to build up the traffic through the use of fast, light boats of special design carrying between eighty and ninety passengers, and by charging about 3s. 4d. (17p) a mile. The boats were built of thin iron sheets, with fabric cabin covering over supports. They were some 70 ft long, 6 ft wide, weighed only 33 cwt and drew 19¼ in when fully loaded. Houston achieved the following results:

Year ending 30th Sept	*Passengers carried*	*No. of boats each day each way*
1831	79,455	4
1832	148,516	7
1833	240,062	9
1834	307,275	12
1835	373,290	12

In this last year Houston cut the fares for the 8 miles from 9d. (4p) to 6d. (3p) cabin and from 6d. (3p) to 4d. (2p) steerage, and still further increased his trade, until his long white boats and scarlet-jacketed postillions became well known. Other canal companies heard of William Houston's boats and ordered similar ones, or bought them second-hand: we find them on the Don, Lancaster, Carlisle and Bridgewater canals, the Grand Canal of Ireland and even the Kennet & Avon.

A writer of 1835 says of these Scottish canals:

> If any one had stated five years ago, that by improvements, in the build of Canal Passage Boats, a speed of ten miles per hour would be regularly maintained on Canal routes; and that the charges to passengers, carried at this speed, would be the same as at the previous slow speed, of four or five miles per hour; that in one small district of Scotland alone, distances amounting in all to nine hundred miles each day . . . should be performed by these improved light Boats at the above speed . . . the assertion would have been received with unlimited ridicule. Yet such is now the case.[7]

When railway competition came prices were cut, until both canal and railway were carrying passengers from Paisley to Glasgow for 2d. (1p). Then, in 1843, the canal company gave up passenger and parcel carrying in return for an annual payment, and its horses and boats were sold.

In England there are records of passenger carrying on many canals. For instance in 1802 the Lancaster Canal was advertising trips from Lancaster to Preston, saying

> for safety, economy and comfort no other mode of conveyance could be so eligible; for there the timid might be at ease and the most delicate mind without fear.[8]

A daily service between Kendal and Preston was operated from 1820 with boats that covered the 57 miles in 14 hours, with tea, coffee and other refreshments being served on board. In 1833 an express boat was introduced to compete with the stagecoaches, which cut the time from Kendal to Preston to 7¼ hours. In the first six months 14,000 passengers were carried. Passenger boats did not finally leave the canal until 1846.

Regular services were operated on such waterways as the Bridgewater, Mersey & Irwell, Leeds & Liverpool, Aire & Calder and Yorkshire Ouse; for shorter periods on the Birmingham, Chester, Ellesmere and Grand Junction; while on others market boats were run, as on the Gloucester & Berkeley and the Derby Canal, on which 'a market-boat, decked over, with seats, and a fire-place, for the accommodation of passengers, starts from Swarkestone every Friday morning, to carry market-people to Derby, at 6d. each; which again leaves Derby at 4 o'clock for Swarkestone.'[9]

The oddest collection of passengers was perhaps that reported in the *Derby Mercury* of 19 April 1826:

> On Saturday last arrived in this town by canal, a fine Lama, a Kangaroo, a Ram with four horns, and a female Goat with two young kids, remarkably handsome animals, as a present from Lord Byron to a Gentleman whose residence is in this neighbourhood, all of which had been picked up in the course of the voyage of the *Blonde* to the Sandwich islands in the autumn of 1824.

In Ireland the Grand Canal Company maintained long-lived passenger services between Dublin and the Shannon, later Ballinasloe, and to the Barrow, and also built fine hotels, though these proved less successful than the boats. First put on in 1780 between Dublin and Sallins, packet-boat services were extended and then curtailed, until they ended in 1852. The importance given to packet-boats is shown in the following rule for lock-keepers made by the Royal Canal Company in 1813:

The Grand Canal at Shannon Harbour, with the ruins of the company hotel on the left. Charles Lever's novel included some very uncomplimentary comments on this hotel, which was built in 1806, shortly after the completion of this final length of the Grand Canal in 1804. Not a great success, it seems to have last been used as a hotel in 1847, and was vacated after 1925 (Ruth Heard)

> If a Lock-Keeper has not his Upper-Chamber full, and his Gates open to receive the Packet-Boat the moment she arrives on her Passage to Dublin, he shall be liable to a Fine of Two Shillings & Six Pence.

Here is a description of Irish canal travelling from one of Charles Lever's novels:

> Little, does he know, who voyages in a canal boat, dragged along some three miles and a half per hour, ignominiously at the tails of two ambling hackneys, what pride, pomp, and circumstances, await him at the first town he enters . . . suddenly the loud bray of the horn breaks upon his ears – the sound is re-echoed from a distance – the far-off tinkle of a bell is borne along the water, and he sees before him, as if conjured up by some magician's wand, the roofs and chimneys of a little village. Meanwhile, the excitement about him increases; the deck is lumbered with hampers and boxes, and parcels – the note of departure to many a cloaked and freize-coated passenger has rung . . . the large brass bell at the stern of the boat is thundering away with its

> clanging sound; the banks are crowded with people; and as if to favour the melo-dramatic magic of the scene, the trackrope is cast off, the weary posters trot away towards their stable, and the stately barge floats on, to its destined haven, without the aid of any visible influence.[10]

Excursion travelling by canal was also quite common. As early as 1776 the Chester Canal company was running special boats from Beeston to Chester Races. A handbill of the Edinburgh & Glasgow Union in 1834 offers 10 miles for 6d. (3p) amid most pleasant scenery and over highly interesting aqueducts, at one of which fruits, confectioneries and a variety of refreshments could be had.

Later, excursion steamers were run, especially on rivers like the Thames, Severn, Wye and upper Dee (above Chester), but also, for instance, on the Forth & Clyde Canal, on which the famous 'Queens' worked from 1893 to 1939. Today many private firms, individuals and bodies of enthusiasts run excursion trips on the canals.

It is interesting to note that the battle for passengers between water and rail was not known to be lost in 1835, when a prospectus was issued for a new canal in Scotland to connect Stirling with the Forth & Clyde Canal. This statement of the promoters says:

> In regard to the comparative amenity of the two modes of travelling, the noiseless smoothness of the Canal boats is unequalled. Nor must it be forgotten, that while a very large portion of the Liverpool Railway passengers are conveyed in uncovered waggons, exposed to wind and weather, all the Canal passengers have the privilege of well-lighted, comfortable, and elegant cabins.[11]

Since the canal was never built, presumably the investing public thought better of the railway.

Although a boat drawn by horses on a canal may not seem a dangerous mode of travelling, accidents did occur. The following newspaper account in 1810 tells of one incident:

> Paisley. Nov. 11. Yesterday about half-past 12 the boat which tracks on the Ardrossan Canal, was about to set off for Johnstone: it was one of the days of our quarterly fair, and a great many boys and girls being off work – were attracted by its novelty (being the fifth day it had sailed); some had not got out from Johnstone, while others were crowding on board to go there; the boat was lying at the quay in the basin; the water about six feet deep, some were below, but most part on the top of the cabins or the deck. The boat was raised pretty high out of the water,

GRAND CANAL.

Cheap Travelling,

Between DUBLIN and ATHLONE, by TULLAMORE,

Commencing on Friday, the 15th day of November, 1811.

FARE.

Boat, between Dublin and Tullamore, 45 Miles.	s.	d.	*Coach, between Tullamore and Athlone, 19 Miles.*	s.	d.	*Total.* s.	d.
First Cabin, -	13	0	Inside, - -	5	0	18	0
Second Cabin,	8	8	Outside, - -	3	4	12	0

Coach Fare, from Tullamore to Clara, Inside, - 1s. 8d.—Outside, 1s. 8d.
Ditto, - - - to Moate, - - 3s. 4d.— - 2s. 1d.

LUGGAGE allowed in Coach——Inside, 40lb.—Outside, 20lb.

Extra Luggage to be paid for, at the rate of one penny per lb.

A Passage-Boat departs from Dublin, every morning, at seven o'clock; and arrives in Tullamore, at ten minutes after eight o'clock, in the evening;—and another Boat departs from Dublin, every afternoon, at two o'clock, and arrives in Tullamore, at half after three o'clock, next morning.—And a COACH, capable of conveying six inside and ten outside Passengers, departs from the Company's Hotel at Tullamore, every morning, at five o'clock; and, passing through the towns of Clara and Moate, arrives at half after nine o'clock, at Mr. JOHN GARTY's Hotel, in *Athlone*.

NOTE.—Under this arrangement, a passenger, leaving Dublin in the Boat, at two o'clock in the evening, will arrive in Athlone, about nine o'clock next morning.

The Coach departs, from Athlone, every afternoon, at half after two o'clock, and, passing through Moate and Clara, arrives at seven o'clock, in the evening, at Tullamore Hotel: whence a Boat proceeds, at half after nine o'clock, for Dublin; where it arrives at twenty minutes after eleven o'clock, next morning:—and, another Boat proceeds from Tullamore, every morning, at seven o'clock, and arrives in Dublin at ten minutes after eight o'clock in the evening.

N. B. No charge made in the Boat for any child, under the age of one year; and only half price charged for the passage and ordinary of any child between that age and seven years.

Breakfast, Dinner, and Supper, provided in the Boats, as usual.

Small parcels carried in the Boat and Coach, between Dublin and Athlone, at moderate rates.

Seats for the Coach, from Tullamore to Athlone, may be engaged from the Boat-Masters on the Passage; and Seats from Athlone to Tullamore to be engaged at Mr. JOHN GARTY's Hotel, in *Athlone*.

By Order,

15th November, 1811. DANIEL BAGOT, *Sec.*

DUBLIN: PRINTED BY WILLIAM PORTER, GRAFTON-STREET,
Printer and Stationer to the Grand Canal Company.

A notice for a combined boat/coach service run by the Grand Canal Company between Dublin and Athlone. This had to compete with direct coach services, but some combined services lasted until they were overcome by railway competition

Two of the Queens, *passenger excursion vessels on the Forth & Clyde Canal* (British Waterways)

> and the weight getting too great above, she suddenly swayed on one side, and all on deck fell over. Some were able to leap upon the quay on the first motion: but upwards of 100 persons, men, women, boys and girls, and even children were precipitated into the basin. A few swam out, and others were got out before they sunk: but the greater number sunk to the bottom. Drags were got, and before one o'clock about 50 were got out. Every aid was given by the surgeons and inhabitants, and on Saturday night 18 or so were recovered. The dragging continued all the afternoon. About 90 have been dragged out in all; but owing to the great number of families the sufferers belong to, it is not accurately known how many are dead . . . Those in the cabin of the vessel were safe, the boat uprighting as soon as the crowd fell off.[12]

The historian of Bury tells of another accident that happened on the Manchester, Bolton & Bury Canal:

> The catastrophe . . . was caused by the insensate folly of a party of passengers, drunken men, numbering near twenty, who overawed the

> quieter portion on board, and persisted, for amusement and to frighten the women, in swaying the boat, heavily laden and overcrowded, from side to side, until the window-sills of the cabin, below the deck, were almost on a level with the water of the canal. The brutal wretches, maddened with drunkenness and riot, paid no heed whatever to the remonstrances of the captain, the shrieks and piteous entreaties of the women, or the tears and cries of children who were on board; for the journey was a favourite Sunday trip, many families going that day to visit friends or relatives in Bolton. Opposition led only to more strenuous efforts, and they were blind to danger; and at length the dreaded apprehension was changed to reality. The heavily laden boat, urged by powerful impetus, gave one fatal dip below the water-line, turned upon its side, with its living freight, a hopeless multitude, and rose no more . . .[13]

Such events were, fortunately, rare, but accidents involving the passenger boats operating on the Royal Canal in Ireland also took place. In 1845 six people died when a boat full of emigrants at Longford harbour keeled over and capsized; sixteen died when a packet-boat, in the hands of an inexperienced steerer, struck a rock in Clonsilla cutting and sank.

The carrying of passengers and the working of fly-boats were affected by experiments in 1832 and 1833 on the Forth & Clyde, Oxford and Grand Junction canals to increase the speed of boats. It was found with specially built light boats that if speed was increased beyond the normal 3–4 mph a wave was built up in front of the boat, but that a further increase in speed enabled the boat to pass the wave, rise in the water and to travel at a speed of 11–12 mph. Frequent changes of horses were, of course, necessary. As a result of these experiments, fast passenger services were operated successfully on the Glasgow Paisley & Ardrossan and other canals.

In 1839 the Forth & Clyde Canal experimented with locomotive haulage from the bank on a ½ mile stretch near Lock 16, but concluded that it would prove too expensive. Half a century later more trials were held, this time on railway initiative, when Francis W. Webb, the mechanical engineer of the London & North Western Railway, initiated trials on the Middlewich branch of the railway-controlled Shropshire Union. These showed that loaded boats could be towed at 8 mph. Mechanical towage from the towpath using tractors was used on British Transport Commission waterways in the 1950s, but on the Continent both locomotive and tractor towage had a long life until self-propelled craft made them unnecessary.

Just as it is difficult now to realize the canal activity of those times, when much of the heavy goods, some of the lighter merchandise and many passengers were all moved by water transport, so it is not easy to generalize about the prosperity of the canals without complete figures for every company. A few concerns, which were extremely prosperous, are often quoted as examples of the high profits made by navigation companies in the days before their monopoly was threatened. In 1833, for instance, the figures for seven of the leading companies were as follows:

Name	*Nominal value of shares* £	*Dividend paid per cent*	*Market value of shares* £
Loughborough Nav	142	108	1,240
Erewash	100	47	705
Mersey & Irwell	50	40	750
Trent & Mersey	100	75	640
Oxford	100	32	595
Coventry	100	32	600
Forth & Clyde	100	25	545

A number of other companies were very satisfactory investments, such as the Staffordshire & Worcestershire, Cromford, Shropshire, Shrewsbury, Swansea and Grand Junction. Others were paying only small dividends but had good prospects if locomotive railways were to prove only a flash in George Stephenson's pan, such as the Brecknock & Abergavenny, Peak Forest, Macclesfield, Ashby de la Zouch, Kennet & Avon, Rochdale, Stratford-upon-Avon and the Regent's, none of which paid as much as 5 per cent in 1833.

Hundreds of thousands of pounds had, however, been spent on canals that were financially unsuccessful, and which never paid a dividend in their working existence, such as the Grand Western, Salisbury & Southampton and Leominster. Canals in Ireland and highland Scotland had, of course, not been built in the main by investing companies.

The following details of the dividends paid by three important companies are fairly representative. The Oxford was built before the wartime rise in prices, and its high dividends reflect its low construction cost of about £300,000. The Grand Junction and the Kennet & Avon were both built during the war, and each cost about £1 million. One was financially very successful, the other less so. All three were of great commercial value.

Year	*Oxford (opened 1790) Dividend on £100 shares per cent*	*Grand Junction (opened 1805) Dividend on £100 shares per cent*	*Kennet & Avon (opened 1810) Dividend on £40 shares per cent*
1809	25	5	-
1819	32	9	2 1/4
1829	32	13	3 1/8
1839	30	10	3 3/8
1849	20	5	15/16

The dividend figures should be compared with those of toll receipts. These are roughly, but not exactly, comparable with each other:

Year	*Oxford* £	*Grand Junction* £	*Kennet & Avon* £
1809	78,848	127,404	4,472 (not yet opened)
1819	78,876	157,633	35,595
1829	89,992	181,144	43,818
1839	85,570	138,263	44,328

(The Kennet & Avon figures include tonnage receipts from the Kennet Navigation from 1814.)

It is odd that waterway interests met the threat of railways bravely and progressively up to a point, and then resigned themselves to passive defence of their positions or to active efforts to get themselves bought out at favourable prices. The force of private enterprise in railways overcame that of the waterways, and the latter succumbed. In France, Germany and lowland Europe, on the other hand, State or local authority intervention early in the struggle led to partial nationalization, the coordination of water and rail transport, and the modernization and standardization of the waterways.

Here and there a canal company believed in itself, for a time at least. In 1841 the Birmingham Canal company wrote:

> The circumstance . . . of the Birmingham Canal being kept in a navigable state during the winter, whilst the neighbouring Canals were closed, affords strong proof of what can be done by energy and determination, and is well calculated to add to the impression, now rapidly gaining ground, that the low price of Canal stock and diversion

> of Traffic, is less to be ascribed to opposing railways, than to the inactivity, want of foresight, and absurd jealousies of the Canal Companies themselves.[14]

A striking example of inactivity was the Staffs & Worcs company, a neighbour of the Birmingham. This was a very prosperous concern in a key position, run by a small group of apparently able proprietors. Yet throughout its long career from its opening in 1772 it spent no substantial sum on the improvement of its winding narrow line and single locks, except to build reservoirs. It watched the Worcester & Birmingham take part of its Birmingham–Severn trade, and then the Birmingham & Liverpool Junction take most of that from Liverpool to Birmingham, with no action more effective than petitions against the Bills and, in the second case, provision for heavy compensation payments.

A few concerns stood up, fought and succeeded. It never seems to have occurred to the Aire & Calder proprietors that they might be defeated, though even they were willing to sell to a railway group at one time. They were broad-based, prosperous and well managed, and they showed what could be done. If more companies had been like them, more could have been saved. Across the Pennines the Weaver's reactions were much the same. This navigation was publicly owned, by Cheshire County Council, and is the main British example of what happened so often on the Continent. The Weaver trustees also stood up and fought, and, indeed, were so formidable that railway companies treated them with respect. It is significant that both the Aire & Calder and the Weaver, many times modernized, are today among Britain's principal commercial waterways.

On the whole each waterway lived for itself. Very few working agreements were made to pass traffic, and those that were often broke down. There were few canal amalgamations in pre-railway or early railway times. Only the Ellesmere with the Chester, and later with others to form the Shropshire Union, the Mersey & Irwell with the Bridgewater, the Birmingham with the Wyrley & Essington and the Dudley, and the North Wilts with the Wilts & Berks spring to mind, though sometimes canal ownerships were interlocked by shareholders prominent in the affairs of more than one company. Even during the railway period amalgamations were few.

So ended the canal age, which had made the already navigable rivers a basis for an inland waterway system of some 4,000 miles in all, serving nearly all of the important towns and industrial areas as well as many country districts. In the eighty years to 1840 it had provided the chief means of transporting goods in bulk and had fostered the process known as the Industrial Revolution. Britain and Ireland now stood on the threshold of a new era – the Victorian or railway age.

CHAPTER EIGHT

The Rivers during the Canal Age

As Chapter One indicated, over a thousand miles of river had been made navigable before the Duke of Bridgewater promoted his canal. Further miles were added throughout the canal age by work under a number of Acts for small rivers, and by efforts to improve drainage, which resulted also in better navigation facilities.

River navigations were built in a variety of ways. In some very early cases individuals were appointed to do the work, while later some river Acts named commissioners, local people with property near the river, who in turn appointed undertakers, sometimes called trustees, to do the actual work. Money was then borrowed, usually at a fixed rate of interest. The Weaver to Winsford was made navigable like this. In other cases commissioners themselves undertook the work, as on the River Ure, Calder & Hebble and, indeed, the Thames. Where drainage was part of the exercise, trustees were sometimes given local rating powers, as under the River Axe Act of 1802 and the Adur in 1807.

Joint stock companies were also formed, as for building the Aire & Calder, the Don and the Mersey & Irwell. During the second half of the eighteenth century, and afterwards, the joint stock type of company organization became more usual, the Calder & Hebble and later the Ure changing to this type.

The coming of canals caused great changes in transport patterns, and rivers usually benefited, for they became the trunks from which canals branched out. Some promoted linking canals – as the Aire & Calder did the Barnsley, and the Don did the Dearne & Dove and the Stainforth & Keadby. Others found their interests so closely linked with canals that amalgamation took place – as did the Kennet and the (Bristol) Avon rivers with the Kennet & Avon Canal – or the river was let to the canal – as was the Upper (Warwickshire) Avon to the Stratford-upon-Avon Canal. Some, however, found themselves in bitter competition with a canal – like the Tone with the Bridgwater & Taunton Canal, and the Upper Trent Navigation with the Trent & Mersey Canal – and a battle took place that often ended with the new canal buying the old river, as later in other circumstances new railways bought old canals. Finally there were the great rivers of the Thames and Severn, throughout the canal age always to some degree navigable, yet never fully so until after that era was over.

In 1778 the opening of the Aire & Calder company's new Selby Canal provided an artificial bypass to the difficult natural navigation of the lower Aire. Almost fifty years later the Selby Canal was itself bypassed when the company opened a new large-scale canal from Ferrybridge on the Aire to Goole on the Ouse, engineered by George Leather junior. Immediately afterwards the Aire & Calder's routes upwards from Ferrybridge to Castleford, and then to Leeds and Wakefield, were rebuilt to the same standard, to a depth of 7 ft and with locks 18 ft wide. It was during this rebuilding that the tied-arch aqueduct at Stanley Ferry (bypassed from 1981 by a new one) was constructed.

The port of Goole was the creation of the Aire & Calder. From 1826 it grew throughout the nineteenth century and into the twentieth, new lock entrances being added as traffic – by canal and later by rail – increased. This company demonstrated how a river company that was connected to canals, and that used the science of canal building to shorten and make easier its own line, could attain and maintain prosperity. As we shall see in later chapters, the Aire & Calder was still a leading waterway concern when it was nationalized and its routes are still active today.

To the south the Don Company, controlling the river from Tinsley near Sheffield to the Dutch River, was nearly as energetic. Authorized in 1726 and 1727, the line to Tinsley was finished in 1751, with seventeen locks and a number of cuts bypassing river sections. During the canal mania the company took the lead in getting the Dearne & Dove and Stainforth & Keadby canals built: the first connected the Don to the coalfields north of Barnsley, the second provided an outlet to the Trent more efficient than the Dutch River passage to the Ouse. Later, in 1819, the Sheffield Canal was opened to the Don at Tinsley, and from 1821 onwards the Don company rebuilt much of the line so that, when the railway age began, they were well placed to meet it.

An example of a river closely connected with a canal, and later incorporated with it, is the Kennet, the navigation of which ran from Newbury to within 1½ miles of the Thames at Reading, where it came under the jurisdiction of the Thames Commissioners. In that distance there is a fall of 126 ft.

The first Bill to make the river navigable was introduced in 1708. It was supported by towns like Westbury and Hungerford, and opposed by Reading, which feared the loss of its transhipment trade, and by one Finch, a pensioner of the turnpike on Reading road. He presumably feared that, if the navigation was successful, the road would no longer be able to pay his pension.

The Act was passed in 1715 in favour of seven partners, who held between them the thirty-two shares in the navigation. In 1718 John Hore was taken on as engineer. He built 21 locks and made several artificial cuts to join sections of river, the whole, apart from the towpath, being ready in 1723. He became a surveyor of the river and wharfinger at Newbury, and a relative of his was later an engineer on the Kennet & Avon Canal. The proprietors were not successful, until

> about the year 1767 when, instead of being under the direction of a large body of men who were continually at variance with each other, the late Mr Page purchased the whole of the shares which were intitled to any profit . . . and giving up his time and attention to it he raised it from the ruinous state in which it was getting . . .[1]

The Pages, first the father, Francis Page, then the sons, Frederick and Francis, did their own carrying. By 1798 they had built up the trade to 20,000 tons a year and the tolls (apart from freight) to £2,140 a year; three years later the effect of the still uncompleted Kennet & Avon Canal had raised the tolls to £3,115. At that time there was a trade in malt, flour and timber to London; peat to Marlow and Henley; coal, and Baltic and West Indian goods, from London to Bath, Bristol and Salisbury by land carriage from Newbury.

The building of the Kennet & Avon Canal greatly increased the profits of the Pages. Soon afterwards in 1809, therefore, when the canal company interested itself in a possible link from Newbury to Old Basing on the Basingstoke Canal, which would have bypassed the Kennet, Frederick Page opposed the proposal on behalf of himself and the Thames Navigation. For this he earned some criticism from 'A Friend of the People', who pointed out that, as owner of the Kennet Navigation, he charged 5s. (25p) for transporting a load of timber for 18½ miles, while the Basingstoke Canal charged 6s. 2d. (31p) for 27 miles, and 2½d. (1p) per ton per mile for corn against the Basingstoke's 1¾d. (0.7p). Page's opposition, probably combined with a little pressure behind the scenes, caused the canal company to buy him out for £100,000 in 1812. A few years earlier his property had been valued at a little over £23,000, so he drove a hard bargain, though the increased prosperity brought by the canal had increased its value.

It is amusing to find that in 1824, when the Basingstoke link was again being discussed, Frederick Page was this time representing the Kennet & Avon Company, and was giving evidence in favour of the link and against his former ally, the Thames Navigation. Later, for a short time, he became chairman of the canal company, until his death in 1834.

Frodsham Bridge on the Weaver, on a formerly tidal length which was bypassed by the construction of the Weston Canal which extended the Weaver Navigation to Weston Point. The boat is the Panary, *used to carry grain from Seaforth for forwarding by road to a mill in Stockport. The* Panary *was the last craft used to carry grain into Warrington through Walton Lock; the latter has been unnavigable since 1984, and the subject of closure proposals in the early 1990s*

A number of rivers were physically independent of the main waterway systems of Britain and Ireland. Some were great rivers, like the Tay, Tyne and Tees; others were small affairs, like the Adur, Eastern Rother, Boyne and Slaney. All to their capacities performed a useful service in opening up inland areas to trade. Of these a prosperous example was the Weaver. This Cheshire river was first made navigable in 1732 under an Act of 1721; a further Act of 1760 put it under the control of a body of county trustees, which continued to be responsible for the waterway until the Transport Act of 1947.

The first locks were made of wood, taking boats of about 40 tons, while the river itself could only be entered from the Mersey estuary at highwater ordinary spring tides. From 1760 onwards, however, the locks were rebuilt and the navigation improved, with a new lock built at Frodsham, near where the river entered the Mersey, so that it was accessible at most states of the tide. At this time the trustees made great efforts to connect their river to the proposed east–west canal that later became the Trent & Mersey. Failure, however, hardly affected the salt trade, which was the staple of the Weaver, and in 1810 the trustees opened an improvement, the Weston Canal. This avoided the difficult navigation of the lower Weaver by linking it to a new basin at Weston Point (the ancestor of the later docks), where craft could wait for the tide, with a river lock.

By 1830 the waterway was receiving some £30,000 a year from its trade and was handing considerable sums to the county authorities in relief of rates. Traffic was mainly in salt (432,000 tons) and coal (124,000 tons). From 1832 onwards the trustees carried out major improvements by increasing the depth from 6 ft (itself an increase on the original 4 ft 6 in) to 7 ft 6 in and enlarging the locks to 88 ft by 18 ft, which could then take vessels carrying 100 tons or more of cargo. Oddly, not until well into the railway age was this well-managed river connected to the canal system, first by the building of the short Runcorn & Weston Canal in 1859, linking it to the Bridgewater Canal docks at Runcorn, and later by the Anderton lift in 1875, connecting it with the Trent & Mersey Canal and enabling narrow boats from the latter to pass down the river to Weston Point.

The most interesting of the failures among river navigations was the Norwich & Lowestoft. The ancient communication of Norwich with the sea had been by way of Yarmouth, but this line of waterway grew so shallow as to be of little use. In order to make Norwich once more a port, therefore, a plan was put forward for a ship canal to Lowestoft. After great opposition from Yarmouth this was authorized in 1827. The River Yare was deepened from Norwich to Reedham, from where a cut of 2½ miles was made to the River Waveney, taking the line to Oulton Dyke, which was enlarged to Oulton Broad. A short cut took the line into Lake Lothing, which was made into a tidal harbour by cutting through the bank separating it from the sea. The ship canal, which cost £150,000 to build, was opened in 1833 and was a financial failure, the expenses of maintaining the channel exceeding the revenue. Money borrowed from the Exchequer Loan Commissioners could not be repaid and the canal was sold by the commissioners to a new company, which soon afterwards resold to a group of railway promoters. The older route to Norwich continued to be used and in 1908 there was a further proposal for a major ship canal to Norwich.

The rivers that were either independent of the canal system or fitted well into it were a large group. Some, however, found themselves directly in competition with canals. In Chapter Nine we will see what effect the competition of railways had on waterways, with the price-cutting and

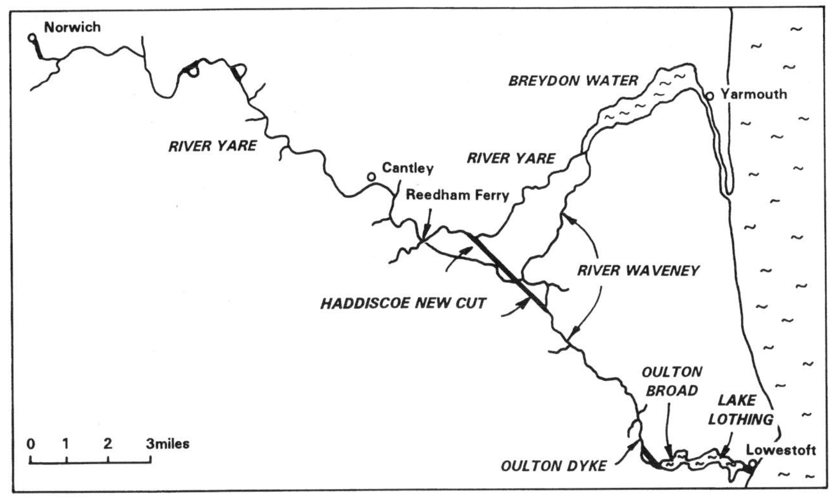

Map of the Norwich & Lowestoft Navigation, the thick lines showing the new cuts created to improve the navigation

acquisition of waterways by railways that resulted from the impact of an efficient on a less efficient means of transport. During the canal age we can trace the same development in the impact of the newer canals on the older river navigations. This impact was very local and occurred whenever a canal was projected, sometimes at the very end of the canal age.

The case of the River Tone is typical. This little river, running down from beyond Taunton in Somerset to its confluence with the River Parrett near Bridgwater, on the Bristol Channel, had been made navigable to Taunton under an Act of 1699, which set up conservators to keep the navigation open from Bridgwater. Under the General Proposals signed in 1697–8 by the thirty-four gentlemen who moved for an Act, Article Five said:

> 'Tis agreed that when the Moneys Subscribed shall be paid and the work wholly finished; That every Subscriber shall be reimburst both the Principal Money and Profit at the Rate of Seven pounds per Cent with all Cost and Charges they shall be at for the Carrying on and effecting the said work, and after such ample satisfaction made out of the Profitts, Touls, or Customs that shall be settled by Act of Parliament on Coals or other goods brought up the said River, That then the remainder shall be to the said Company and every one of them, their Heires and Assigns for ever, In Trust for the use of the Poor of Taunton and Taunton St. James.[2]

The navigation to Taunton, completed in 1717, with one lock and at least two half-locks, had been a small affair but had slowly increased in prosperity through the eighteenth century, and more rapidly in the nineteenth, as the figures below show:

Date	*Tolls received*
	£
1728	388
1789	668
1821	2,369

When the Bridgwater & Taunton Canal Bill was put forward the conservators bitterly but unsuccessfully opposed it. The canal was opened in 1827 and price cutting followed. The tolls became absurdly low and the canal company felt the strain to such an extent that, in spite of the strong opposition from the conservators, they sought parliamentary powers to acquire the Tone Navigation and so get the trade into their own hands. While the Bill was before the House the two parties agreed to various obligations, including payments by the canal company to discharge the charitable trust for the poor, and the only powers left to the conservators were those of inspection, to see that the communication between Bridgwater and Taunton was kept free and available. These powers of the conservators to complain at Quarter Sessions were used at various times up to nationalization.

In some cases the river navigation succumbed to the competition and ceased to be used. The River Salwarpe gave way to the Droitwich Canal, as did the River Idle from Bawtry to the Trent when faced with the Chesterfield Canal. In other cases amalgamation took place. For instance in 1783 the Leeds & Liverpool Canal bought the Douglas Navigation; when it was authorized in 1795, the Derby Canal bought the Derwent Navigation and closed it; and the Bridgewater Canal bought the Mersey & Irwell Navigation in 1844. The competition between these latter companies had been long standing. The navigation company had failed to oppose successfully the building of the Duke of Bridgewater's Canal from Manchester to Runcorn. Thereafter followed a competition for Manchester traffic that lasted until 1844. During this time the river company shortened its line by artificial cuts and overcame shortages of water. In the last years of its life it took such a progressive line that it was worthwhile for the Bridgewater trustees to buy it up. The river company started a plan to deepen the rivers to allow vessels of 300 tons to reach Victoria Bridge, Manchester, and successfully promoted the Manchester & Salford

Junction Canal (buying it in 1840), which joined their navigation to the Rochdale, already linked to the Bridgewater.

Another type of river navigation usually had a more fortunate history: that which formed an integral part of a through line of canal. The Kennet & Avon proprietors, for instance, found that, if traffic was to be efficiently handled, they must own the two rivers connected by their canal. As we have seen, they bought the Kennet Navigation at a high price, and at the Bath end they acquired a majority of Avon shares.

The outstanding example of a river that prospered from the connection it made with canals was the Soar, usually known as the Loughborough Navigation. Originally built during canal times as an inexpensive project to make navigable the River Soar from the Trent to the town of Loughborough, this company, with an authorized capital of only £10,000, had the good fortune to find itself connected in 1794 with Leicester, and then in 1814 with the Grand Junction Canal by means of the Leicestershire & Northamptonshire Union and (old) Grand Union canals. As a result its earning capacity was greatly increased, the average dividend rising from an average of 1½ per cent in 1782–94 through 40 per cent in 1797–9, 108 per cent in 1812–14 to 154 per cent in 1827–9, before falling to 107 per cent in 1839–41.

Three great rivers, the Thames, Severn and Shannon, need to be dealt with. The first two were vital to the English canal network, for both carried great quantities of goods not only for the towns along their own banks, but also to and from the many river and canal navigations that joined them. How important these two arteries were can be seen from maps of the waterways system, yet neither was improved to a good navigation standard during the canal period. This failure not only prevented the canal system from functioning as efficiently as it might, but also contributed to its inability to compete with the railways.

The Severn, but not the Thames, was a free navigation at the beginning of the canal age. The general responsibility of the City of London for the Thames before 1730 was only strictly exercised below Staines, while the only other authority was the Oxford-Burcot Commission set up in 1624 to build three pound-locks between Oxford and Abingdon and so improve the navigation of the part of the river between those towns. In 1695 a commission was set up for the river, and from 1751 the commissioners included all persons rated to the land tax for an estate of £100 a year in the seven upper riverside counties, together with various official members from the towns along its banks. It was not until 1771 that the commissioners, now increased by including more representatives of local authorities and other interested bodies, as well as clergy and Members of Parliament, obtained powers to borrow and to regulate charges. Three years later the river downwards from Staines was formally transferred to the City of London. They were now able on the part above Staines to build pound-locks and make towpaths, to buy the old flash-locks and to arrange for regular flashes. However, it was provided in the Act that the same tolls as before had to be paid to the owners of the old flash-locks, even though barges passed through new pound-locks on which tolls were also payable. A result of improvement was therefore to turn some old lock owners from mill owners into landowners or publicans, with a second and substantial source of income. Only very slowly over the following decades were the flash-lock owners bought out.

The navigation of the Thames at that time entirely used flash-locks, except for the three pound-locks built in the previous century by the Oxford-Burcot Commission (absorbed by the Thames Commission in 1790). So bad was it in the light of the improved waterway standards set by canals that, in 1770, Brindley proposed a London Canal to avoid a long stretch of the river from Monkey Island below Maidenhead to Isleworth. This project, and another for a Reading–Monkey Island canal, gave place to the Act of 1771 to improve the navigation of the river itself, under which the commissioners built 8 timber pound-locks on the length between Reading and Maidenhead. Between 1777 and 1795 a new series from above Reading to Oxford was built. The river below Oxford, as far as Maidenhead, was now in fair condition, with locks able to take 150 ton barges, but the dredging of the channel, and the layout and construction of the older locks was not always good, while many of the old weirs still remained, on which tolls were payable. The improvements had not, however, been able to prevent the building of the Grand Junction Canal from the Oxford Canal at Braunston to London. This broad waterway diverted much Midlands traffic from the older route via the narrow Oxford and the Thames.

Below Maidenhead only one lock had been built before 1800: Romney near Windsor in 1797. Expecting that the new Kennet & Avon Canal, opened in 1810, would bring additional trade to the Thames between Reading and London, the City built 6 locks below Staines between 1811 and 1815. The Thames Commissioners followed with others in the length between Staines and Windsor, and more to fill gaps, until Bray lock in 1845 completed the series below the junction with the Oxford Canal at Oxford.

However, to the proprietors of the Thames & Severn Canal, which entered the Thames at Lechlade and which had opened in 1789, it was the state of the Thames above Oxford that was especially important. In 1784 the newly formed canal company had interested itself in a scheme for a canal from Lechlade to Abingdon, but the Bill failed. Jessop surveyed the upper river, which at that time had no pound-locks, and four bridges with small navigation arches. Osney lock was then built and Radcot bridge enlarged. Five more locks followed, by which time the Thames Commissioners reckoned they had done well by the new and unproven canal. However, they called in the elderly, rather cantankerous but expert Robert Mylne to make a survey. On behalf of the commissioners he wrote: 'I consider the Navigation, across the Island, from the Severn to the Thames, is totally barred and locked up; unless, it is opened by the means herein recommended; or some other way, that may appear proper.'[3]

Eventually the question was taken before a committee of the House of Commons in 1793. Among the witnesses, Christopher Chambers, a Thames & Severn shareholder, complained about the condition of the Thames:

> he recollects the Improving of the River being objected to, until such Time as the Trade was brought thereon from the Canal, sufficient to satisfy the Expence; that if the Thames was put into as perfect a State as possible he thinks he should receive a fair Dividend for his Money, but now receives none; that the Canal was made in full Confidence that the Commissioners of the Thames Navigation would complete their Navigation by the Time it was opened, but the Proprietors have been disappointed.[4]

The committee concluded that the commissioners had both neglected the upper river and opposed canal improvements. In 1811, however, the commissioners were unrepentant, stating:

> In the district above Oxford, these [towing-paths] are the only expences of any magnitude which your Committee think themselves justified in recommending, and . . . the favourable expectations formerly entertained, of the accession of trade, to be expected from the Thames and Severn Canal, have not yet been realized. Of the four canals, namely, the Kington and Leominster, Hereford and Gloucester, Berkeley, and Worcester and Birmingham, which were stated by Mr Josiah Clowes, in his evidence in 1791 [sic], before the House of Commons, as then forming; and all the goods from which were expected to pass down the Thames and Severn Canal, not ONE has yet been finished.[5]

This tactless expression of home truths was too much for the Thames & Severn company, which in 1813 joined with the Wilts & Berks to promote the North Wilts Canal to join them together and so allow narrow boats to avoid the upper Thames altogether. Thenceforward a good deal of trade left the Thames, but whether the Thames lost profit as a result of its diversion is doubtful. It was not until the 1890s, in the last active days of the Thames & Severn Canal, that a number of new locks were built to bring the upper river to the standard of the lower, or until the twentieth century that the last flash-lock disappeared from it.

By the time that the Thames Conservancy was set up (in 1857 for the part below Staines, until then controlled by the City of London, and in 1866 for the whole river) and modern administration established, the Thames & Severn, Wilts & Berks, Basingstoke and Wey & Arun tributary canals were moribund, the Kennet & Avon had passed into railway ownership and the Londonwards traffic brought from the Midlands by the Oxford Canal had long ago been diverted to the Grand Junction. So low had the commissioners fallen through railway competition that, in their last year of existence, the £100 stock units were valued at 2s. (10p) and the annual income from tolls, which had once been £13,000, was only £3,000. From that time the development of pleasure boating became the main priority.

The story of the Severn shows less movement still. Throughout the canal age the river had no controlling authority at all, for the Severn Commission was not set up until 1842, and then only for the portion between Stourport and Gloucester. Before the canals the river had been a great artery of trade in spite of its imperfections, and such it remained. For instance in 1797 seventeen trows went weekly between Bristol and Bewdley, and twenty-eight between Bristol and Stourport. Although for the rather abnormal year of 1796 Telford claimed that barges could only be navigated for two months with a paying load, only two serious efforts were made to do something about the river's condition, by the Staffs & Worcs and Gloucester & Berkeley companies.

The Staffs & Worcs Canal entered the river at Stourport, and, when another canal from Birmingham to the Severn, the Worcester & Birmingham, was projected to join the river lower down, the former company obtained an Act in 1790 to deepen the river channel between Stourport and Worcester. This it achieved not by using locks, but by building projecting jetties to increase the speed of the current and thus its scouring effect on the river bottom. However, the boatmen found these obstacles to navigation and they were removed. Lower down, the Gloucester & Berkeley Canal (see Chapter Six) was promoted in 1793 to bypass the worst stretch of the river, where shifting shoals and strong tides made navigation difficult.

One other improvement was carried out under various Acts between

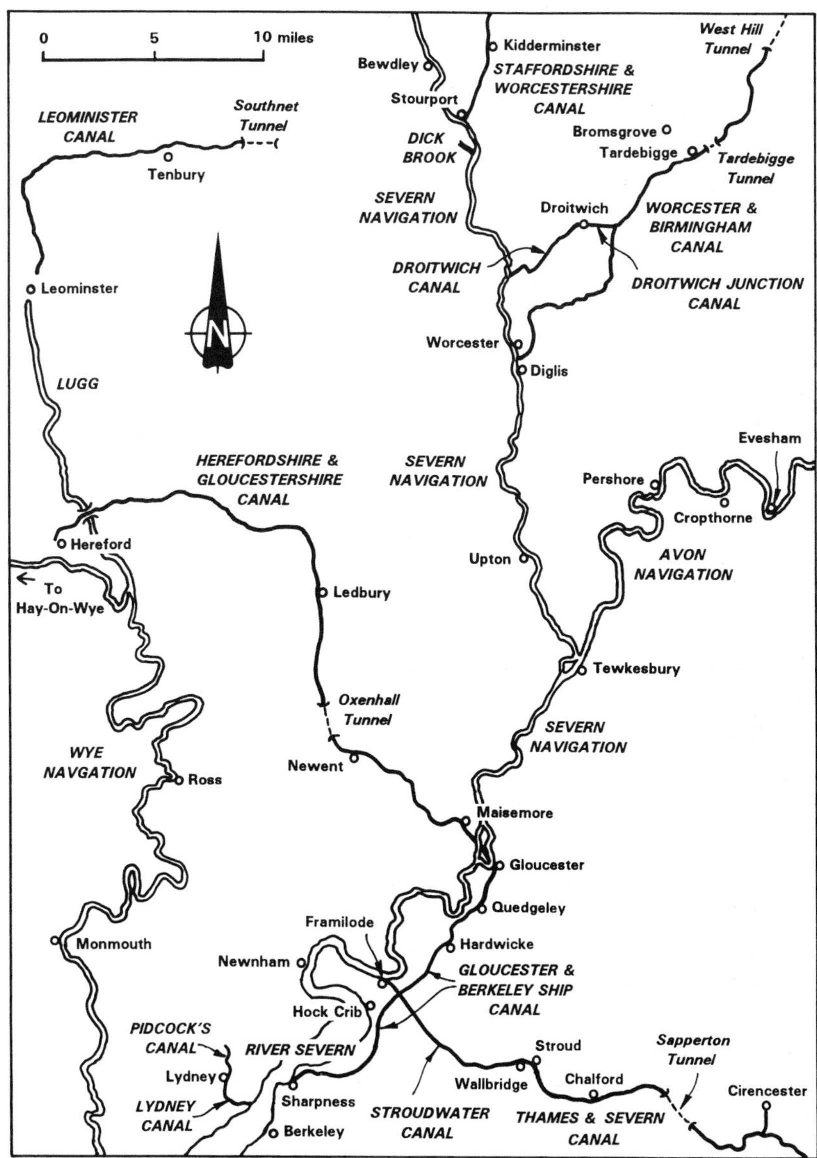

The waterways associated with the Severn, along with those of border England

1772 and 1811 to incorporate companies to build horse towing-paths from Shrewsbury to Gloucester. On the Severn, as well as on the Thames and many smaller rivers, the towpath was an addition of the canal era. Before the building of the Gloucester & Berkeley Canal, which was opened in 1827, the trows went up to Gloucester under sail and with the tide, and from there to Worcester and Stourport, partly under sail on the tide and partly by bow-hauling by gangs of men who could get past the obstructions of the river bank better than horses before the towpath was built. The heavy river barges needed gangs of men just as later they needed teams of horses – as many as twelve horses on one barge was usual on the Thames when working upwards. Before the opening of the Gloucester & Berkeley Canal goods going downstream were normally transhipped to trows at Worcester or Stourport, though a few narrow boats that worked from Stourport or Worcester to Maisemore for the Herefordshire & Gloucestershire Canal, or to Framilode for the Stroudwater and the Thames & Severn canals, were given sails or bow-hauled. Later, bow-hauling died out, and many narrow boats worked down from Stourport or Worcester to Gloucester without transhipping their cargoes.

The only effort at this time to deal with the river channel was by the Severn Navigation Company, formed at Worcester in 1835. Its proposal for a series of locks and weirs to give 12 ft of water to Worcester and 6 ft from there to Stourport affected a number of interests. In favour were the merchants of Worcester, who would have found themselves at the head of a ship canal made up of the Gloucester & Berkeley and the newly deepened Severn from Gloucester to Worcester, and also the Staffordshire & Worcestershire Canal, which was always in trouble because of the lack of water below Stourport to carry its Midlands' goods down to Worcester. Opposition came from the Gloucester & Berkeley Canal and the merchants of Gloucester, who foresaw that the transhipment trade of Gloucester would be transferred to Worcester, and feared that the imposition of charges on the river would in any case injure traffic by waterway. This too was the fear of the Worcester & Birmingham proprietors, who also had an interest in diverting to their waterway Midlands' trade that might otherwise go up the Staffs & Worcs. The opposition proved the more powerful and the Bill was thrown out. While the Navigation Company then put forward a smaller scheme, for a depth of 6 ft 6 in, an opposition company, the Severn Improvement Company, was sponsored by the Worcester & Birmingham Canal with support from the Gloucester & Berkeley, which sought to get 5 ft to Worcester only, by means of two movable weirs.

The Navigation Company's Bill was again defeated. A compromise was agreed whereby the Gloucester & Berkeley would support a Bill for the improvement of the river by public commissioners, and the Navigation Company dissolved itself. A Bill was introduced in 1841 for this purpose, but by this time the canal interests (except for the Staffordshire & Worcestershire) had gone back on their support, fearing damage to the river. Only when it was agreed to put no lock lower than Diglis, near Worcester, but to dredge from there to Gloucester, did the Bill pass in 1842. A commission was then constituted, representative of the towns and navigation interests on the river, and at last the Severn had a controlling authority.

Compared with the Severn the Shannon had much more attention paid to it, as well as money spent on it, prior to 1842. Afterwards development was somewhat similar.

The Shannon, the longest river in the British Isles, includes canal sections and also lakes or loughs, some of considerable size. Navigation started at Lough Allen, with a section via Battlebridge and Carrick-on-Shannon to Jamestown below, and then via Lough Boderg, Roosky, Lough Forbes, and a section to Lough Ree (18 miles long). At Lough Ree's far end is Athlone, from where the river runs past Shannon Harbour and Banagher to Portumna, where it enters Lough Derg (24 miles long). From Killaloe beyond the lake lies the final section to Limerick, below which the estuary begins.

This great river has several natural tributaries, which include the River Boyle, joining the Shannon above Carrick-on-Shannon, itself made navigable into and just beyond Lough Key. In the course of time three canals were to join it. The Ballinamore & Ballyconnell, entered by the Leitrim river just north of the Boyle, an ambitious effort opened in 1842 to connect with Belfast and Newry, was a total failure. The Royal Canal from Dublin, 7 miles above Lough Ree, was completed in 1817. This was the canal mania's contribution to Ireland. At Shannon Harbour the Grand Canal from Dublin was opened in 1805. From 1828 the Ballinasloe line continued the Grand Canal across the river.

There had been proposals to make the river navigable even before the general enabling Act of 1715, which included the Shannon's improvement from Limerick to Carrick-on-Shannon. However, action waited until 1755, when Thomas Omer, on behalf of the Corporation for Inland Navigation, began work on both the Limerick–Killaloe section and the upper Shannon. The first, an example of optimistic estimates, insufficient technical supervision and therefore highly intermittent progress, was transferred to the Limerick Navigation Company in 1767 but not opened until 1799, and then only for small boats. The Directors General of Inland Navigation had to take over this section in 1803 to complete this system which comprised three bypass canals with two intervening river stretches, and 14 locks – a tidal lock and 12 in staircase pairs, together with a flood-lock at Killaloe. They kept the section, finished it and handed it back to the company in 1829. It had cost £96,000 and took craft 74 ft by 14 ft, but was still imperfect.

Athlone Lock on the Shannon about 1910, part of the improvement works carried out in the 1840s. By this time, traffic above Athlone was minimal (National Library of Ireland)

Higher up, the length from Battlebridge to Lough Allen was begun, but not completed until 1822, with two slightly smaller locks. Between Roosky and Killaloe the river was reputed to be navigable in 1769, with locks and half-locks. The remaining bypass, the Jamestown Canal, was considered navigable a few years later. So, while the Jamestown–Killaloe section had early been canalized, though unsatisfactorily, the top and important lower sections had to wait until the 1820s to be perfected.

In the 1790s the directors of the Grand Canal, which was to join the Shannon in 1805, began to take an interest in the condition of the middle length between Portumna, at the top of Lough Derg, and Athlone, at the bottom of Lough Ree. If they could get a grant towards the cost they were willing to take it over and improve it. William Jessop was called in. He reported on the river up to Lough Allen, and on the basis of his proposals the company asked for a government grant of £130,000. This failed to go through, but a modified scheme for the middle Shannon (Portumna–Athlone) received a £54,634 grant in 1806, the year after the canal's opening, and was finished by 1810. However, even after the whole river was open, tonnage was negligible: in 1835 under 9,000 tons north of Athlone and under 20,000 on the middle Shannon; in 1836 just over 36,000 tons on the Killaloe–Limerick section.

Thereafter a concern for public works to relieve unemployment combined with a drive from passenger steamboat interests produced reports from the engineer Thomas Rhodes in 1832 and 1833, proposing major improvements. As a result Shannon Commissioners were appointed under an 1845 Act to take charge of the whole river. Their work was done in the middle section, from Killaloe northwards to Battlebridge. This they rebuilt, enlarging some lock cuts but eliminating others and using the dredged river channel instead to take steamers of 102 ft by 30 ft. Below Killaloe dimensions remained smaller and bridges lower, as also on the unimportant Lough Allen section above Battlebridge. The improvements increased traffic: in 1845 16,113 passengers were carried on the river and 105,084 tons conveyed, 31,537 tons of which was interchange traffic with the canals, mainly the Grand Canal. To get these increases nearly £600,000 had been spent.

During the canal age works to improve drainage in parts of lowland England also resulted in better navigation facilities, as with the Ancholme, Witham, Nene, Great Ouse and associated waterways. Towards the end of the canal age one scheme, in the north of Ireland, which served both navigation and drainage and which would experience conflict between these uses, was the Lower Bann.

Several rivers drain into Lough Neagh, the largest inland lake in the British Isles, but its shallow nature meant that flooding occurred when its only outlet, the Lower Bann, could not discharge all flood waters. In 1822 it was proposed to remove the locks on either side of the summit level of the Newry Canal and thus allow lough floodwaters to drain through the Upper Bann and south along the Newry Canal, on which navigation would be maintained. No work resulted, but in the 1840s several studies indicated that the Lower Bann, running north to Coleraine, could be made navigable and improve the drainage of Lough Neagh. This was to involve lowering the level of the Lough, works on the Upper Bann and Blackwater, which linked to the Newry, Ulster and Coalisland Canals, and the construction of a 32 mile long navigation with six locks, including a staircase pair. Work began in 1847 under the Board of Public Works but was not completed until 1858. By this time £144,214 had been spent on drainage works and £101,081 on navigation works, both well over the total estimate of £183,775. Control of the Lower Bann Navigation passed to a trust whose annual deficits were to be made up by two local county councils.

By the time that the navigation opened, railways already served both ends of the Lower Bann Valley at Toomebridge and Coleraine, and by

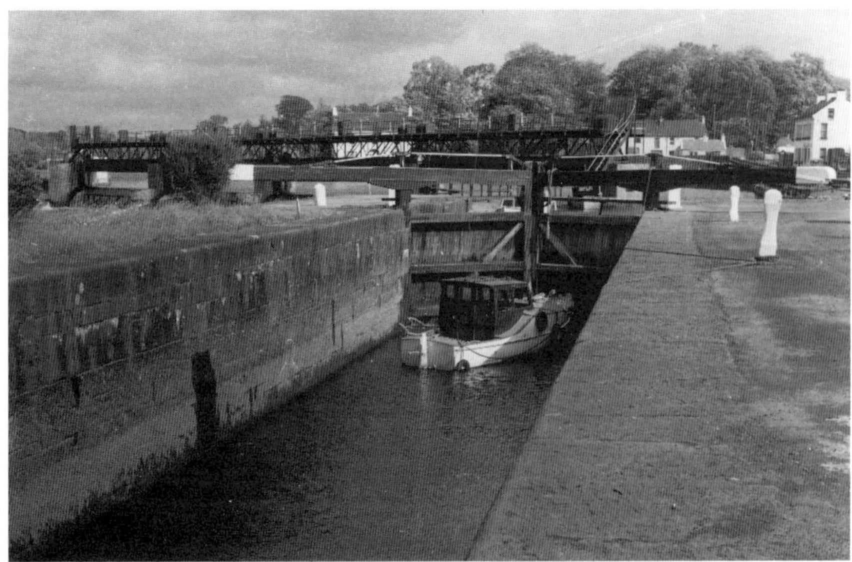

The lowest lock on the Lower Bann Navigation, at The Cutts, near Coleraine. The railway bridge above the lock was completed in 1860, only two years after the navigation opened (McCutcheon Collection)

1880 a direct line paralleled the navigation. In 1887 receipts were averaging only £70 a year and navigation works were inhibiting proper drainage. It was suggested that, if navigation ceased and the river could be altered to improve drainage, about £10,000 could be saved annually. The waterway was only later kept open to preserve the possibility that a significant volume of traffic might be attracted, although closure was advocated from time to time up to 1929, when the Trust was abolished and its powers transferred to the Ministry of Finance of the Stormont government, which continued to make up its continuing financial losses.

CHAPTER NINE

War with the Railways

Although the early railways had mostly been built as feeders to canals, and the early locomotives had been used on such lines – Trevithick's on a canal feeder in South Wales, Stephenson's on a coal line to the Tyne – even before the days of steam, railways and canals had competed. For instance the Surrey Iron Railway had struggled with the Croydon Canal for the carriage of goods from the Thames to Croydon. No existing navigation interest was affected by the building of the Stockton & Darlington Railway (though a canal had first been proposed), but during the two years 1824 and 1825 that saw the opening of that historic line, a number of railway Bills were put forward, and some Acts obtained, which foreboded the coming struggle.

For example a meeting was held in Gloucestershire in 1824 to promote a railway, for which locomotives were recommended, from Framilode on the Severn or from Frampton on the Gloucester & Berkeley Canal to Stroud, with a capital of £50,000, to be called the Stroud & Severn Rail Road.

It is not quite clear whether the promoters seriously intended to proceed with a railway, for they authorized their committee to begin negotiations with the Stroudwater Navigation for a reduction in rates of tonnage. When the canal company refused to do so, the railway committee decided to go ahead with the promotion of a Bill. This attitude of the railway promoters seriously frightened the canal company, the members of which pointed out that they were not profiteers – for over forty years their average profit had been only 5⅜ per cent – but they agreed to reduce their tonnage rate for the whole length of their navigation from 3s. 6d. (18p) to 2s. 9½d. (14p) per ton, and to reduce it by another 6d. (3p) if the railway project were abandoned. However, the railway promoters insisted on presenting their Bill in the Session of 1825, saying that

> they did not consider the suggested reduction of Tonnage to be a sufficient inducement to them to enter into any negociation [sic] for the abandoning the Railway.[1]

The Bill was opposed by landowners, the Stroudwater and the Thames & Severn Canal companies, and was defeated.

The lesson that competition would reduce canal tolls was not lost on businessmen as there was no other way, so long as the companies did not exceed the maxima laid down in their Acts. The very high profits of many canal companies, and the refusal of reductions when railway competition threatened – for not all companies were as accommodating as the Stroudwater – led to railways being regarded by the trading public as their saviours from a canal monopoly. The story of the Erewash valley coal trade, told at the Canal Conference of 1888, illustrates the point. While in the 1790s there had been an abortive attempt to link the Leicestershire collieries to Leicester by means of tramroads and a canal through Charnwood Forest, Leicester had only been supplied by the Derbyshire and Nottingham collieries. Then

> the opening of the Swannington line, in 1832, placed the trade in the hands of the West Leicestershire colliery people. A reduction of 3s. 6d. per ton on coal delivered at Leicester, from the Erewash valley, was needed to enable the Derbyshire and Nottinghamshire proprietors to retain the trade. As this traffic amounted to 160,000 tons a year, it was a great question . . . whether coal-owners or canal proprietors should make the sacrifice. The Erewash Canal received, for toll and wharfage, 2s. per ton for 12 miles; Loughborough, 3s. per ton for 8 miles; Leicester, 1s. 8d. for 14 miles – total, 6s. 8d. per ton (exclusive of boating and haulage charges) for 34 miles, or 2⅓d. per ton per mile. Conferences were held with the canal committees, who decided each to allow a drawback of 6d. per ton 'on such coal only as shall be delivered at Leicester at 10s. per ton'. The coal-owners, who held that the canals should allow 1s., 'promptly rejected' these proposals, and the meeting broke up, with the colliery proprietors determined to free themselves from the monopoly of these canals by making a railway . . . The result was, the railway secured the traffic to the detriment of the canals, who are now, in 1888, glad to pass coal at 2d. per ton each, or 6d. per ton for the whole 34 miles.[2]

The development of railways was seen by some to overcome the disadvantages of canal transport and to encourage further industrial progress. As a prize-winning essay at the Ystalyfera Eisteddfod of 1860 asserted about the Swansea Canal,

> It is very often the case for managers of collieries, iron and tin-works, etc., to fail to produce the articles demanded by the order at the specified time for shipment in consequence of the slowness and difficulty of conveyance by canal; and the result is that they have to

The lower section of the Swansea Canal, some sixty years after it was acquired by the Great Western Railway, whose line was built so close here as to overshadow the canal. This length was closed and drained after 1928, while the middle portion remained in use by trading craft until 1931 (Boat Museum)

defray the expenses of the vessel as long as it is detained, and sometimes to make up losses. Now, by railway, these things could be brought from the works to the vessel in less than an hour's notice and this expense prevented. Also, conveyance by rail is safer than by canal. Most merchandise brought and taken along the Canal is liable to be damaged, either by water bursting into the boat, which is seldom devoid of that element, or from exposure to the weather . . . The Railway, also, is vastly superior to the Canal from its being open for traffic in all kinds of weather. But extremes of heat or cold prevent all communication by canal, the warm weather from scarcity of water, and the cold by reason of the water being frozen up. At such periods traffic is not only checked but the Ystalyfera Forge and Tinworks are stopped from want of coal, which can be obtained no nearer than Pontardawe, it being carbon; and the blast furnaces cannot remain for long without it in the shape of coke. It greatly hinders every work in the Valley; and if these stoppages continue long, they occasion the most pitiful misery by making many a pantry empty.

The Swansea Vale Railway was completed up the valley shortly afterwards, and in 1872 the Great Western Railway Company acquired the Swansea Canal; much traffic nevertheless remained on it into the twentieth century.

The use of locomotives on a railway that competed directly with navigations began in 1830 when the Liverpool & Manchester Railway was opened. With it a new situation was created, for steam traction brought to the railways two advantages: speed and the ability to haul heavy loads. The waterways bitterly opposed the early railway Acts and made it expensive for the railway shareholders to obtain them. Indeed, inducements had to be offered to them to persuade them to withdraw their opposition.

A curious situation then developed. Early railways were thought of much as if they were land canals: proprietors said they only wished to be toll-takers; and Parliament in some cases empowered any carrier who wished to to run trains, landowners to make branch lines to connect with the railways, and lords of the manor to use free of charge those parts of the lines that passed through their property. In 1845 the Upper Medway Navigation indeed bought its own locomotive to haul coal trains on the South Eastern Railway, but quickly found that parliamentary powers were little use against the railway's determination not to allow their locomotive to run. On the London & Birmingham all carrying was done by private carrier for a time, the company only providing waggons and engines, while on the Great Western and the Grand Junction Railways carriers competed with the railway company.

Nowadays all trade is usually considered in national terms, and it is difficult to realize that both the canals in their day and the railways in theirs began as essentially local affairs. While the canals had joined up with each other and thus grown into national systems, they continued to be owned by small, independent and jealous units, often competing with one another as well as with rival methods of transport such as roads, coastal shipping and horse tramroads. They were constructed of all sizes and shapes, and traffic passed from one to another with difficulty.

The railways began in the same way, as local affairs. The Stockton & Darlington, Liverpool & Manchester and the Canterbury & Whitstable were built to improve communication between two towns, or along one route. Even the bigger projects, such as the London & Birmingham, were still local in the sense that they were not thought for practical purposes to be part of a national scheme.

Competition therefore began between a local waterway and railway for the same passenger and goods traffic between two points, as happened between Manchester and Liverpool. In the 1830s the annual reports of almost every canal company carried some statement to the effect that a railway in competition with that undertaking was projected. An extraordinary general meeting of the Basingstoke proprietors, for example, was called for 22 September 1831: 'to adopt such measures as may be necessary for the Interests of this Company, in regard to the proposed Railway, from London to Southampton.'[4]

Just as the river navigations had bitterly opposed in the parliamentary committees the making of canals, so now the canals set themselves to oppose the railway Bills in a way that, until the railway mania of 1845–7, did not differ much from a standard pattern. First, pamphleteering, meetings and a little misrepresentation; then petitions and the organizing of parliamentary opposition; then, if the canal was important enough, compensation or possibly purchase. In 1835 the Kennet & Avon Committee reported that

> The necessity of watching and opposing the Great Western Railway Bill, during the last two years, has materially added to the law expenses of the company; but the committee beg to inform the proprietors, that such arrangements have been made as rendered unnecessary a continuance of opposition to the Bill, and as cannot, in the opinion of the committee, fail (if the bill should pass) to be satisfactory to the proprietors.[5]

These arrangements consisted of a payment of £10,000 by the railway company, less the value of lands carrying a rentcharge of £100 a year that were transferred to the railway. Since the gross annual receipts of the canal company for the previous five years had averaged £45,213, the compensation payment was not large and reflected the bad bargaining position of the canal.

The railway Bills having been obtained, the canal companies then gained a few years of extra prosperity by carrying the materials to build their rivals' lines. One bizarre instance of new traffic was the carriage of a railway engine, in sections, along the Newry Canal to the Great Northern Railway at Portadown, just before the parallel railway line was completed in 1852. The receipts of the Kennet & Avon rose from the average (given above) to a peak of £48,269 in 1840. Then the railway opened and competition began, fly-boat services being affected first. Takings on the Kennet & Avon in three years dropped to £32,045, caused not by a loss of tonnage but by the drastic cut in tolls necessary to keep the traffic.

Price cutting was the most common competitive weapon, and it was

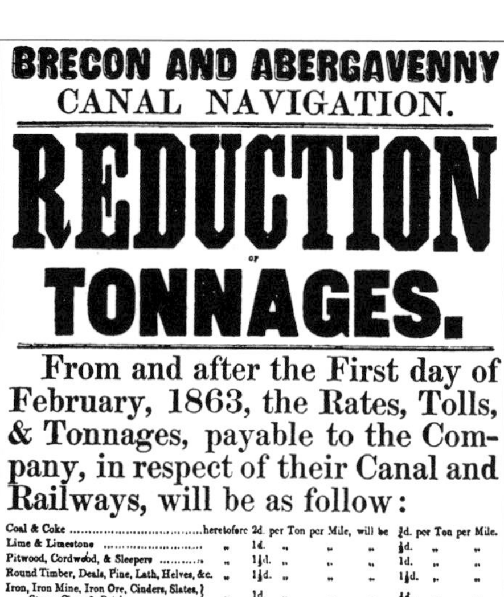

BRECON AND ABERGAVENNY
CANAL NAVIGATION.

REDUCTION
OF
TONNAGES.

From and after the First day of February, 1863, the Rates, Tolls, & Tonnages, payable to the Company, in respect of their Canal and Railways, will be as follow:

Coal & Coke	heretofore	2d.	per Ton	per Mile,	will be	¾d.	per Ton	per Mile.
Lime & Limestone	"	1d.	"	"	"	½d.	"	"
Pitwood, Cordwood, & Sleepers	"	1½d.	"	"	"	1d.	"	"
Round Timber, Deals, Pine, Lath, Helves, &c.	"	1½d.	"	"	"	1¼d.	"	"
Iron, Iron Mine, Iron Ore, Cinders, Slates, Stone, Clay, & Bricks	"	1d.	"	"	"	½d.	"	"
Hay, Straw, & Compost	"	1d.	"	"	"	1d.	"	"
Goods and other Merchandise not above described.	"	2½d.	"	"	"	1½d.	"	"

Canal Office,
Llanelly, Nr. Abergavenny,
January, 29th, 1863.

By Order,
GEORGE L. HILEY,
Clerk to the Company of Proprietors

PRINTED BY J. HILEY MORGAN, HIGH STREET, ABERGAVENNY.

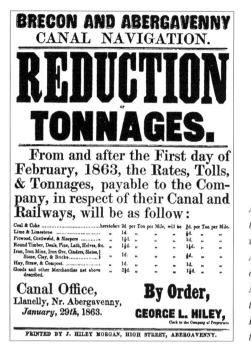

An example of heavy price-cutting, in the face of railway competition which was affecting traffics on the Brecon & Abergavenny. Two years later this amalgamated with the connecting Monmouthshire Canal, which was in turn acquired by the Great Western Railway in 1880. There was very little traffic on either canal after that

sometimes taken to the point where a weak canal company charged no toll at all, only freight charges being taken by the carriers. At the same time steps were taken to improve the service, as when in 1844 the Gloucester & Berkeley Company agreed to a proposal from Pickfords, the carriers, that trows should be permitted to move at all hours of the night to expedite carriage and so enable water carriers to compete more successfully with the railways.

This lengthening of the permitted hours during which boats could move through locks and tunnels, in some cases to the extent of 24 hour working, combined with the religious revival of the time, brought pressure on canal companies against Sunday canal work. In 1839, for instance, 140 boatmen at Shardlow petitioned the Trent & Mersey Company to close the canal on Sunday, and in the next year the company in turn petitioned Parliament 'for the general prevention of Traffic on all Canals and Railways on Sundays'.[6] The Lancaster and Worcester & Birmingham companies took the same view. Protests against Sunday working also came in from canalside towns, such as Stourport in 1839. Companies varied in their attitudes: on the Manchester to Wakefield line the Calder & Hebble closed its line on Sundays from 1836, but the

Rochdale did not agree and, in one instance, defended a boatman accused by the Calder & Hebble of contravening their by-law.

Most of the money of the early railways was made from passenger carrying – rather against the railway companies' expectations – the heavier goods remaining for the time being on the canals, though at a lower rate of toll. In 1843 the railways received £3,110,257 from the carriage of passengers and £1,424,932 from goods. In 1848 the receipts from passengers had risen to £5,720,382 and those from goods had reached £4,213,169. Canal dividends had by then suffered little from the railway competition that so far existed: the Oxford paid 25 per cent in 1846, compared to 32 per cent in 1833; the Coventry 25 per cent compared to 32 per cent; the Trent & Mersey 30 per cent compared to 37½ per cent.

There is a close parallel between the development of canals – first the building of isolated lines of waterway, then the evident success of the new type of transport, and then the canal mania – and that of railways. From 1830, the date of the opening of the first really successful railway operated by locomotives, to 1844 was a time of construction. Towards the end of the period the local view of railways gave way to the national. ?The importance of through routes, the necessity for spheres of influence seized on such enterprising railway directors as George Hudson, and so the railway mania began. It consisted of a mad scramble to promote companies and to buy up competitors. In 1843, 23 railway Acts were passed; in 1844, 48; and in 1845, 108. These competitors were either other railways or canals, and anyone who reads the annals of that time realizes that railway directors saw little difference between the two types of competitor – both represented a threat to the golden dreams created by the dividends of the Stockton & Darlington or the Liverpool & Manchester.

The government at first doubted the wisdom of allowing an unrestricted amalgamation policy, whether of railways with railways, or of railways with canals, and it was laid down that the Board of Trade must examine all amalgamation Bills to determine whether they were in the public interest. The tide was, however, coming in too strongly, and the decision was soon reversed, with no further attempt to control the leasing or sale of one line of transport by another until the railway mania was over. The policy of control had, however, reversed the leasing in 1843 of the Calder & Hebble to the Manchester & Leeds Railway, following protest by the Aire & Calder.

In 1846 a committee of the House of Commons recommended precautions to be taken before railway and canal amalgamations were allowed, such as the provision in authorizing Acts to ensure low maximum canal tolls, and to ensure that railway-owned canals were kept in repair and supplied with water. It led to an Act of the same year that set up a policing Railway Commission. However, *laissez-faire* ideas caused its abolition in 1851, its duties going to the Board of Trade.

Parliament then chose to put railways and waterways on a basis of competitive equality. Canal companies' Acts had bound them to charge the same tolls for any mile of their line as for any other and not to discriminate between customers, although this rigidity was a little lessened by drawbacks on tolls for cargoes carried a minimum distance and discounts for those passing a minimum annual tonnage over the canal. In 1844, however, when a railway Bill sought power to vary tolls, representatives of canal companies, led by the Aire & Calder, met in London, calling themselves the United Body of Canal Proprietors.

Canal companies' Acts, again, unlike railway Acts, did not specifically authorize the companies to operate carrying craft; neither had they forbidden the practice. Some companies had carried extensively in the past, others occasionally, while others had operated through nominally independent firms. In their carrying role they could quote *ad hoc* rates which, as toll-takers, they were prevented from doing, and the resulting anomaly must have looked unsafe to the United Body. They therefore drafted what became the Canal Tolls Act of 1845 – empowering canal companies to charge different rates per ton-mile on different parts of their line, though the varied rates had to be applied equally to all – and the Canal Carriers' (or Clauses) Act enabling companies to carry and provide towage services on their own or other waterways, though not to discriminate between customers in doing so. This second Act also empowered companies to make traffic agreements with railway or other canal companies and to lease themselves to any other canal or navigation company, in a section whose implications were not then seen. In 1847 a third Act enabled companies to borrow money to set up carrying departments.

Very few canal companies seem to have had any feeling that there was a general waterway interest opposed to a general railway interest, or that the one kind of transport was locked in battle with the other. One of the few was the Staffs & Worcs, which proposed to send a circular letter to other canal companies (probably never sent) which said:

> An experience of seventy years has established the utility and importance of Inland Water Communication. It has become intimately interwoven with the great manufacturing, trading, and agricultural industry of this country, and has been mainly instrumental to the development of its resources and the growth of its power and

> importance. But although your Committee are quite ready to admit the advantage and necessity of Railways as a great step in advance of the old modes of conveyance for passengers and many articles of commerce, they conceive that a stoppage of any part of the great chain of inland water communication, would cripple the whole system and produce irremediable mischief to the interests of the Canals and Navigable Rivers and to those of the Community at large . . . they afford to the public the only salutary check to and control over those charges and regulations which the Railway Companies may at pleasure impose if left uncontrolled by such check.[7]

A month later, however, when it seemed likely that the Regent's, Warwick & Birmingham and Warwick & Napton canals would all be bought for conversion to railways, such a powerful company as the Grand Junction could write mildly to the Board of Trade saying that

> altho' this Committee is not aware that any reasonable objection can be urged to the whole, or even the greater portion, of any thorofare line of Canals being converted into Railways, it is to be hoped that with a view to protect the inland navigation of the Country Her Majesty's Government will be disposed to oppose in Parliament, the principle of partial conversion.[8]

The first incident of the war with the railways was a case of desertion to the enemy, for in 1831 the Manchester, Bolton & Bury Canal proprietors obtained an Act authorizing them to make a railway at or near the line of the canal, and altering their name to the Company of Proprietors of the Manchester, Bolton & Bury Canal Navigation & Railway. Following a successful takeover bid by a group of railway promoters, it was decided not to turn the canal into a railway, as intended, but to build a railway alongside the waterway. The line was opened in 1838. In 1846 the company amalgamated with the Manchester & Leeds Railway, which the following year changed its name to the Lancashire & Yorkshire.

Other canal companies later followed the example of the Manchester, Bolton & Bury, and turned themselves into railways, among them the Ellesmere & Chester, Liskeard & Looe Union, Thames & Medway, Monmouthshire, and the Carlisle. The important Don company followed its own path in order to dominate south Yorkshire traffic, on the one hand absorbing three other waterways – the Stainforth & Keadby, Dearne & Dove and Sheffield canals – while on the other encouraging the formation of what became the South Yorkshire, Doncaster & Goole Railway. In 1850 the Don Company amalgamated with this line to form the South Yorkshire Railway & River Don Company, which operated as a combined rail-waterway transport concern until it was leased in 1864 by the Manchester, Sheffield & Lincolnshire Railway, whereupon the waterway side of the business became much less important.

Before the mania began only one or two other waterways had been sold or leased to a railway company, such as the Croydon, bought by the London & Croydon Railway for conversion, and the Kensington, vested in the West London Railway in 1839. By 1845, however, there was a double interest at work: the railways wishing to eliminate a competitor and using their shareholders' money to do so; and canal proprietors who had experienced a year or two of what railway competition meant, and who were in many cases anxious to sell out while the golden shower continued. In 1845 five navigations, beginning with the Norwich & Lowestoft, with a total length of 78¼ miles, came under railway control; in 1846 seventeen navigations with a total length of 774½ miles; and in 1847 six navigations with a total length of 96¼ miles. These figures include the canals that turned themselves into railways. In these three years about four-fifths of the mileage of all railway-controlled canals was acquired, being one-fifth of all the navigable waterways in Great Britain. These included the 160 miles of the Birmingham Canal Navigations and the 204 miles of the Shropshire Union system, on which railway control did not become effective for some time.

There was one curious case of the reverse process – of a canal company that leased a railway. The Lancaster Canal, on which carrying had increased from 459,000 tons in 1825 to 617,000 tons in 1840, was seriously hit by the opening, in 1840, of the Lancaster & Preston Railway – as after 1846 by the Lancaster & Carlisle. The canal company therefore obtained a lease of the Lancaster & Preston in 1842 for 21 years, for an annual rent of £13,300. In 1848, however, the Lancaster & Preston, wishing to sell itself to the Lancaster & Carlisle, offered the canal proprietors £4,875 a year for the remainder of their lease, as well as the cessation of the annual rent. This offer was accepted. In 1859 these lines were leased (and later sold) to the London & North Western Railway, in 1864 the canal itself was leased to the same railway and in 1885 it was bought outright. In 1864 the separate southern portion of the canal – from Walton Summit to Wigan – was leased to the Leeds & Liverpool Canal Company, since it formed part of that company's line.

Whereas railway competition greatly affected Irish waterways, most of which were economically less secure than those in Britain, only one waterway was bought by a railway and another leased for a time. The Royal Canal, less prosperous than the Grand Canal, received an offer to purchase from the Midland Great Western, at some £300,000, 40 per cent

The Royal Canal at Pike Bridge, near Maynooth, in 1965 (shortly after closure). The second bridge carries the parallel railway, demonstrating how closely it followed the canal. After closure this would prevent the blocking of the canal by the removal of road bridges, since any new road crossings between Dublin and Mullingar had to clear the railway line, and culverting, which affected several crossings in County Longford, did not take place (Ruth Heard)

of its written-down capital and over one fifth of original cost. The railway wanted canalside land to build their line for over 50 miles between Dublin and Mullingar. The canal company was agreeable and the purchase was authorized in 1845. Thereafter it remained open, but in a steadily deteriorating condition.

The same railway then tried to buy the Grand Canal. The Grand company had been working a haphazardly observed rates agreement with the rival Great Southern & Western Railway since 1847, and in 1848, in financial difficulties, had had to write down its capital. In 1850 the Great Southern & Western ended the agreement and in 1852 offered to buy the Grand Canal. The Midland Great Western made a higher offer, which was accepted. The authorizing Bill was, however, defeated by the Great Southern and Western and the Midland Great Western then leased the Grand Canal for seven years from 1853 at £19,564 a year. During the lease the two railway companies agreed to buy the canal jointly, but the Midland Great Western had been losing money on it and, when in 1860 the proposed canal rates seemed too low, the Bill was dropped and the canal returned to its own company, which then negotiated rates agreements with both railways.

Railways bought canals for three reasons: because they could not get their Bills without coming to an arrangement with their principal opponents; because they were actual or potential competitors; and because they wanted to use the line of the canal for a railway.

The purchase of some canals was authorized as part of the Bill giving powers to a railway company to construct its line. These included the Stratford-upon-Avon, the Stourbridge Extension, the Ashby de la Zouch and the Cromford, which were in a position to make a good bargain and also to make sure that the acquisition by a railway company did the least possible harm to other waterway interests. For instance in the Act for the sale of the Ashby Canal, in 1846, it was laid down that the maximum tolls charged should not exceed the railway charges, and that

> if, owing to railway competition, coal from the Moira collieries is diverted from the Oxford Canal (which is a continuation of the Coventry Canal, and is in communication of course with the Ashby Canal), and in order to meet such diversion the Oxford Canal lower their tolls for this traffic, then the Midland Railway must lower the tolls on the Ashby Canal proportionately, provided that the tolls shall not be reduced below ¼d. per ton per mile . . . There is a further clause to this effect, that if any one or more of the canals forming the route to London, combine to reduce their rates, the Midland Company are bound to reduce the tolls on the Ashby Canal correspondingly.[9]

The situation envisaged in this Act later came about.

Many canal companies, whose opposition to railway Bills had not brought forth an acceptable offer, or which at first were prepared to ride the whirlwind, later became uncertain of their ability to compete and tried to bring the railway companies to the point of making a proposal. One way of doing this was to promote a Bill for a rival railway. In 1845, for instance, the Kennet & Avon committee considered converting the canal to a railway, proposing a survey and information to decide how to proceed.

The canal owners were on a good wicket. It was with crocodile tears the following year that

> The Committee regret to report the loss of the Bill which was applied for in the present Session of Parliament . . . for making the London, Newbury and Bath Direct Railway, in conjunction with the Kennet and

> Avon Canal, but they trust that as a General Meeting will be shortly held, the explanations which will there be given, of the arrangement come to with the Great Western Railway Company and the Wilts, Somerset and Weymouth Railway Company, will be satisfactory.[10]

In 1852 the Great Western Railway finally agreed to take over the canal for a payment capitalized at £210,415. The capital cost of the waterway had been just over £1 million, but the highest dividend paid had been 3¾ per cent, and since the railway had been opened the usual distribution had been under 1 per cent.

Again, railways were sometimes forced to acquire canals by the extent of the competition that developed, and the losses on carriage by rail that showed themselves. The opening of the Bristol & Exeter Railway by way of Taunton in 1844, and especially of its Tiverton branch in 1848, brought it into direct competition with the Grand Western Canal from Tiverton to Taunton.

After 1845 this canal company was unable to pay its mortgage interest and had to maintain itself with further loans. It was, indeed, a matter of life or death to defeat the railway, even though a forlorn hope. The canal and the railway proceeded to cut rates against each other. In about 1851 the former charged tolls on coal from Taunton to Tiverton of ¼d. per ton per mile, to enable the canal traders to sell at Tiverton at the same price as the railway company delivered. Later the traders were able to carry coal free of any toll. At the same time the railway was losing money, but was able to recoup the losses elsewhere. The situation was only appreciated by the consumers at Tiverton.

The extent of the price cutting can be seen by comparing the figures for tolls and tonnage in the years 1849 and 1853. In each year the canal carried 37,000 tons, but while it received £2,351 in tolls in 1849, this had fallen to £734 in 1853. The canal company had, however, succeeded in raising the tonnage carried on the through haul from Taunton to Tiverton from 1,961 in 1850 to 4,373 in 1852.

It was estimated that the railway was losing £6,000 a year as a result of the competition, so both parties were anxious to come to terms, and did so after the railway had opened negotiations with the Bridgwater & Taunton Canal, so threatening the source of the Grand Western's coal supplies.

The railway refused to buy the canal but agreed to lease it for £2,000 a year, and in 1853 the tolls on it and on the Bridgwater & Taunton were raised to the full parliamentary levels, while the railway charges rose also. Traffic then left the canal almost entirely, and ten years later, when it was clear that the canal company was unable to revive its business, the railway

HEREFORDSHIRE AND GLOUCESTERSHIRE CANAL.

In the Matter of The Newent Railway Act, 1873, and
In the Matter of The Ross and Ledbury Railway Act, 1873.

TAKE NOTICE, that in pursuance of the powers in that behalf contained in the Newent Railway Act, 1873, and the Ross and Ledbury Railway Act, 1873, it is intended on and after the 30th day of June, 1881,

TO STOP UP AND CLOSE

so much and such part of the CANAL known as the Herefordshire and Gloucestershire Canal as is situate BETWEEN the Worcester and Hereford Railway at LEDBURY in the County of Hereford and the River Severn in the City of GLOUCESTER, and that all rights of way or navigation and other rights and privileges if any along, upon, or over such part of the said Canal with the Banks and Towing Path will as from the said 30th day of June cease and determine accordingly.

AND FURTHER TAKE NOTICE, that all persons who will be affected by the closing of the said portion of the Canal are required, on or before the said 30th day of June, to remove their Barges, Boats, and other Craft accordingly.

Dated this 2nd day of June, 1881.

BY ORDER.

One of the later canal closures to allow a railway to be built along its site. It was rumoured that the section from Ledbury to Hereford, which opened in 1845, was constructed so that its line could be converted to a railway. However, it was the older section which was converted to a railway

made an offer for its purchase of £30,000, which was accepted. The Taunton to Holcombe Rogus portion was dismantled, but the part that carried the stone traffic from Holcombe Rogus was preserved. This isolated local traffic passed until 1924.

Lastly, in a few cases canals were bought or leased in order that they could be converted into railways, the rails being laid along their banks, such as the Croydon, Aberdeenshire, Glastonbury, Oakham, Andover and part of the Leominster.

Financially the waterways that sold out made no bad bargain for their shareholders, who fared far better than did most of those who remained owners of independent canals. For instance the Stratford-upon-Avon, owing to a cost of construction far above the estimate, had never been a great success. Authorized in 1793, it was not completed until 1816. In 1824 it paid its first dividend of 3½ per cent, which rose to a maximum of 6½ per cent, for seven years. Altogether it had cost some £300,000, and the owners of bonds and shares received between them £160,434 for their property from the Oxford, Worcester & Wolverhampton Railway Company. The little Stourbridge Extension Canal was sold to the same company for more than its stated capital value. The proprietors of the

Cromford Canal, which had cost about £79,000 to build before the wartime rise of prices had become severe, judiciously agreed during the railway mania to sell to the Manchester, Buxton, Matlock & Midlands Junction Railway before the most seriously competitive line, the Erewash Valley Railway, was opened in 1847. Since by 1850 the canal tolls had fallen from £14,198 in 1840 to £7,588, although the traffic had only fallen from 346,208 tons to 284,889 tons, the Cromford Canal Company was perhaps lucky to get £103,500 for the property. The Fossdyke Navigation was leased for 894 years to the Great Northern Railway for a yearly rent of £9,570, and the Witham to the same company for 999 years at £10,545 a year, and the interest on mortgages amounting to £24,692. These rents were calculated on the basis of the previous three years' profits, plus 5 per cent.

The canals that the railways acquired while they were consolidating their position became, in most cases, an embarrassment to them. The companies were bound to maintain them in good order by statute, and therefore many waterways were fortunately kept in more or less navigable condition up to the time of nationalization; they would have decayed if they had remained in private hands.

On the other hand the railway companies naturally wished to carry traffic by rail and not by water, since otherwise they would have been maintaining a competition with themselves. Partly by intention and partly by neglect the general effect of high tolls, a lack of dredging, closures for leisurely repairs, decaying warehouses and wharves, failure to provide or maintain cranes and no effort to obtain business was to divert trade from the water to the land.

There were exceptions, either because the canals were indispensable for certain purposes or because they served an area or attracted traffic not otherwise available to the railway company. The two most important were the Birmingham Canal Navigations and the Shropshire Union system.

The Birmingham Canal Navigations came under railway control by deferred action. The canal company was a powerful one with a near monopoly position in the Birmingham area, which had been strengthened by its amalgamation in 1840 with the Wyrley & Essington, and the making, almost immediately afterwards, of two additional links between the Walsall lines of the former and the Wednesbury canals of the latter. Yet the beginnings of railway competition caused strain, and when the London & Birmingham Railway Company proposed a joint venture for a railway taking in Birmingham, Wolverhampton and Dudley, the canal company agreed. Because the Dudley Canal Company would obviously be affected, an amalgamation was arranged in 1846 between the two waterway concerns, a second railway, the Shrewsbury & Birmingham, being taken into the partnership. In 1846 the canal company subscribed to the new railway, the Birmingham, Wolverhampton & Stour Valley, and at the same time came to an arrangement with the London & Birmingham Railway, by which the latter would guarantee the dividends of the canal company at 4 per cent and nominate half of the canal committee. However, so long as the canal company did not need the guarantee the canal directors should have the casting vote; but in any year in which the guarantee was needed, the railway directors should have the casting vote. With the exception of 1868, however, the dividends of the canal company did not need support from the guarantee until 1874. Thereafter the canal company's income never reached the sum required to pay 4 per cent on its stock in any year, and the company came under continuous railway control. However, in the original agreement a clause provided that the canal company should not vary its tolls without the consent of the railway, which thus gained much immediate advantage in the competition for business.

In 1878 the then chairman asserted that

> The company would concur in thinking that the directors had done wisely in placing themselves under the tutelage of the L.& N.W.R. instead of leaving themselves to contend against the continually increasing encroachments of the railways, which were now more than ever going on in the district. They might rest under the shadow of the £4 per share which the L.& N.W.R. Company guaranteed to them.[11]

The case of the Birmingham Canal Navigations illustrates how precarious was any unity of waterway interests in face of the problems with which each company's self-interest confronted it. In December 1844 the Staffs & Worcs, one of the few canals that maintained an anti-railway policy throughout the mad year of 1845, proposed a meeting with the Birmingham 'to confer on the propriety of arranging a Coalition of the Canals in this District, in opposition to the projected Lines of Railway'.[12] The meeting took place, a joint fund was set up and agreement reached to oppose railway Bills at any rate to second reading. Alas, only a fortnight later the Birmingham had had second thoughts, in the light of the moves by the London & Birmingham Railway, and wrote to say that 'under all the Circumstances . . . [it is] no longer expedient to carry on any united opposition to the various projected Railways'.[13]

The Birmingham Canal Navigations remained busy from the time they came under railway control to the present century. Indeed, the important Cannock Extension and Wyrley Bank branches were constructed, and the

The railway/canal interchange basin at Hockley, off the Soho Branch of the Birmingham Canal, opened at the same time as the adjacent railway. Cargoes were exchanged here with the Great Western Railway; railway-owned craft were used until 1954 (Boat Museum)

Netherton Tunnel was built with a double towing-path after the agreement with the London & Birmingham Railway. However, the high figures of trade done on these canals mask the change that in fact took place. Birmingham and its neighbourhood were intersected with this elaborate network of some 160 miles of canal, along the banks of which had grown up hundreds of works (there were some 550 private basins), which depended on the waterway for their coal and raw material supplies, and in many cases for the removal of their finished products. It would have been impossible to divert all of this traffic from canal to rail without causing intense dislocation, since in many cases the construction of rail sidings was impossible in such a crowded area. Instead the railway policy was to use the canal like the road – for a collection and delivery service. Instead of goods being sent from the canalside works for long hauls by waterway to London, Hull or Liverpool, they were sent by water to a railway basin, where they were transferred to rail for the remainder of their voyage. Figures put before the Royal Commission of 1906 show that between 53 per cent and 63 per cent of the goods transhipped could not have completed their journey by waterway. Taken in reverse, the figures show what a large tonnage could in fact have remained on the water for long hauls.

Railway basins were built on the Birmingham system by three railways: the London & North Western, Midland and Great Western. Only for short hauls within the Birmingham system did goods remain on the water. In 1905, out of 7,546,453 tons of goods conveyed on the Birmingham Canal Navigations only 1,376,165 tons moved outside the system.

Within these limits the Birmingham Canal Navigations were well maintained and improved. The widening and deepening of channels, widening under bridges, installation of new pumping machinery and extensive walling of banks were all carried out under railway control, which showed a gross profit on canal working as well as an indirect gain to the railway system. For instance in 1905 gross receipts were £190,873 and the working expenses £99,207, but the balance was enough to pay the guaranteed 4 per cent dividend to the shareholders and £39,861 was paid to the canal company by the railway company.

The Shropshire Union system, which afterwards controlled over 200 miles of waterway, was authorized in 1846 to include the Ellesmere & Chester (already united with the Birmingham & Liverpool Junction), Shrewsbury and the two parts of the Montgomeryshire Canal. The object of the company, in which two railways were given powers to hold stock, was to convert part of the canal line to railway and to build certain new lines of railway. One of these lines, from Wellington to Stafford, was in fact built. Then in 1847 the whole system was leased to the London & North Western Railway, and later part of the Shropshire Canal was added. Since this system covered an area not fully served by the railway owner it was encouraged to receive trade. Later, when the Manchester Ship Canal was built, Ellesmere Port, which was the outlet on the Mersey for the canal system, became a port on the ship canal. This fact was important enough to persuade the railway to operate the canal as fully as possible, as supplementary to their own system, and to avoid a loss on the heavy maintenance cost of the waterways. The railway company spent over £250,000 on new quays, warehouses and a barge dock at Ellesmere Port, and became carriers on the canal. In 1905 469,950 tons were carried, having increased from 371,978 tons in 1898. After deducting the cost of maintenance and the carrying business the company was still making a profit of £6,765, but without any contribution towards interest on capital.

When the railway mania ended in 1847 the greater part of those canals that were destined to pass into railway ownership had already done so. Only fifteen more, with a mileage of 300 miles, were subsequently transferred, though others came under railway direction for a time.

Chirk Aqueduct on the Shropshire Union Canal, with Chirk Tunnel in the distance. The parallel railway viaduct and tunnel, opened in 1848, were constructed by the Shrewsbury & Chester Railway, which rapidly became a rival to the London & North Western Railway Company which owned the Shropshire Union. Traffic, including regular flyboats to Llangollen, was organized in Shropshire Union craft until 1921

Of the remainder of the canal network, which continued an independent existence in competition with the railways, it was the canal with plenty of factories on its banks that survived, often making its money from only a small portion of its waterway, while long hauls fell away. It benefited from the long time-lag that intervenes before a user changes from one method of transport to another. All along the banks of canals in Manchester and London stood works that had been built during a time of water transport that might go back eighty years. It was often impossible to build sidings, and the historian of Manchester wrote quite truly in 1836 that

> Railroads have one disadvantage in the carriage of coal for manufactories, which appears likely to give the canals a permanent superiority over them in this branch of traffic. The banks of the latter being generally studded with manufactories (to which such a supply of water as canals afford is indisputable); coals conveyed in boats is lodged

DERWENT NAVIGATION.

NOTICE IS HEREBY GIVEN,

That it is intended to commence some Repairs and Alterations at Stamford-Bridge Lock on the River Derwent, on *Monday the 16th of July instant;* On and after which day no Vessels can pass the said Lock to and from Malton until further Notice.

The stoppage is expected not to exceed a Month.

MALTON, 2nd July, 1849.

C. SMITHSON, PRINTER, YORKERSGATE, MALTON.

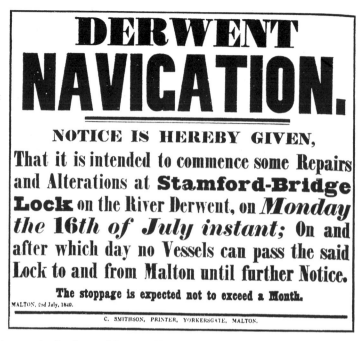

A stoppage notice for the rural Derwent Navigation, some five years before its owner, Earl Fitzmilliam, sold out to railway interests. When the threat of railway competition first became evident, the earl had improved the river by dredging; but by 1849, despite reductions in tolls, traffic was so light that a lengthy stoppage would not prove a major inconvenience

> without any second expense, at their very doors. The railroads are otherwise circumstanced. The coal is necessarily deposited regularly at the 'stations', whence it must be carted to its destination . . .[14]

The advantage was with the canal, though usually only if it cut both tolls and freights from their accustomed levels. It was clear to most manufacturers, however, that the railways were more efficient and offered a wider distribution system. Therefore new factories tended to be situated alongside the rails rather than the waterway, and branches were built where a change in the type of transport used was practicable. Indeed, it was often the case with an industrial canal that it was not the original line of competing railway that did the serious damage, it was the subsequent building of branches and sidings into works after works which had formerly sent their goods by canal.

While the industrial canals kept their tonnage at the expense of their receipts, the independent waterways that ran through agricultural districts and had no wealth of works on their banks (like the Wilts & Berks), or the heavily locked long-haul canals such as those over the Pennines (like the Rochdale), mostly succumbed sooner or later to the competition of the railway. During the railway mania, and afterwards, the railway companies had brought under their control over one fifth of the navigable waterways of Britain. In the century between the mania and nationalization another quarter was driven out of active existence by the competition of newer forms of transport: first railways, then motor lorries. It was the relentlessness of this pressure, quite as much as the actual purchase of waterways by railways, that broke the waterway system of the country up into units and forced it back to the local trade from which it had sprung.

CHAPTER TEN

The Years of Decline

The completion of the Birmingham & Liverpool Junction Canal in 1835 marked the end of major canal development. It was Telford's great effort to show that an improved canal, straight and comparatively level, even though narrow, could compete with a railway, and it cost so much more than the estimate that at one time there was doubt whether it could be opened. A few waterways were built later, such as the Tame Valley and Netherton Tunnel lines of the Birmingham Canal Navigations, and its link to the Warwick & Birmingham Canal known as the Birmingham & Warwick Junction; the Chard Canal from Chard to the Bridgwater & Taunton at Creech St Michael; the continuation of the Herefordshire & Gloucestershire from Ledbury to Hereford; the Manchester & Salford Junction to link the Rochdale Canal with the Mersey & Irwell Navigation; the Droitwich Junction to join Droitwich to the Worcester & Birmingham; and in the twentieth century one further important link, the New Junction Canal (see Chapter Eleven) in Yorkshire. In addition, some new branches were built onto existing lines, notably the Bentley, Rushall and Cannock Extension canals on the Birmingham system, and the Slough branch of the Grand Junction.

In the previous chapter we saw what happened to those canals that, in their war with the railways, were taken prisoner or disarmed. What of the remainder, the independent waterways that continued to compete, either from choice or because they could not find a rich enough captor?

The Oxford Canal was built in the days before the Napoleonic Wars inflated construction costs. It had been prosperous from the time that its line, from the Coventry Canal to Oxford, had been completed in the first days of January 1790. It additionally benefited when, by the building of the Grand Junction to Braunston, a portion of its line became incorporated in the through route from London to Birmingham because of the substantial compensation payment to which it became entitled. If we take the year 1870 as marking the date by which the affairs of the waterways had attained some sort of stability in their relationship with the railways, we can see at once that the Oxford had in fact lost no traffic, measured in terms of tonnages carried, as follows:

1828	450,000 tons
1838	520,000 tons
1848	420,000 tons
1858	400,000 tons
1868	482,000 tons

Tonnages rose from 1828 to 1838, partly through the natural increase of trade and partly because the canal was carrying railway constructional material. Then the effect of railway competition drove down the tonnages for twenty years, after which the effect of both improvements on the waterway itself and of generally expanding trade brought an increase.

Financially, however, the position of the Oxford Canal greatly deteriorated, for its tonnages were maintained at the expense of a steady decrease in tolls and compensation receipts, and so in dividends. Only the fact that its position had been so good at the beginning of the period enabled it to reach the end still in a reasonably strong position. These are the figures, taken every ten years:

Year	*Toll receipts* £	*Rate of dividend per cent*
1830	92,962	32
1840	84,159	30
1850	46,198	20
1860	25,898	8¼
1870	23,632	8½

The receipts at the end of the period had thus fallen to about a quarter, while the tonnage carried remained constant. No exact comparison can be made, however, because of variations in the tolls on the kind of goods carried and in the length of the hauls, but a great change took place in the balance of the trade and the traffic became much more local.

The three great interchange points of Hawkesbury (to the Coventry Canal), Braunston (to the Grand Junction Canal) and Napton Junction (for Birmingham) had accounted in 1830 for 67 per cent of the total receipts. By 1869 the long hauls had fallen away so far that the proportion of total receipts taken at these three points had dropped to 47 per cent, Hawkesbury having suffered least and Napton Junction most. Oxford had not had much interchange traffic with the Thames within the period of comparison and must be counted as a local centre. Trade to Oxford, Enslow, Aynho, Cropredy and Hillmorton (for Rugby) had fallen away heavily owing to railway competition, but where that competition was less, takings could be maintained, as at Banbury, or indeed increased, as at Stretton.

The Oxford was a major canal that formed part of important through lines of waterway. The Stour was a minor river not joined to any other navigation. Yet this small concern, through whose minute and account books run the names of Gainsboroughs, Constables and Lotts, met the railway threat, made the most of a good competitive position and survived into the twentieth century as a going concern.

The Stour Navigation from Manningtree to Sudbury had been authorized by an Act of 1705 and by 1835 was paying a dividend of 14 per cent on its nominal capital of £4,800. On 10 February of that year the minute book recorded the appointment of a surveyor to investigate and report on the state of the river, and stated

> That it be a particular instruction to the surveyor that his attention be drawn to the possibility of there being shortly established two lines of Rail Roads through Colchester and Bury Saint Edmunds to Yarmouth and Norwich, and how they are likely to affect the interests of all parties concerned.

The proprietors at once got back the lease of the tolls from a lessee who had held them for many years and proceeded to manage the river themselves. They decided to abolish all staunches, build a number of new locks, dredge and clean the river, improve the towing-paths, cut tolls and revise schedules of rates. The improvements were paid for partly by issuing twelve new £100 shares at £400, thus raising £4,800, and partly by taking considerable amounts from revenue during two and a half years when no dividends were paid. The result of these measures of reconstruction was to increase the rate of dividend on the larger capital to 20 per cent in 1840 and 30 per cent in 1846.

In 1845 a railway company offered to buy the shares, and the proprietors with spirit offered them at £1,000 each, the market price having reached £850. They seem to have been sure that the railway would accept the offer, but it was refused, and the proprietors began a long and losing battle. They had the advantage of connection with the sea, and thus the opportunity to handle seaborne imports, mainly of foreign corn for the mills along the river, and coal for Sudbury and other towns. Exports, chiefly flour, and also bricks from Sudbury for the building of the suburbs of south London, also went by sea for many years. They reduced tolls when they had to, got every possible competitive advantage from quoting special rates, kept the river in good repair and even experimented with a steam barge. Though the gross income from tolls, which had reached £3,415 in 1847, was less than £2,000 in 1849, it did not actually fall below £1,000 until 1869. A dividend of 15 per cent was still being paid in 1863, and of 6 per cent in 1871. The last, of 1½ per cent, was declared for 1890.

The canal boom of 1888 brought a moment of hope to the weary proprietors, when a vague proposal was made to join the Stour with the Ouse and the Cam. Thereafter mills began to close, the new county councils set up in 1888 began to insist on more expensive standards of maintenance for bridges, and money to keep the navigation alive and in repair was only found from sales of land and property. At last, in 1913, the shareholders resolved to wind up the company. It was revived, unsuccessfully, as a public trust in 1918, and again collapsed in 1935. While a campaign for revival began in 1947, only limited restoration has been possible.

Such was the decline of prosperous companies. Those other concerns, which at the beginning of the competitive period did not have the small capital and high earning power of such waterways as the Oxford Canal or the Stour Navigation, found that, by being forced to cut their tolls, they eventually brought their receipts below their maintenance costs. These costs were indeed an important factor, for they slowly rose throughout the century and formed one jaw of the financial pincers, the other being falling revenue per ton carried. On the Basingstoke Canal, for instance, an estimate of tonnage and receipts made by the company in 1787 was 30,700 tons and £7,783, or 5.07s. per ton carried; in 1801–2 the actual tonnage carried was 18,737 tons and the tolls 4.08s.; in 1814–15, at the end of the Napoleonic War, the position was similar at 21,695 tons and 4.17s.; and in the boom year of 1825–6 the figures were 15,258 tons and 4.06s. By 1838–9 the tonnage had risen to 33,717 tons because of materials being carried for railway building, but tolls were 3.2s. The next year the figures were down to 26,965 tons and 2.79s.; by 1865–6 they had fallen further to 20,598 tons and 1.03s. a ton. (While these figures are only roughly comparable, the general trend is clear.) At this point the company went into liquidation, though it was later revived more than once under various names before passing into decrepitude or dereliction, except for the small portion between the Wey and Woking. In 1949 it was bought by a new company, which obtained revenue from the sale of water but let navigation decline. The canal was bought by the Surrey and Hampshire county councils in the 1970s and most of it was re-opened in 1991.

All canals suffered from this tendency. For instance the revenue of the very prosperous Somersetshire Coal Canal fell from 2.61s. per ton carried in 1828 (113,442 tons and £14,809) to 0.84s. per ton in 1868 (140,112 tons and £6,120); and that of the Leeds & Liverpool from 1.59s. per ton in 1828 (1,436,160 tons and £114,518) to 1.13s. per ton in 1868 (1,884,140 tons and £94,207). It will be noticed that the tonnage carried increased in both these cases, as it did in many others.

Some of the smaller concerns went into voluntary liquidation, retiring with dignity from a contest to which they were not equal, such as the Wey & Arun Junction, which from 1830 to 1865 paid a dividend in all but three years. In 1864 it went into liquidation while there were still assets to divide. Many followed, especially in the seventies, including the Tavistock, Baybridge, Coombe Hill, Ivel, Melton Mowbray and Sleaford navigations. A few, like the Wilts & Berks, just faded away. The receipts became less and less, until meetings ceased to be held and offices were shut for the lack of means to pay wages. The long pounds became slowly unnavigable and stagnant, and a nuisance to towns and villages. Then some public authority would take steps to end the life of the canal and stop the inconvenience.

In the Fens, where the waterways had been built or enlarged primarily for drainage reasons, a great waterborne trade had grown up before and during the canal age. The coming of the railways saw this trade up and down the rivers and drains of the fenlands slowly die away, except here and there where the railways did not quite serve local purposes. In these cases, however, the waterways themselves continued to be maintained for their primary purpose of drainage.

By the early 1850s a considerable mileage of canals was railway-controlled. The Railway & Canal Traffic Act of 1854 specified that these railway canals should provide 'reasonable facilities' for traffic and should not hinder through freights to or from independent waterways. Complaints were to go to the courts. The Act was well-intentioned but had no teeth, and not until the appointment of commissioners under the Regulation of Railways Act of 1873 did policing become effective, or the quotation of through rates compulsory.

Some canals were bought by railways long after the railway mania. This was not illegal, given parliamentary approval, but as the 1850s moved on Parliament became less and less inclined to see canal companies absorbed. Railways therefore looked for expedients whereby they could control canals without having to go before Parliament. One way was to use the leasing clause of the 1845 Canal Carriers' Act in an unintended way. If a railway already owned a canal company, that company could legally lease others. Thus a consortium of three canal owning railways in 1850 jointly leased the Leeds & Liverpool Canal for 21 years, and in 1855 another consortium of four companies leased the Rochdale Canal for 36 years, thus killing the trans-Pennine canal trade in

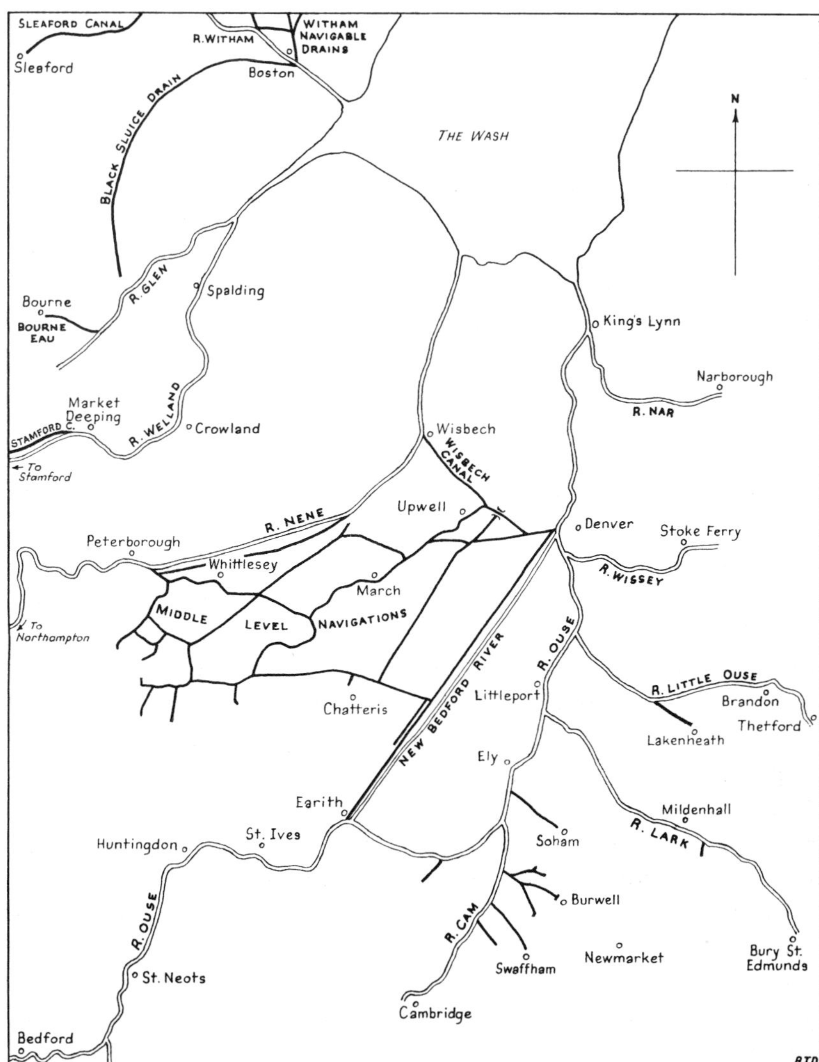

The main waterways of the Fens. Apart from the seaports of Boston, Wisbech and King's Lynn, navigation was generally an incidental adjunct to drainage by the end of the nineteenth century

finished textiles. As the Huddersfield was already owned by the London & North Western Railway, all three Pennine canals were for a time railway-controlled.

The Rochdale case – taken to the Board of Trade by the vigilant and powerful Aire & Calder – and an effort by the Oxford, Worcester & Wolverhampton Railway – also to use the Canal Carriers' Act to lease the Worcester & Birmingham Canal, taken also to the Board of Trade, in this case by the Gloucester & Berkeley Company – led to the government inserting a clause into the Cheap Trains Bill, then before Parliament, to prevent the practice except after a special Act.

Another way was never prevented. In 1855 three officials of the North Eastern Railway bought, in their own names, the Yorkshire Derwent Navigation from Earl Fitzwilliam, then leased it to their own company. The same technique was used in 1859 when the Upper Avon was sold to an individual who resold it to the Oxford, Worcester & Wolverhampton Railway, and, more importantly but differently, in 1871, when the Bridgewater trustees sold their waterways to the chairmen of the Midland and the Manchester, Sheffield & Lincolnshire railways – these then formed the Bridgewater Navigation Company to take over their purchase.

From the 1840s to the 1870s the impression is that the waterways were becoming more and more old-fashioned and unable to cope with the changing world of the mid-nineteenth century. The independent canals seemed mostly to lose heart from the beginning of railway competition. They had been created as local lines of communication and local they largely remained. There was little sign of the race to amalgamate and to form national lines of communication that gave its driving force to the railway mania. From time to time, however, the bigger of them met together to try to evolve a common policy. For instance in May 1841 a conference of all the companies on the Liverpool and Manchester to London route met to complain about the excessive tolls demanded at that time and of acute competition by the Oxford company. The Regent's, Grand Junction, Coventry, Trent & Mersey, Macclesfield, Peak Forest and Ashton-under-Lyne companies were represented; the Oxford was not. These were the figures produced at the meeting of the companies' share of the through toll from Manchester via Preston Brook, Fradley and Braunston to Paddington:

Canal	*Miles*	*Toll*		
		s	*d*	
Bridgewater	25	1	0	(5p)
Trent & Mersey	67	2	9 ½	(14p)
Coventry (Fradley section)	5 ½	0	2 ¾	(1p)
Birmingham (Fazeley section)	5 ½	0	5 ½	(2p)
Coventry	21 ¼	0	11	(5p)
Oxford	23 ⅝	2	11	(15p)
Grand Junction	101	4	2 ½	(21p)
Total	248⅞	12	6 ¼	(63p)

These figures are for tolls only. At the time the freight charge for the distance made by the carriers was £2 2s. 5½d. (£2.12), making £2 15s. (£2.75) in all, which was a quite inadequate differential in favour of the canals compared with the railway charge of £2 17s. 6d. (£2.87) for the same distance, which had recently been reduced from £3 5s. (£3.25).

The meeting resolved that 'the course which the Oxford canal is pursuing is destructive of the thoroughfare trade'.[1] The Oxford did nothing, and the situation got worse. In July 1845 there was another meeting, this time with the Oxford present. The Oxford took the offensive, complaining that the Grand Junction was giving preference for coal traffic to the Leicestershire line over its own. The Grand Junction replied that the Oxford charged 1¾d. (0.7p) per ton for coal to London, and 3d. (1.3p) for other goods, compared with their own rates of ¼d. (0.1p) and ½d. (0.2p), respectively, 'by which exactions the Oxford Canal Company had been and were still enabled to Share a Dividend of 30 per Cent, while the Grand Junction Canal Company were sharing one of only seven per Cent'.[2] Still the Oxford Company refused to lower its tolls or to go to arbitration. The Grand Junction then approached the two Warwick canals and others for 'a general amalgamation of their common interests'.[3] This proposal does not seem to have been meant seriously but to have been intended to force the Oxford's hand by isolating that company. It worked, and the Oxford agreed to arbitration and a lowering of tolls. No more was heard of amalgamation for many years.

This episode shows the difficulties that a number of long-established and independent canal companies faced in competing against railways. For a time the tonnage carried was to be unaffected, but the heavy fall of revenue that resulted from price cutting might have been to some extent counteracted, and the conservatism of management and engineering policy mitigated, by amalgamation into bigger units, or at the least by following a common policy.

There was one water line where such a policy was pursued with a good deal of success: that from Birmingham or Liverpool by way of the Staffs & Worcs Canal to the Severn and the Gloucester & Berkeley. The initiative came from the Staffs & Worcs, the energetic management of which combined much foresight in respect of other waterways with an inability to improve its own canal. From the beginning in about 1835 of serious proposals to improve the navigation of the Severn, the Staffs & Worcs had supported them with money and parliamentary influence. When the Severn Commission was at last set up in 1842 the canal company agreed to guarantee the commission's bonds up to £180,000, which enabled locks to be built between Stourport and Diglis, and the river to be dredged lower down.

When the railway mania began, two or three railway companies interested themselves in the Severn, offering to guarantee its revenue in exchange for a clear run with their Bills. Of these the offer of the Oxford, Worcester & Wolverhampton Railway was accepted, so that the Severn bond-holders were doubly protected: the railway company guaranteed the revenue of the waterway, and the Staffs & Worcs the capital and interest of the bonds.

Through many years and manoeuvres it then became the object of the Staffs & Worcs, which had meanwhile entered into guarantees for additional capital for improvements to the river, to get rid of the influence first of the Oxford, Worcester & Wolverhampton Railway, and then of the Great Western Railway behind it. It took the canal company until 1890 to do so, and at a heavy cost, and there was then once more an independent waterway route to Gloucester. It was ironic, however, that the Staffs & Worcs' old rival for the Birmingham trade, the Worcester & Birmingham, was now owned by the Gloucester & Berkeley, and therefore had an automatic preference, while all three main feeders into the Staffs & Worcs, which should have contributed most to this water line – the Shropshire Union, the Trent & Mersey and the Birmingham Canal navigations (including the Dudley line) – were railway-controlled. Only the small and extraordinarily supine Stourbridge Canal was independent, though its feeder, the Stourbridge Extension, was not.

Again, a waterway company could stay in business if it could encourage traffic originating on its line to remain, was largely self-contained, well managed and had reasonable access to funds. This was the case with the Aire & Calder. The company was well-placed to meet competition for, between 1820 and 1826, it had built the broad and deep Ferrybridge & Goole Canal as a more modern alternative to its older line to the Yorkshire Ouse via the Selby Canal, and had then developed Goole as a port. It had also enlarged and straightened its main lines from Castleford to Leeds and Wakefield between 1828 and 1839, so that it entered the railway age with a recently modernized waterway.

The navigation's basic traffic was coal, much of it from collieries beside its own waterway, with East Anglian corn as back carriage upwards. To enlarge the area from which coal could be drawn the company leased the largely coal-carrying Barnsley Canal in 1854 (later purchased and its locks enlarged) and the Calder & Hebble for 21 years in 1865. To keep traffic on the water it followed a vigorous carrying policy. Steam tugs had been used since 1831, and by 1855 the company was steam-hauling two thirds of its own carrying mileage, after which it put on public tugs to haul bye-traders' craft.

It is difficult to say that railway ownership of or influence over important canals prevented a movement to bring the waterways closer together, because there were so few signs of such a movement even along routes that remained independent, but it was undoubtedly one of the factors working against an energetic canal policy. The difficulty in getting a quotation for a through toll from a railway-controlled canal such as the Trent & Mersey, for instance, was a discouragement in itself. By the time the law compelled railways to quote through tolls, under the Railway & Canal Traffic Act of 1888, the possibilities of keeping long-haul traffic on the canals had largely gone.

Part of the drag that kept canals back was the result, of course, of their many sizes and shapes; part, especially in agricultural areas, came from the repeal of the Corn Laws and the transfer of mills to the ports; part also resulted from changing industrial techniques, such as the substitution of a few large steelworks served by railways for many small ironworks alongside canals.

In sum, the canals fell behind because the investing public no longer believed in inland water transport. Railways were seen as more efficient, more speedy, more flexible and more widely spread. In consequence, canal proprietors and officials lost heart; doing so they found capital for improvements almost impossible to obtain.

Throughout the period the canals that were successful in retaining their trade did so by keeping the short hauls, which stayed with them because old-established industry was located on the canal banks. The long-distance trade decreased a good deal, not only because of the difficulty of passing goods from one company to another with different tolls and classifications, a different size of lock and depth of waterway, but also because portions of many through routes were in railway hands. The tendency towards the short haul can also be seen on the system of a single waterway. In 1905 on the 145 miles of the Leeds & Liverpool, for instance, the average haul for a ton of goods was 19.6 miles; on the 189 miles of the extended Grand Junction it was 23.2 miles; and on the 144 miles of the Thames Navigation it was 16.7 miles.

Canal companies were hampered by several factors in any effort they made to extend their hauls. The first was the old distinction between toll-taking and carrying.

A number of navigation and canal concerns had always had their own carrying fleets, like the Aire & Calder, the Mersey & Irwell and the Bridgewater; others had organized the business of carrying by accepting goods freight-paid, and then themselves employing independent craft to carry them, like the Don or the Calder & Hebble; others again had agreed with carriers that they would run regular services – the so-called contract vessels of, for instance, the Rochdale Canal. However, the majority of companies had only intermittently or never been concerned with carrying, and had confined themselves to taking tolls from anyone who wished to put a boat on the waterway and use it for the carriage of goods. We have seen that this system was abandoned in the early days of railways, and its maintenance on many canals meant that the necessary business organization for successful competition of offices, regular services, warehouses, cranes and so on was not available to the trader.

The carrier might have been the owner of a single boat, a manufacturer, or a carrying company like Fellows, Morton & Clayton, which carried goods over many canals. As the canal, unlike the railway, did not usually do its own carrying it did not have the same vital interest in the state of its line. If a carrier's boat went aground the company did not feel the same urgent sense that a railway company did when a train was derailed. Again, manufacturers who wanted goods moved by water had to go to more trouble: they had to find carriers and then entrust them with the necessary money to pay tolls and charges. Sometimes the money was otherwise spent, especially by small carriers, or there was pilfering from the cargo, compensation for which was difficult to recover.

A number of companies continued to carry; others adopted the powers of the Canal Carriers' Act; while others made no attempt to go beyond their toll-taking functions. One well-managed concern, set up by the Grand Junction company, is worthy of examination.

While the Grand Junction was only a toll-taker it had only been indirectly concerned with rate cutting against the railways through pressure from the independent carriers for reduced tolls. Once it set up a direct carrying business in 1848, soon after the authorizing Act, it became directly involved, and as early as 1851 agreed with the London & North Western Railway that both companies would not cut rates against each other. In this agreement the Grand Junction was bound to peg not only its own freight charges but also those of the independent carriers. This, not surprisingly, it found itself unable to do. In 1854 it had to inform the railway, which then began to cut rates again, causing further reductions in both tolls and rates on the canal. In October 1857, at a meeting of canal companies and carriers, the Grand Junction chairman reported that he had been to see the managers of the London & North Western Railway and the Great Western Railway, who had complained that 'they could not retain their fair proportion of the heavy Trade in consequence of the Carriers on the Canal being enabled to carry at such low rates'.[4]

The meeting must have decided not to fight further, for in December a rates agreement was concluded with both railways that gave small fixed differentials to the canal carriers, which the Grand Junction accepted for itself and undertook to enforce on the independents. This was perhaps made easier by some rises in rates on both railway and canal as a result of the agreement. Over this tendency the (old) Grand Union company warned that 'any decided combination between the Railways and Canals may materially affect the interest of the Canals with the Board of Trade',[5] refusing to join the understanding on tolls that the Grand Junction, in the light of its agreement with the railways, had now reached with the Oxford and other canals.

Price cutting by the independent carriers caused further trouble, however, and for a moment the company thought of following the example of the Bridgewater trustees, controlling the Duke of Bridgewater's Canal. Faced with the same difficulty, they had converted the independent carriers on their canal into their agents, to whom certain working expenses and a commission were paid in exchange for agreements to charge uniform rates.

All seems thereafter to have gone well until the Regent's Park explosion of 1874 (see Chapter Three), which, although on the Regent's Canal, involved Grand Junction carrying craft. The damage brought 632 claims totalling £74,418, and the final cost of the settled claims, together with legal costs and those of reinstating Macclesfield Bridge, proved so daunting that in 1876 the company closed its carrying business.

Not until the 1880s were serious efforts made to negotiate through tolls, even on lengths of waterway that were not interrupted by railway ownership. At no time did the canal companies set up an equivalent to the Railway Clearing House for the settlement among themselves of mutual debts (although this had saved railway companies and railway users immense time and trouble), though they were expressly authorized to do so by the Railway & Canal Traffic Act of 1888. There was not even an association to promote the interests of the waterways during the critical early period of their history. In the canal age there had from time to time been *ad hoc* meetings, or groups of meetings, between representatives of canal companies, such as the group of proprietors of inland navigations who called a meeting in 1797 to protest against a proposed tax on goods carried by canal.

Common action had to wait until 1844, when the United Body of Canal Proprietors helped to push through the Canal Tolls and Canal Carriers' Acts of 1845. This body continued in loose form to watch current Bills and consider the future of the canal interest. In 1855 it became the Canal Association, with an Aire & Calder chairman and secretary. This lasted until nationalization. There was no journal devoted to canal affairs until the short-lived *Canal Journal* of the 1890s, though several periodicals covered railway interests.

Boating for pleasure on the tidal Arun in 1867, from J.B. Dashwood's account of his voyage in Caprice. *The journey was not without difficulties, given the decaying condition of the Wey & Arun Junction Canal, and the problems involved in persuading the horse to negotiate the gates across the towing-path on the Arun*

Meanwhile a steady deterioration of the condition of many canals took place. As receipts fell, maintenance was cut in order that dividends might still be paid. Money for capital expenditure was hard to find in the face of dropping revenues with which to pay interest on borrowings. Canals began to look less prosperous, and that did not attract new customers. Mud accumulated, boats could not carry full loads, delays increased and even long-standing customers began to look for alternative transport.

The decline of the canals introduced a new figure to the scene, the tourist, who always arrives when the ordinary is becoming exceptional. Earlier there were occasional references to short pleasure trips on canals, such as the 'Barge with a party of Ladies and Gentlemen'[6] for whom tolls on the Swansea Canal were remitted in 1809. The Reverend John Skinner, rector of Camerton in Somerset, describes in his diary such an occasion in 1823 on the Somersetshire Coal Canal:

Loading sugar beet at Ludham Bridge on the Ant, some 7 miles south of its junction with the North Walsham canal. The tractor indicates that this dates from as late as 1959, but otherwise the vessel is similar to those operating in the late nineteenth century. This photograph was taken in October, towards the end of the pleasure boating season; the traffic was itself seasonal and loading rarely took place in summer (L.A. Edwards)

> Having engaged one of the coal barges, I had it fitted up for the ladies with an awning and matting against the sides, and tables and chairs from the public-house, in which we proceeded to Combe Hay . . . As the day was delightful, the whole party much enjoyed the excursion.[7]

In 1867 a party took a boat through the Wey & Arun Junction and down to the sea at Littlehampton shortly before that canal closed, and published the results of their adventures as *The Thames to the Solent by Canal and Sea* in 1868. The following year a similar book, *The Waterway to London,* described a canoe trip by three men from Manchester to London by way of the Mersey, Shropshire Union, Severn, and Thames & Severn canals, and the Thames. Both accounts are written as if their authors were pioneers of this type of amusement, and in neither case do they regard the canals themselves, or the people on them, as picturesque. Both are taken for granted, as might be expected when the waterways were still a familiar means of transport.

Day pleasure trips on rivers, such as the Wye at Tintern or the Dee at Chester, were popular from the 1860s, while after 1866 the new Thames Conservancy soon concerned itself with pleasure craft, the Thames Preservation Act of 1885 aiming at 'the preservation of the River above Teddington Lock for purposes of public recreation, and for regulating the pleasure traffic therein'. From the 1880s regular services of steamers ran up to Oxford, mainly for pleasure rather than travel purposes, while boat rollers for small craft were provided at the new locks built by the Conservancy.

The first developments towards the modern hiring industry began on the Norfolk Broads, where trading wherries were being hired out from 1860, with visitors attracted in large numbers from the 1880s. In 1888 Press Brothers of North Walsham advertised five trading wherries for hire. Unusually, these millers also owned the North Walsham Canal, which they had acquired in 1866. When they sold the canal in 1907 there was still some income from pleasure tolls. This hiring operation was probably the first on an artificial canal in England. It was still in being in 1899, when four craft were in use. Purpose-built broads hire craft were first advertised in that year.

All of these early hired craft were sailing vessels, and hire charges usually included the services of a skipper and a steward who would act as cook. One problem for visitors was the difficulty in organizing bookings at a distance. One visitor recalled of the 1900s that 'the novice might . . . find on his arrival that he had booked a boat which had halyards and sheets in a deplorable condition, several important items of gear missing, and a 6 ft tiller occupying the whole of the cockpit'.[8]

One solution to this problem was the development of booking agencies, which could ensure minimum standards. Following a holiday organized by members of a Dulwich tennis club, Harry Blake set up a booking agency in 1907, the catalogue of which listed forty-three sailing yachts by 1908.

Interest in canal trips was more limited, although a long-standing service of horse-drawn day boats between Llangollen, Berwyn and Chirk, on the Shropshire Union Canal, began with *Maid of Llangollen* in 1884. This and the river developments were facilitated by the same railways which had removed much waterborne goods traffic. These were able to exploit the growth of holidays and excursions in the latter part of the nineteenth century.

CHAPTER ELEVEN

Time of Hope

Until the 1870s the development of the railway system was so astonishing and so apparently beneficial that many thought the waterways obsolete and overlooked the dangers of railway monopoly. A letter written at the time of the Canal Conference of 1888 asserted that: 'Sixteen years ago anyone advocating water transport was promptly accused of galvanising a corpse . . . '.[1] In Britain, a change of heart was brought about by a number of factors all operating over the same period.

The dangers of a railway monopoly began to be understood when, for the first time since the Industrial Revolution, foreign manufactured goods began seriously to compete with British ones in the home market, held open to them because of the universally held doctrine of free trade. It began to be said that cheap transport was vital, and that on the Continent both railways and waterways were cheaper than British railways, the latter by a good deal. There were complaints that railway rates on imported goods were less than those the home manufacturer had to pay, and statements that manufacturing firms were moving from the interior of the country to the seaboard to avoid the high railway rates. Critics of the railways pointed to their high capital charges and suggested that new capital was being raised to carry unprofitably heavy traffic, which could better go by water.

The 1873 Regulation of Railways Act was the first to provide machinery adequate to control railway influence over canals. It compelled railway and canal companies to quote through tolls or rates and to publish them, forbade railways to acquire a controlling interest in a canal unless approved by commissioners appointed under the Act and stated that railways already controlling canals must maintain them 'so that the whole of such canal or part may be at all times kept open and navigable for the use of all persons desirous to use and navigate the same without any unnecessary hindrance, interruption or delay'. The Act set up Railway Commissioners to whom matters of dispute were to be referred, who were to see that through rates were fair and who were to be the guardians of the public interest.

Between the 1870s and the Royal Commission of 1906 an argument raged between two groups of interests. Supporters of waterways transport argued that it could play an important part, but only if existing companies were amalgamated, probably with the help of the central or local government, followed by modernization. This would ensure a uniform gauge on the major through waterway routes, an enlarged sectional area to increase speed, the substitution of lifts for flights of locks, the protection of canal banks by walls and the use of steam haulage. On the other side railway supporters pointed out that the canal network was not nearly as comprehensive as that of the railways, that storage in railway waggons was an essential convenience to coal and other merchants, that speed of conveyance was becoming increasingly important as traders held smaller stocks and traded on less capital, and that the enormous expenditure involved in any major reorganization of the waterways system would be out of all proportion to the possible benefits.

By the 1880s so active had interest become in the revival of the waterways that in 1888 the Royal Society of Arts held a two-day conference on the subject, involving leading waterways engineers and managers. It was revealed that private enterprise was unlikely to raise the necessary capital and that, in any case, a strong hand was needed to make sure that railway influence was still not exercised over waterways. Several speakers supported nationalization, or the formation of public trusts under local authorities. Nationalization had not then acquired its later political contentiousness and proposals for state acquisition were judged on their merits in furthering transport improvements. As one speaker put it: 'The traditional independence of Englishmen is opposed to Government interference, and yet the descendants of Englishmen in Canada and the United States are now enjoying the benefits of artificial waterways provided by their Governments.'[2]

The conference resolved to press the Council of the Society of Arts to petition Parliament to consider the necessity of improving waterways transport. The proposals covered the use of State acquisition and the amendment of the Railway & Canal Traffic Bill to give power to local authorities to form public trusts that would take over and develop canals. The Act did include the latter and, as we shall see, was used. From then to the end of the century the controversy continued, but with very little action before the appointment of a Royal Commission in 1906 to study the whole matter.

This revival of interest in waterways, which began in the 1870s, led to developments along several lines. These included a number of proposals for ship canals and other waterways developments, coloured by the progress of the slowly maturing Manchester Ship Canal. Again, the purchase in 1874 of the Worcester & Birmingham and the associated

Droitwich canals by the Gloucester & Berkeley, and the negotiations by the Staffs & Worcs which led in 1890 to the freeing of the Severn from railway influence, were forward moves of importance by waterways concerns. In the case of the Worcester & Birmingham Canal this also marked the defeat of a long effort by a railway company to acquire the canal.

In Ireland, in contrast to the British mainland, the railways took a large share of a much slower growth in trade, and there was a continuing conflict between the interests of navigation and drainage. Navigation tended to be put first by a Royal Commission of 1880, chaired by Lord Monck, which considered the future of the very unsatisfactory north–south waterways that nominally existed from Belfast or Newry to Lough Neagh, and then by way of the Ulster and Ballinamore & Ballyconnell canals to the Shannon and so to Limerick. Subsequent commissions – the Allport of 1887 on Irish Public Works and that of 1905 on Arterial Drainage – thought navigation, drainage and other water interests should be the responsibility of a single government department.

Earlier editions of *British Canals* devoted a whole chapter to the Manchester Ship Canal, but as this has now been fully detailed elsewhere, in books by Dr D.A. Farnie and Dr David Owen, a briefer summary must suffice.

We earlier noted the formation of the Mersey & Irwell Navigation, and the reasons behind the Duke of Bridgewater's Canal. The river company, carriers as well as toll-takers, had not been prosperous even before the Duke had opened his Runcorn extension in 1776, and in 1779 it had sold out to a new group for £10,000. This group worked to build up the fleet, improve the navigation – notably by a canal extension from Warrington to Runcorn – and to put on a passenger service. It benefited a good deal from its connection with the Manchester, Bolton & Bury Canal, but much less from the Manchester & Salford Junction Canal to link the river to the Rochdale Canal, to which the Bridgewater was already joined. Keen competition developed between the two concerns, each of which shared in the prosperity that good water transport and the rise of the cotton industry brought to the district. In 1844, when Egerton of the Bridgewater bought the river navigation and so united the two waterways, the Mersey & Irwell Navigation £100 shares (£70 paid up) were still valued at £800 each, in spite of railway competition.

The Liverpool & Manchester Railway had opened in 1830. It had been promoted partly because the rapid growth of trade had been greater than the waterways' ability to carry the increased traffic efficiently, in spite of improvements, partly because it seemed to the railway promoters that there were lucrative pickings to be had. In fact, the railway company found its principal source of revenue was not, as it had thought, goods but passengers. Ten years after the railway had opened it was still only carrying a third of the total goods traffic available.

There was a proposal as early as 1824 for a small ship canal to carry 400 ton vessels to Manchester – not from the Mersey but from the Dee – by a line 45 miles long at a cost of £1 million. The scheme reached Parliament in 1825 but was thrown out. It would have been strongly opposed by the port interests of Liverpool. However, Manchester remained interested in a ship canal, and references to it occur at intervals during the next fifty years. As the century wore on there was increasing criticism, both of the exactions of the Liverpool port authorities and of the railway transport monopoly that was growing up between Liverpool and Manchester, and which was solidified in 1872, when a new railway-influenced company, the Bridgewater Navigation Company, bought the canal, carrying interests and waterway property of the Bridgewater trustees for £1,115,000.

The beginning of the process that led to the building of the ship canal was probably a walk beside the river by Mr George Hicks in 1876. He saw barges stuck on the mud and wrote to the *Manchester Guardian*, pointing out that a good waterway was neglected. This letter was noticed by a London engineer, Hamilton Fulton, who wrote to express his interest in helping any scheme to improve the navigation of the Mersey. The two men met and Fulton's preliminary report was put before a meeting of the Chamber of Commerce. A trading slump set in, however, and nothing was done until, in 1881, Sir William Harcourt made a speech in which he praised the energy of the citizens of Glasgow in making the Clyde navigable for ocean-going steamships. Further newspaper correspondence followed and interested a man who was to be prominent in ship canal affairs, Daniel Adamson. He consulted an engineer friend, James Abernethy, over the project and, getting a favourable reply, took the lead in organizing a lobby for a canal.

The slump also played its part, for it was especially severe in Manchester, where it was attributed 'to the excessively keen competition to which Manchester was subjected by reason of the great cost of transit of goods from this district as compared with that to which other manufacturing centres were put'.[3]

The effort towards a ship canal really dates from a pamphlet of 1882, backing up the proposals with statistics, which went quickly through a number of editions. In June, Adamson called a meeting of sixty-eight prominent businessmen and representatives of interested towns to meet Fulton and Edward Leader Williams, then engineer of the Bridgewater Navigation Company. The meeting was enthusiastic and plans were made to fund preliminary expenses. Fulton's proposal, for a tidal canal without locks costing £4.5 million, was set aside until the autumn, following the advice of Leader Williams and James Abernethy in favour of a canal with locks, which was more practicable.

Meetings were held, newspaper correspondence sprang up, money was raised and even songs were written. The Manchester and Salford city councils supported the project, and before the end of the year the plans for the Parliamentary Bill had been deposited. Up to August 1885 there raged a parliamentary war, during which two Ship Canal Bills were thrown out amid opposition from the railway companies, the Bridgewater Navigation Company and Liverpool interests. The parliamentary battle was matched by newspaper wars in Liverpool and Manchester.

The third Bill was passed after various alterations had been made to placate Liverpool interests, especially by altering the route so that the canal, instead of passing down the estuary, left the river at Eastham and ran beside it. Liverpool opinion greatly feared that the works would, in the former case, have damaged the estuary farther down. The estimated cost of the works was £6,311,137, but among additional commitments were those to acquire the Bridgewater Navigation Company for £1,710,000, nearly £600,000 more than the railway interests had paid for the waterway a few years before. The Act provided for a capital of £8 million in shares, with power to raise a further sum by loan, of which £5 million, as well as the purchase price of the Bridgewater concern, was to be raised before 6 August 1887.

While the Act did not give power to pay interest on capital during construction, Adamson was optimistic that the money needed would be raised without difficulty. It was a shock to the promoters when only £750,000 came in, and a Bill was quickly prepared to authorize the company to pay interest while the canal was being built. The Act was passed, only to be followed by an issue of shares that failed, chiefly because investors were not sufficiently impressed either by the strength of the Board of Directors or by the soundness of the estimates.

The board then wisely set up a consultative committee, which included men like C.P. Scott, editor of the *Manchester Guardian*, who had not strongly supported the scheme, which was asked to study the practicality of the ship canal. After a careful inquiry the committee reported that the estimates were satisfactory and that the project was thoroughly sound commercially, but suggested that the board should be strengthened. Eventually Adamson resigned as chairman in favour of Lord Egerton, a kinsman of the Duke of Bridgewater, whose canal had first connected Liverpool and Manchester.

Then began a rush to raise the money. Meetings were held all over the Midlands, and before 6 August 1887 two-thirds of the share capital authorized had been issued and accepted in accordance with the Act of 1885. An agreement was signed with the contractor T.A. Walker, builder of the Severn Tunnel, and on 11 November 1887 the first sod was cut by Lord Egerton on the site of Eastham Lock, where the canal was to enter the Mersey.

Within a year eleven thousand men were at work and cutting was on schedule. Then Walker died, and his death was followed both by arguments between the company and his executors, and also natural disasters in the shape of floods, that delayed work and added to its expense. This led the company at the end of 1890 to take the work into its own hands, unfortunately at a time when bad weather was to cause further difficulties, and when the price of labour and materials was to rise beyond the estimates.

It soon became clear that the company had insufficient capital to finish the canal. The chairman therefore approached Manchester Corporation, which so well understood the seriousness of allowing the works to stop that it promoted a Bill allowing it to lend £3 million to the company in debentures, and to have five directors on the board.

The influence of the corporation led to a tightening up of the canal administration but, while work progressed, in 1892 it became clear that still more money would be needed to finish the canal. While the corporations of Salford and Oldham promoted Bills to allow them to lend money to the company, Manchester had offered to lend a further £2 million, and this was accepted by the company in debentures. It was agreed that until half of the total of £5 million owing to the Manchester Corporation had been paid off, it should appoint a majority of the directors. This majority existed until 1988.

Among the last works to be completed was the Barton swing aqueduct, a unique structure that carries the Bridgwater Canal over the ship canal. At the same time Brindley's old aqueduct was pulled down, the oldest large piece of engineering on an English canal making way for the newest.

So on 1 January 1894 the canal was opened for business by a procession of boats headed by the *Norseman* carrying the directors, followed by a trail of merchant ships, seventy-one of which entered the docks. On 21 May the formal opening took place. The total cost was £14,347,891, compared to the £8,408,936 estimated in the prospectus of July 1886. Given the vicissitudes through which all great works pass, this was not excessive, but the greatly increased cost did mean, as so often when the earlier canals were being built, that it was many years before the Ordinary shareholders saw a dividend.

The canal had 179 acres of water space in its docks at Manchester and Salford alone, and 5⅝ miles of quays. The largest entrance lock to the canal at Eastham was 600 ft by 80 ft, the upper locks being 600 ft by 65 ft.

The Irlam Locks, looking west, as pictured in the Illustrated London News *on 30 December 1893, just before formal opening. The railway bridge is one of the five bridges built on the elevated deviation lines. The Ship Canal Railway passed through the arches on the right (now occupied by a main road); it is not yet shown on this drawing. The Partington Coaling Basin lay shortly beyond the railway bridge*

The early years of the canal were filled with difficulties. Among them were a lack of cooperation from the railways, which caused the slow handling of goods, and the practice of conferences of shipping companies to bind shippers by means of rebates to use certain channels that were not easy to change. For the first year or so it was thought possible that the canal would have to close, then slowly its fortunes changed. Cheaper costs attracted imports to Manchester, and the total tonnage handled rose from 1,826,237 tons in 1896 to 2,595,585 tons in 1898. With the canal rose the prosperity of Manchester.

The indirect benefit in lowered freight rates to Manchester was great, both on canal-borne and railway goods, since the railways had lowered their Liverpool–Manchester rates when the canal was opened.

Early developments included its close association with Trafford Park Estates in 1896, which was developed for new industry likely to use the canal, and in 1898, with Christopher Furness of the shipping line, the formation of Manchester Liners Ltd, intended to increase the carrying of Canadian produce to industrial England, and which soon added services to the USA too.

The largest entrance lock at Eastham, looking out onto the tidal Mersey. The approach channel also serves the Queen Elizabeth Dock, which is part of the Port of Manchester but not part of the Manchester Ship Canal. The craft consists of four tanks carrying Venezuelan orimulsion, carried from land storage at Liverpool, pushed by Ordale H

Then came the provision of facilities especially for the import trade, mainly in timber, grain, cotton, oil, cattle and, later, wood pulp. Since outside interests were reluctant to provide such necessaries as warehouses for raw cotton, grain elevators, cattle lairages, cold stores and oil tanks, the Ship Canal Company had to act, directly or indirectly, to provide them. Manchester was to remain a mainly importing port: imports as a proportion of total traffic were 60 per cent in 1900, 70 per cent in 1920, 71½ per cent in 1950 and 75 per cent in 1970. The greatest battle of all was with Liverpool for raw cotton, especially American cotton, and Manchester never succeeded in winning a dominant share of the trade.

Exports were mainly coal, salt, manufactured goods and machinery, the mechanized Partington Coaling Basin of 1894 being the forerunner of a continuous development of mechanized handling of varied cargoes.

The next chapters will outline the later history of the Manchester Ship Canal. The influence of the scheme on proposals for improved navigation elsewhere was almost as great as that of the canal on the prosperity of Manchester.

Proposals for a ship canal from Birmingham to the sea arose from complaints about the high railway rates from Birmingham during the trade depression of 1885. On 5 April 1887 Birmingham Town Council passed the resolution

> That this Council deems it to be of the utmost importance to the trade and commerce of Birmingham and the surrounding district that improved canal communication should be opened up, which should connect this great centre of industry with the sea . . .

and a committee was set up to make investigations. There were two principal candidates: the Birmingham & Liverpool ship canal project, for a line 64¼ miles long from the Weaver at Winsford by way of the Potteries to Stafford, Wolverhampton and Birmingham; and the Birmingham & Bristol Channel Improved Navigation, to include a Worcester & Birmingham Canal enlarged to 200–250 ton capacity. A third line, to London, had less support.

The committee reported in March 1888, pointing out that, although the Severn was the greatest channel for Birmingham's imports, its exports went to London and Liverpool, and it was these routes that needed most attention. It recommended that action should be taken by public trusts to rebuild the main lines of canal – those joining the Trent, Mersey, Severn and Thames – to a uniform depth of 8–10 ft and a width of 70–100 ft, to take steamers of 600 tons. Lifts were to be substituted for locks wherever possible. It was thought that the cost of acquiring and converting the waterways concerned would be about £8–12 million each. This proposal was reflected in the recommendations of the Royal Commission some twenty years later, discussed in the next chapter. Little was done. In 1891 the North Staffordshire Railway obtained an Act to enlarge the Trent & Mersey to Stoke-on-Trent, but did not implement it, although it enlarged the canal between Anderton and Middlewich to barge standard. In the 1920s and 1940s there would be various schemes for ship or barge canals to Birmingham from the Mersey, Severn and London.

The danger from the railway monopoly had been perceived in the 1870s. One way of limiting it was to revive the waterways. A series of Select Committees from 1872 to 1883, and the Royal Commission on the Depression of Trade of 1886, all recommended that waterways should be developed and freed from the railways. The 1883 Select Committee also recommended that the Irish canals should be taken over by public trusts or local authorities. Several Acts from 1858 to 1888 protected canals against railways, encouraged canal amalgamations, gave canal companies and carriers additional powers, such as those of compulsory reduction in certain conditions of the tolls of railway-owned canals, and empowered local authorities to take over canals that their owners wished to abandon. But to legislate was easier than to take action.

Apart from the acquisition of the Worcester & Birmingham and the Droitwich lines by the Gloucester & Berkeley, two important canal amalgamations took place towards the end of the century. In 1894 the Grand Junction Canal Company, one of the most powerful, bought the Leicestershire & Northamptonshire Union and the old Grand Union canals. These purchases were followed by an agreement on through tolls with the Loughborough, Leicester and Erewash companies, under which the Grand Junction offered a guarantee of minimum tolls and was given options to purchase. The agreement aimed to obtain the coal trade of the Erewash Valley, but this was partly frustrated by the bad condition of the railway-owned Cromford Canal and the abandonment of the privately owned Nutbrook, and partly by competition from other coalfields in the Grand Junction market. As a result the Grand Junction had to pay out on its guarantees of receipts, relinquish its options to purchase and drop its proposals of 1895 to amalgamate with the Warwick Canals on the Birmingham route.

The Butterley Tunnel of the Cromford had been seriously affected by mining subsidence in 1889 and closed. It was re-opened in 1893 after £8,000 had been spent on it, but when H.R. De Salis went through he found it very low and in a bad condition, 'unsurpassed by any other I have ever seen'. In July 1900 worse subsidence closed the tunnel completely, and it never re-opened. The canal below the tunnel, which served most of the collieries and connected with the Erewash Navigation, was also reported by De Salis to be 'in very bad condition'.[4] The condition of this canal, and that of the railway-owned Nottingham Canal, also affected traffics to Nottingham.

While the law allowed an appeal to the Board of Trade to compel the railway company to reinstate the canal, as the hard-headed Grand Junction told the Royal Commission of 1906, 'It has always been considered that there would be a very great deal of risk for one independent canal to endeavour to compel a railway company to reopen its canal or to make it navigable.'[5] Their opinion was not unique.

In the north of England local interests maintained that the navigation linking Sheffield with the Aire & Calder system should be removed from railway control. The River Don Company had encouraged the building of the Stainforth & Keadby and Dearne & Dove canals, and had later absorbed them, along with the Sheffield Canal. Amalgamations with railway interests had brought the navigation into the hands of the

Manchester, Sheffield & Lincolnshire Railway (later the Great Central) in 1864, which then built a line from Mexborough past Rotherham to Sheffield. This used part of the navigation's Rotherham Cut, which was replaced by a more circuitous route via two new cuts and a section of the old river, which opened in 1868.

In 1888, as a result of strong local initiative, a new company, the Sheffield & South Yorkshire Navigation, was formed to purchase the former navigation from the railway, and to modernize and enlarge the main line. After years of negotiation, agreement was reached in 1894 on a price of £1,140,000, payable as £600,000 in cash and the balance in ordinary shares, to be held by the railway until bought from them at par by the Sheffield & South Yorkshire Navigation. However, the enthusiasm for waterways in the years between 1888 and the opening of the Manchester Ship Canal in 1894 had diminished, and the company could not raise the capital to acquire all of the shares. The railway therefore retained a very strong influence on the company, which in turn prevented the Aire & Calder from giving the Sheffield & South Yorkshire Navigation the financial support it might otherwise have been willing to provide.

The Aire & Calder was the most successful of the independent concerns. Its prosperity largely depended on traffic generated on its own system, that to and from the Barnsley, Calder & Hebble and Leeds & Liverpool adding palatable icing to an already satisfactory cake. It had been fortunate in being managed from the late 1770s onwards by an energetic board and served by highly competent officials and engineers, who had overseen the founding of the port of Goole and the rebuilding of the lines to Leeds and Wakefield.

Steam tugging had been introduced in 1831. By the 1850s most of the company's own craft were steam-hauled. The resultant barge trains suggested much longer and wider locks. The first of these, Pollington – 206 ft long and partially widened to 22 ft – opened in 1860, followed by all others to Castleford by 1867, and throughout the navigation by 1873. Meanwhile, in 1862, the company's engineer, William H. Bartholomew, got the board's approval for the experimental construction of his newly patented invention of compartment boats. These, later called 'pans' or 'Tom Puddings', were rectangular iron boats that could be built up into trains. Each was then fitted with spring-loaded buffers and a protruding vertical iron bar, in front of which fitted a corresponding slot at the back of the boat ahead. By putting a steam tug at the back, running cables through fairleads on each boat to a false bow at the head of the train and working the cables by windlasses it was possible to bend the train to pass round curves in the waterway. At Goole these coal-carrying compartment boats were then separated, raised in a hydraulic hoist and tipped into ships' holds.

Over the years Bartholomew modified his invention: he dropped push-towing from behind, together with his elaborate steering system, in favour of a tug in front pulling a long train of boats that adjusted themselves to curves. The boats' design was also simplified. The system was a tremendous success. By 1897 0.5 million tons a year were being carried in four hundred boats, and 1.5 million tons in 1913 in some thousand pans, which operated, of course, alongside conventional barges and steam tugs. From the 1880s onwards locks began to be further enlarged, and in 1896 the company began to build the New Junction Canal, 5½ miles long with one lock, to join the Sheffield & South Yorkshire to the Aire & Calder, mainly to introduce to the Don line compartment boat trains working to the Goole hoists. Finally from 1884 onwards the company took control of the River Ouse from Goole downwards to its junction with the Trent at Trent Falls, and enlarged it so that bigger ships could reach Goole, where the port facilities had been greatly enlarged and extended in the previous half century.

The effect on revenue of operating a large modern waterway with big barges or long barge trains, compared with narrow-boat canals, whether highly industrialized and short-haul like the BCN, or long-haul on a good sized waterway like the Grand Junction, can be seen from the following figures of revenue earned and tonnage carried in 1905:

Company	*Tonnage*	*Revenue*
Birmingham	7,546,453	£190,873
Grand Junction	1,794,233	£101,926
Aire & Calder	2,810,988	£317,468

In the last thirty years of the century, therefore, there were prosperous concerns such as the Aire & Calder and the Weaver, viable but less secure companies like the Grand Junction, and one or two efficient railway-owned canals like the Trent & Mersey and the Shropshire Union main line. There were also many canals in difficulties. Some became entangled in railway companies; others just died. Perhaps the story of the later years of the Thames & Severn will epitomize the first process, and that of its neighbour, the Wilts & Berks, the second.

As long ago as 1836 the Thames & Severn put forward a Bill to turn itself into a railway, when the broad gauge Cheltenham & Great Western Union Railway was promoted to run from Swindon to Stroud, Gloucester and Cheltenham, with a branch to Cirencester, along a route paralleling the canal between Cirencester and Stroud. The advantages of the canal's existing line and its possession of a ready-cut tunnel led the canal company not only to oppose the railway Bill, but to promote its own. The canal company also supported a rival scheme for a standard gauge railway from Tring through Aylesbury, Oxford and Burford to Cheltenham, as the latter would not have affected its own traffic. However, the Swindon line was authorized and the other two Bills lost. By the time the Swindon line was completed, in 1845, it had been absorbed by the Great Western. This line seriously affected the canal's revenues.

By the early 1860s the canal company was in a bad way: its last dividend was paid in 1864. There were at the time a number of railway proposals for new lines, and the company now planned to use the canal to link up a standard gauge network across the Cotswolds. It suggested that the Severn & Thames Railway joined the proposed Stroud branch of the Stonehouse & Nailsworth at Stroud, through the Sapperton Tunnel on a single line, then following the canal to a point beyond South Cerney, where the railway would swing away to Fairford to join the Witney branch from Oxford. The part of the canal between Stroud and Brimscombe was to be maintained, supplying water for the Stroudwater and Gloucester & Berkeley canals through pipes from Thames Head. This latter feature lost the Bill in 1866, with opposition to the transfer of Thames water to the Severn Valley, though other factors in railway politics also had an influence.

Richard Potter, a director of the Great Western Railway for several years, resigned as chairman in 1865 to pursue other interests. In 1876 he began to buy shares in the Thames & Severn Canal, apparently seeking to convert it to a railway to compete with his old company. Eventually he controlled over 2,000 of the 2,450 shares issued. In 1882 he and the canal company promoted a Bill for a railway to join a proposed Swindon–Cheltenham line at Siddington, near Cirencester, and to run to Stroud, to connect there with the Stroud branch of the Midland. As the Severn Bridge had opened in 1879, Welsh trade would have a direct link with the places served by the new line and its connections. This time the whole of the canal was to be closed.

On the initiative of a section of the Board of the Gloucester & Berkeley Canal, a number of navigations opposed the Bill and approached the Board of Trade. Potter failed to persuade the navigations that the Thames & Severn and its connection to the Wilts & Berks could never compete successfully with the railway, and the Bill was withdrawn. The Great Western Railway, nervous lest the rival railway scheme might re-emerge later, sought to ensure that the Thames & Severn remained a canal by buying control from Potter at a comfortable profit to him, and adding shares held by others. The company acquired 2,205 shares through nominees in order to avoid contravening the Regulation of Railways Act of 1873.

The railway had not bought the canal to work it but to make sure that it was not converted into a rival railway, and would instead remain a canal until it could safely be abandoned. The associated navigations had been discussing rather vague proposals for leasing the canal and now offered to do so for 21 years, but the railway asked a prohibitive price and instead allowed the canal to deteriorate. On local initiative a Board of Trade inspection took place in 1886, recommending the canal's transfer to owners more committed to keeping the canal in good repair, for 'the harmonious working and development of the Canal system . . . cannot be effectually carried out if this duty is neglected and the interests of the public will suffer so long as it is neglected'.[6]

Nothing happened until a memorial was presented to local MPs in 1893, signed by 152 traders, boat owners and others, which brought from the Great Western Railway notice to close 26 miles of the canal, leaving only 4 miles open. Thereupon the local authorities took action. The Gloucestershire County Council and the Cirencester and Stroud Boards of Health headed a deputation of members of Chambers of Commerce, navigation concerns and others to the Board of Trade. This reiterated the willingness of the associated navigations to take over the canal, and in 1895 an Act set up a Trust for the canal, giving the associated navigations and local authorities powers to improve and manage it, but not to turn it into a railway. The Act allowed £15,000 to be raised to carry out repairs estimated at £10,000 and to pay off debentures. While this, together with a further £4,000, was to be spent (as well as £20,000 by the Thames Conservancy to improve the river between Lechlade and Oxford), it was not enough to restore the canal. In 1900 the canal was transferred to Gloucestershire County Council, after five years under the Trust during which it had only been open throughout its length for three months.

The chief hindrance was the chronic leakage on the summit level, so the council spent some £20,000 in completely clearing out and repuddling about 2½ miles. The waterway re-opened in 1904, but traffic never recovered and it was finally closed in 1927, except for 6½ miles between Stroud and Chalford, which were transferred to the management of the Stroudwater company and finally closed in 1933.

The Wilts & Berks was an independent canal. As we saw in Chapter Four its earlier years were not without excitement and, until the Great Western came along the Vale of White Horse, it brought coal and took away produce from the area between its junctions at Semington and Abingdon. The coming of the railway ruined the concern, which struggled on until 1876, by which time the annual tolls had fallen from some £15,000 to £1,158. After the Great Western decided not to buy the canal the original company sold out to a new group, reducing the capital from £321,613 to £30,000. The new company in turn leased the waterway in 1882 for 21 years to a group of Bristol merchants, who thought that they could make the canal pay. Having lost some £16,000, after six years they paid a premium of £1,000 to break the lease. The previous company then worked the canal until 1891, when, with the tolls down to £671, a fresh company was formed. This spent about £7,000 in dredging and other improvements, and put on a fleet of twelve fly-boats, which ran regularly to Bristol.

Once again no money could be made from the canal, and in 1897 the company applied for a warrant of abandonment. Neighbouring waterways and landowners (who needed the water for their farms) opposed the closure, which broke down on a legal point. The company survived but traffic did not, and it ceased entirely by 1906. Swindon Corporation found their local canal such a nuisance that they applied for, and obtained in 1914, an Act for closure, taking over Coate Water, the canal reservoir, for local purposes. Shortly after, road bridges in Swindon were removed, parts there were filled in and the line was sold to local landowners.

It is very noticeable during this period that the best progress was made by the river navigations, though more could have been done had the non-tidal portion of each river been under the control of a single authority. Some rivers, like the Severn, for a long time had no authorities, while others had several: in the case of the Witham, at one time seventeen. Increases in capacity could be obtained more easily and at less cost on rivers, even if partly canalized, than on pure canals. However, the smaller river navigations still suffered from the old trouble of the rights of millers to draw off or withhold water and to charge tolls, but the improvement of large rivers was general. The Severn and the Weaver will serve as examples.

The Severn Commission, representing interested local authorities and neighbouring navigations, was set up in 1842 to improve the waterway from Gloucester to Stourport, the rest of the river being left without a controlling authority. Its work was, however, hampered by the existence of two parties on it, one representing the interests of Gloucester and the other those of Worcester. The former wanted no other improvement than dredging to be carried out below Worcester, in order to keep tolls low; the latter, supported by the Staffs & Worcs Company, wanted locks to be built in order to increase traffic above Worcester, both on the river and on the canals. Work proceeded under the enabling Act, the bonds of the commission up to £180,000 having been guaranteed by the canal company. Four locks were built between Diglis (near Worcester) and Stourport, while below Diglis the river was dredged to a depth of 6 ft, thereby meeting Gloucester's wish that the channel should not be obstructed. It was found impossible to maintain the dredged depth and, after much opposition, a proposal for a lock and weir at Tewkesbury was sanctioned, and completed in 1858.

When the Severn Commission's engineer, Leader Williams, wrote in 1864 a pamphlet on the state of the river, he advocated major improvements to bring a foreign as well as a coasting trade to Worcester, and Gloucester interests so far withdrew their opposition as to support a plan for obtaining a firm 6 ft to Worcester by a lock on each branch of the river at Gloucester. Clegram, the engineer to the Gloucester & Berkeley, pointed out that the shallow state of the river prevented the full use of steam tugs and caused expense through the lightening of deep-draughted vessels, remarking that it 'greatly interrupts that regularity of traffic which is essential to keep the water communication between Gloucester and the interior of the country in fair competition with the railway system'.[7]

The waterway interests had seen where the danger lay. When in 1868 the commission announced its intention to apply for an Act, the Gloucester & Berkeley agreed to guarantee £750 a year to the commission, and the Staffs & Worcs helped also. The Act provided for complete canalization through the construction of two locks and weirs at Gloucester.

When the Oxford, Worcester and Wolverhampton Railway obtained its Act in 1845 for a railway that largely paralleled the river and the Staffs & Worcs Canal from Worcester to Wolverhampton, the Severn Commission represented that £180,000 had been spent on the river and that the estimated annual yield from tolls was £14,000. The railway therefore undertook to make up the tolls to this amount should they fall short of it. However, further bond guarantees for improvements to the river with the encouragement of the Staffs & Worcs put the railway guarantee into abeyance. It was renewed in 1868 by an agreement between the Staffs & Worcs and the Great Western Railway, which had absorbed the Oxford Worcester & Wolverhampton Railway, and was, as we have seen, eventually commuted in 1890 for cash payments and mortgage cancellations totalling £129,000, much of which was used to repay part of the debt owed by the commission to the Staffs & Worcs Company.

In 1888 the river had a minimum depth of 6 ft, with 9 ft in most parts. Tugs towing ten or twelve boats navigated it and in that year carried 323,000 tons. While in 1890 further improvements were made to the river, including the enlargement of the lock at Gloucester, which connected the river with the ship canal basin, and the condition of the

The Anderton Lift, photographed from the Weaver below. This was still in regular use when this photograph was taken; the lift continued in commercial use until 1968
(British Waterways)

navigation remained adequate, the tonnage carried declined to 120,000 tons in 1927, in spite of great efforts by the Severn Commission and the Severn & Canal Carrying Company to obtain traffic.

The River Weaver depended for its traffic on an export trade in salt and an import trade in coal, raw materials and china clay, much transhipped at Anderton for the Potteries. From the late 1840s to the 1870s the eleven locks were reduced to nine. Most were also doubled, new 100 ft by 22 ft by 10 ft locks being built alongside the old 88 ft by 18 ft by 7 ft 6 in ones. An additional dock and Mersey entrance lock were also built at Weston Point, and opened in 1856. The result was to increase both tonnage and revenue by 50 per cent between the 1840s and the 1870s.

Then Edward Leader Williams, son of Leader Williams of the Severn Commission, was appointed engineer. Further dock extensions began, a steam tugging service for Weaver traffic was inaugurated on the Mersey and the Anderton vertical boat lift opened in 1875, thus providing a direct connection between the docks, the Weaver and the Trent & Mersey

Canal to the Potteries. This structure, the prototype of many lifts on the Continent, raised boats 50 ft 4 in, each caisson being 75 ft by 15 ft 6 in by 5 ft, and able to take two narrow boats or one barge. In 1903 electricity replaced steam power at the lift, and in 1908, when the hydraulic rams and cylinders were worn out, the lift was provided with a new framework that enabled each caisson to be separately worked using counterbalance weights.

In the early 1870s, following recommendations Leader Williams had made in 1865, the Weaver trustees began to build new locks of 220 ft by 42 ft 6 in by 15 ft, able to take craft carrying 1,000 tons and, except for the Manchester Ship Canal, the biggest inland waterway locks so far built in Britain. Four of these were constructed in parallel with the larger of the earlier pairs, to replace all existing locks down to the old entrance at Frodsham, and the new one at Sutton, where a new duplicate lock was also built. The gates of these new locks were power-operated by two Pelton wheels to each gate. The programme was completed by 1885, the year a further dock was opened at Weston Point. By the 1880s the income of the Weaver Navigation had reached £60,000 a year, and £10,000 or more was being handed over to the relief of the Cheshire rates by the 105 trustees. The principal traffic was salt, carriage of which had grown from 14,524 tons in 1732 to 1,250,543 tons in 1880–1, when another 500,000 tons were being sent by rail. Thereafter the salt traffic tended to move to pipeline and rail. Coal carrying fell also, but thanks to modernization these losses were replaced by a rapid growth of traffic for the chemical works that had been built near the Weaver from the 1870s.

The last half of the century saw a number of major engineering improvements on waterways. In 1850 the Blackhill inclined plane had been completed on the Monkland Canal. With a rise of 96 ft its twin caissons carried 70 ft by 13 ft 4 in barges longitudinally down its 1 in 10 slope. Steam engines provided the power. Blackhill plane did not replace the duplicate flights of four staircase pairs of locks beside it, but supplemented it – loaded boats coming down the locks, empties passing up the plane.

Next came Foxton inclined plane on the Leicester line of the Grand Junction, after the Grand Junction Canal Company had taken over the two canals between Norton Junction and Leicester. The Foxton incline replaced the ten locks of the Foxton flight. Opened in 1900 and steam-powered, it had a rise of 75 ft, each of its caissons taking two narrow boats or one barge. Unlike Blackhill, which had closed in about 1887, Foxton's caissons carried boats sideways down the slope. The hoped for trade did not materialize, however, and the incline was abandoned in 1910 and the old locks reinstated. Some waterways themselves were also improved. For

A contemporary drawing of the Foxton Inclined Plane

instance the Bridgewater Canal was walled and a depth of 7 ft obtained on the towing side, road bridges were rebuilt to give greater canal width, and additional water supplies were found. Traffic was by then normally worked by a tug towing four boats with a total cargo of 200–240 tons. A more modest but valuable improvement was the opening out of the two lengths of the Fenny Compton Tunnel, totalling 778 yd, on the Oxford Canal in 1868 and 1870, and their replacement by a cutting – the longest such tunnel to be opened out.

Though steam-driven craft had been used experimentally on canals from early days, and soon came into use as tugs in tunnels and on the bigger waterways, they did not seriously threaten horse-drawn boats on the narrow canals until about the 1870s. These 'steamers' were similar in design to diesel-engined craft, with an engine room separate from the living accommodation and an overhanging counter to protect the propellor. The earlier craft were adapted from horse-drawn boats by adding a separate counter. Later they were specially built.

Coke-fired boilers were designed to take up the least space: they were 6 ft long by 4 ft in diameter, and worked at a pressure of 140 1b to the square inch. The boats had tall brass funnels, hinged so that they could be lowered under bridges if necessary, and a brass steam whistle. The engines usually had one high-pressure and one low-pressure cylinder in tandem vertically, operating on a single crank, and were fitted with Stephenson link motion for reversing.

Two main disadvantages of 'steamers' compared with semi-diesel-engined craft were the greater space needed for the engine, boiler and coke supplies, and the heavy crew. There were usually two men on the 'steamer' and two on the butty, or, if the boats were working 'fly' round the clock, four on the steamer and three on the butty, of whom three were off duty at any one time. The whole crew was employed by the captain. Later a family sometimes took over the butty, but not the steamer.

In about 1910 the biggest canal carriers, Fellows, Morton & Clayton, began to fit single-cylinder two-stroke semi-diesel units to their boats, and other carriers followed. The last 'steamer' was to leave the Grand Junction in 1932, but on the northern canals occasional steam-driven craft, usually maintenance boats, lasted much longer. From the early 1930s two-cylinder four-cycle diesels began to be fitted, which did not need the pre-heating of the older type.

One great operational reform in the late Victorian period was the reclassification of the freights carried on waterways and the fixing of new tolls for each waterway. An inquiry on rates resulted in the Railway & Canal Traffic Act of 1888, which laid down that each waterway company had to submit a revised classification of traffic and schedule of rates to the new Railway and Canal Commission, which succeeded the Railway Commission set up by the 1873 Act. Much work was done by the commission, and in 1894 a series of Acts gave the new classifications and charges (generally lower than before) the force of law. This Act was damaging to some of the smaller canals, and to the Leeds & Liverpool, since it reduced their already small revenue, collected perhaps from a single article over which they had a local monopoly.

In about 1887 Henry Rodolph de Salis, a director of the carriers Fellows, Morton & Clayton, and a seeker after greater efficiency, began an examination of the waterway system of England and Wales, travelling 14,000 miles in eleven years. His survey was published in 1904 as *Bradshaw's Canals and Navigable Rivers of England and Wales*, a handbook intended to inform commercial users of the possibilities of water transport. The third and last edition appeared in 1928.

Finally, what of the human side of canals during, and after, the long time of decline? Since the first edition of *British Canals* historians, notably Harry Hanson, have devoted much interest to this question, and some impressions must suffice here.

Earnings had fallen in terms of real wages as the prosperity of the industry declined, and in Britain (but not Ireland) this tended to bring

THE PADDINGTON

CANAL BOATMAN'S

Magazine.

No. 1.] APRIL, 1829. [Vol. 1.

INTRODUCTORY ADDRESS.

In commencing a new Periodical, it is usual to state the necessity that exists for such a work, and also the end likely to be promoted by such a publication.

The necessity of the work is simply this: There is no publication, at present, for the specific purpose of placing before the Christian public an account of the means employed to promote Christianity among those useful labouring men, who are employed on the Canal and on the various Wharfs at the Paddington Basin. Nor is there any publication which records the proceedings of that Society, whose members are so interested in the welfare of this class of men;—and those friends who have contributed to its support, know not whether the efforts used are successful or not. To supply this information, and to establish a publi-

B

The churches were interested in canal people from before the Victorian era. This is the title page of a church-backed magazine, which ran until December 1832

more families onto the boats. The canal people – the men and women who lived on the boats – brought up children, aged, died and were ignored by legislators, reformers, novelists and clerks of canal companies alike. Because they moved about they did not fall within the jurisdiction of any local authority; the Factory Acts did not apply to them, and Acts prohibiting the employment of women and young children, or Sunday work, had no application to the canals. No Engels studied them as he studied the condition of the working classes in Manchester in 1844; no Royal Commission investigated hours or conditions; no Charles Kingsley took canal people for his theme.

Now and then a glimpse of their lives appears: of the part played by canals in spreading cholera, for instance, as at Braunston in 1835, 'it appearing that the disease first attacked a woman who had been employed in washing the bedding of a boatman who had died of it';[8] of poachers, when a Cromford Canal by-law prohibited any boat from stopping at night in Crich Chase, or in any wood or coppice; of drunken boatmen, when the lock-keepers on the Staffs & Worcs were told to report them to the committee; of sober boatmen on the same canal, at a temperance meeting at Penkridge in 1891, when some took the pledge.

In the mid-Victorian period the churches acted when no one else cared. Little schools were opened, Boatmen's Institutes were started, religious services for boatpeople were held, and the vicars of Paddington and Acton, Cheshire, married boat couples, many of whom had dispensed with the ceremony until late in life.

It was a Nonconformist, George Smith, who first took an interest in boat people. He had earlier pursued the cause of children working in brickyards, securing through persistence and publicity an Act to regulate their employment, losing his well-paid job as manager of a large brickyard in doing so, and from then on being boycotted by employers all of his life.

Since he lived near a canal he then turned his attention to the plight of the canal people, especially children. His two books, *Our Canal Population* (1875) and *Canal Adventures by Moonlight* (1881), provide lurid accounts of the state of the floating population when canals were crowded. They do not paint a pleasant picture to any lover of what is imagined to be the 'good old days'.

While later research has pinpointed many inaccuracies in Smith's books, some truth underlies their portrayal of a population that was mostly irreligious and illiterate, with children worked hard for seven days a week. There was no statutory limit on the number of people who could occupy a boat cabin, and no powers for any public body to inspect boats for health reasons. The Canal Boats Act of 1877, much influenced by his campaign, provided for the registration of boats and certificates, which limited the number of adults and children who could live aboard. While this system would provide later researchers with invaluable data for boat genealogy, it proved to have little impact on the problem. It was permissive only and was rarely enforced, and much less comprehensive than what Smith wanted – in his opinion children should not live on the boats at all.

Finding that the Act was of no practical help, Smith began the struggle again, helped by another Nonconformist, the Reverend Guy Mark Pearse, the author of a tract in 1878 entitled *Rob Rat: a Study of Barge Life*. In 1884 another Canal Boats Act provided for the central supervision of local authorities, instructing the latter to make sure that children attended school. This did much to improve the sanitary conditions of canal boats and to reduce overcrowding, although the difficulties of enforcing school attendance only disappeared with the boat people themselves. George Smith later focused his efforts on the gypsies, but this time unsuccessfully. He died in 1895.

In 1921 a Ministry of Health committee reported on the practice of living-in on canal boats, finding that there were less than a thousand children of school age, of whom 85 per cent were almost illiterate. While the committee recommended that such children should be prohibited from living on boats during term time, no such provision was included in the Education Act of 1921, and many children did not receive regular education.

A somewhat fanciful portrait of an oppressed canal child, from the tract Rob Rat; *note the bearded sailor ogre-figure on the boat!*

This view, showing the work of the London City Mission at Brentford early in the twentieth century, indicates conditions much more clearly. Despite the attentions of Father Christmas, the well-scrubbed angelic child, and the Lady Bountiful figure, the children on board Foxton *do not look impressed.* (K.C. Ward/Boat Museum)

The life of boat crews and canal workers, whether involved in carrying or maintenance, was a hard and often dangerous one. One of the last narrow-boat carriers later asserted that boat people 'worked eighteenth century hours, for nineteenth century wages, until three-quarters of the way through the twentieth century'.[9] Long hours, poor pay and harsh working conditions were indeed to drive many from the waterways in the twentieth century.

Some examples from the 1930s, when conditions had improved, indicate how hard working life on canals must have been in the Victorian period. James Unsworth, born in 1906, recalled moving from regular work on the Leeds & Liverpool to more casual work:

> . . . I went working with . . . Dick Abraham. Dick owned his own barge, the *Mary*, and carried anything - coal, wheat, or muck. If there was nothing else, we could always get refuse from Liverpool Corporation, but the last load finished us off, 3½ tons of dead cats followed by a load from Hartley's jam works on a hot summer's day. I don't know which was worse the smell, the flies or the wasps. When we got to the dump we shouted for the unloaders, and beat it as fast as we could to the nearest pub.[10]

Charlie Morris from Chester, who worked during the 1930s on barges on the canals around the Mersey, recalled recently that in his youth

> an owner thought more of his horses' welfare than the men and women who worked his craft. The horses must be in the stable for 7 pm bedded down, watered and fed, but the boaties could go hungry, and many times they did . . . All the boaties I knew had a dog, a good safeguard against hunger, many a rabbit or pheasant went into the pot that way, and I went to the cook on many a ship looking for food.[11]

This deprivation was none the less the product of very long working hours, which applied also to bankside workers. Ireland's leading canal historian, Ruth Delany, described conditions on the Grand and Barrow:

> The position of lockkeeper in particular stayed with the same family through several generations. The house and garden were the attraction because the wages were very poor; the Barrow lockkeepers were still getting as little as 11s. per week in 1930 and the others not much more. The hours were very long, as boats had to be locked through at all hours of the day and night. On one occasion, Thomas Murphy, lockkeeper at Lowtown, was asked by the chairman of the company

James Street Harbour on the Grand Canal, around 1949, with a Grand Canal Company boat loaded with barrels of Guinness porter. There appear to be four boatmen on board; a very long and hard voyage lay ahead for them (Guinness Museum)

> how long he had worked in the service of the company and he received the reply, 'A hundred years, fifty by day and fifty by night.'
>
> The boatmen were also drawn from the same families . . . It was a hard life and poorly paid. The four men lived in the tiny cabin in the bow, conditions were very primitive and they often shared their meagre meal from a communal enamel basin. Until 1946 they were expected to travel night and day, with twenty-four hours a week off on Sundays . . . In 1946, in an early example of a productivity deal, the men agreed to man the boats with only three men and work a sixteen hour day. This gave them more opportunity to get home because they could stop over and make up the time by travelling through the night.[12]

While the waterways themselves would require modernization in the twentieth century, so would the conditions of those who worked on them. The next century would bring only limited progress in both track and craft modernization and working conditions.

CHAPTER TWELVE

From Royal Commission to Nationalization

The opening of the Manchester Ship Canal increased public interest in waterways, while a greater knowledge of the achievements of overseas waterways was provided by such books as J.S. Jeans' *Waterways and Water Transport in Different Countries* (1890), and the second rewritten edition of L.F. Vernon-Harcourt's two-volume engineering work, *Rivers and Canals* (1896). The development of waterways was viewed as one means of reducing railway rates, especially on the raw materials on which British industry increasingly relied, and in 1900 the Associated Chambers of Commerce asked the government to appoint a Royal Commission to consider the whole question of the waterways. The same body fostered a series of waterways Bills between 1901 and 1906. While none proceeded, the memorandum attached to the 1906 Bill conveys their general object:

> To constitute a strong Central Canals Board for the purpose of obtaining provisional orders authorising the board to take over, improve and manage, in the first instance, certain canals which form a chain of navigation between the principal ports in England. . . . The object of the Bill is, by such a consolidation of interests and management, to improve the facilities for water carriage and to establish a complete system of intercommunication.[1]

This pressure led eventually to the appointment of the Royal Commission of 1906, which presented its Report in twelve volumes in 1911. This Report remains the most comprehensive study of the waterway system of the British Isles. The commissioners also studied carefully the waterways of continental Europe, attempting to balance the undoubted progress there against the very different commercial and economic conditions in the British Isles.

They summed up the position, as they saw it, as follows:

> On a few waterways or sections of waterways, favoured by special conditions, combined in two or three cases with enterprising management, traffic has been maintained and even increased. On other waterways it has declined, on some it has virtually disappeared. Everywhere the proportion of long-distance traffic to local traffic by water has become small. Considered as a whole, the waterways have had no share in the enormous increase in internal transport business which has taken place between the middle of the nineteenth century and the present time. Their position, so far as regards their total traffic, has been at best one of a stationary character, since the development of steam traction on railroads and on the sea, while the whole transport business of the country, including that taken by railways and that taken by coasting vessels, has multiplied itself several times over.[2]

The commission recommended that the trunk waterway routes of lowland England, known as the Cross, which connected the Thames, Severn, Humber and Mersey to a centre at Birmingham, should be widened and deepened. It was thought that the reconstruction of these lines to take larger barges, with the elimination of many of the locks, would result in large savings in time and thus in labour costs.

It was considered impossible to widen the Birmingham area canals, and this system was regarded as a collecting ground for the enlarged waterways. It was suggested that after the Cross waterways had been dealt with, one of the trans-Pennine canals should also be enlarged.

The enlargement proposals would have meant the complete reconstruction of the trunk waterways to enable them to handle a great deal more traffic in an efficient way. For instance, consulting engineers for the route from Birmingham to Sharpness suggested that 7 inclines and 6 locks should replace 62 existing locks.

The cost of improving 533¾ miles of main waterways was estimated at £15,238,909, with an extra £2,295,001 for 514 miles of branch canals, which would be in close communication with the Cross, that would need some improvement. These estimates did not include acquisition costs or subsidiary charges such as the provision of new warehouses. The commission placed the annual charge for the improvements at £1,098,025 compared with a revenue for the existing owners of the waterways affected of £567,971. This would suggest that the revenues would have to be doubled if there was to be an economic return on the capital invested in improvements.

The commissioners were realistic about the interest of private investors in improvements, stating that 'we are convinced . . . that private enterprise cannot be expected to take the improvement of canals in hand, because, as things stand now, there is no prospect of adequate remuneration, except perhaps in a very few cases'.[3]

They therefore recommended nationalization of the trunk waterways and their branches in England and Wales, under a Waterways Board, which was not, however, to have powers to act as carriers. This board was to assume control of the two existing State-owned canals, the Caledonian and the Crinan.

It was clear that, if the waterways were improved on the lines recommended, there would be a great saving in transport costs to certain users. For instance a reduction in the cost of carrying coal from Leicestershire to London from 6s. 8d. (33p) to 3s. 10d. (19p) a ton was envisaged. However, the work of the commission was deeply criticized in two influential books by Edwin Pratt – *British Canals* (1906) and *Canals and Traders* (1910) – who was employed by the Railway Companies Association to present, *inter alia*, the case against the work of the commission. In the latter book, Pratt practically accused the Liberal Party of organizing the Royal Commission as a means of helping them to nationalize all transport: by improving waterways at government expense, the value of railways would fall and the costs of acquiring the railways with it.

There were some powerful arguments against the commission's proposals. Only certain waterways were to be improved, and their improvement would virtually subsidize certain traders at the expense of all others on railways or unimproved waterways. The proposal that a State-owned system of waterways would compete with a privately owned system of railways was in contrast to the practice in continental Europe, where both railways and waterways were State owned or State assisted, and where the transport system was planned as a whole.

In the event the attention of the Liberal Government was diverted away from the problems of transport towards the problems posed by Irish home rule and the long struggle with the House of Lords, up to the outbreak of the First World War. An early pressure group, the Waterways Association, was formed in 1912 to press for waterways improvement under State ownership, but this made little progress, despite the support of many Midlands local authorities and MPs.

As regards Ireland, the commission's report was less radical. It noted the problems of drainage on the Shannon and from Lough Neagh, and recommended State control of both navigation and drainage by a single water authority. While it considered proposals to enlarge the line between Limerick and Belfast to a single gauge, it confined full approval to the enlargement of the locks on the Shannon between Limerick and

Killaloe, along with a replacement for the Newry Ship Canal. After the struggle for Irish independence the Canals and Waterways Commission, appointed by the Irish Free State in 1922, also recommended public ownership, and enlargement of the lower Shannon.

An opportunity to rebuild the latter section came with the building of hydroelectric works at Ardnacrusha between 1925 and 1930. The old locks were now eliminated, the navigation channel remaining in the river to Parteen, where a new navigation cut led to the power station and a staircase pair of locks, one 60 ft and one 40 ft deep. While these have by far the largest fall of any locks in the British Isles, they were built 105 ft by 19 ft 6 in, still narrower, curiously, than those above Killaloe.

On the outbreak of war the railway-owned canals were immediately put under State control through the Railway Executive Committee, along with the railways themselves. Nothing was done to control the independent waterways, however, and their tonnage fell as their men left to join the Forces. It was not until March 1917 that most of them were brought under a Canal Control Committee of the Board of Trade. While this committee tried to restore some of the lost traffic to the canals, much had gone for good. In 1913 31,585,909 tons were carried on canals in the British Isles, and in 1918 this had reduced to 21,599,850 tons.

On 31 August 1920 the canals reverted to private control, although the Ministry of Transport agreed to continue nominal government control of certain waterways for a time after 1920 in order to raise tolls to an economic level pending new legislation. The removal of control placed a number of navigations into crisis: the war had disrupted trade, maintenance had been neglected during the period of control, and the prices of materials and labour were rising without any corresponding increase in revenues. The main railway-owned canal-carrying concern, the Shropshire Union, ceased to carry in 1921 as losses were too great, owing to the eight-hour day, higher wages and higher costs of materials. Before the war this concern had operated 670 craft of various kinds. Other canal companies with carrying departments, like the Rochdale and Leeds & Liverpool, soon followed.

Bye-traders could not offer the same integrated services as their predecessors and tonnages carried dropped. In the case of the Rochdale Canal, for instance, which had carried 554,597 tons in 1905, tonnages declined as follows:

1922	180,269
1927	100,092
1932	38,638
1937	19,187

Much of this was local coal traffic in Manchester: mill closures and road competition meant that there was almost no traffic over the summit by 1925. This company, as would others like the Stroudwater or the Neath, increasingly concerned itself with revenues from water supplies and property.

The postwar inflation made it unlikely that the recommendations of the Royal Commission would ever be carried out, and, to review the post-war position, the government appointed a committee chaired by Neville Chamberlain MP, who was leader of the Waterways Association. A first interim report in February 1921 suggested immediate action to improve the Trent, while a second, in May, recommended against nationalization on the grounds of the financial liabilities involved, as the waterways had deteriorated further since the Royal Commission report, and both prices and wages had risen.

At this time the railways were being formed into four great groups, and the committee suggested the formation of seven regional groups of waterways, including railway-owned canals, each under a public trust made up of representatives of local users, public bodies, the Ministry of Transport and the stockholders, and financed by the state and the local authorities concerned. These trusts were to have carrying powers, though not to the exclusion of bye-traders, and the railways were to be debarred from uneconomic competition with them. The groups proposed were: the canals based around the Trent and its connections; the Yorkshire canals; the Lancashire canals; the canals between Liverpool and the Midlands; the canals based on the Severn; the Thames and its connections with the Midlands and Bristol; and the canals in the Birmingham area.

It was recommended that the groups should not all be formed at once, but that an experimental start should be made with the Trent group, since Nottingham Corporation was already committed to an improvement scheme on that river.

The committee did not produce a final report, and nothing was done to follow up its recommendations. The Waterways Association decided that it was defeated, and thus disbanded, although the National Council for Inland Waterways was formed to continue the campaign for development. No action followed the Royal Commission on Transport of 1930, which also suggested that public trusts should take over the waterways of the Cross if voluntary amalgamations did not take place.

While the time between the wars was one of steady contraction, there were some developments. Three are of especial interest.

The River Trent has always been of great importance as a navigation, and the building of the Trent & Mersey Canal made it a link in a through

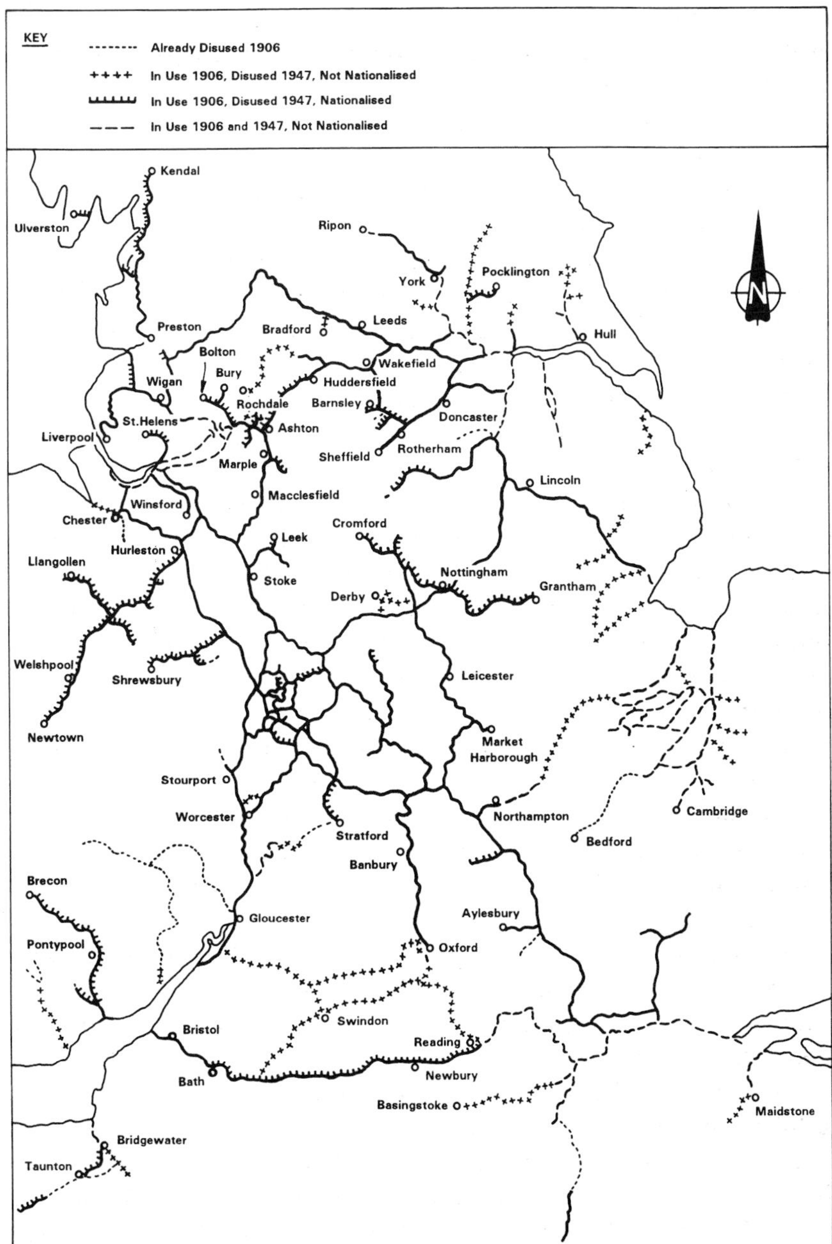

This map of the main waterways in England and Wales shows the way in which the system contracted between 1906 and 1947. Those shown in thick black lines show the most significant waterways to be nationalized

route from the Humber to the Mersey. The original Trent Navigation Company, formed in 1783, was concerned with the state of the river, especially that part below the canal entrance at Wilden Ferry, while the Newark Navigation Commissioners controlled the cut of 4 miles at Newark. Later the Humber Conservancy Board was formed to control the portion of river from Trent Falls, where the river joins the Humber, to Gainsborough, where the control of the Trent Navigation Company began.

The navigation was good from Trent Falls to Newark, but between there and Nottingham lay a shallow and fast-running part of the river, with a fall of up to 19 in to the mile. This meant that goods had to be transhipped at Newark to smaller craft, which added to the transport costs of those carried up to Nottingham. Nottingham Corporation had long been interested in improving the navigation, and it welcomed an Act obtained by the Trent Navigation Company in 1906 to dredge the river to a minimum depth of 5 ft and a width of 60 ft, and to build six new locks and cuts. The Act specified that the works were to be completed within ten years. However, financial shortages meant that, before war broke out in 1914, only one new lock and cut, at Cromwell, 188 ft by 30 ft, had been built, while the river had been dredged below Newark so that 120 ton vessels could come up to that town.

Nottingham Corporation then sought to ensure that the works would be completed before parliamentary powers expired. This resulted in an Act in 1915, obtained against opposition from the railway companies, allowing it to finance the remaining works. Nothing was done, however, as by then the war had caused money to be tight and labour scarce. Not until the war was over was the river dredged and new locks, the same size as that at Cromwell, built. These could take three Trent boats and a cargo-carrying tug at once, each 82 ft 6 in by 14 ft 6 in, and carrying between them up to 600 tons. The single-boat lock at Newark Nether was replaced by a four-boat lock, and a new channel later provided at Holme lock so that the biggest craft using the river could work through to Trent Bridge, Nottingham. Above Nottingham to Shardlow and Leicester, however, the waterway still only took Upper Trent boats of 71 ft 6 in by 14 ft 6 in.

Nottingham was now less than twenty-four hours away by river from Hull, where craft could be loaded direct from seagoing ships. The work authorized under the 1906 Act was completed in 1927, and Nottingham Corporation, which had spent about £450,000, took over the navigation. In 1932 the corporation opened a new basin at Trent Lane, forming a major new head of navigation, while a new oil terminal opened at Colwick in the early 1930s. Traffic increased from 66,960 tons in 1928 to

The oil terminal at Colwick, shown here in the early 1960s. The craft operated by John Harker of Knottingley carried petroleum from the 1930s until 1971, with a later revival (British Waterways)

230,514 tons in 1936; oil carrying rose from 7 per cent to over 50 per cent of the tonnage. In 1936 the Trent Navigation Company took a lease of the Nottingham Canal in Nottingham from the London & North Eastern Railway, and approached the same company to lease the Fossdyke to Lincoln in 1939.

A second important development was the formation of the Grand Union Canal Company and the modernization of its route. In 1894 the Grand Junction Canal Company had absorbed the Leicestershire & Northamptonshire Union and the (old) Grand Union, and so had carried its waterway to Leicester. In 1929 it joined with the Regent's Canal in London and the three canals on the Birmingham route – the Warwick & Birmingham, the Warwick & Napton, and the Birmingham & Warwick Junction – to form a new company, the Grand Union. A through route from Regent's Canal Dock (now Limehouse Basin) and Brentford in London to Birmingham was now under one ownership, with running powers over a short length of the Oxford Canal.

Three years later the amalgamated company absorbed the Leicester and

Lock widening on the Warwick section of the new Grand Union Canal in the early 1930s, with the original narrow locks still in use on the left. Note the broken balance beam on the offside bottom gate of the nearest lock. The new locks were built partly on the site of wide pounds and side ponds serving the narrow locks. Replacement side ponds are shown under construction (British Waterways)

Loughborough navigations and the Erewash Canal, extending the line past Leicester and Trent Junction to Langley Mill. The length of the new combined waterway was over 300 miles. With the help of a government guarantee of interest for a number of years about £1 million was then spent on the London to Birmingham route. As it stood, this had been built as a barge canal to Braunston, while the remainder was narrow. On the Braunston to Birmingham section 51 new broad locks were built to take two narrow boats at once. In order to work 14 ft beam barges through the canal it would, however, have been necessary to rebuild so many bridges that it was decided for the time being to maintain the 14 ft standard from London to Berkhamsted, and a 12 ft 6 in standard from there to a newly developed depot at Sampson Road, a mile from Birmingham. While the Grand Union Company intended to build boats of 12 ft 6 in beam, and prototypes were constructed, there were so many lengths where two 12 ft 6 in craft could not pass that the canal north of Berkhamsted continued to be worked by narrow boats in pairs.

Much dredging was done, and over many stretches of the canal the cross-sectional area was increased by walling and piling the sides, thus enabling the boats to travel faster. Most of this programme was completed by 1934.

Meanwhile the canal company had begun carrying by buying the small firm of Associated Canal Carriers Ltd, and in 1934 changing its name to the Grand Union Canal Carrying Co Ltd, greatly expanding its fleet. It had also acquired the Erewash Canal Carrying Company, which the Erewash owners had formed in the 1920s to carry from Leicester and Loughborough, developed shipping and property subsidiaries, and provided lorries for deliveries in the Birmingham area.

It proved to have over-expanded: there were shortages of crews and many boats were laid up. The carrying operation had to be considerably cut down and reorganized before heavy losses could be ended. These had repercussions on the canal company itself, which paid no dividend on its ordinary shares between 1933 and 1945.

The Weaver Navigation formed part of the proposed Wolverhampton–Mersey route of the Royal Commission. The rebuilt Anderton Lift passed craft more rapidly, and through traffic increased to a record 226,000 tons in 1913. Much of this traffic served the Potteries, and plans for a new canal there continued, but only got as far as a conference of Potteries local authorities in 1912.

Plans for a Birmingham Ship Canal, to the Severn or Mersey, were revived in the early 1920s, but all that emerged was a guarantee to cover losses on the Worcester & Birmingham Canal, to prevent its closure and thus safeguard the Severn route. The Weaver Navigation cleared its debts in 1934 and the Trustees promptly reduced tolls. New opening bridges, similar to those on the Manchester Ship Canal, had been built, and the last low bridge at Hartford was removed in 1938.

Until the 1930s only one seagoing vessel regularly used the river, most traffic relying on transhipment at Weston Point, Liverpool or Birkenhead. From 1938 the Weaver trustees sought to develop direct traffic to waterside industries, especially to the ICI works around Northwich, using diesel-engined coasters with a greater carrying capacity. Improvements, mainly dredging and the easing of corners, continued into the war years. The trustees then promoted a Bill to extend navigation up the Weaver valley to Audlem, and then south on an enlarged Shropshire Union Canal to Wolverhampton. This endorsed wartime government proposals for a new line for 100 ton craft, but railway opposition meant that only an extension to Nantwich was authorized.

The Manchester Ship Canal had a considerable effect on the trade of Manchester, in the growth of waterside industries in Trafford Park and near its waterside, served by its private railway. The first oil installations had opened at Mode Wheel in 1896, along with Barton Oil Berth in 1902, but the growth in oil traffic was to direct development to the lower reaches up to Runcorn. In 1922 the Ship Canal Company opened a new dock at Stanlow to accommodate imported petrol, while refining started on the opposite bank in 1924, where there was soon established a major centre for oil storage and distribution. Distribution routes included the canal to Chester and the Midlands, and up the Weaver.

Before 1907 the whole canal had been deepened from 26 ft to 28 ft in order to accommodate larger vessels, and in 1927 it was deepened further between Eastham and Stanlow by 2 ft. By the 1920s plans to complete the final Dock No. 10 at Salford had been shelved.

Ellesmere Port was also gradually developed for Ship Canal traffic, especially after 1922, when the Shropshire Union leased its property there to the Ship Canal Company. This built on existing installations based on the Shropshire Union, in milling, ironworks and a cement works, and that benefited both waterways. In the interwar years the importance of the smaller canal diminished, with greater reliance on direct shipments to Ship Canal locations and forwarding via the Ship Canal Railway.

Most smaller waterways lost traffic in the interwar years, and a number became disused entirely. The latter included the Neath, Swansea, Tennant, Monmouthshire and Brecon canals in South Wales; the Edinburgh and Glasgow Union and Monkland canals in Scotland; and, in England, the Grand Western, the Stratford-upon-Avon, Pocklington, and most of the Dearne & Dove and Huddersfield Narrow canals. Of these, only short lengths of the Swansea Canal were formally closed, and some closures awaited future development, like the upper part of the St Helens Canal, which was closed in 1931 to facilitate new road crossings in St Helens. Others, like both Droitwich canals, and the Louth, Wisbech, Aberdare and Bradford canals, were abandoned as derelict or unnecessary.

One major contributor to this decline was the rise of the motor lorry, competition from which removed much short-haul and rural canal traffic, penetrating to waterside locations that railway sidings and railway cartage services could not have reached. Between 1919 and 1939 the number of licensed road goods vehicles in Great Britain increased almost eightfold from 62,000. Road competition also forced railway rates down, which sharpened competition with canal traffic and made their operation even less remunerative. However, that quietude – in whatever sense - had fallen on old rivalries is shown by the agreement reached in 1933 between the four railways and the Canal Association for joint traffic conferences and the elimination of price cutting and the quotation of uneconomic rates.

The Nottingham Canal at Wollaton Top Lock at the beginning of the twentieth century. Note the poor condition of the lock brickwork and the leaking top gates – indications of neglect. Even by this date traffics from this colliery and others along the line were very limited (British Waterways)

Other canal traffics were lost owing to the further working out of coal seams and quarries on canal routes, and the replacement of coal by electricity from the grid as a source of power. Tonnages therefore diminished from about 17 million tons in 1924 to about 13 million tons in 1938. The condition and use of most waterways deteriorated, and pleasure boating was then only in its infancy.

The fate of the Nottingham and Grantham canals illustrates the difficulties involved in pursuing formal closure of disused waterways. Both were owned by the Great Northern Railway Company, passing to the London and North Eastern company on Grouping. The lower part of the Nottingham Canal was part of the through Trent route and was kept in satisfactory condition. However, the upper Nottingham and the mainly rural Grantham Canal suffered from the stifling of trade owing to night and Sunday closures, water shortages exacerbated by industrial sales of water, objections to the use of steam-powered boats, a lack of ice-breaking and refusals to quote through tolls. In 1905 the Grantham Canal, which had carried 34,291 tons in 1898, carried only 18,802 tons, much of it in manure from Nottingham conveyed a short distance to local farms. By 1924 this tonnage was down to 1,583, with no traffic by 1929. The upper portion of the Nottingham Canal had lost almost all traffic by 1928, and the prospects of traffic from the decrepit Cromford Canal (see Chapter 11) were remote.

The London & North Eastern company sought to close both canals, but only obtained an Act in 1936 after agreeing to maintain water levels and measures to ensure public safety. The lower section of the Nottingham Canal was leased to the Trent Navigation Company, which purchased it in 1946. While the locks on the closed sections were converted to weirs, and bridges could be converted to low crossings, the watercourses had to remain. The railway thus regarded the closure as one that conferred little financial benefit, and the closure of further disused lines, such as the Hollinwood and Stockport branches of the Ashton Canal, was not seen as worth the effort and expense involved. As a result a number of railway-owned waterways survived into the postwar era for restoration, although this did not include the Nottingham Canal or, to date, most of the Grantham Canal. Parts of both are available as local amenities and an isolated section of the latter is under restoration.

Similar objections inhibited the formal closure of parts of the Shrewsbury and Newtown lines of the Shropshire Union Canal, when Shropshire County Council sought closure in 1935 to construct new low road crossings. While this was defeated by objections over the loss of rural water supplies, the railway company owner was able to leave unrepaired a breach at Perry Aqueduct on the Newtown line in 1936. These lines were eventually closed in 1944.

The Kennet & Avon Canal, between Bath and Newbury, was almost devoid of traffic by the interwar period, owing both to railway competition and to poor maintenance, but similarly expensive conditions for closure led the Great Western Railway to abandon closure plans in 1929. Instead it embarked on a programme of repair, albeit to low standards, and occasional pleasure boats were able to use the canal until the late 1940s. It nevertheless then became largely unnavigable, and a long campaign for its retention and restoration was fought, successfully, until the 1990s.

In the Irish Free State the recommendation of the Canals and Waterways Commission of 1923, to set up a Waterways Board, was not implemented. In the south the Grand Canal Company from 1927 onwards built up extensive road services, providing a flexibility that small consignments by canal could not achieve. Canal carrying on all waterways fell, except during the Second World War. Although it comes from the description of a pleasure journey in 1946, the following passage conveys

Unloading porter barrels at Ballinasloe, the extension of the Grand Canal across the Shannon, around 1954. This was a part of a network of stores owned by Guinness and served by the Grand Canal Company (later CIE) fleet. The Ballinasloe branch closed in 1961 and much has since been destroyed by turf workings (Guinness Museum)

the flavour of Grand Canal transport, bearing out the 1923 commission's assertion that 'primitive conditions still exist':

> We soon discovered that our 'tug' was the canal equivalent of an 'ordinary goods' train on the railway, and in consequence our day's journey proved as slow as it was eventful. Our first stop was at Philipstown Wharf to pick up some empty porter barrels . . . After performing this arduous task the crew adjourned to the bar which was conveniently situated near the canal bridge and proceeded to do their best to empty another porter barrel . . .
>
> At the next bridge . . . we stopped again, this time to deposit two sacks of sugar. There was no wharf or warehouse, in fact no sign of habitation. Apparently the sugar was destined for the shop in the little village of Road just over a mile distant. Here there was no convenient bar to detain us, and we were just congratulating ourselves on having

> got under way smartly when our 'tug' suddenly slewed across the canal and ran her bows into the bank while one of the crew jumped ashore. He had apparently arranged to call at the neighbouring cottage upon some errand or another.[4]

In the north, too, the largely rural canals gradually ceased to be used for commercial traffic: the Ulster in 1929, the Strabane in 1932 and the Newry Inland Canal, oldest of all, in 1938–9. Traffic on the Coalisland Canal held up well until road competition started to undermine it in the early 1930s. The decline in the traffic of the Lagan Navigation was such that from 1938 the government made up any financial deficits, until 1952. The Lower Bann, which featured some limited commercial and pleasure traffic, had been threatened with closure by drainage and hydroelectric schemes.

Among sparsely populated, mainly agricultural areas of England, traffic was especially badly affected by the flexibility of the motor lorry, such as in the fen districts, characterized in 1907 as

> the only district where navigation is utilized by the agriculturist . . . The roads in those districts are abominable; the soil is magnificent, soft alluvial deposit; they float barges or small craft up these drains; they load and take them off to some staith, where they can put the produce on to a railway truck or take it to their own yards.[5]

Once roads and vehicles were improved, traffic disappeared rapidly, although barges serving the beet industry and fuel deliveries to isolated pumping stations lasted until after the Second World War. The waterways continued in being for drainage purposes and, usually, for occasional pleasure use. While the fen areas today provide solitude for pleasure boaters, the Great Ouse upstream of St Ives to Bedford, largely derelict by the start of the century, was kept open for a short period from 1906 by the River Ouse Locks Committee, representing pleasure users. In three months of that year nearly two thousand boats passed through Bedford Lock. Not until after the war would a long campaign, from 1950 to 1978, secure the re-opening of the river to Bedford for pleasure cruising.

Chapter Ten mentioned some early pleasure boating on the canals, although river cruising remained much more popular. It was probably George Westall who first made cruising by canal popular when he published an account of a tour through 870 miles of waterway by motor boat in twenty-five days, which he had carried out in 1907. He later became the President of the National Inland Navigation League, which existed for a time after the First World War.

A hazard to early pleasure boating: an example of one of the Shropshire Union Canal 'swing' bridges (actually lift bridges) which gave A.E. Neal's friend William so much trouble. Most of the original bridges have been modified, but this one, on the Prees Branch and thus in lesser use, survived into the 1990s, being renewed in preserved appearance after its collapse in 1997

Other accounts followed, notably E. Temple Thurston's *The 'Flower of Gloster'*, a possibly fictional account of a tour through the Oxford, Stratford and Thames & Severn canals. P. Bonthron's popular *My Holidays on Inland Waterways*, comprising staccato descriptions of explorations of many canals, some no longer navigable, was published in 1916.

In Scotland, passenger steamers had run for many years on the Crinan and Caledonian canals, and on the Forth & Clyde the five *Queens* plied from 1893 to 1939. There were some regular trip boats on smaller canals, such as the steamers like *Compton Queen* run by Arthur Beech of Compton on the Staffordshire & Worcestershire and Shropshire Union canals, which lasted until around 1930.

Early pleasure boating was not without incident, as a detailed log of a trip just before the First World War suggests. A.E. Neal owned a succession of craft at Derby, from where he travelled to Llangollen in 1913, near where on 19 July 1913

> Poor William got his hand rather badly bashed against the wall in Chirk Tunnel while he was holding a flashlight over the side to guide

> my steering; but he soon forgot the pain caused by this in the agitation resulting from his dealings with the swing bridges. As he was a shorter man than Basil he could only just reach the uplifted bridge with the boat-hook, and being unable to give a sufficiently long and strong pull to return the bridge to the horizontal, it occasionally took command of the proceedings, and, when about a third of the way down, majestically uplifted itself again, carrying the struggling William into the air with it.[6]

These difficulties with a canal operated for transport rather than pleasure were also marked by Neal's trip to Oxford in the summer of 1914, when he succeeded in draining a pound at Claydon, which held up traffic. Technically infringing the by-laws, he was 'discharged with a caution' by the lock-keeper.

The attitudes of canal owners towards pleasure boating varied. Some, like the Birmingham Canal Navigation or the Bridgewater Department, were very reluctant to admit pleasure craft, while the London, Midland & Scottish Railway strongly discouraged boats on its Lancaster and Manchester, Bolton & Bury canals, but welcomed enquiries about the Shropshire Union and Trent & Mersey canals. The London & North Eastern Railway positively welcomed pleasure boating on its Ashton, Peak Forest and Macclesfield canals, with very reasonable charges. Pleasure use was often discouraged on the more congested waterways. As one Grand Union worker at Brentford later recalled:

> In my youth, we would do anything in our power to prevent pleasure boats, and we would make it pretty plain to them. The boatmen regarded them as a nuisance, that's all. The idea of people using the canal for pleasure didn't seem to occur to us then.[7]

Usually an exception to this was the annual outing, often on Sundays or bank holidays, when there was less traffic. On the Swansea Canal, for instance, trips at Whitsun were part of an annual celebration:

> The carnival field, usually the local farm fields such as Norton fields at Ynystawe or the tinplate works field such as the 'Bryn' tinplate works at Ynysmeudwy was the destination for the boat trips. Tents and stalls would be erected on the field and all types of sports and games would be played throughout the day . . .
>
> A canal barge would be hired from one of the local industries or the Great Western Railway Company, which had several maintenance barges on the canal . . .

> On the Friday and Saturday preceding the event the barges would be scrubbed clean and sawdust sprinkled on the floor. The barges were decorated in various ways, principally to brighten the boats up but also to protect the best clothes of the occupants . . . Seats or benches would be placed in the boat for the older passengers whilst the youngsters stood up.[8]

One canal that featured a number of early pleasure boating initiatives was the Shropshire Union. The horse-drawn passenger boats from Llangollen continued into the 1930s and even, on a very reduced basis, during the Second World War. The popularity of the longer trips to Chirk, which connected with the Glyn Valley Tramway, declined with the growth of short charabanc outings and the ending of passenger carrying on the tramway in 1932. A shorter-lived service, run by a coach proprietor, ran from Ellesmere in the 1930s. While various individuals began to hire out their own boats at this period, from about 1933 one carrier at Whitchurch began to hire out a narrow boat, complete with horse and boatmen, during slack trading periods. This was a precursor of the later camping boats. Both the Whitchurch and Ellesmere operations had ceased by 1939, despite being situated on one of the most attractive, if increasingly decrepit, canals in Britain. One firm that drew on this attraction was the Inland Cruising Association, formally founded (following some earlier private hiring) in 1935 by G.F. Wain and others at Christleton near Chester, a week's trip away from Llangollen. This became the first successful hire boat firm on a British canal, expanding rapidly to run a fleet of purpose-built craft by 1939.

Boat clubs began to be formed in the 1930s, of similar character to the many river cruising clubs like the Ripon Motor Boat Club, formed on the short Ripon Canal in 1931. The earliest, the Mersey Motor Boat Club, was founded at Litherland on the Leeds & Liverpool Canal in 1932. Both this and the West London Motor Cruising Club, founded in 1938 at Alperton on the Grand Union Canal, were on heavily trafficked, urban, broad canals, but close to major rivers. The North Cheshire Cruising Club, at High Lane on the narrow and mainly rural Macclesfield Canal, was formed in 1943 to oppose the rating of boathouses. This formalized moorings that dated back to before the First World War.

Fuel restrictions brought most pleasure boating to an effective close in 1939, some for good. This included the steamers on the Forth & Clyde Canal from Port Dundas to Craigmarloch, where the *Gipsy Queen* was withdrawn and sent to the breakers in 1940. No service would be revived after the war, although this canal stayed open for a time and saw the sea-to-sea passage of pleasure yachts. The traditional annual outings, usually in working craft, still operated, although charabanc excursions reduced their appeal. On the Swansea Canal, devoid of traffic since 1931, the last such trip, from Pontardawe to Ynysmeudwy, was made in 1939. After the war the canal was impassable.

In Britain, wartime conditions brought the main connected traffic waterways, along with all of the railway-owned waterways, under central control, an arrangement that would persist until nationalization. At first the Ministry of War Transport did not bring the independent canals under control, on the grounds of cost and the assumption that much traffic would find its way to them without assistance. The war caused a great shift in trade, away from east coast ports facing Europe towards those on the west coast, while traffic also changed in character and usual destination. The limited mileage and flexibility of the waterways compared with rail and road transport meant reduced traffic, and the canal companies began to lose revenue. Subsidies to canal carriers were introduced in June 1940, aiming to make canal transport competitive with other forms of transport, along with pegged tolls. The latter soon proved insufficient to enable the canal companies to maintain their waterways, which deteriorated in consequence.

In 1941 the government appointed Frank Pick, the head of London Transport, to investigate the use of canals in the war effort. Pick recommended that the government should assume responsibility for them, and the advisory central and regional canal committees that had been set up at the beginning of the war were strengthened. He also recommended amalgamations of ownership on certain routes and the closure of lightly used canals. One major owner, the London Midland and Scottish Railway, implemented part of these proposals, transferring part of the Huddersfield Canal to the Calder & Hebble Navigation in 1945. The London Midland and Scottish Act of 1944 involved the largest single closure of canal mileage, covering much of the Cromford, Huddersfield and Shropshire Union canals, along with shorter lengths. This was generally on similar conditions to those for the Nottingham and Grantham canals, so that watercourses had to be maintained.

Pressure on transport in Britain became such that it was clearly necessary to maintain in reasonable order those waterways that could contribute to the war effort. Therefore eighteen undertakings and a number of carriers were taken under State control in 1942. All income went to the Ministry of War Transport, which paid fixed annual sums equivalent to average revenue in the last three pre-war years, plus outgoings considered necessary for war purposes. The cost to the government up to the end of the war was £2.6 million.

While efforts were made to direct and divert as much traffic as possible to the waterways, the canals suffered from the previous poor standards of maintenance, and from the drain of skilled men and women, not only from the boats themselves, but from such ancillary industries as the boat-building and repairing yards. The different gauges of the canals made it almost impossible to transfer craft from less used parts of the system to others, such as the Mersey and Severn areas, where more traffic could have been carried by water if boats had been available.

The chief transfer carried out was that of petroleum tank barges from the Humber to the Severn. These helped to build up what later became a substantial trade in petroleum by water from Avonmouth to Gloucester, Worcester and Stourport. The Severn line had suffered from the interwar depression, railway competition, and fragmented management, and its fortunes were only revived by the growth in oil traffic after depots were established in 1927 at Stourport and Diglis, Worcester. Sharp bends and draught restrictions above Gloucester prevented fully loaded petroleum craft from passing.

The carrying of general merchandise on the Severn was also improved by wartime developments. The link provided by the narrow Worcester & Birmingham Canal was of reducing importance, and Pick advised its closure. From the early 1930s new riverside wharves had been developed at both Worcester and Stourport to serve large craft that could not get into the canal basins there, and Pick recommended that the Severn should be enlarged to take estuarial craft directly from Avonmouth and elsewhere to new waterheads at Worcester and Stourport for roadborne forwarding. In 1942 the Nelson Wharf was opened below Stourport, and in 1944 a new wharf and transit shed were opened at Diglis.

Towards the end of the war the coalition government considered the prospects for postwar redevelopment and commissioned four schemes for the waterways of the Cross. Based wherever possible on the enlargement of river navigations rather than canals, these were to use the Severn to Stourport; the Weaver to Audlem and Shropshire Union south to Wolverhampton; the Trent and Tame to Tamworth; and the Thames between London and Oxford, the Oxford Canal and the Grand Union line into Birmingham. While none of these schemes proceeded, those for the Weaver and Severn spurred further studies to enlarge and extend those navigations.

Women had long partnered men on some canal boats, sometimes being captains in their own right. As a result of the enterprise of two, later three, women who ran a boat in 1941 on the Worcester &

Birmingham Canal, a scheme was started to train women to work pairs on the Grand Union. While only a maximum of eleven pairs of boats was worked by women at the same time, it was none the less valuable. The scheme was later taken over by the Ministry of War Transport and was wound up at the end of 1945, when the last woman volunteer left. Four books, by Emma Smith, Susan Woolfitt, Eily Gayford and Margaret Cornish, describe these experiences. A smaller scheme involved women on Leeds & Liverpool Canal barges.

The tonnage carried on canals had dropped to 13 million in 1938. The wartime dislocation of trade caused a further fall to about 10 million tons by 1946, of which about half was coal. As well as the major closure in 1944 the war years saw the closure of most of the Glamorganshire and Manchester, Bolton & Bury canals. On both canals, breaches had been left unrepaired.

Public interest in waterways was raised from December 1944 with the publication of L.T.C. Rolt's *Narrow Boat*. Written in 1940–1 about a journey made on the eve of war on his converted narrow boat, *Cressy*, on which he lived, it pictured, in somewhat arcadian manner, a world of narrow-boat carrying, which was in danger of disappearing, on canals that could themselves be lost. The book's success aroused interest in canals from various perspectives, reflected in the six people who gathered in Robert Aickman's London flat in 1946. They founded the Inland Waterways Association, and the first officers included Aickman as chairman, Rolt as secretary, and Charles Hadfield and Frank Eyre, co-authors of *English Rivers and Canals* (1945). The new association began to campaign against closures, such as those of the Llangollen, Derby, Rochdale and Huddersfield canals, and for the revival of derelict waterways, such as the Suffolk Stour. Tom Rolt's book about the Irish canals, *Green and Silver* (1949), increased public interest and goodwill in the Republic and influenced the founding of the Inland Waterways Association of Ireland in January 1954.

The nationalization of most British waterways, which had been seriously debated since 1888, came about almost without controversy through the Transport Act of 1947. This was part of a much broader nationalization of transport, centred on railways and road transport; the battle over the Bill was chiefly fought over the nationalization of road transport and there were few mentions of canals in the debates. Waterway concerns represented by the Canal Association soon concentrated any opposition on the grounds of compensation, which proved fairly generous. Companies like the Stourbridge and Staffs & Worcs, owning waterways whose traffic was fast disappearing, would have faced a disastrous financial future once wartime subsidies had ended, and the main opposition to nationalization came from the Weaver Navigation, where the loss of local control was opposed.

In the south of Ireland partial nationalization came with the Transport Act of 1944, followed by the setting up of the road–rail amalgamation, Coras Iompair Eireann (the Transport Company of Ireland), in 1945. Coras Iompair Eireann took over the railway-owned Royal Canal, on which the minimal traffic would cease in 1951. Meanwhile the Board of Works had controlled the Shannon Navigation since the nineteenth century.

During the Emergency of 1939–45 the severe fuel restrictions in road transport brought increased traffic to the Grand Canal, but this declined after 1945 as road transport revived. State ownership of transport throughout the Republic was authorized in 1949, and in 1950 CIE, now a public corporation, acquired the Grand Canal Company, and so the Grand and Barrow. This was not without controversy, although the Grand company had been subsidized for some time and was losing traffic. Coras Iompair Eireann's main interest was, however, in the company's road services.

In the north the nationalization of rail transport took place through the Ulster Transport Authority from 1948, but no waterways were in railway hands and none was nationalized. However, in 1954 the Lagan Navigation Company was dissolved and its property, the Lagan, Coalisland and Ulster canals, transferred to a succession of government departments, largely in connection with their drainage functions. The Stormont government had subsidized the Lagan Company since 1938 in order to avoid a statutory transfer of responsibilities for moribund waterways back to the government. Traffic on both the Coalisland and the canal section of the Lagan had ceased by 1948, and both were closed in 1954. It would remain to be seen whether this would be the effective fate of many other publicly owned waterways in the British Isles.

CHAPTER THIRTEEN

Between Transport and Amenity

The period between the Transport Act of 1947 and the end of the 1960s involved a transformation for the smaller canals, on which amenity uses largely replaced commercial carrying, while the larger waterways retained a significant transport role.

Although most artificial canals in Britain were nationalized, many important inland waterways, including estuarial navigations and those in East Anglia, were not. The most significant exception was the Manchester Ship Canal, viewed as a port, and the Bridgewater Canal, viewed as part of that port operation rather than as part of a national transport system. From 1948, the Bridgewater Department concentrated its canal carrying services on lighterage from the docks into the Trafford and Warrington areas, the canal being deepened to the Kelloggs mill at Stretford in 1947. Other carrying services were withdrawn, although bye-traders continued to use the canal, including long distance traffics to the Midlands until the 1960s. From 1952 pleasure boating on the canal was encouraged, and several boat clubs were formed in the 1950s. This new role for one of Britain's oldest canals, concentrating solely on the development of profitable traffics, and developing revenues from pleasure boating and water sales on the rest, indicated a possible course for those now in public ownership.

Many other waterways which stayed in private hands were canals with minimal or no traffic, like the Stroudwater, Basingstoke, North Walsham & Dilham, or Rochdale, for which water and property revenues were significant. Such revenues were also important on some canals, especially those in railway ownership, taken over by the British Transport Commission (BTC) and its subsidiary Docks and Inland Waterways Executive (DIWE), of which the 'Inland Waterways' component was very much the junior partner.

The BTC attempted to integrate all transport in Britain, in place of competition between transport modes, but financial and organizational problems thwarted progress in this direction, and policies to re-introduce competition followed the change of government in 1951. Competition for freight traffic between the partly denationalized road haulage and the state-owned railways intensified after 1953, when the DIWE was abolished and substituted by a Board of Management, still under the BTC. Until 1963 the inland waterways were a very small part of a large transport organization, whose centre, the BTC, was much more sceptical about the future of waterways than those who managed them on a day to day basis. From 1963 waterways were fully separated, along with other transport sectors, removing the cross-subsidization which had shielded the loss making parts of the BTC's operations, including most waterways and carrying operations.

Many canals were irrelevant to a national transport system; as early as 1949 the DIWE asserted that 'the future of the artificial waterways is obviously considered doubtful'[1]. It then considered only the Severn, Weaver and Trent routes as worthy of major improvement, later adding the lower Lee (to Enfield), lower Grand Union and Aire & Calder and Sheffield & South Yorkshire Navigations to form a group, linked to the major estuaries, which were capable of enlargement to take larger craft.

While most of the smaller DIWE canals formed a network throughout lowland England, this primarily relied on narrow boat carrying, which Pick had dismissed in 1941 in the following terms:

> canals are heavily handicapped in competing with the roads, except where craft carrying large loads are concerned, or where narrow boats worked in pairs are possible. For all canals with locks capable of holding only one narrow boat at a locking, the prospect is bleak and unpromising, and should be faced. They are definitely uneconomical and their financial position is unsound.[2]

While some long distance traffics survived between the major navigations and the Midlands, most traffics on the smaller waterways were short distance, with especially large tonnages around the Birmingham Canal Navigations (BCN) area. The DIWE wished to retain those canals which still held traffic but doubted the wisdom of investment to develop them. Investigations revealed that while many canals had no serious traffic future, they could be retained for pleasure boating, water supply or general amenity; early candidates included the Lancaster Canal and the canal to Llangollen, but not the Kennet & Avon, for which the costs of retention for pleasure boating were considered prohibitive.

The BTC, however, refused at first to allow the DIWE to foster pleasure boating or amenity, ordering the transfer of non-trafficked waterways to other authorities such as catchment boards, river boards or local authorities, which could develop these for other purposes. In the early 1950s these orders were largely thwarted, except for parts of the Nottingham and Dudley Canals, when these authorities refused to take over the heavy responsibilities and minimal revenues involved. Meanwhile, tonnages carried on DIWE waterways increased, but by 1953 98 per cent of traffic was being generated on 1,250 miles out of a total of 2,172, and a Board of Survey was appointed to determine future policy; this reported in 1955.

Its report proposed to retain (for the time being) the Class II waterways, mainly narrow trafficked canals, but endorsed the BTC policy to transfer a total of 771 miles to other bodies. Proposals to close the Kennet & Avon and other canals followed, and protests in Parliament and elsewhere led to the appointment of an independent committee, the Bowes Committee, whose brief was to consider the future of all inland waterways in Britain.

Meanwhile, there was considerable disquiet in Parliament over two independent disused canals, where closure involved a further loss of amenity. Most of the Rochdale Canal was closed in 1952. Local authorities in Lancashire had failed to force its owners to fill in sections and to pay for the culverting of former bridges; this canal soon became a unsightly water channel but a profitable source of water sales. The closure of the Stroudwater Canal in 1954 aroused a different controversy, carefully orchestrated by the IWA. Concern was expressed at the loss of a potential cruising route solely to permit highway crossings to be reconstructed with embanked culverts. The Bowes Committee had to consider problems posed by disused canals, including those in private ownership, which had first been exposed in the 1930s over the Nottingham and Grantham canals.

The committee's Report of 1958 endorsed similar groupings to those of the Board of Survey, recommending that all the transport waterways (Classes A and B) be put into good order and maintained for at least twenty-five years. The government refused to provide this guarantee, or to subsidize the smaller Class B waterways, or to base carrying on such canals on the licensing of craft rather than toll payments. However, it did agree that the remaining waterways, along with disused private canals, should be dealt with by an independent Inland Waterways Redevelopment Advisory Committee (IWRAC), which would consider schemes for redevelopment, sometimes for pleasure boating, sometimes involving total elimination.

IWRAC, which included L.T.C. Rolt, and Lionel Munk, owner of a major hire boat firm and later leader of the IWA, began work in 1959; many of its recommendations over the next three years were accepted, and several waterways were closed up to 1962. These included sections which remained navigable, such as parts of the Chesterfield Canal and part of the Erewash. One controversial closure in 1962, of the Dudley

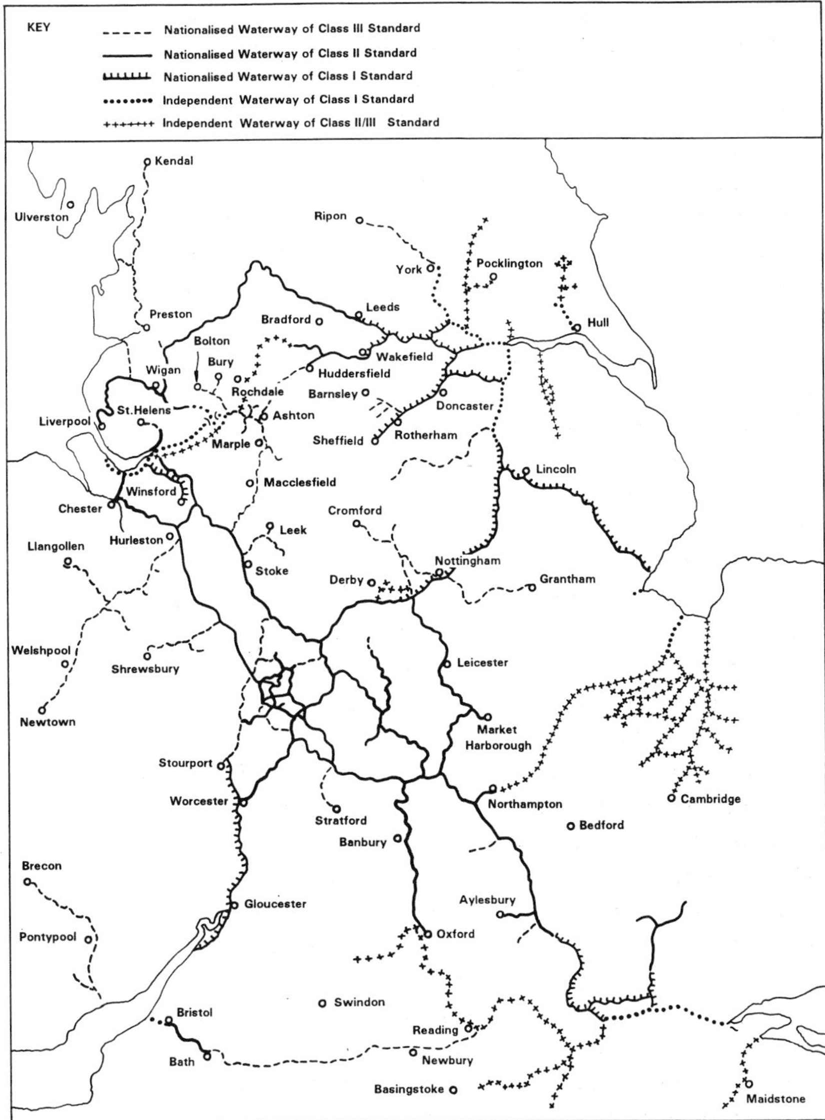

The classifications produced by the Board of Survey in 1955, with suggestions as to the status of linking independent waterways. These roughly correspond to the usefulness of such waterways for traffic purposes. The very limited mileage of Class I waterways will be noted. The Bowes Committee would follow much the same classifications except for the Avon from Bristol to Bath, which was placed in Class A

Tunnel line, soon led to the formation of a preservation society, which secured its restoration in 1973; this was probably the first formally closed navigation to be reopened.

Bowes also fostered investigations into the enlargement of the London–Birmingham and Weaver–Wolverhampton lines, but no firm proposals emerged, probably due to government investment in parallel motorways, and the difficulties of developing sufficient new traffics.

After the Board of Survey, the docks were separated from the inland waterways. Improvements to the major Group I waterways were embodied in the Development Plan of 1956, put into effect over the period to 1962. The largest expenditure involved widening, deepening and dredging to ease the passage of larger craft, while the enlargement and duplication of locks, such as those at Brentford, and on the Lee to Enfield, accounted for £1 million out of £5.5 million. New craft and improvements to handling facilities were also provided. Further developments on some of these waterways continued in the 1960s.

Public support for waterways was partly reflected in, and partly encouraged, by the growth of a waterways literature from the late 1940s onwards, much written by early IWA members. This included L.T.C. Rolt's outstanding *Green and Silver* (1949) and *The Inland Waterways of England* (1950); Robert Aickman's popular *Know Your Waterways*; Eric de Mare's superbly illustrated *The Canals of England* (1950); and Charles Hadfield's *Introducing Canals* (1955). These together fostered interest in cruising and in canal history, and began a continuous stream of waterways publications, encouraged by journals like the IWA's *Bulletin* and the BTC's *Lock and Quay* and *Waterways.*

Canal history in Britain began to be studied and written about. In 1950 Charles Hadfield published the first edition of *British Canals*, and four years later helped to found the Railway and Canal Historical Society, which had originally proposed to study railway history alone. In 1955 Hadfield's *The Canals of Southern England* appeared, the first in what became the *Canals of the British Isles* series. Since then much has been written on canal history, but little was then accurately known; it was not certain that canals like the Chard Canal had been built at all! Nationalization greatly helped students of history by bringing together the scattered archives of canal and railway companies in a single collection, British Transport Historical Records, later housed in the Public Record Office. The *Canals of the British Isles* series provided a basis for the history of many individual waterways.

The history of the IWA has been detailed at length elsewhere, but some developments can be emphasized. Beyond campaigns for individual canals, such as the abortive attempt to acquire and manage the

Basingstoke Canal in 1949, it put much pressure on successive governments to produce a national waterways policy for both carrying and pleasure boating; as Robert Aickman put it in 1950:

> our impoverished economy can no longer afford to ignore what is the cheapest form of transport for a wide range of loads; and holidays with pay for millions require that the waterways be made available for pleasure boating on a vastly increased scale.[3]

While this proved unrealistic for the commercial use of narrow canals, it was brilliantly prophetic for the amenity use of canals, which was very limited in the late 1940s; public support grew considerably into the 1960s, reflected in the changing views of Parliament and local authorities. Public interest was greatly increased by a series of national and local boat rallies, beginning with that attended by a hundred craft at Market Harborough in 1950. Shortly after this, a serious upset occurred in the IWA, partly over priorities; some original members, including Tom Rolt and Charles Hadfield, were expelled, and independent local canal societies, such as the Kennet & Avon Canal Association, formed. Under Robert Aickman, the IWA grew rapidly in size and influence into the mid-1960s, although its often confrontational approach perhaps limited its direct influence on government and other decision-makers.

Efforts to support carrying by narrow boat were partly at the expense of practical plans for new and enlarged waterways; the latter had to await the formation of the Inland Shipping Group in 1971, when many opportunities had been lost. The decline of narrow boat carrying in the 1950s removed all traffics from the Ashton, Macclesfield, the southern Trent & Mersey and the Leicester line, and left many others with minimal traffic. Campaigning to save such carrying helped to save some waterways for amenity use, but the decline in traffic proved inexorable, and once British Waterways ceased to subsidize its own carrying, traffics carried by narrow boat were insignificant.

The goodwill created by rallies and local campaigns was enlarged by the progress of restoration schemes, which began on the river navigations with the revival of Linton Lock in 1949. The first major scheme sought to rescue the Lower Warwickshire Avon, from Evesham to the Severn at Tewkesbury. This had decayed until it was almost unnavigable, as the navigation company had insufficient funds to repair it. Local people joined Midlands IWA members under Douglas Barwell's leadership, and early in 1950 they bought the navigation for £1,500, forming the Lower Avon Navigation Trust.

The navigation was re-opened throughout twelve years later, after

The last regular traffic on the Macclesfield Canal was in coal to the Goyt Mill at Marple, which ended in 1953. The remains of the unloading area were still in place forty years later, although the mill building has been divided into small business units. There have been later traffics in domestic coal on this canal

£35,000 had been raised, with volunteers assisting works which included the reconstruction of weirs, the removal of flash-locks and other obstructions, and the renewal of lock gates. Barwell had shown what volunteers, efficiently managed, and supported by professionals when necessary, could accomplish. What he taught for waterways, L.T.C. Rolt and the Talyllyn Railway Preservation Society were teaching for railways.

The earliest major canal restoration project to be completed was the southern Stratford Canal, a waterway disused since the 1930s and unnavigable after 1947. Warwickshire County Council refused to accept any transfer from the DIWE, but, seeking to lower a bridge at Wilmcote, announced its intention in 1958 to seek the canal's abandonment. In 1956 the Stratford-upon-Avon Canal Society had been formed (succeeding an earlier canal club) to press for restoration. When the county council acted, the society linked itself with the IWA and the National Trust to restore the canal, whereupon the council retreated. The National Trust was mooted as a prospective owner of several canals, including the Southern Oxford, Staffs &

Worcs, and Caldon, and, as an initial experiment it leased the southern Stratford in 1960 for five years.

David Hutchings was appointed manager, and some £20,000 was provided by the government, £7,500 and free water supplies by the BTC (and later BWB), £10,000 by the Pilgrim Trust, and the balance by the IWA and public subscription. Work began in 1961 at Kingswood, and the canal was reopened to Stratford in 1964. The restored section was 13 miles long with 36 locks; almost every lock gate had to be replaced, while many lock chamber walls had to be rebuilt, the whole length had to be dredged and many damaged banks repaired.

The progress of the Stratford restoration provided publicity and an example to be followed elsewhere. A succeeding development was the formation of the Upper Avon Navigation Trust to rebuild the long disused connecting link between the Lower Avon and Stratford Canal. David Hutchings took charge of this operation, with the through line being reopened, after many difficulties, in 1974.

Meanwhile, the freehold of the Stratford Canal, along with its management, passed to the National Trust in 1965. Unfortunately, this proved to be an unhappy venture for the National Trust, given the continuing and inevitable losses on the canal's operation. In the early 1980s it became possible that the Southern Stratford might close, till it was transferred back to BWB in 1988 with an endowment of £1.5 million towards maintenance arrears; the latter included an almost total lack of dredging since reopening.

The transfer to the National Trust of the Wey and Godalming Navigations, in 1963 and 1967, was more successful; they were in reasonable condition, and supported by accompanying property income. An Taisce, the Irish National Trust, took over the Boyne from private owners in 1980, but resources for restoration were limited, and it was passed to the Office of Public Works in 1991.

Pleasure boating had revived slowly after 1945, with shortages of fuel and suitable craft; the latter included many converted wartime pontoons and lifeboats, along with a growing number of converted narrow boats. A growing number of boatyards began to design and build purpose built canal craft, including Taylors of Chester, with *Teal* in 1954, later preserved (as *Amaryllis*) at Ellesmere Port, and the fleet for hire and private use built by Holt Abbott of Canal Pleasurecraft Ltd at Stourport from the late 1940s.

One unintended consequence of nationalization was to allow the amenity use of certain waterways to develop for the first time, and to remove the need to obtain permits from separate authorities for different waterways. By 1958 the toll system had been replaced by a general system of licensing, encouraging long distance cruising. In contrast, on the privately owned Chelmer & Blackwater Navigation, still carrying timber traffic, pleasure boats were not allowed through locks before this traffic ended in 1972.

By 1950, the Inland Cruising Association's much reduced fleet was joined by new hire firms at Stone and Market Drayton. Hotel boats began to be operated by Waterborne Tours of Penkridge in 1951, and there were sufficient hire firms to form a trade association, the Association of Pleasure Craft Operators, in 1954.

Day trip boats were also developed on a commercial basis. One early example, initiated by Waterways (Morecambe) Ltd, between Hest Bank and Carnforth on the isolated Lancaster Canal in 1948, did not prove viable. Despite bus and publicity links with the seaside resort of Morecambe, this collapsed in 1953 with heavy debts. Other trip boats, on a more modest scale, were more successful, such as that started in 1951 by John James and *Jason* along the Regent's Canal in London.

The number of cruising licences issued on BTC canals rose from 1,500 in 1950 to 10,500 in 1961. New boat clubs were formed, often formalising existing moorings. Some were founded with a campaigning role, like the Wey Cruising Club, formed in 1950, which campaigned for the Basingstoke Canal, fast falling into dereliction; or the Nantwich & Border Counties Yacht Club, formed in 1953, whose early members were prominent in the North Western Branch of the IWA. Both clubs included sailing sections which later separated from the parent club.

The administrative changes within the BTC from 1955 coincided with a more progressive leadership under Sir Reginald Kerr. While he firmly favoured the retention only of selected waterways under him, the BTC encouraged the promotion of pleasure cruising, publishing a series of cruising guide booklets from 1956 onwards, and developing a small hire fleet, based first at Chester, and later at Middlewich and Oxford. As well as these self-drive boats, the BTC inaugurated hotel boats on the Oxford Canal and the Trent, which lasted into the 1960s, and day trip boats, running regular trips or on charter, of which the best known (and longest lived) was the Zoo Waterbus, serving London Zoo, alongside the Regent's Canal, which began to operate in 1959.

Despite these beginnings, transport remained the remit of the BTC. Nationalization involved the carrying fleets of the Aire & Calder Navigation, including the coal compartment fleet, and the large narrow boat fleet of the Grand Union Canal Carrying Co. While much carrying remained in private hands, the BTC could acquire fleets by agreement, and acquired Fellows Morton & Clayton (in which it was a major shareholder) when this went into voluntary liquidation in 1948. This

Basin End at Nantwich, with the long-standing moorings of the Nantwich & Border Counties Yacht Club on the right and, in the distance, the British Waterways hire boat base, which moved here in 1968. The latter closed after the end of the 1993 season

added 176 craft, along with road vehicles, warehouses and depots, to make the DIWE fleet the largest recorded, at almost 1,500 craft; this was soon reduced by diminishing traffics. It tended to retain loss-making fleets wherever toll revenues exceeded their losses, and later acquired firms like Mersey Weaver, attempting to retain their traffics and toll revenue.

The Transport Act of 1962 abolished the BTC, and in January 1963 the new British Waterways Board (BWB), took office; members included Sir Frederick Parham, who had chaired IWRAC, and Charles Hadfield. Under the Act, the canals were to be maintained until firm policies could be decided. Despite the end of the cross-subsidization ensured by common BTC ownership, BWB sought to shift emphasis away from transport and towards amenity. It decided to cease most abandonments of canals, and sought to end the antagonism that had existed between the BTC and the IWA and canal societies, and to create instead a feeling of partnership.

BWB soon produced a report, *The Future of the Waterways*, in which it noted that

> We have taken over an undertaking which cannot as a whole be any longer regarded solely as a national transport system. As such, some of it is manifestly out of date. On the one hand, the waterways cannot be neatly and separately arranged as those usable, and those, not usable, for transport; nor in fact can they be each separately labelled as particular waterways usable for single particular purposes . . . the rational way of managing them is probably to manage them as one single, though varied, whole.[4]

It became the first public body to formulate what the IWA had long advocated, and that the Bowes Committee had acknowledged, that most waterways had amenity value and that this should be the subject of subsidy. It enlarged this case by stressing that ownership, even of unnavigable waterways, presented an irreducible deficit for which government subsidy would be required, and that a larger subsidy could secure the future of much of the system for pleasure boating. It was not then clear that all navigable canals could be kept open, but that water sales, general amenity and pleasure boating would form additional criteria for retention, and that pleasure use required a coherent network rather than individual stretches. Once any network had statutory authority and hence long-term stability, private investment in hiring, moorings and boatbuilding could take place, and their future would then be unquestioned.

The Facts about the Waterways, published in 1965, attempted to estimate the additional costs involved in retaining navigation for traffic or pleasure purposes; it proved that deficits were inevitable, and made a strong case for government support. The White Paper which followed in 1966 proposed five-yearly reviews of canal viability that would have stultified enterprise; widespread protests headed by the IWA followed, and a new White Paper led to the Transport Act of 1968.

This Act provided that a small group of Commercial waterways were to be maintained and developed for 'the commercial carriage of freight'. BWB had rapidly given up most of its own narrow boat carrying, introducing an experimental licensing system for specific carriers. It had also sought to continue the work of the Development Plan, examining the potential of the Sheffield & South Yorkshire Navigation, and enlarging the Aire & Calder to accommodate new oil and coal traffics.

The 1968 Act classified a large network, including waterways previously retained for transport purposes, as Cruiseways, which were 'to be principally available for cruising, fishing and other recreational purposes', with their operations subsidized. By now there was very little traffic on such waterways, and even less on the final group, classified as

Remainder Waterways, which were to be 'dealt with in the most economical manner possible'; this could include retention for cruising, water channelling or elimination, or disposal. An Inland Waterways Amenity Advisory Council was established to advise BWB and the minister on developments for amenity purposes, and on any changes in the classification of waterways.

This effectively provided, twenty years after nationalization, a future for most waterways for cruising purposes. The IWA had played a major part in arousing public opinion, and convincing successive governments, that this was a proper use of canals originally nationalized to develop a national transport system.

The 1960s saw the growth of a large movement of volunteers interested in practical involvement with the restoration of derelict waterways. Partly spurred by the Stratford restoration, which recruited volunteers from a distance, the voluntary movement became more organized in the 1960s. In 1966 *Navvies Notebook* (*Navvies* since 1971) was founded by Graham Palmer, initially based on the London Working Party Group, which had worked on the decaying Basingstoke Canal in the early 1960s. This informed volunteers about the growing number of schemes throughout England and Wales, and enabled major working parties to be organized to coordinate voluntary efforts on distant canals.

Restoration was spurred by a co-operative approach from BWB. This began with the Stourbridge Canal, barely navigable by 1961, with closure expected. However, obstruction from the BTC over the campaigning rally in Stourbridge in 1962 was soon replaced by cooperation between the new BWB and volunteers from the Staffordshire & Worcestershire Canal Society. The main line was restored with volunteer input alongside renewed BWB maintenance operations, and reopened in 1967.

Navvies Notebook enabled major working parties to be organized; perhaps the most celebrated example was 'Operation Ashton' in 1968. This was held at Droylesden on the Ashton Canal, which had been unnavigable since 1961–2, and several local authorities had favoured elimination. Working parties had started on the adjacent Lower Peak Forest Canal in 1965, mainly clearing undergrowth. As the greatest opponent of restoration was Droylesden Council, 'Operation Ashton' aimed to clear a 700 yd section of the canal there to show that it could be an amenity. Graham Palmer pictured activities on the first morning, on 21 September 1968:

> To stand on Crabtree Lane Bridge and look down the site was a very emotional experience. As far as could be seen were hundreds of volunteers scurrying here and there clutching large, heavy, muddy

The eastern end of 'Operation Ashton' in Droylesden was marked by the two Fairfield Locks which lead to the summit level of the Ashton Canal. The pound between the locks has been used for some years by this club for young people, showing that waterways in urban areas can be put to wider purposes than summer use by holiday-makers. Two lock chambers, one gateless, can be seen through the bridge; traffic was once so heavy that the top lock had to be duplicated

> objects, hauling on ropes, pushing wheelbarrows. Amongst them were the brightly painted dumpers and looming over the whole scene a string of old cars suspended from the jib of a red mobile crane brought along by our friends from the Caldon Canal Society. To add atmosphere were the raging orange-yellow flames from countless fires and billowing black smoke from the old car tyres found in abundance in the canal – and it still kept raining![5]

Despite the poor weather, some 2,000 tons of rubbish were removed by over 600 volunteers in one weekend. The canal was classified as a Remainder waterway in 1968, but local authority support for restoration grew, full restoration was agreed in 1971, and the canal was reopened in 1974.

The *Navvies* organization, renamed the Waterway Recovery Group in 1970, coordinated the work of growing numbers of local restoration bodies from the 1970s, going from the recently derelict waterways like the Ashton to assist the gradual revival of the Kennet & Avon, last fully navigable in 1949, and on to work on canals like the Rochdale or Huddersfield canals which had long been derelict. For a time in the mid 1970s, a similar group, around *MacNavvies*, worked in Scotland, starting restoration and improvement works on the Forth & Clyde and Union canals, which had closed in 1963 and 1965 respectively.

The 1968 Act provided a secure framework for Commercial waterways, but it could not reverse trends in traffic. One area of traffic growth in the 1950s was the bulk carriage of liquids, especially on the Severn line, one of the large commercial waterways which the DIWE considered worthy of improvement.

Nationalization unified the administration of the Severn Commission's line to Worcester and Stourport with the Gloucester & Sharpness Canal, owned by the Sharpness New Docks company. Improvements enabled estuarial craft to bring oil, grain, metals and general merchandise directly from Bristol Channel ports, especially Avonmouth, to depots at Stourport and Worcester for onward road distribution to the Midlands.

Petroleum traffic from the Bristol Channel ports grew after nationalization, to Diglis and Stourport on the Severn, and increasingly in coastal tankers, to Monk Meadow Dock in Gloucester. New oil wharves were added at Diglis in 1954, but despite further improvements under the Development Plan, traffics fell away in the early 1960s, especially above Worcester. Petroleum movements to Stourport, using smaller craft, declined from 201,477 tons in 1956 to 35,779 tons in 1963, as a result of pipeline developments. These later affected traffics to Worcester, where only small loads unsuitable for pipeline transfer were carried; by 1971 these had transferred to road and rail transport and regular movements above Gloucester had ceased.

The BTC handled the carrying of general merchandise, for which four new craft were built under the 1956 plan. However, the opening of the M5/M50 route helped to divert traffics from Avonmouth and Sharpness to the road-served South Wales ports, while all Bristol Channel ports were affected by the general diversion of shipping towards continental Europe. When Sharpness revived, this largely relied on rail or roadborne forwarding. Facing increasing losses, BWB withdrew its fleet in 1969, after which the main regular traffic above Gloucester was a longstanding grain traffic to Healings' Mills at Tewkesbury (and one up the Avon to Pershore), which continued until 1984, with later revivals.

The greater capacity of the Canal to Gloucester enabled the development of larger craft. A new oil depot opened at Quedgeley in the early 1960s to relieve congestion at Monk Meadow; this was mainly served

Healings' mill on the Avon at Tewkesbury, the source of long-standing grain traffic. Photographed during a revival of traffic in 1993, Chaceley *has been unloaded. This and other craft were retained as floating storage after regular traffic ceased in 1984*

by coastal tankers. Traffics in grain to mills in Gloucester Docks continued until the last one closed in 1977, while timber shipments to various waterside wharves in Gloucester lasted into the 1970s. While BWB opened a new depot at Monk Meadow in 1965 for timber and general traffics, diminishing trade led it to cease all handling at Gloucester in 1987. Quedgeley was to close in 1985, while the last petroleum was delivered to Monk Meadow around 1991. By 1993, there were no major regular traffics above Sharpness, and the Severn Corridor plan, to enlarge the line for 2500t craft to Gloucester, and 1500t on to Worcester, which had been agreed in 1983, had been quietly shelved.

Coal remained a major, if declining, canalborne cargo between 1947 and the early 1970s. Some traffic was diverted to road or rail, with the growth of merry go round trains from pit to power station. Traffics were affected by the declining use of coal, through smokeless zones, changing energy use in industry, the closing of old waterside power stations and the opening of new non-coal stations, and the closure of gasworks as gas-making from coal ended in the 1960s. This was exacerbated by the obsolescence of much loading and unloading equipment, and the failure to invest in new.

Westwood Power Station at Wigan in the early 1960s. This was served only by canal and rail from its inception; only when the loading equipment needed to be renewed, in 1972, was a road access constructed and the canal traffic brought to an end (British Waterways)

Positive developments were mainly confined to the opening of new waterside power stations such as Westwood on the Leeds & Liverpool (1952), and Skelton Grange (1949) and Ferrybridge C (1967) on the Aire & Calder. Walsall Power Station, at Birchills on the narrow BCN, opened in 1949; by 1963 one of the busiest points on the whole BWB system was the length between this and Holly Bank Basin, with trains of narrow boats hauled by tugs, but this traffic ended in 1965.

The Leeds & Liverpool Canal relied heavily on coal carrying, mainly to power stations, gas works and waterside factories. General merchandise traffics mainly originated in Liverpool for delivery to a network of warehouses on both sides of the Pennines, along with grain movements.

The opening of Westwood Power Station in Wigan, fuelled largely by canalborne coal from the Leigh Branch, added to existing traffics to power stations at Whitebirk (Blackburn) and Kirkstall (Leeds), the latter served by pits on the Aire & Calder Navigation. Two gas works and sugar refineries in the Liverpool area also received coal into the 1950s.

Most general merchandise was carried in BTC craft, and a number of

A rather grey view of Litherland Lift Bridge and Calder, *one of the BTC general merchandise craft built of high tensile steel in the 1950s. The bridge was removed in 1975; before this it formed a discouragement to the passage of pleasure craft. Ironically, the earliest canal boat club was located near here* (British Waterways)

new craft were constructed in high-tensile steel in the 1950s; this increased carrying capacity by 10 per cent. There was a shortage of traffics that could be carried so as to undercut rates for road transport, and by the mid-1950s many of the warehouses were being used for roadborne storage. Pit closures and changes to industrial fuel use reduced traffics, such as that to Tate & Lyle in Liverpool, withdrawn in 1958. The BTC acquired a Bootle coal carrying fleet in 1962 in a bid to retain traffics, but the hard winter of 1962–3 had a major impact. Most coal traffic was suspended, and most was switched to road during this period, and did not return afterwards. By the end of 1964 the only traffic bar that to Wigan power station was a lighterage traffic in grain at Liverpool, which lasted till 1966. Grain carrying from Liverpool by H & R Ainscough, to their own mills at Burscough and Parbold, and into storage at Wigan and elsewhere, had ceased in 1961.

The Leeds & Liverpool presented major financial problems for the BTC, accounting for 30 per cent of its deficit in 1956. Maintenance and operating responsibilities included major mining subsidence on the Leigh Branch, numerous locks, large reservoirs, two tunnels, and a large number of old warehouses inherited from the Leeds & Liverpool company.

Once the coal revenues collapsed in 1963, closure became a serious possibility, especially when pleasure boats were rarely seen outside the Lydiate and Keighley/Skipton areas; the heavy traffic and locks had deterred many boats. There were problems at both Liverpool and Leeds ends; a pleasure boat passage of River Lock, Leeds, took 6 hours in 1964, while crowbars were needed to open the swing bridges on the Yorkshire side. The terminal length into Bootle and Liverpool was subject to vandalism, while prior notice was required to raise Litherland Lift Bridge. BWB stated gloomily in its *Future* report of 1964 that 'given the present and (as far as they can foretell) the future usage they must give serious consideration to further reduction of expenditure even though this may mean a reduction of facilities.'[6]

The 1965 report estimated the annual costs of maintaining the main line to water channel standards at £77,800, and to navigable standards at £122,653; it appeared that £44,853 pa was required to allow a few pleasure craft to pass. It was thus clear that 'On the main line . . . the deficit could be reduced considerably – though it would remain very substantial – by conversion to a water channel.'[7]

The IWA perceived the threat to navigation, and organized a National Rally at four sites on the canal in August 1965, with 130 boats reaching the main site at Blackburn alone. Its *Bulletin* stressed

> the genuine delight of all British Waterways lock-keepers and maintenance men along the entire route of the canal, that now, at last, someone was determined that traffic should return to the Leeds & Liverpool . . . Immediately craft entered the canal, both at Leeds and at Wigan, there was startling evidence of the willingness of British Waterways men to offer every assistance. Lock-keepers turned out on duty at all manner of unaccustomed hours feverishly tarring and painting gates and balance beams, and greasing swing bridges. While the work they did was sometimes of a superficial nature, the waterway was generally easy to navigate; it cannot be too strongly emphasized that increased use by boats will improve conditions as will nothing else.[8]

This rally, as with earlier ones, helped to demonstrate the potential amenity value of the canal to local authorities which would not then support any closure proposals. As the canal formed a significant link in the future Cruiseway network, it was so retained under the 1968 Transport Act, except for 8 miles at the Liverpool end. There were proposals to use the latter for a road, and local campaigns to fill it in to remove danger to local children (there were several drownings), and most of this length remained behind gates, with the towpath inaccessible. By the early 1990s this remained one of the least used sections of navigable canal in Britain, although the towpath had been opened up.

The several lines of the Shropshire Union illustrate the fate of narrow boat carrying, and of campaigns for the retention and restoration of disused sections.

The main line to Autherley took mainly long distance traffic to and from Ellesmere Port and, via the Middlewich Branch, from the Weaver and Port of Manchester. By 1947 the 243,527 tons carried in 1937 had diminished to 72,591 tons. The main traffic through Ellesmere Port was in fuel oil carried from Stanlow, on the Manchester Ship Canal, to Langley Green at Oldbury, a traffic which had commenced in 1924. By the time that this had ceased in 1955, all general merchandise traffic through Ellesmere Port, carried in BTC craft to Birmingham and Wolverhampton, had ended. The main cargoes carried – sugar, cocoa and flour – had partly moved to road. Traffics from Weston Point were mainly in metals and bentonite, which benefitted from backloads of coal and gravel on the Trent & Mersey Canal, as well as one in 'tank house slime' carried from Darlaston to Manchester; as these backloads were lost, the viability of this carrying operation diminished further.

The BTC kept its Northern fleet operating, despite growing losses in the face of increasing competition from road transport, so as not to lose both traffics and accompanying toll revenues. It even provided new craft in the late 1950s, but the loss of Midlands traffics continued, dropping from 29,012 tons in 1957 to 5,779 tons in 1960.

In 1964 BWB closed its narrow boat fleet, and Willow Wren, one of the more enterprising carriers, took over the remaining traffics. This, however, could not make these pay, and gave up after the loss of bentonite and aluminium traffics to Wolverhampton in 1966 and 1967. The recently formed Anderton Canal Carrying Company then took over, carrying aluminium to Wolverhampton until 1968. This was forwarded by lorry to Bridgnorth, while a traffic in silicon carbide for a Stafford factory was forwarded from Norbury by tractor until it ended in 1970. As maintenance priorities were increasingly centred round the summer passage of pleasure craft, a satisfactory service to customers could no longer be assured.

The closure of the branches to Newtown, Llangollen and Shrewsbury in 1944 was based on the maintenance of water levels, so that while locks

This bridge at St Martins on the Llangollen Canal was programmed by Shropshire County Council to be rebuilt without navigable headroom, but it was rebuilt in 1952 after the Denbighshire, Shropshire and Cheshire county councils agreed to retain navigation

and bridges could be dismantled, draining and infilling would require Ministry of Agriculture approval.

The Llangollen line had remained navigable after 1944, supplying water to the lower Main Line and various industrial users. The closure Act transferred highway bridges to local highway authorities, which soon proposed two culverted crossings in Denbighshire and one in Shropshire. As maintenance was mainly waterborne, the Divisional Waterways Officer in the North West, Christopher Marsh, convinced Denbighshire that the culverting of Wenffrwd Bridge, near Llangollen, would involve the Council in heavy future maintenance costs, and it was agreed in 1949 to build a new bridge instead, a policy confirmed by all the canalside highway authorities in 1951.

In the early 1950s the DIWE offered the canal to the Mid and South East Cheshire Water Board, which planned to use it to transfer domestic water abstracted from the Dee near Pontcysyllte into Cheshire, using the canal reservoir at Hurleston for storage. The Water Board refused to take over the canal, and in 1952 produced alternative plans for a pipeline to Cheshire. Only when loan sanction for this was refused was it agreed that the BTC should retain ownership and obtain powers to permit the water supply scheme. The canal was duly put into good order between 1956 and 1959, when the abstractions began. The water sales revenue made the Llangollen line one of a handful of profitable canals by the mid-1960s, and enabled it to stay open for pleasure traffic. Its popularity expanded rapidly in the 1960s, and it was classified as a Cruiseway in 1968.

While water supplies to industry were long known in Britain, the use of canals to transfer domestic water was new; a further scheme followed on the Gloucester & Sharpness Canal (for Bristol), and later the Bridgewater & Taunton Canal. In 1993 studies were published to use a number of midlands waterways to transfer water between regions. In Ireland, both the Grand and Royal canals had supplied Dublin with drinking water into the nineteenth century; the Grand Canal still supplies the Guinness brewery.

One of the DIWE's few successful transfers in the 1950s was of the terminal length of the Shrewsbury Canal to the local council; while this was drained and filled in, the rest of the line remained, obstructed by a number of road crossings west of Wellington. IWRAC approved plans to dewater both the Shrewsbury and Newtown lines once alternative drainage and farm water supplies could be secured; negotiations had reached a late stage on the Shrewsbury line by 1965, when a restoration campaign was launched, partly inspired by the Stratford example. While there were limited physical obstacles to restoration on the eastern length, BWB declined support due to the high restoration costs and the advanced stage of negotiations; the draining of the canal and its sale to local farmers began in 1966, and by 1970 much had been sold and filled in. A later revival of interest involved some work near Berwick Tunnel.

The Shrewsbury and Newport campaigners formed the Shropshire Union Canal Society, which turned its attention to the line to Newtown (now known as the Montgomery Canal). By 1949 this was obstructed by five low road crossings and two dry sections, and by the mid-1960s the length into Newtown was destroyed and a dewatering scheme prepared for the rest, although negotiations with landowners were not completed. In 1967 the campaigners tried to persuade BWB to repair the supplies to the Tanat feeder and hence the centre section of the canal. A new Welshpool bypass was proposed along the line of the canal in 1969, and in October a campaigning dig, including volunteers from the *Navvies* group, cleared the canal in Welshpool. This assisted the defeat of the bypass plans in 1972, and BWB decided to repair the Tanat feeder.

Restoration began on Welshpool Lock, aiming to develop a length of 2 miles between lowered road crossings either side of Welshpool. A

Welshpool Lock on the Montgomery section of the Shropshire Union Canal; the building in the offside distance, formerly the Shropshire Union warehouse, now houses the Powysland Museum. The regular trip boat which is just entering the lock is also based alongside the museum. While for twenty-five years after the restoration campaign started this section was an isolated cruising length of 2 miles, by the mid-1990s it formed part of an 11 mile section between Burgedin and Berriew

further 6 miles north to Burgedin re-opened in 1978; volunteers gradually restored the locks at Carreghofa, Frankton and later Aston, and BWB improved the channel of the watered lengths. Meanwhile, amid much disquiet, further road crossings were lowered, but plans for restoration south of Welshpool were enhanced by the insertion of a navigable culvert under the new Abermule bypass in 1973.

In 1983 a report by the consultants W.S. Atkins recommended the full restoration of the canal, including the Guilsfield Branch and a new line into Newtown. The costs involved were seen as justified by the external economic benefits, while such benefits would be maximized if restoration was achieved within three years. A private Act to permit restoration was obtained, but in 1989 the Secretary of State for Wales refused loan sanction for the various public bodies willing to finance restoration. A more gradual approach followed, joining the Welshpool and Burgedin lengths by the provision of a new Gallowstree Bank Bridge in 1992, with the length south of Welshpool extended to Berriew in 1996.

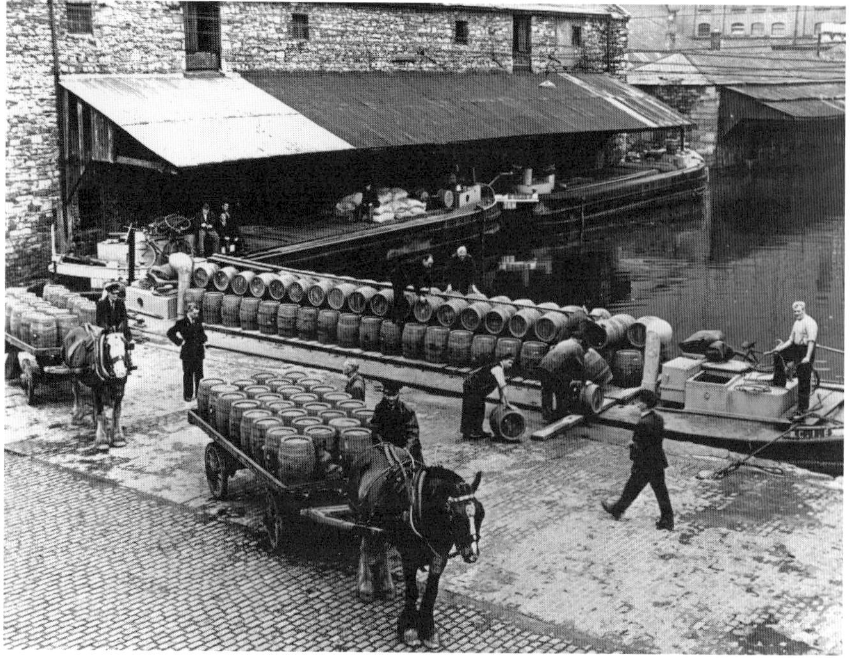

Loading porter barrels into CIE boats and discharging empties at James Street Harbour, Dublin, towards the end of the carrying era, around 1957. Note the simple loading methods, the use of the horse and cart (still viable over short distances for collection and delivery), and the numerous staff. This harbour and the connecting length of canal were filled in during the early 1970s (Guinness Museum)

Developments in lowland England and North Wales were not followed elsewhere. The Inland Waterways Association of Ireland was formed in 1954, following consultation with the IWA in Britain, by, among others, Colonel Harry Rice, author of *Thanks for the Memory* (1952), about the Shannon, and Vincent Delany; both were boating enthusiasts, and the latter and his wife, Ruth, became the leading historians of waterways in Ireland. The IWAI would be spared the internal problems which affected its British counterpart, although the position of the Irish waterways was potentially a desperate one. It was unable to campaign for the retention of commercial carrying, and at first fought proposals to replace swivel bridges over the Shannon with low fixed spans, which would have prevented navigation. In 1955 CIE was persuaded to introduce passenger launches on the river which required 14 ft headroom, and, while carrying ceased in 1959, the river remained open.

The CIE fleet continued to operate on the Grand, Barrow and

Shannon in the 1950s, but under the Transport Act of 1958 CIE withdrew its services to transfer traffics to the ailing rail network. The final traffics, for the Guinness Brewery, the main customer, were carried in 1960. Only intervention by the IWAI prevented the closure of the canals, although CIE were empowered to close canals which had been disused for three years, and all the main Grand Canal branches were closed, along with the Royal Canal, in 1961.

Hire boating in the Republic had been as limited as that in Britain; in 1946 Tom Rolt located only three craft on the Shannon, and found that only through traffic was permitted on the Grand Canal. After the 1950s, encouraged by the IWAI campaigns and the annual Shannon rallies from 1961, several hire firms started operations on the Shannon, while private pleasure boating grew. Albert Lock, in the northern part of the Shannon at Jamestown, was used 70 times in 1959, 1,672 times in 1964 and 2,240 times in 1969. In the mid-1960s three hire firms were operating on the Grand Canal, although growth was not inexorable; by the 1990s there were only two.

Proposals by Dublin Corporation to fill in the Circular line, linking the Grand to the Liffey at Ringsend, were defeated by a long IWAI campaign between 1963 and 1969. Campaigning included picketing the City Hall, then a most unusual form of protest in Ireland. The Circular line remained open, but the terminal length of the main line in Dublin was filled in by 1974.

Little public interest was aroused in the waterways of the north of Ireland, although the IWAI covered this area and an active Erne branch was formed. In the 1960s the construction of a new motorway destroyed 8 miles of the canal line of the Lagan, including the aqueduct at Spencer's Bridge and the Union Locks. The Lower Bann Navigation had limited commercial and pleasure traffic, but from 1962 the Lower Bann Association successfully opposed proposals for closure. The last major traffic left the Newry Ship Canal in 1966, and this closed in 1974, when the owning trust went into liquidation; the development of alternative port facilities at Warrenpoint made this canal obsolete.

In Scotland, the final traffics had passed on the Monkland and Union canals in the 1930s; the Monkland closed in 1950, and part of its line was used to construct the Monkland motorway (M8) in the 1960s. The Union was also a barrier to road developments, and was closed in 1965, after a brief period during which British Waterways introduced small hired pleasure craft. While the Forth & Clyde had long been obsolete for most seagoing traffic, a small oil traffic developed in the early 1950s, and fishing boats regularly used it. The Bowes report dismissed the canal's usefulness as merely the source of a hidden subsidy to the fishing industry, and closure in 1963 obviated the need to provide new opening bridges.

There was little public support for the retention of canals in South Wales. Both the Swansea and Monmouthshire Canals were closed in stages to 1962, with parts being retained for water supplies; on the Monmouthshire through Cwmbran New Town, locks were converted to ornamental cascades, with new roads crossing at water level.

Only the Brecon & Abergavenny length, disused since 1938, remained navigable. Maintained primarily for water supply, only rowing boats used it until 1952, when a rally of trailed boats at Brecon awakened interest, and helped to defeat proposals to close it to culvert highway crossings. After the partial restoration of the locks south of Talybont from 1959, boating on the lower length grew; the Govilon Boat Club was formed in 1963. Although part in Brecon was filled in after 1960, and the canal was classified as a Remainder waterway in 1968, an agreement with local authorities to fund restoration and some maintenance costs led to the reopening in 1970 of the length from Talybont to Brecon, including new lift bridges. Between 1969 and 1971 the number of boats on the canal increased from 136 to 217. While a major breach closed the canal in the 1970s, it was later repaired and the canal reclassified as a cruiseway in 1983.

Long distance carrying by narrow boat was seen to end in 1970, when the coal traffics from Warwickshire to Croxley and Southall ceased. Of the carriers involved, Willow Wren soon went into receivership, while Blue Line concentrated on hire boating. The remaining major carrier by narrow boat, the Birmingham & Midland Carrying Company, launched with much optimism in 1964–5, mainly used its fleet as camping boats after 1971. Decreasing financial viability accompanied lack of traffics and crews, exacerbated by declining maintenance standards, including winter closures, on Cruiseways.

The Regent's Canal and lower Grand Union (to Berkhamsted and Uxbridge) had been classified as major transport waterways in the 1950s, although improvement works were mainly confined to the duplication and mechanization of the locks at Brentford, and the development of the depot there. While BWB closed its south eastern fleet in 1963, ending most traffics from Brentford to Birmingham, it retained one traffic, lime juice in barrels to Roses' at Boxmoor, transhipped at Brentford. In other hands, this lasted until 1981, perhaps the last medium distance narrow boat traffic carried on strictly commercial lines, which outlived barge traffics on the Regent's and lower Grand Union. In 1966 numerous timber yards and manufacturers such as Heinz at Harlesden or J Lyons at Greenford were still receiving goods imported through the London docks; by 1972 increasing craft size, and dock reorganization, especially the closure of Surrey Commercial Docks where much of the timber

Unloading lime juice in barrels for Roses' of Boxmoor from a British Waterways' narrow boat in the early 1960s. Note the rather primitive, but mobile, crane and the pleasure boat in the background. This was BWB's last narrow-boat traffic (British Waterways)

traffics originated, had reduced regular barge traffics to a minimum. These waterways were classified as Cruiseways in 1968.

The long level of the Paddington Branch and Regent's Canal above the locks at Camden had developed for pleasure boating since the 1950s, with trip boats which introduced many people to waterways. From the early 1970s BWB removed the restrictions on the weekend use of locks, converting the duplicate locks on the Regent's Canal to weirs by 1975. The towpaths had been used for tractor towing, and those on the Regent's Canal were inaccessible. During the 1960s the London Canals Consultative Committee considered the recreational possibilities of the towpaths through London, and in 1968 Westminster City Council opened up the first section along the Regent's Canal by the London Zoo. This was the forerunner of the London Canal Way opened through central and west London in 1977.

One unusual long term traffic began in 1967 on a Remainder waterway in the Potteries, the Caldon Canal. Johnson Bros, a subsidiary of Wedgwood, began carrying tableware between two factories in Hanley and a packing plant four miles away in Milton, using a special narrow catamaran, *Milton Maid*; this later expanded with two more craft, reducing to two craft and a much shorter run after the Milton store closed in the 1980s. These effectively used a roll-on, roll-off principle, loading cargoes onto trolleys which were wheeled off onto ramps at the unloading points.

After 1970, inland waterways traffic would develop in ways which bore little relation to the traditional craft, track and trading of the canals of the industrial revolution; by the end of the 1980s, even regular movements by barge would be rare. Concerns that traditional carrying might disappear altogether were met by varied responses. These included the development of boat preservation, sometimes allied to museums, and the development of carrying on a partly commercial basis. The assertion in *The Future of the Waterways* in 1964 proved prophetic:

> the scale of commercial transport operations over the narrow waterways is small. It appears that, if there is a future for it, it may lie more in the use of some kind of relatively small, and perhaps 'profit-sharing', organization than in normal terms of large scale company undertakings.[9]

The remaining carrying by narrow boat into the 1970s mainly involved domestic coal. Perhaps the most professional operator was the Ashby Canal Association, which succeeded in retaining traffics from Gopsall Wharf until 1981, on a canal upon which carrying almost ceased in 1959. From here and from Atherstone Wharf, coal was carried to various canalside locations in Southern England. Several other individuals or groups became coal merchants, supplying bagged coal to various locations, some of which, like the Macclesfield Canal, had seen no traffic since the 1950s. The Narrow Boat Trust, formed in 1971 to preserve working narrow boats in action, acquired three Willow Wren craft; volunteers would assist the carrying of domestic coal on to the Thames into the 1990s. A periodic gravel traffic developed on the Soar near Leicester, initially in wide craft, then in narrow boats, and most recently in special narrow craft.

Another aspect of the preservation of craft and historical sites was the development of museums. The earliest museum, based traditionally on artifacts in glass cases, was opened by BWB at Stoke Bruerne in 1963. Visitor numbers grew from 14,000 in 1963 to 48,000 in 1970, when the original displays and visitor facilities had been enlarged, making Stoke Bruerne itself an added attraction, with a boat operating trips to Blisworth Tunnel from the 1968 season. By 1974, when visitors were at a

The Boat Museum at Ellesmere Port, showing the top gate of the Whitby Locks, the entrance opened in 1993 and the associated trip boat. Before the museum opened in 1976, on a much smaller scale, there were proposals to build a container terminal to serve the Manchester Ship Canal on this site

record level of nearly 108,000, it had been joined by the Canal Exhibition Centre at Llangollen, linked to the horse-drawn trip boats there, and the small private Dewsbury Canal Museum, which concentrated on the waterways of Yorkshire.

Other museums which involved waterways, and which began work in the 1970s, included the Open Air Museum of the Ironbridge Gorge Museum Trust, which includes a visual restoration of the Hay Inclined Plane and part of the Shropshire Canal; and Morwellham Quay, which included part of the Tavistock Canal among the reconstructed historical scenes. In 1970 a group was formed which fostered the Boat Museum at Ellesmere Port; this originally aimed to preserve a small collection of historic boats, but expanded rapidly after it first opened in 1976. Finally, the Black Country Museum, which included some floating exhibits, first opened in 1977, on a site next to Dudley Tunnel. In the 1980s a new tunnel was opened to link limestone caverns under Dudley and to create a return route for trip boats into the main tunnel. Measured in terms of passenger numbers, this soon became the most extensively visited point on the British canal system.

CHAPTER FOURTEEN

In Transformation

The growth in amenity uses of waterways, encouraged by the Transport Act of 1968, led to the expansion in use and extent of the then navigable network. Public perceptions of canals changed, so that local authorities, for instance in the West Midlands, which had sought the destruction of their local canals, came to regard them as important recreational assets. During the same period there was a somewhat insidious process of commercialization which was seen by some to compromise the essential character of historic waterways scenes and structures. The facilities upon canals had changed greatly since the beginnings of pleasure boating in the interwar years, and their appearance was also often transformed.

The administration of Britain's waterways did not greatly change after 1970, despite proposals in 1973 to merge BWB, as a water supplier, with the regional water authorities. These were successfully resisted, but other independent navigations, such as the Thames, Nene and Great Ouse, were transferred to the new water authorities. Campaigning ensured that one major new owner, the Anglian Water Authority, retained navigation as a significant priority alongside water supply or drainage. When the water authorities were privatized, navigation responsibilities were transferred to the new National Rivers Authority; in the early 1990s proposals arose to merge the BWB waterways with these interests, probably to the detriment of commercial transport and possibly to amenity interests.

In Ireland, the former CIE canals, the Grand, Royal and Barrow Navigation, were finally transferred in 1986 to the Office of Public Works, which had long controlled the Shannon. A more positive approach followed; the OPW was able to develop pleasure boating and amenities in ways which had been beyond CIE's remit. The OPW also took over the Ballinamore & Ballyconnell Canal in 1990 prior to restoration, and the Boyne in 1991, unifying the ownership of most significant waterways in the Republic, in contrast to the continued patchwork in the north.

The legal protections in the 1968 Act did not directly guarantee finance or maintenance provision. A 1974 survey by the consulting engineers, Peter Fraenkel & Partners, into maintenance standards and costs on the BWB canals, identified maintenance arrears on both commercial and cruising waterways of some £60 million at 1977 prices. While special grants to tackle the maintenance backlog followed, major problems persisted. On the cruiseways between 1973 and 1978, there were long closures of Harecastle, Blisworth, Netherton and Braunston tunnels, Pontcysyllte and Alvechurch aqueducts, and Anderton Lift. If substantial commercial traffic had persisted on these lengths, it could not have lasted for long.

In 1977–8 a Select Committee on Nationalized Industries examined BWB and its affairs, and recommended acceptance of the Fraenkel report and continued financial support for maintenance. This was somewhat reluctantly accepted, and the Transport Act 1978 duly laid a duty on the Secretary of State 'to promote a national policy for the use of inland waterways for commercial transport'. However, while work started on the Sheffield & South Yorkshire enlargement, this had to be financed from the National Loans Fund at commercial interest rates on the basis that tolls must be set at 'an economic price for traffic', criteria not applied to road improvements.

In 1984, in line with government policy to commercialize nationalized industries, a Statement of Objectives for BWB insisted that it 'should, as far as practicable, run its affairs on a practical basis',[1] and thus minimize its call on Exchequer funds. BWB stressed that

> While continuing their traditional role and commitments as custodians of part of the National Heritage, the Board have in their Plan sought to adopt a commercial approach necessary to attract more private sector finance to the waterways.[2]

This approach lay behind such policies in the 1980s as the (unsuccessful) privatization of cargo handling at Weston Point Docks, which finally collapsed in 1993; the closing of BWB's London lighterage fleet and operations at Brentford; a move into the general holiday market with the use of a cottage at Nantwich Basin as a holiday home; and the start of a joint venture to develop property at Gloucester Docks. In 1987, the Board sold its last carrying craft, ending the practice of canal carrying by canal owners; in 1988 four freight depots were closed and the rest sold to the private sector. Finally, hiring ceased from the base at Nantwich at the end of the 1993 season.

The IWA increasingly concentrated on issues of interest to pleasure boat navigation and amenity, including canal restoration, within a framework of critical support for BWB and other owners. In 1971 it helped form what became the Inland Shipping Group (ISG), founded by Charles Hadfield. The ISG focused interest away from traditional carrying, and from such ambitious schemes as J.F. Pownall's Grand Contour Canal; the latter, which the IWA had endorsed as late as 1965, had advocated a new canal for 1,350 ton barges, at the 310 ft contour, between Preston and Hertford with branches to the Midlands. ISG instead soberly investigated new traffics, track improvements, and new approaches to craft and cargo handling.

ISG soon redefined inland waterways transport, to include many waterways which fall outside the traditional canals and river navigations discussed earlier in this book. These were found to contribute much more to domestic waterborne freight than those owned by BWB. Newly revised statistics (very different from those quoted in earlier chapters in this book) indicated that in 1980 87 per cent of inland waterway traffic moved in ships, and 81 per cent passed direct to the open sea.

Seagoing vessels included low profile coasters which could pass under low bridges. To admit traffics on to the larger canals and river navigations, barge carrying ships, such as LASH (Lighter Aboard Ship), used in the Medway, or BACAT (Barge Aboard Catamaran), were developed; craft could move inland directly from these vessels without any need to tranship cargoes. Despite promising developments, union opposition at Hull led to the withdrawal of BACAT craft from the Yorkshire waterways in 1975. One problem was the heavy capital investment involved in the building of special vessels whose alternative uses were limited, and the consequent requirement to secure long term traffic commitments.

Proposals developed both to enlarge existing canals, and to build new canals, where there was traffic potential. Proposals in the 1970s included a line from the Trent into the new South Nottinghamshire coalfield, and a Trans-Anglian waterway to link the growing East Coast ports with the Midlands. More modest schemes were pursued by BWB in the early 1970s to develop transhipment depots at Winsford and Rickmansworth, to provide barge feeder services to the congested Mersey and London docks; declining traffic on the former, and the need to destroy historic structures to enlarge the lower Grand Union from Brentford, led to their eventual abandonment. Only the modest Sheffield & South Yorkshire enlargement was completed; nevertheless, experience in continental Europe suggested (and continues to suggest) a considerable potential for new waterways.

The collapse of narrow boat carrying was matched by the decline in barge traffics by the 1990s, due both to the reorganization of traffics and to the increasing carrying capacity of craft required. The closure of coal mines and power stations affected coal traffics, such as the withdrawal in 1981 of the last short West Country barges on the Calder & Hebble

Navigation to Thornhill Power Station. Developments in timber packaging and the distribution of imported timber, increasingly via continental ports, helped to end important traffics on the London waterways, to Gloucester, and the Lydney Canal; on the latter, timber was the final traffic. The oil crisis in the early 1970s accelerated the reorganization of petroleum distribution, and the closure of depots like Quedgeley on the Gloucester & Sharpness in 1984 followed smaller ones such as that at Exeter in 1972.

Traffics in bulk grain, which relied on port storage and overside loading, declined with the increasing use of home-grown grain and the concentration of most imports into two major terminals at Seaforth (Liverpool) and Tilbury. This led to the end of most traffics from Hull, such as that up Beverley Beck in 1981, and on to the Sheffield & South Yorkshire and Aire & Calder Navigations. Smaller upstream mills tended to close, like Coxes Mill at Weybridge in 1983, which ended a revived traffic from Tilbury. New highway developments improved the capacity, flexibility and speed of motor vehicles, serving ports which had no upstream connections, making it more and more competitive with waterborne transport. This affected the use of general terminals; of the BWB depots sold in 1988, those at Knostrop, Brentford, Enfield and Nottingham had not been used for waterborne transport for some time.

Future traffic opportunities were increasingly lost due to the conversion of waterside terminals for commercial or residential property, especially during the property boom of the late 1980s. While this was most marked in the development of London's docklands, it also affected such sites as the timber yard and mill in Norwich which provided the final traffics to that city in the late 1980s.

Two commercial waterways which were developed were the adjoining Aire & Calder Navigation (ACN) and Sheffield & South Yorkshire (S&SYN), which had been identified soon after nationalization as suitable for development. This enthusiasm had not extended to the smaller Barnsley Canal, breached in 1946, where the DIWE secured closure in 1953; from the 1980s there were plans to restore parts for amenity use. The depot provided at Knostrop under the 1956 Development Scheme was soon further enlarged, and the line to Leeds was enlarged in the 1960s for new oil traffics to Leeds and for increased coal traffics, especially to the power stations at Ferrybridge.

On the smaller S&SYN, under the Development Plan, Long Sandall Lock was enlarged in 1959 to allow trains of compartment boats through to Doncaster. After 1963 the Sheffield Basin facilities were replaced by a new Rotherham Depot, and the Sheffield Canal section declined until

The Aire & Calder Navigation above Pollington Lock in the 1960s. Craft include Esso Leeds, Liliane *and British Waterways'* Waterdog. *This is now the busiest of the BWB freight waterways, with bulk liquids to Castleford and coal to Ferrybridge passing regularly in 1997* (British Waterways)

the last traffic passed in 1970, and this length was classified as a Remainder Waterway.

BWB's early proposals to enlarge the S&SYN to attract new traffics were rejected in 1966; a revised scheme for enlargement from the New Junction to Rotherham, submitted in 1971, was authorized in 1974. Finance was finally secured in 1978 with EC and South Yorkshire County Council support, and work began in 1979. The scheme, which involved channel widening, dredging and piling, bridge alterations, and 10 new locks, to provide a 700 ton waterway to Rotherham, opened in April 1983; a new Rotherham depot followed in 1985. This was described as the 'first major improvement to a waterway in the United Kingdom since 1905';[3] the 1905 waterway, the New Junction Canal, linking the new navigation to the ACN, was improved by BWB at the same time. The total cost was about £12 million.

This improvement accompanied new interest in improvements to major waterways, including the Severn Corridor proposals and studies to enlarge the Trent to Nottingham. However, by the time that the S&SYN improvement opened, many traffics, including that to Doncaster Power Station, had ended, while some potential customers had failed in the recession and industrial closures of the early 1980s. Few new traffics materialized beyond a limited increase in general merchandise carried from Goole to Rotherham and Swinton. While a new stone wharf opened at Cadeby in 1985, the only major traffic, in limestone to Hull, was short-lived.

In 1978 a more gradual programme to improve the ACN for 700t craft to Leeds, including the widening of the locks, was completed. In 1977 the tanker *Humber Jubilee*, the first craft to be built for the ACN since 1968, was launched to carry petrol from Immingham to Leeds; in that year 400,000t in liquids was carried on the Navigation, out of a total of over 2 million tonnes, a level which was maintained into the 1990s.

This improved line brought proposals for new traffics, such as minestone waste from the Castleford area to a land reclamation site in the Humber estuary in the early 1980s. Other plans sought to exploit the proximity of major power stations on the Aire and Ouse to the Castleford coalfield and to the new Selby coalfield, the latter being served from a single railhead at Gascoigne Wood.

Despite this potential, many traffics were lost. The end of the BACAT operation through Hull affected traffics to the depots, and those at Wakefield and Castleford closed, while Caldaire Terminal, opened in 1985 to assist transhipment at Goole, did not realize the anticipated traffic.

By the mid-1970s coal traffics to Skelton Grange Power Station and into Leeds had ceased. The rapid rundown of the coal industry in the 1980s reduced loading points to one deep mine, Kellingley, opened in 1965, and an open cast site at Astley, opened in 1974; the latter was replaced by a new loading point nearby in 1988. From 1986, when the compartment trains, now carrying smokeless fuel to Goole, ceased altogether, only the power stations at Ferrybridge received coal. Of these, Ferrybridge 'A', the first to be served by the Navigation from 1927, had closed in the 1970s, and Ferrybridge 'B' in 1992.

Coal to Ferrybridge 'C' accounted for a increasing proportion of traffic on BWB waterways into the 1990s. Here push-towed Cawoods-Hargreaves compartment boats in trains of three pans, carrying 500t, were emptied by a special lift, operational from 1967, in a more efficient development of the much earlier Bartholemew system. A record tonnage of 2,045,630 tonnes, one-third of the coal consumed by Ferrybridge 'C', was carried in the year ending 31 March 1993. This single traffic represented over half of the tonnage on all BWB waterways.

By 1994, the sporadic traffics in sand to Leeds or Knottingley were very much reduced, as were those in bulk liquids, affected by the movement of Humber loading points downstream to Immingham. Limited oil deliveries to power stations on the River Aire, Ouse, ACN and S&SYN did continue, but those to bulk terminals at Leeds and Fleet ceased. The Aire & Calder, BWB's most modern waterway, indicates a future for inland waterways carrying with waterways and craft unfamiliar to the canal pleasure boater. On the East Coast, for instance, small ports like Rochester, Colchester, and Wisbech take considerable seaborne traffics, while Fosdyke Bridge, on the Welland, was revived from 1979. While the Trent Navigation above Gainsborough saw very limited traffics in the 1980s, the River Trent below, controlled by Associated British Ports, saw considerable traffics to wharves reached by 3,000 ton craft, such as Keadby, Gunness, Grove Wharf, Neap House, Flixborough, Burton-on-Stather and Gainsborough, with over 2,000 seagoing vessels handled in 1990.

The Manchester Ship Canal was increasingly affected by the same factors as the surviving smaller commercial waterways, and also by the changing direction of trade towards continental Europe. It would form the subject of an unprecedented public campaign for retention during the 1980s.

The Ship Canal Company (MSCCo) had steadily disengaged itself from small canal traffic, closing Runcorn Locks in 1966 to develop traffic at the Runcorn docks, where tonnages handled increased from 52,832 tons in 1958 to 435,318 tons in 1968. On the Bridgwater Canal, the grain traffic to Kelloggs mill at Stretford ended in 1974 with a transfer to road transport from Seaforth, while the last main coal traffic passed to Trafford Park Power Station in 1973. A major breach at Lymm in 1971 brought unexpected proposals for closure, but the IWA National Rally there in 1972 encouraged its repair and the reopening in September 1973. Local authorities then formed a Bridgwater Canal Trust to cover operating losses, and the development of the canal for pleasure boating continued.

As early as 1962 an official Committee of Inquiry endorsed the MSCCo's policy to concentrate development at the Ship Canal's deeper western end, which could accommodate larger ships, and on bulk liquid traffic, concluding that:

> we cannot believe that the port has any great development potential. The ability of ships to berth right inland is a factor of decreasing importance in these days of cheap and rapid road transport, whereas the limitations on the size of ship which can use the port are likely to become more serious as the average size of ship continues to grow . . .[4]

At the end of the 1960s the upper reaches, above Runcorn, still remained in considerable use. Regular liner services linked the Terminal Docks at Salford to Canada and the Mediterranean, while between Mode Wheel and Barton there were oil installations, with cereals carried to Barton. Below Barton Lock, sewage sludge from the Manchester Corporation works was loaded for dumping in Liverpool Bay, while at Partington Coaling Basin coal for export, chemicals and petroleum products were handled.

While lighterage traffic at Warrington, through the Black Bear Canal to Howley Quay, had ceased at the end of the 1960s, traffic still passed through Walton Lock onto the upper Mersey into Warrington until 1984.

Container handling, which was to transform dock handling employment, and to greatly speed the turn-round of ships, had begun on the canal in 1965. Britain's first container terminal for fully-cellular dedicated container ships, in Manchester Liners vessels for Canada, opened in November 1968 in No. 9 Dock at Salford; from 1971 the terminal was enlarged to accommodate regular Mediterranean services. Increasing containerization overseas, coupled with the long transit time up the Canal to Manchester, and proposed motorway links, led to the development of a new container terminal at Ellesmere Port; after this opened in 1972, Ellesmere Port's export trade exceeded that of Manchester.

In 1981 the MSCCo chairman reported that 'No longer is there any demand for deepsea general cargo vessels in the heart of the greater Manchester area – the purpose for which the Ship Canal was originally constructed.'[5]

The long transit times up the canal, along with increased ship sizes and turnround times, led to the withdrawal of traffic on the upper reaches above Runcorn. In 1980 the National Coal Board declined to modernize the coal exporting facility at Partington, which dated back to 1894, and transferred operations to Garston, while in 1981 another longstanding service, by the Clan Line to India was withdrawn. In July 1983 Manchester Liners moved its remaining container service to Ellesmere Port, followed by the Atlant Line.

In April 1984 the MSCCo announced its intention to close the upper reaches after 1987, when the North West Water Authority would withdraw its sludge ships from Davyhulme, with a major loss of revenue in consequence. At that time, the only traffics in the terminal docks were a regular scrap movement for Spain, which soon moved downstream, and an occasional heavy-lift ship to Pomona Docks.

The closure announcement aroused controversy in Parliament and locally, and a Steering Committee including local authorities and other interested parties was soon formed to study the future of the upper reaches. However, the MSCCo chairman, pointing out that in 1985 the upper reaches lost £2.2 million against a profit of £1.6 million on the lower reaches, asserted that:

> the only commercial solution which I can see is to run a viable port on the canal between Eastham and Runcorn and to turn the Upper Reaches back into a river, a safe river but with no through navigation. . . . Should it be that an overriding public interest requires an ocean link to be maintained, then I believe that the public should meet that cost.[6]

As with the smaller BWB canals, the Ship Canal involved irreducible maintenance costs; its course drained much of Greater Manchester, and there were fears that if it was not dredged for navigation purposes, it would silt up and flooding would result. Dredging vessels would probably need to pass through locks and bridges, whether or not the waterway was open to shipping or even to pleasure craft.

The steering committee commissioned a report which asserted that new traffics could be attracted, and that the least expensive solution would be to keep the Canal open and to encourage leisure uses and property development. The MSCCo did not accept this report, but a takeover bid from a property company was soon made, and as part of an arrangement whereby the City Council directors were removed, it was agreed in 1988 that the Canal would stay open indefinitely, while property development unrelated to water transport would be encouraged on its banks.

Traffic continued to decline, although about 300 ships used the upper reaches each year. After the heavy lift berth at Pomona closed, Trafford Road Swing Bridge was fixed in 1992. The most significant traffic is in maize to CPC (later Cerestar) at Barton, amounting to 400,000 tons per annum, carried in barges from Seaforth until 1986. Since then it was carried directly from France by ship; new ships were specially commissioned for this traffic in 1993.

From the mid-1980s, the former Salford Docks were transformed into 'Salford Quays', with new residential and business space alongside the former docks, which were adapted for recreational use, including the construction of two short new linking canals.

Redevelopment around Salford Quays, and at Pomona, continued into the 1990s, but an area next to No. 9 dock was refurbished for possible port activities. While several shipments of timber from Portugal arrived

The Manchester Ship Canal at Barton, taken from the Swing Aqueduct looking upstream. The Arklow Villa *is carrying grain from France to the Cerestar wharf, in the far distance. In the right foreground is Barton Oil Berth, whose use ended in the early 1990s*

during 1990, the transformation of the surrounding area, and the Trafford Park estate, makes it unlikely that substantial traffic will ever return.

The loss of traffics in the Port of Manchester also involved the lower reaches. Although the container terminal at Ellesmere Port was enlarged both in 1987 and 1989 for a new traffic in exported coal in containers, by 1991 the Mediterranean container traffics had ceased, while the coal traffic proved to be short-lived. The terminal closed in 1992 and the cranes were dismantled and re-erected at Seaforth.

In the early 1990s one positive development, although carrying a cargo of some environmental controversy, was a new traffic in Venezuelan orimulsion for Ince power station, carried in special tank craft from Liverpool. By 1993 this traffic amounted to 1 million tons, but the power station closed in 1997.

Traffic on the Lee relied on lighterage from and to the London docks. The 1956 Development Plan sought to develop the lower 13 miles to Enfield, upon which the locks were doubled and mechanized, halving the

One of the terminal docks of the Ship Canal, now transformed into part of Salford Quays. This ia a bizarre sight for anyone who knew the docks when they were working – model yachts, a dog paddling, cranes preserved as curiosities? Even the barge in the distance is a floating bar! This represents a potential vision for many of the smaller waterways, with water space preserved but sanitized, the past dressed up to add flavour to the present and waterways built for transport used to enhance the value of commercial or residential property. Transport historians are not the only people to feel some unease about this development. The future use of the tidal Thames for modern water transport has been greatly diminished by the development of property which seeks to exploit the waterside location for aesthetic ends only

transit time from the docks. By the early 1980s, the main traffics were timber lightered from the docks to various waterside yards, copper to Delta Enfield Metals, and exported goods grouped at the Enfield Depot, which BWB had opened in 1970.

These traffics were affected by the reorganization of the London docks and the accompanying collapse in lighterage. Following liquidations and mergers of the remaining lighterage companies, in 1982 BWB formed its own company, Lee & Brentford Lighterage, to try to retain traffics. However, with the rundown of the older London docks, competition with road transport to Tilbury could not be withstood, while one of the last significant traffics, to Delta Enfield Metals, ended when the cargo ceased to be imported through London. Lee & Brentford Lighterage terminated operations in 1984 (ending

Timber traffics and wharves on the Lee navigation in the early 1960s. Before the development of modern timber handling techniques and packaging, such traffics were easily handled by lighters, stowing logs and planks with ease, and emptying ships carrying imports rapidly. Timber yards grew up alongside the Lee, Regent's, the lower Grand Union and the Grand Surrey Canal, but while traffics remained significant in the late 1960s, most had ended by the end of the 1970s (British Waterways)

traffic to Brentford), and all traffics on the tidal length, Bow Creek, ended in the early 1990s.

The Transport Act secured a long-term future for the Cruising waterways, and marked the end of the general campaign to retain waterways which were already navigable, strengthening campaigns to revive those which were unnavigable. In the Republic of Ireland, these battles had, effectively, been fought in the early 1960s by the IWAI, although there was an attempt to remove the safeguards for the CIE waterways in the Transport Act 1958; this had to be countered by the IWAI before the Canals Act 1986 transferred the canals and the Barrow from CIE to the Office of Public Works.

The growth in both private and hire boating in Britain, especially between 1965 and 1975 is indicated by the following statistics for powered craft on BWB canals and rivers:

	1965	*1970*	*1975*	*1980*	*1984/5*	*1989/90*
Licensed (canals)	-	-	14,751	13,385	14,090	17,146
Registered (rivers)	-	-	4,605	5,451	4,792	5,072
TOTAL Licences	9,241	12,845	19,356	18,836	18,872	22,218
Hire craft	441	663	1,511	1,983	1,590	1,603

While the basis of licensing changed during this period, the growth, especially in the numbers of hire boats, is clear. Hiring did expand, using better quality craft, and more professional management. However, like many sectors of the holiday industry, it did not prove as profitable as it might and the recession of the early 1980s caused the failure of companies and reductions in fleets. Craft changes were reflected in the boatbuilding industry, which developed through the conversion of commercial craft, through new wooden boats and fibreglass hulls, to the steel hulls which became commonplace in the 1980s.

The development of waterways for cruising did arouse some objections, recalling earlier controversies about the commercialization of the Broads. In 1968 BWB noted that linear moorings could present problems, and from 1974 sought to control their growth by encouraging the construction of off-line moorings and marinas. Some canals became congested by pleasure boats; at Grindley Brook on the Llangollen line, the Fraenkel report of 1974–7 recommended a duplicate flight of locks.

The growth of cruising reflected the concerns presented by growing numbers of visitors to the countryside. Planning controls did not always prevent the development of unsympathetic canalside properties, and sometimes natural habitats which had survived in waterways were destroyed. In the late 1980s the latter was experienced as a major inhibition on navigation, when the Nature Conservancy Council (later English Nature) declared lengths of canal as Sites of Special Scientific Interest, and sought to restrict boat movements. This seriously affected the newly reopened Basingstoke Canal from 1991, upon which proposals for an extension through a rebuilt Greywell Tunnel were inhibited by the latter's use as an important roost for bats.

In the Irish Republic, the IWAI began to perceive a threat to the character of the Shannon from pollution and its development for powered boats, and sought the development of sympathetic harbour facilities.

The IWA in Britain tended to see a threat to the character of waterways from waterside development unrelated to navigation, many in urban areas. The property boom of the late 1980s produced many developments, including the demolition or conversion of historic waterside buildings, which sought to exploit waterside locations. Often these seemed to threaten character, as with the plans for Coventry Basin; others, like the restoration of Spiers Wharf by the Forth & Clyde Canal in Glasgow, enhanced the character of a waterway which was itself under revival.

The 1968 Act did not protect the remainder waterways, which BWB had to treat in the most economical manner possible. After maintenance agreements were negotiated with local authorities, restoration between 1972 and 1974 was carried out over the Caldon Canal and the Ashton and lower Peak Forest Canals, the latter completing the Cheshire Ring of canals. The future of the Erewash was secured by the reopening of the bottom lock and adjacent basin on the Cromford Canal in 1973. This modest scheme involved perhaps the earliest instance of the re-excavation of a canal (filled in only in 1967 in this case). The first short stretch was enlarged by 1977, and a marina established; meanwhile the scenic but isolated top 5 mile length of the Cromford was transferred to Derbyshire County Council, followed by some restoration work.

While most of the BCN system was classed as remainder waterway, several sections still featured regular commercial traffic in 1967-8. The final regular traffic in waste from the Chemical Arm to the Gower Branch ended in 1975, while floating tube storage at Coombswood lasted to 1976. While the BTC had organized regular day trips from Gas Street along the Worcester & Birmingham Canal in the early 1960s, pleasure boating had been slow to develop, apart from moorings on the Cannock Extension and the Longwood Boat Club at Daw End. The 1969 IWA National Rally in Birmingham fostered support for the retention of the remainder sections and the promotion of pleasure boating.

BWB argued successfully that waterborne maintenance was essential if the BCN was to continue its water supply and drainage functions, and thus most sections which were still navigable in 1968 remained so. Exceptions were perhaps, on a national scale, insignificant, the last being the Ridgacre Branch, which attracted major protest when it was closed in November 1992 to accommodate a low road crossing.

Some revival and restorations took place, including the Titford Canal and the Dudley Canal to Coombswood, where work was completed in 1974; at the end of the latter, Hawne Basin, disused since 1967, was cleared by the Coombswood Canal Company in the late 1970s to provide new moorings. The most significant reopening was that of the Dudley Tunnel line, which was the first canal which had been formally closed (in 1962, with no safeguards) to be reopened in 1973.

Most other remainder waterways that were revived after 1968 were re-classified as Cruiseways under the BWB Act of 1983. Once the future of many remainder waterways appeared secure, attention could turn to the restoration of other waterways. Among the many schemes, the progress of the Rochdale Canal has been outstanding. This scheme grew from improbability to maturity from 1974 onwards, by dint of careful campaigning and developing local authority support.

After most of the Rochdale Canal closed in 1952, the line was obstructed by road crossings, including two motorways, piped sections in Sowerby Bridge and Failsworth, and a 3 mile length in Manchester shallowed to a depth of 6 in by 1970. Water sales and property rents had long been the main interest of the canal's private owners, and its attempts to close the remaining length in Manchester, which links the Ashton and Bridgewater canals, were defeated in 1965 after a long IWA campaign.

Interest in the canal as a local amenity began at Littleborough in 1971, while in 1973 the Canal Company's survey of possible uses for the closed length made no mention of any boating activities. Meanwhile the Calder Navigation Society and North Western IWA carried out a feasibility study into restoration. Some waterways enthusiasts doubted whether full and partial restoration should be sought; however, as Ralph Kirkham of the Calder Navigation Society stressed:

> the object is to consider all possibilities not only to restore a through route but also to link up existing pounds by restoring locks to form linear parks and to permit boating.
>
> There is no plan at the moment to re-open the Rochdale and it is possible that after the research at present being conducted we shall arrive at the conclusion that the ultimate aim is not feasible. It will, however, be a considered opinion whereas the objectors do not seem to have made any such study.[7]

The survey preceded the formation of the Rochdale Canal Society in 1974, which aimed initially to restore an isolated section near Todmorden, holding working parties and a trail boat rally on the summit pound in 1975. Early support for eventual restoration came from Greater Manchester Council and Calderdale Council.

Work began, somewhat unexpectedly, in Rochdale itself, under a job creation scheme to restore two locks as part of local environmental improvements. This became a pilot scheme for further work in Rochdale, at Chadderton, and in Calderdale, aiming to restore the canal's appearance as a local amenity before pressing for any removal of major obstructions. Volunteers restored East Summit Lock, and boats passed through at a dinghy rally in 1980.

Late in 1981 Calderdale Council obtained MSC approval for a proposal to restore the section between Todmorden and Hebble End Bridge, 3½ miles long with 10 locks, in order to introduce a trip boat upon it.

The Rochdale Canal at Hebden Bridge, with the re-excavated wharf between the two boats on the offside. The wharf, formerly used by the Rochdale Canal Company when it was engaged in carrying, was let in 1922; later it was filled in and a garage built on its site. During the late 1960s there were proposals (and much local support) to fill in the whole of the canal within Hebden Bridge

The first section, of 3 miles from Todmorden, opened in the summer of 1983. This was soon extended through to Hebden Bridge, and on 18 April 1984 a new Hebble End Bridge opened, the first bridge in Britain to replace a culverted crossing. During 1984 local authorities along the line agreed that eventual full restoration was desirable; the Rochdale Canal Trust, which included local authorities and the Rochdale Canal Company, was formed to oversee restoration and subsequent navigation.

By 1986 the wharf and basin at Hebden Bridge was re-excavated to form the base for a horse-drawn trip boat, the *Sarah Siddons*, while in 1985 a hire boat was introduced onto the isolated but steadily expanding length.

The initial form of the crossing by the proposed M66 Manchester Outer Ring Road at Broadway, Chadderton, would have made restoration insurmountable. In 1981 a campaigning working party cleared the canal at the Broadway site, and a Trailed Boat Rally followed in 1986, helping to increase support for navigation. When the Public Inquiry into the M66 was eventually held, only the Department of Transport favoured destruction of the canal line, and in 1988 this was rejected in favour of a diversion and bridges. In 1986 consultants reported that £10 million of public money had already been spent, and that another £10 million would be needed to complete restoration.

By 1988, restoration to Sowerby Bridge, bar the Tuel Lane blockage, was complete. Work on this length had included four new bridges, including one at Fallingroyds, built in 1986, where the new 'bridge' was practically a cut and cover tunnel, much more ambitious than that at Hebble End. Attention then turned to the length south of Todmorden, where restoration to Littleborough, including three crossings and removal of an infilled section, was completed in 1990.

By 1993, a length of 15 miles with 44 locks was in use by two hire craft, a trip boat and over thirty private boats, the latter mostly organized in the Rochdale Canal Boat Club. Clearance of the Tuel Lane blockage, including a new tunnel, was expected to be completed by 1996 at a cost of £2.7 million; four crossings were to be removed to provide access to Rochdale; and a trip boat was operating on another isolated length in Oldham.

This major project, like many from the 1970s, relied not so much on physical restoration by volunteers as upon the enthusiasm of local authorities who saw that restoration could assist local economic regeneration through the promotion of tourism and local amenities. By 1991, consultants estimated the costs of the remaining restoration works at £15.9 million, but the social and economic benefits at £29 million.

Two long-standing revival and restoration schemes were completed in the early 1990s. The restoration of the Basingstoke Canal, which had been largely unnavigable since 1961, depended on a campaign to transfer it into local authority ownership. The acquisitions were completed by 1976, and restoration, using volunteers, job creation schemes, and with local authority support, was finally completed from the Wey to Greywell Tunnel in 1991. The Kennet & Avon Navigation, partly unnavigable since 1949, was restored lock by lock after closure was resisted in the 1950s; it reopened in 1990, although water supply problems on this (and indeed on the Basingstoke) remain a problem.

By 1990, these revivals had been joined by much more ambitious schemes, to restore such long lost waterways as the Wey and Arun Junction and the Herefordshire & Gloucestershire; limited stretches of these canals have been re-watered. One useful restoration would involve the Dudley Canal between Hawne and Selly Oak, but to achieve this, the Lapal Canal Trust will need to secure the rebuilding of the 3,795 yd

The Sankey Navigation Canal between Bradley and Hey Locks, one of the few lengths of the 1757 canal to have survived with anything like its original appearance. This length was in regular use until the sugar traffic ended in 1959, but it then closed in 1963. Some clearing works were carried out in the 1970s, but the bridge does not open, and much of the canal above Bradley Lock has been destroyed

Lapal Tunnel, which collapsed in 1917 and was later partly filled by concrete, the provision of two major road crossings, and the re-excavation of much of the rest of the filled-in line.

There were also proposals to provide new waterways, such as the Higher Avon to Warwick and the upper Severn to Ironbridge. These attracted much opposition, as did the campaign to restore the Yorkshire Derwent, which involved major legal expenses.

Other schemes aimed to revive short lengths for amenity purposes, which might eventually be joined to form longer lengths. These included the Wilts & Berks Canal, 51 miles long, with the whole length through Swindon destroyed, and that to restore the Swansea Canal, of which only the isolated 5 mile length from Clydach to Ystalyfera had not been eliminated and redeveloped by 1981, when revival began. Similarly, much of the Sankey Canal was destroyed in the 1970s, and restoration could only be a gradual process.

Restoration schemes in Scotland, of the Union and Forth & Clyde

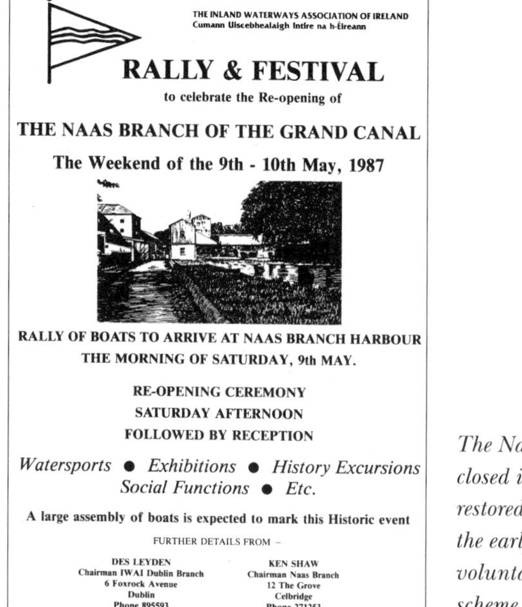
THE INLAND WATERWAYS ASSOCIATION OF IRELAND
Cumann Uiscebhealaigh Intíre na h-Éireann
RALLY & FESTIVAL
to celebrate the Re-opening of
THE NAAS BRANCH OF THE GRAND CANAL
The Weekend of the 9th - 10th May, 1987
RALLY OF BOATS TO ARRIVE AT NAAS BRANCH HARBOUR
THE MORNING OF SATURDAY, 9th MAY.
RE-OPENING CEREMONY
SATURDAY AFTERNOON
FOLLOWED BY RECEPTION
Watersports • Exhibitions • History Excursions
Social Functions • Etc.
A large assembly of boats is expected to mark this Historic event
FURTHER DETAILS FROM –
DES LEYDEN
Chairman IWAI Dublin Branch
6 Foxrock Avenue
Dublin
Phone 895593
KEN SHAW
Chairman Naas Branch
12 The Grove
Celbridge
Phone 271253

The Naas Branch of the Grand Canal, closed in 1961, was the first branch to be restored. Restoration proposals began in the early 1970s, and it was restored with voluntary and government employment scheme assistance

canals, proceeded on a more piecemeal basis, partly because there was no existing navigable network to which restored sections could connect. After the defeat of County Council plans to fill in much of the Union Canal in Stirlingshire, navigation was gradually revived on the long lengths between obstructions. One former obstruction at Linlithgow was replaced by a new bridge in 1992, while trip boats for the disabled were introduced on both this canal and the adjacent Forth & Clyde. On the latter, boats operated on the summit level, and on the parts of the Glasgow Branch and adjacent sections of the main line restored under the Glasgow Canal Project from the late 1980s.

In the Irish Republic, the IWAI founded schemes to restore most of the Grand Canal branches, with that to Naas reopening in 1987; its Corbally extension may follow. The Ballinasloe Branch was mostly destroyed by peat workings, but a new navigation to Ballinasloe, using the River Suck, was partly opened in 1990, with completion anticipated in 1994.

The IWAI had not felt it practicable to revive the Royal Canal, whose main line was 90 miles long with 56 locks, and which closed in 1961. By 1974 the section west of Mullingar had been drained, with eight major obstructions, while there were proposals to use its line in Dublin for a motorway and other obstructions. The Royal Canal Amenity Group was rapidly formed to restore sections with a view to possible full restoration. The motorway proposals and another road obstruction were defeated, and local authority and CIE support for the protection of the line was gradually won; CIE was persuaded to repair the top gates at Lock 12, to allow work on the seven mile pound west of Blanchardstown. Support from AnCo and later the Social Employment Scheme (similar to the UK job creation schemes) led to the provision of two large lock gate workshops.

By 1990, the canal from Lock 12 to Mullingar was reopened, with completion of the 6 mile link to the Liffey programmed for 1994. Dredging and rewatering works had reached Toome Bridge, 75 miles from Dublin, with a dry length 15 miles long, with 7 locks but 6 lowered road crossings, separating this from the Shannon.

Probably the most ambitious restoration to be completed in the British Isles has involved the Ballinamore & Ballyconnell, upon which work commenced only at the end of 1990. Financial backing from the EC, for a waterway which crossed the border between the North and the Republic, through an area of exceptional rural depression, secured restoration and reopening in 1994. At a cost of £28 million, work on this canal, 38 miles long with 16 locks, included the rebuilding of several lock chambers, the raising of the level of Lough Scur and dredging through two other loughs, and the widening of the former channel. Land acquisitions alone involved 450 farmers and 650 acres.

In the North, restoration had been proposed by the early 1990s for all of the major canals. This included proposals to clear the terminal basin on the Coalisland Canal, and the clearance of a short section of the Ulster Canal, at Benburb, as part of the Blackwater Valley Museum project. In 1994 voluntary work here by WRG would be its first outside the British mainland. Following the example of the Ballinamore & Ballyconnell, proposals emerged to restore the Ulster, which crosses the border into the Republic, and of which some 10 miles have been filled in. Even the short Strabane Canal, mostly filled in, drew local authority support for restoration, which was perceived to develop tourism; here the restoration project itself was viewed as a potential tourist attraction.

The earliest restoration plans were for the Newry Canal, for which a full restoration scheme was costed by the job creation agency Enterprise Ulster in 1980. Actual restoration progress was at first limited to voluntary clearance work near Scarva in 1982, but the entrance locks on the Newry Ship Canal and the 4 miles to Albert Basin were restored in the late 1980s. This followed the acquisition of the length within Newry by the local council in 1987; the three other canalside authorities had all

The last coaster to use the Newry Ship Canal to Newry was the Saint William, *which carried its last cargo of timber to Newry in 1966. After the canal was acquired by Newry & Mourne District Council, permission was given for a number of pleasure boats to use the canal. On 26 September 1987 the gates were pulled open by a tractor and the craft passed through. Since then the lock has been fully restored* (McCutcheon Collection)

acquired their sections, for nominal sums, by 1992. One study carried out for the new owners recommended a gradual approach to restoration, restoring water levels to the summit, re-establishing the towpath, and generally clearing and maintaining structures like surviving bridges and lock chambers. A more ambitious plan, awaiting finance, would see the canal restored from the Bann to Newry, where lowered road crossings present major difficulties.

These attempts to rescue historic waterways and structures for future use and interest were matched by attempts to preserve traditional carrying craft, the growth of museums, and developments in waterways history. The preservation of craft was partly linked to the demise of traditional carrying, and to attempts to not only retain and restore historic craft, but also to develop their use. One example is the Wooden Canal Craft Trust, based on the Ashton Canal, which was founded in 1986 to restore wooden craft and to put them to various community-based uses. In 1992 this acquired *Raymond*, the last wooden narrow boat to be built, in 1958, which had been used on the last run to Croxley in 1970.

In 1990 a number of owner/carriers, not all owners of traditional craft, grouped together to form the Commercial Narrowboat Operators Association, backing enthusiasm with professional organization; based mainly in the South Midlands, the carrying craft involved had grown from an initial nine to forty in 1993.

These enthusiasts have succeeded in preserving the appearance of traditional narrow boat carrying operations, while many private owners, such as those in the Narrow Boat Owners Club, have also contributed to preservation. This interest in craft has led to what may be termed 'boat genealogy', striving for comprehensive and minute detail and authenticity; this has sometimes extended to the genealogy of boatpeople and canal workers, reflecting the explosion in interest in family history from the 1970s onwards.

Larger traditional craft did not attract the same enthusiasm as narrow boats, but some were preserved in floating collections. The largest of these was at the Boat Museum at Ellesmere Port, which expanded after 1976 to include the preservation of much of the historic port site as the craft and exhibits, along with a large archive collection. Much restoration work on craft, buildings and artefacts was carried out by volunteers, with considerable input from MSC schemes until the late 1980s.

In contrast, the National Waterways Museum at Gloucester was mainly founded by BWB, and opened in 1988. This was also located in a historic canal port setting, although not quite as ruinous, with the main exhibitions sited in the former Llanthony Warehouse. BWB secured the future of many of the port buildings, by promoting sympathetic property development, which have made the Docks area a tourist attraction in its own right. The older Stoke Bruerne operation was renamed the Canal Museum in 1989.

Smaller museums or exhibition centres elsewhere sought to highlight the history of local waterways, such as that in Nottingham and the London Canal Museum. The development of Summerlee Heritage Park at Coatbridge in the 1980s involved the digging out of an infilled length of the Monkland Canal. Developments like that at Wigan Pier, including a trip boat to the nearby Trencherfield Mill, helped to preserve canal buildings with some interpretation of their setting.

Museums in Ireland, with a much smaller population, have been slower to develop; that at Robertstown, in the former Grand Canal Hotel, closed due to financial difficulties, although several museums include canal exhibits. One aim of the Dublin Nautical Trust, founded in 1986, is the preservation of historic canal craft, including Grand Canal barges, at

Ringsend. The OPW opened a Visitor Centre at Ringsend in 1993, which will probably feature floating exhibits in due course. In the North, a small exhibition centre in the former stables at Moneypenny's Lock, on the Newry Canal, opened formally in 1992.

The major histories completed in the 1970s were followed by many smaller, often locally produced, publications on canal history. Some used documentation which was newly deposited in archives, while others developed the practice of oral history. Many articles based on the memories of former boatpeople and canal workers began to appear; perhaps the most prominent historian is Mike Taylor, who has done much, especially for the Yorkshire waterways, to preserve memories from many whose personal testimony is no longer available. This was encouraged by the growth of magazines taking historical articles, such as *Waterways World* and *Canal and Riverboat*, both founded in the 1970s, along with BWB's *Waterways News* before it was replaced by a house magazine in 1989.

The growth of local archives, supplementing the collections in the Public Record Office, has provided canal historians with solid written evidence on a subject which had, as Charles Hadfield stated in an earlier edition of this book, 'been somewhat at the mercy of guesswork and catchwords'. Some of this examination of documentation has led to the revision of what had been accepted wisdom, indirectly over the role of Brindley and the Gilberts, in Peter Lead's *Agents of Revolution* (1989), and directly for Jessop and Telford, in Charles Hadfield's *Thomas Telford's Temptation* (1993).

New fields of history and new approaches have also yielded insights. Social historians, like Wendy Freer and Harry Hanson, have examined the working and living conditions, organizations and everyday lives of canal workers. Industrial archaeology, extending to excavations on the Bude and Grand Western Canals, or to the history of industries served by canals, has yielded many insights since its first formulations in the 1950s. Finally, the early 1990s saw the beginning of interest in the history of pleasure boating, reflecting perhaps the demise of many early pleasure boaters and their craft.

The growing popularity of towpath walking from the 1970s was reflected in expanding numbers of publications. Many have experienced waterways by walking their banks, and towpaths had long been used for informal walking where there were accessible. However, as the BWB Annual Report of 1967 stated:

> Hitherto a 'trespassers will be prosecuted' policy has been traditional – in the distant past because the towing paths were extensively used for

> their original purpose, and in the more recent past because the uncertainty surrounding the future of the smaller waterways made it difficult to do anything which would tend to establish rights of way.[8]

This resistance was reduced once most horse or tractor towage had ended, while the security provided by the 1968 Transport Act made more positive policies possible. From the 1970s many local authorities funded improvements to paths both in rural and urban areas. Devon County Council acquired and restored the remainder Grand Western Canal in 1972 and opened it into a linear country park by 1974, with boating use limited. In other areas, towpath clearance preceded any restoration of the canal itself, as with the Droitwich Barge Canal, where only the summit level in Droitwich was navigable by 1993.

From 1978 BWB formally permitted the use of all its towpaths. There was potential for conflicts with other users, notably anglers and cyclists, with, from 1983, new restrictions on cycling.

Long distance public footpaths, for which enabling legislation dated from 1949, began to be opened in the 1960s. The Offas Dyke Path, which opened in 1971, included a short length of the Llangollen Canal towpath near Pontcysyllte. In July 1993 the opening of the first long distance towpath, the 145 mile long Grand Union Canal Walk, followed the expenditure of £1 million on bank protection, path laying and signposting. Other formal long distance canal paths may follow.

In Ireland, the OPW has encouraged the clearance and development of towpaths, including that along the unrestored parts of the Royal Canal. The towpath of the Newry Canal now forms part of the Ulster Way.

While many ramblers are keen walkers of towpaths, there was no specific group to promote towpath walking until the formation of the Towpath Action Group in 1987-8. Inspired by the construction of a new wall which obstructed the newly restored towpath of the Rochdale Canal in Manchester, the group went on to investigate access to the whole Rochdale Canal and to protest about the lack of facilities for walkers, especially in restoration schemes which concentrated solely on navigation. By 1993 TAG had about 160 members, the majority in north-west England, and was involved in assisting the restoration of towpaths as well as a campaigning role.

When in 1950 the first edition of *British Canals* was reviewed in a well-known weekly, the reviewer suggested that Charles Hadfield should have given his views on the future of the waterways. But *Hadfield's British Canals* is a history, and I too will resist the temptation to offer predictions. Interestingly though, an age-old pattern is showing through. Before and during the Middle Ages, people and light goods moved by road, most heavy goods, if they could, by water. In those days the maritime link was strong, sailing vessels navigating rivers and the sea alike. The turnpike mania widened and improved road facilities, and the subsequent canal mania did the same for waterways. The two, along with maritime-linked rivers and canals, underlay the first industrial revolution. Then came railways, to sweep away much road and water transport. But now railways are of minor importance for most freight and passenger carrying except for specialized traffics, and we find ourselves back with roads and waterways, fulfilling their old functions, but upon improved roads and (perhaps) improving waterways, and with very different vehicles and craft. There are two changes: rail and to a smaller extent road have lost passengers, though little freight, to a new means of transport, the air, and road, though rail only marginally, has gained a maritime link by means of RoRo ferries, and indirectly through the Channel Tunnel.

Towards the late 1990s, the world of inland waterways has been transformed by the growth since the war of amenity interests, especially pleasure boating, to major significance from almost nothing. Both in Britain and Ireland, this has recreated an obsolete network of small waterways, albeit not always in ways that early supporters of its retention would have wished. On the freight side, inland waterways in Britain (but not in Ireland) no longer represent a losing and old-fashioned transport mode, but one which, over limited routes, has potential if the opportunities presented by changes in technologies, traffics, and vessels are grasped. As many of the significant waterways are estuarial, the history of modern waterborne freight routes has moved away from the artificial waterways whose history is discussed in this book.

The last edition of *British Canals*, in 1983, closed on a note of optimism about the future for waterborne freight in Britain. Experience of developments in the last decade has suggested a more pessimistic view, given the lack of real popular or central government support for inland waterways freight in Britain. Only the unfolding of future policies and developments will reveal which view is correct.

The history of the canals of the British Isles continues.

Notes

Chapter One

1 Quoted in T.S. Willan, *River Navigation in England, 1600–1750*, 1936, p. 106, referring to the Medway Navigation.

2 Quoted in Keith Fairclough, 'A Survey of the River Lea by Sir Christopher Wren' in *Journal of the Railway and Canal Historical Society*, Vol. 31, Pt 1, No. 153, March 1993.

3 *A Report of the Committee of the Commissioners of the Navigation of the Thames and Isis, appointed to survey the rivers from Lechlade to Whitchurch . . .*, 1791 (Institution of Civil Engineers).

4 H.C. Darby, *The Medieval Fenland*, 1940.

5 L.F. Vernon-Harcourt, *Rivers and Canals*, 1882, p. 81.

6 Quoted in H.C. Darby, *The Draining of the Fens*, 1940.

7 Quoted from the Journals of the House of Lords in T.S. Willan, *River Navigation in England, 1600–1750*, 1936.

8 F.G. Blacklock, *The Suppressed Benedictine Minister and other Ancient and Modern Institutions of the Borough of Leominster*, 1898.

9 Mersey & Irwell Act, 7 Geo I c 15.

10 2 Geo I c 12 (Ireland).

11 *Dublin News-Letter*, 30 March 1742.

12 Obituary notice of Henry Berry, *Liverpool Mercury*, 7 August 1812.

13 *Annual Register*, 1760, p. 160.

14 C. Humbert, *The History and Description of the County of Shropshire*, 1837, p. 94n.

Chapter Two

1 Thomas Telford, *A Survey and Report of the proposed extension of the Union Canal from Gumley Wharf, in Leicestershire, to the Grand Junction Canal, near Buckby-Wharf, in Northamptonshire*, 1804.

2 H.F. Killick, 'Notes on the early history of the Leeds & Liverpool Canal' in *The Bradford Antiquary*, July 1897.

3 J.A. Langford, *A Century of Birmingham Life*, 1868, quoting a local newspaper.

4 W. Cobbett, *Rural Rides*, Vol. 2, 1912, p. 93 (Everyman edition).

5 *Thames Navigation. Observations upon the evidence adduced before the Committee of the House of Commons upon the . . . Hants and Berks Canal*, 1825.

6 *Felix Farley's Bristol Journal*, 22 March 1794.

7 E. Meteyard, *Life of Josiah Wedgwood*, 1866.

8 J.S. Padley, *Fens and Floods of Mid-Lincolnshire*, 1882.

9 Gloucester & Berkeley Canal Minute Book, 23 December 1794.
10 Thames & Severn Canal Records (Glos CRO).
11 J.A. Langford, *A Century of Birmingham Life.*
12 Ashby de la Zouch Canal Minute Book, 1 July 1794.
13 Birmingham Canal Minute Book, 14 July 1769.
14 J.S. Padley, *Fens and Floods.*
15 H.F. Killick, *Bradford Antiquary.*
16 Kennet & Avon Canal Minute Book, 10 April 1797.
17 Quoted in D.R. Phillips, *The History of the Vale of Neath,* 1925.
18 Unidentified newspaper cutting (Charles Hadfield collection).

Chapter Three

1 C. Nicholson, *The Annals of Kendal,* 2nd edn, 1861.
2 Swansea Canal Minute Book, 9 June 1803.
3 J.A. Langford, *A Century of Birmingham Life,* 1868.
4 Anon, *An Authentic Description of the Kennet & Avon Canal . . .*, 1811 (Institution of Civil Engineers).
5 J. Plymley, *A General View of the Agriculture of Shropshire,* 1813. Article by Telford on 'Canals' dated 1797.
6 Grand Junction Canal Minute Book, 9 July 1811.
7 Charles Dickens, 'On the Canal' in *Household Words,* 11 September 1858.
8 Grand Junction Canal Minute Book, 10 November 1825.
9 W. Hutton, *A History of Birmingham,* 2nd edn, 1783.
10 Grand Junction Canal Minute Book, 13 September 1808.
11 Driffield Navigation Minute Book, 6 July 1841.
12 J. Plymley, *A General View.*
13 L.F. Vernon-Harcourt, *Rivers and Canals,* 2nd edn, 1896.
14 Birmingham Canal Act, 23 Geo III, c 92.
15 A. Rees, *Cyclopedia,* 1819. Article on 'Canals' written 1805.
16 Illustrated in *Country Life,* 22 December 1955, article 'History in Ceramics', by Stanley W. Fisher.
17 Staffs & Worcs Canal Minute Book, 14 September 1832.
18 Basingstoke Canal Report, 20 May 1802.
19 *Illustrated London News,* 10 October 1874.
20 Swansea Canal Minute Book, 3 March 1818.
21 Peak Forest Canal Minute Book, 16 May 1806.
22 Staffs & Worcs Canal Minute Book, 23 August 1823.
23 Quoted in F.S. Thacker, *The Thames Highway: A History of the Locks and Weirs,* 1920.
24 Regent's Canal Minute Book, 1 December 1830.

Chapter Four

1 *Case of the Birmingham Canal Committee, in opposition to the Dudley Canal Extension Bill,* nd.
2 J. Phillips, *A General History of Inland Navigation,* 4th edn, 1803.

Chapter Five

1 *Exeter Flying Post*, 2 January 1794.
2 J. Latimer, *The Annals of Bristol in the Eighteenth Century*, 1893.
3 Salisbury & Southampton Canal records.
4 Peak Forest Canal Minute Book, 7 July 1794.
5 Article by Thomas Telford in J. Plymley, *A General View of the Agriculture of Shropshire*, 1813.
6 Kennet & Avon Canal Reports, 14 June 1797 and 26 June 1798.
7 Letter to shareholders, 29 January 1798. Kennet & Avon Canal records.
8 Grand Junction Canal Minute Book, 5 July 1797.
9 Basingstoke Canal report, 26 October 1803.
10 *Records of the Borough of Nottingham, 1760-1800*, Vol. VII, 1947.
11 Grand Junction Canal Minute Book, 5 May 1801.
12 Tavistock Canal Report, 16 March 1803.
13 Tavistock Canal Report, 27 September 1816.
14 Ibid.
15 Ibid.

Chapter Six

1 J. Knox, *A View of the British Empire, more especially Scotland, with some proposals for the improvement of that country, the extension of its fisheries and the relief of the people*, 1784.
2 J. Phillips, *A General History of Inland Navigation*, 4th edn, 1803.
3 Quoted in E.A.Pratt, *Scottish Canals and Waterways*, 1922.
4 *Prospectus of the advantages to be derived from the Crinan Canal*, 1792.
5 Daniel Defoe, *A Tour thro' the whole Island of Great Britain*, 1724–6.
6 H.W. Dickinson, *James Watt*, 1936.
7 English & Bristol Channels Ship Canal Report, 23 June 1828.
8 *Canals and Waterways Journal*, January 1982.
9 J. Phillips, *A General History of Inland Navigation*, 2nd edn, 1795.
10 Gloucester & Berkeley Canal Minute Book, 28 October 1794.
11 Ibid., 11 August 1795.
12 Ibid., 2 June 1797.
13 Ibid., 14 July 1818.
14 Ibid., 5 October 1871.

Chapter Seven

1 Basingstoke Canal Report, 21 October 1816.
2 Ibid., 11 October 1822.
3 Kennet & Avon Canal. Minutes of a meeting of the Western sub-committee, 10 November 1840.
4 E.T. Meteyard, *Life of Josiah Wedgwood*, 1866.
5 H.F. Killick, 'Notes on the early history of the Leeds & Liverpool Canal' in *The Bradford Antiquary*, July 1897.
6 E.A. Pratt, *Scottish Canals and Waterways*, 1922.
7 T. Grahame, *Essays and Letters on . . . Inland Communications*, 1835.

8 Quoted in 'The Lancaster Canal and its Connection with Railways', *LMS Railway Magazine*, November 1928.
9 J. Farey, *A General View of the Agriculture of Derbyshire*, 1817.
10 Charles Lever, *Jack Hinton: The Guardsman*, 1843, CLXX.
11 Prospectus of the Stirling Canal, 1813 (Charles Hadfield collection).
12 *Exeter Flying Post*, 22 November 1810.
13 B.T. Barton, *History of the Borough of Bury*, 1874.
14 Birmingham Canal Proprietors' Minute Book, 14 May 1841.

Chapter Eight

1 MS History of the Kennet Navigation, *c.* 1810 (Institution of Civil Engineers).
2 Bridgewater & Taunton Canal records.
3 *A Report of the Committee of the Commissioners of the Navigation of the Thames and Isis, appointed to survey the rivers from Lechlade to Whitchurch . . . ,* 1791 (Institution of Civil Engineers).
4 *Report from the Committee of the Hon the House of Commons appointed to enquire into the progress made towards the amendment and improvement of the Thames and Isis,* 1793 (Institution of Civil Engineers).
5 *Report of a Survey of the River Thames from Lechlade to the City Stone . . .*, 1811 (Institution of Civil Engineers).

Chapter Nine

1 Thames & Severn Canal Report, 25 January 1825.
2 Report of Canal Conference of 1888. Royal Society of Arts. Paper on the *History, Rise and Progress of Canal and River Navigation in Great Britain and Ireland,* by M.B. Cotsworth.
3 Quoted in D. Trevor Williams, *The economic development of Swansea and of the Swansea district to 1921*, University of Wales Press, Page 129.
4 Basingstoke Canal, Notice of Meeting, 12 September 1831.
5 Kennet & Avon Canal Report, 21 July 1835.
6 Staffs & Worcs Canal Minute Book, 7 May 1840.
7 Ibid., 4 September 1845.
8 Grand Junction Canal Minute Book, 23 October 1845.
9 *Minutes of Evidence of the Royal Commission on the Canals and Inland Navigations of the United Kingdom.* Answers to questions 23965 and 23970.
10 Kennet & Avon Canal Report, 21 July 1845.
11 Birmingham Canal Navigations Minute Book, 22 February 1878.
12 Staffs & Worcs Canal Minute Book, 12 December 1844.
13 Ibid., 30 December 1844.
14 James Wheeler, *Manchester: Its Political, Social and Commercial History, Ancient and Modern*, 1836.

Chapter Ten

1 Grand Junction Canal Minute Book, 28 May 1841.
2 Ibid., 16 July 1845.
3 Ibid., 21 May 1846.

4 Ibid., 2 October 1857.
5 Ibid., 7 January 1859.
6 Swansea Canal Minute Book, 5 September 1809.
7 *Journal of a Somerset Rector*, 1930.
8 Recounted in *IWA Bulletin* 71, June 1964.

Chapter Eleven

1 *Report of Canal Conference of 1888* (Royal Society of Arts). Letter from W.M.T. Campbell.
2 Ibid., paper on *The Relative Cost of Transport by Railway and Canal*, by W. Shelford.
3 A. Woodroofe Fletcher, *The Economic Results of the Ship Canal on Manchester and the Surrounding Districts*, 1899.
4 *Minutes of Evidence of the Royal Commission on the Canals and Inland Navigations of the United Kingdom*, 1906–10. Answer to Question 1468, 15 May 1906.
5 Ibid. Answer to Question 19214.
6 *Report to the Board of Trade on the Thames and Severn Canal*, 1888 (Glos CRO).
7 Gloucester & Berkeley Canal Report, 1 April 1864.
8 Grand Junction Canal Minute Book, 6 March 1835.
9 Michael Streat, owner of *Blue Line*, quoted in Tom Chaplin, *The Narrow Boat Book*, 1977, p. 115.
10 James Unsworth, 'Life on the Leeds & Liverpool', in *Waterways World*, April 1981, p. 52.
11 Private correspondence, 25 November 1991 and 20 October 1993.
12 Ruth Delany, *Ireland's Inland Waterways*, 1st edn, 1986, p. 143.

Chapter Twelve

1 *Report of the Royal Commission on the Canals and Inland Navigations of the United Kingdom*, 1907–9. Vol VII. Final report, para 28.
2 Ibid., para 20.
3 Ibid., para 442.
4 L.T.C. Rolt, *Green and Silver*, 1949, pp. 83–4.
5 *Minutes of Evidence of the Royal Commission on the Canals and Inland Navigations of the United Kingdom.* Question 22588, 27 February 1907.
6 Austin E. Neal, *Canals, Cruises and Contentment*, Heath Cranton, London, nd (*c.*1921), p. 134.
7 V. Gregory, quoted in *Waterways News*, January 1976, p. 4.
8 Clive Reed, Social Outings on the Swansea Canal, *Swansea Canal Society Newsletter*, October 1993.

Chapter Thirteen

1 BTC Supporting Papers, 9/9/1949, PRO AN85/2.
2 Frank Pick, *Report on Canals and Inland Waterways to the Ministry of War Transport*, unpublished document, 1941, pp. 49–50.
3 Foreword to Lewis A Edwards, *Inland Waterways of Great Britain and Northern Ireland*, London, 1950.

4 British Waterways Board, *The Future of the Waterways*, 1964, p. 17
5 Graham Palmer, In The Beginning, *Peak Forest Canal Society Newsletter*, No 23, October 1968, p. 9.
6 British Waterways Board, *The Future of the Waterways*, 1964, p. 44.
7 British Waterways Board, *The Facts about the Waterways*, 1965, p. 84.
8 Quoted in *IWA Bulletin* 75, November 1965, p. 39.
9 British Waterways Board, *The Future of the Waterways*, 1964, p. 28.

Chapter Fourteen

1 British Waterways Board, *Report and Accounts for the 15 months to 31st March 1985*, Appendix VI.
2 Ibid., p. 2.
3 Sir Frank Price, in *Waterways News*, No. 91, June/July 1979.
4 Ministry of Transport, *Report of the Committee of Inquiry into the Major Ports of Great Britain*, HMSO, September 1962.
5 Manchester Ship Canal Company, *Annual Report and Accounts*, 1981.
6 Ibid., 1985, p. 3.
7 Ralph Kirkham, letter in *Waterways World*, December 1973.
8 British Waterways Board, *Annual Report and Accounts*, 1967, p. 17.

Further Reading

The following is a selection of useful sources on canals and river navigations in the British Isles. The dates given are those of the first edition, unless otherwise stated.

Periodicals include *Industrial Archaeology*, the *Journal of the Railway and Canal Historical Society*, the *Journal of Transport History*, the *Minutes of Proceedings of the Institution of Civil Engineers* (and its *Journal* and *Proceedings*), *Transactions* of the Newcomen Society, *Transport History*, and the periodicals published by numerous local history and canal societies. Bibliographies are to be found (for material published before 1916) in Jackman's *The Development of Transportation in Modern England* and, most recently, in Edward Paget-Tomlinson's *The Illustrated History of Canal & River Navigations*. Mark Baldwin's *Canal Books* usefully discusses the literature of waterways, while detailed bibliographies are published annually in the *Journal of the Railway and Canal Historical Society*.

Official publications are not listed here, and the *Canals of the British Isles* series are detailed in the index to that series (pp. 328–35).

General transport and canal history

Albert, William, *The Turnpike Road System in England, 1663–1840*, 1972.

Anon., *The History of Inland Navigation*, 1766.

Bagwell, Philip S., *The Transport Revolution from 1770*, 1974.

Barker, T.C. and Savage, C.I., *An Economic History of Transport in Britain*, 3rd edn, 1974.

Baxter, Bertram, *Stone Blocks and Iron Rails*, 1966.

Bonavia, Michael R, *The Nationalisation of British Transport*, 1987.

De Salis, H.R., *A Chronology of Inland Navigation in Great Britain*, 1897.

Delany, Ruth, *Ireland's Inland Waterways*, 2nd edn 1993.

Dyos, H.J. and Aldcroft, D.H., *British Transport*, 1969.

Forbes, U.A. and Ashford, W.H.R., *Our Waterways*, 1906.

Hadfield, Charles, *The Canal Age*, 2nd edn, 1981.

Jackman, W.T., *The Development of Transportation in Modern England*, 1916.

Lead, Peter, *Agents of Revolution: John and Thomas Gilbert – Entrepreneurs*, 1989.

Lewis, M.J.T., *Early Wooden Railways*, 1970.

McCutcheon, W.A., *The Industrial Archaeology of Northern Ireland*, 1980.

Paget-Tomlinson, Edward W., *The Illustrated History of Canal & River Navigations*, 1993.

Pawson, Eric, *Transport and Economy: The Turnpike Roads of Eighteenth Century Britain*, 1977.

Phillips, J., *A General History of Inland Navigation*, 5th edn 1792.
Porteous, J.D., *Canal Ports: The Urban Achievement of the Canal Age*, 1978.
Pratt, Edwin A., *Scottish Canals and Waterways*, 1922.
Priestley, Joseph, *Historical Account of the Navigable Rivers, Canals and Railways, throughout Great Britain*, 1831.
Rees, A. 'Canals', *Cyclopedia*, 1819.
Rolt, L.T.C., *Navigable Waterways*, 1969.
Russell, Ronald, *Lost Canals and Waterways of Britain*, 1982.
Ward, J.R., *The Finance of Canal Building in Eighteenth Century England*, 1974.
Willan, T.S., *River Navigation in England 1600–1750*, 1936.
Willan, T.S., *The English Coasting Trade 1660–1750*, 1938.
Willan, T.S., *The Inland Trade*, 1976.
Wright, Ian L., *Canals in Wales*, 1977.

Single waterways or localities

Bick, David E., *The Hereford & Gloucester Canal*, 1979.
Blagrove, David, *Waterways of Northamptonshire*, 1990.
Blair, May, *Once Upon The Lagan: The Story of the Lagan Canal*, 1981.
Broadbridge, S.R., *The Birmingham Canal Navigations* Vol. I (1768–1846) 1974.
Cameron, A.D., *The Caledonian Canal*, 1972.
Chester-Browne, Richard, *The Other Sixty Miles*, [Birmingham Canal Navigations], 1981.
Clarke, J.N., *The Horncastle and Tattershall Canal*, 1990.
Clarke, Mike, *The Leeds & Liverpool Canal*, 1990.
Clarke, Peter, *The Royal Canal: the Complete Story*, 1992.
Clew, Kenneth, A., *The Dorset & Somerset Canal*, 1971.
Clew, Kenneth, A., *The Exeter Canal*, 1984.
Clew, Kenneth, A., *The Kennet & Avon Canal*, 3rd edn 1985.
Clew, Kenneth A., *The Somersetshire Coal Canal and Railways*, 1970.
Compton, Hugh J., *The Oxford Canal*, 1976.
Corbridge, John, *A Pictorial History of the Mersey & Irwell Navigation*, 1979.
Cuss, Edwin and Gardiner, Stanley, *The Stroudwater and Thames & Severn in Old Photographs*, 1988.
Dalby, L. J., *The Wilts & Berks Canal*, 2nd edn, 1986.
Delany, Ruth, *The Grand Canal of Ireland*, 1973.
——, *By Shannon Shores*, 1987.
Denney, Martyn, *London's Waterways*, 1977.
Duckham, Baron F., *The Yorkshire Ouse*, 1967.
Ewans, M.C., *The Haytor Granite Tramway and Stover Canal*, 1966.
Farnie, D.A., *The Manchester Ship Canal and the Rise of the Port of Manchester 1894–1975*, 1980.
Faulkner, Alan H., *The Grand Junction Canal*, 1993.
——, *The Grand Union Canal in Hertfordshire*, 1987.
——, *The Warwick Canals*, 1985.
Flanagan, Patrick J., *The Ballinamore & Ballyconnell Canal*, 1972.

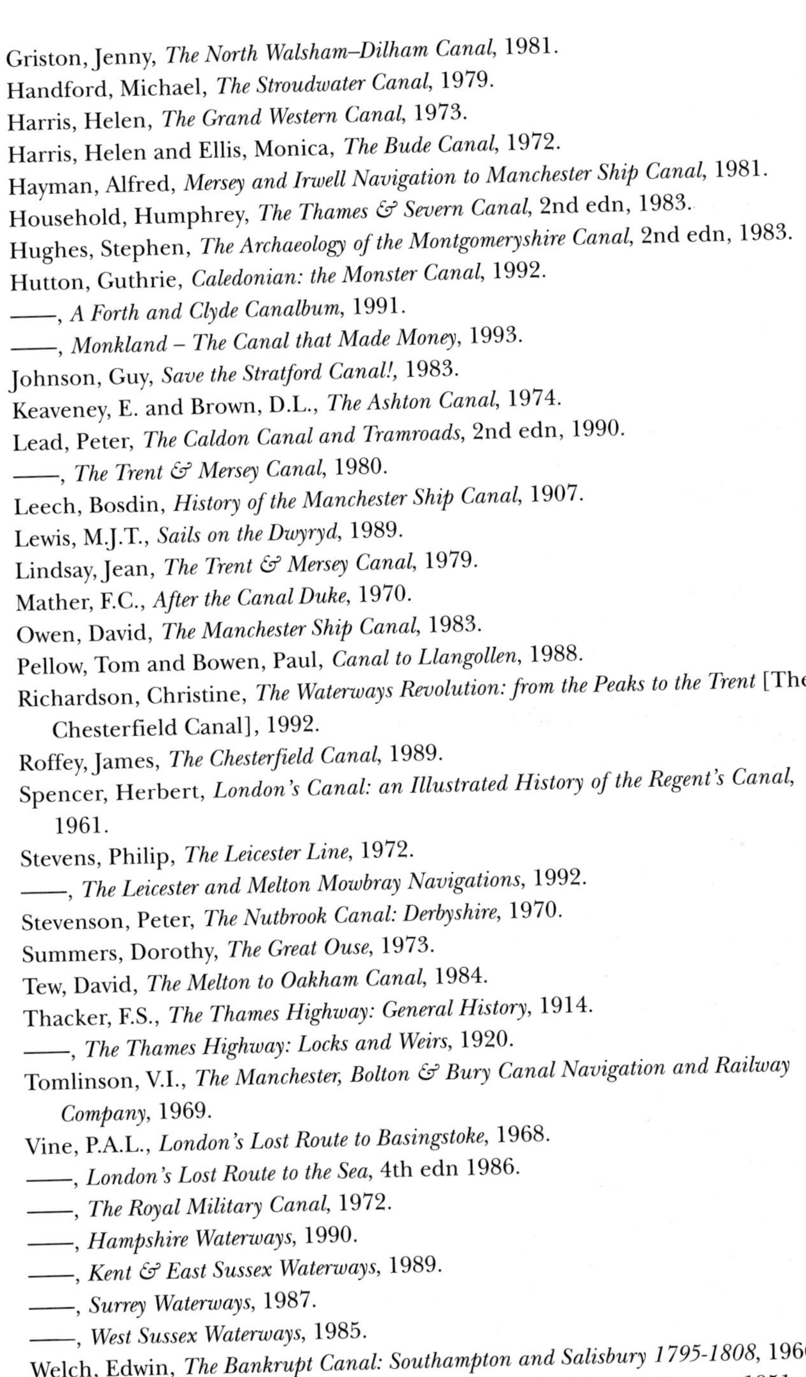

Griston, Jenny, *The North Walsham–Dilham Canal*, 1981.
Handford, Michael, *The Stroudwater Canal*, 1979.
Harris, Helen, *The Grand Western Canal*, 1973.
Harris, Helen and Ellis, Monica, *The Bude Canal*, 1972.
Hayman, Alfred, *Mersey and Irwell Navigation to Manchester Ship Canal*, 1981.
Household, Humphrey, *The Thames & Severn Canal*, 2nd edn, 1983.
Hughes, Stephen, *The Archaeology of the Montgomeryshire Canal*, 2nd edn, 1983.
Hutton, Guthrie, *Caledonian: the Monster Canal*, 1992.
——, *A Forth and Clyde Canalbum*, 1991.
——, *Monkland – The Canal that Made Money*, 1993.
Johnson, Guy, *Save the Stratford Canal!*, 1983.
Keaveney, E. and Brown, D.L., *The Ashton Canal*, 1974.
Lead, Peter, *The Caldon Canal and Tramroads*, 2nd edn, 1990.
——, *The Trent & Mersey Canal*, 1980.
Leech, Bosdin, *History of the Manchester Ship Canal*, 1907.
Lewis, M.J.T., *Sails on the Dwyryd*, 1989.
Lindsay, Jean, *The Trent & Mersey Canal*, 1979.
Mather, F.C., *After the Canal Duke*, 1970.
Owen, David, *The Manchester Ship Canal*, 1983.
Pellow, Tom and Bowen, Paul, *Canal to Llangollen*, 1988.
Richardson, Christine, *The Waterways Revolution: from the Peaks to the Trent* [The Chesterfield Canal], 1992.
Roffey, James, *The Chesterfield Canal*, 1989.
Spencer, Herbert, *London's Canal: an Illustrated History of the Regent's Canal*, 1961.
Stevens, Philip, *The Leicester Line*, 1972.
——, *The Leicester and Melton Mowbray Navigations*, 1992.
Stevenson, Peter, *The Nutbrook Canal: Derbyshire*, 1970.
Summers, Dorothy, *The Great Ouse*, 1973.
Tew, David, *The Melton to Oakham Canal*, 1984.
Thacker, F.S., *The Thames Highway: General History*, 1914.
——, *The Thames Highway: Locks and Weirs*, 1920.
Tomlinson, V.I., *The Manchester, Bolton & Bury Canal Navigation and Railway Company*, 1969.
Vine, P.A.L., *London's Lost Route to Basingstoke*, 1968.
——, *London's Lost Route to the Sea*, 4th edn 1986.
——, *The Royal Military Canal*, 1972.
——, *Hampshire Waterways*, 1990.
——, *Kent & East Sussex Waterways*, 1989.
——, *Surrey Waterways*, 1987.
——, *West Sussex Waterways*, 1985.
Welch, Edwin, *The Bankrupt Canal: Southampton and Salisbury 1795-1808*, 1966.
Willan, T.S., *The Navigation of the River Weaver in the Eighteenth Century*, 1951.
——, *The Early History of the Don Navigation*, 1965.
Wilson, D.G., *The Thames: Record of a Working Waterway*, 1987.
Wilson, E.A., *The Ellesmere and Llangollen Canal*, 1975.

Engineers

Beckett, Derrick, *Telford's Britain*, 1987.
Boucher, C.T.G., *James Brindley, Engineer, 1716–1772*, 1968.
Burton, Anthony, *The Canal Builders*, 3rd edn, 1993.
Dickinson, H.W., *Robert Fulton, Engineer and Artist*, 1913.
Hadfield, Charles, *Thomas Telford's Temptation: Telford and William Jessop's Reputation*, 1993.
Hadfield, Charles and Skempton, A.W., *William Jessop, Engineer*, 1979.
Malet, Hugh, *Bridgewater, The Canal Duke, 1736–1803*, 1977.
Rolt, L.T.C., *Thomas Telford: a Biography*, 1958.
Smiles, Samuel, *Lives of the Engineers*, 1861–2.

Boats, Carriers and Canal People

Alsop, Roger and Dodkins, Graham, *Working Boats*, 1988.
Blagrove, David, *Bread upon the Waters*, 1984.
Carr, Frank, *Sailing Barges*, revd edn, 1971.
Chaplin, Tom, *Narrow Boats*, 1989.
Clark, Roy, *Black-Sailed Traders: the Keels and Wherries of Norfolk and Suffolk*, 1961.
Conway-Jones, Hugh, *Working Life on Severn and Canal*, 1990.
Cornish, Margaret, *Troubled Waters: Memoirs of a Canal Boatwoman*, 1987.
Crabtree, Harold and Clarke, Mike, *Railway on the Water: Tom Puddings and the Yorkshire Coal Industry*, 1993.
D'Arcy, G., *Portrait of the Grand Canal*, 1969.
Faulkner, Alan H., *Barlows*, 1986.
——, *Claytons of Oldbury*, 1978.
——, *F.M.C.*, 1975.
——, *Severn and Canal and Cadburys*, 1981.
——, *The George and the Mary*, 1973.
——, *Willow Wren*, 1986.
Foxon, Tom, *Anderton for Orders*, 1988.
——, *Number One!*, 1991.
Gayford, Eily, *The Amateur Boatwomen: Canal Boating, 1941–1945*, 1973.
Hanson, Harry, *The Canal Boatmen, 1760–1914*, 1975.
——, *Canal People*, 1978.
Lewery, A.J., *Narrow Boat Painting*, 1974.
Malster, Robert, *Wherries and Waterways*, 2nd edn, 1986.
Schofield, Fred, *Humber Keels and Keelmen*, 1989.
Smith, D.J., *The Horse on the Cut*, 1982.
Smith, Emma, *Maiden's Trip*, 1948.
Smith, George, *Canal Adventures by Moonlight*, 1881.
——, *Our Canal Population*, 1875.
Smith, Peter L., *'Ethel' and 'Angela Jane'*, 1976.
Stammers, Michael, *Mersey Flats and Flatmen*, 1993.
Sullivan, Dick, *Navvyman*, 1983.

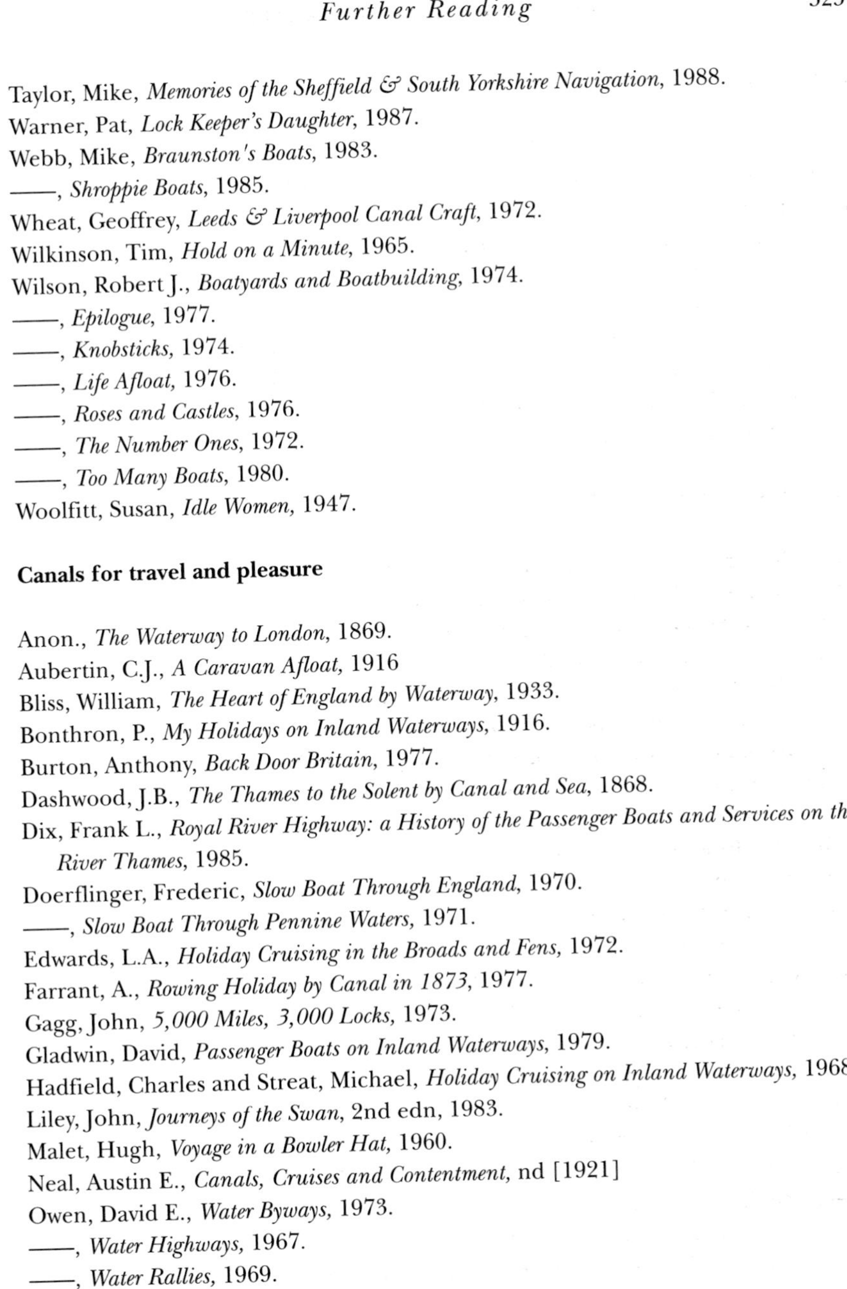

Taylor, Mike, *Memories of the Sheffield & South Yorkshire Navigation*, 1988.
Warner, Pat, *Lock Keeper's Daughter*, 1987.
Webb, Mike, *Braunston's Boats*, 1983.
——, *Shroppie Boats*, 1985.
Wheat, Geoffrey, *Leeds & Liverpool Canal Craft*, 1972.
Wilkinson, Tim, *Hold on a Minute*, 1965.
Wilson, Robert J., *Boatyards and Boatbuilding*, 1974.
——, *Epilogue*, 1977.
——, *Knobsticks*, 1974.
——, *Life Afloat*, 1976.
——, *Roses and Castles*, 1976.
——, *The Number Ones*, 1972.
——, *Too Many Boats*, 1980.
Woolfitt, Susan, *Idle Women*, 1947.

Canals for travel and pleasure

Anon., *The Waterway to London*, 1869.
Aubertin, C.J., *A Caravan Afloat*, 1916
Bliss, William, *The Heart of England by Waterway*, 1933.
Bonthron, P., *My Holidays on Inland Waterways*, 1916.
Burton, Anthony, *Back Door Britain*, 1977.
Dashwood, J.B., *The Thames to the Solent by Canal and Sea*, 1868.
Dix, Frank L., *Royal River Highway: a History of the Passenger Boats and Services on the River Thames*, 1985.
Doerflinger, Frederic, *Slow Boat Through England*, 1970.
——, *Slow Boat Through Pennine Waters*, 1971.
Edwards, L.A., *Holiday Cruising in the Broads and Fens*, 1972.
Farrant, A., *Rowing Holiday by Canal in 1873*, 1977.
Gagg, John, *5,000 Miles, 3,000 Locks*, 1973.
Gladwin, David, *Passenger Boats on Inland Waterways*, 1979.
Hadfield, Charles and Streat, Michael, *Holiday Cruising on Inland Waterways*, 1968.
Liley, John, *Journeys of the Swan*, 2nd edn, 1983.
Malet, Hugh, *Voyage in a Bowler Hat*, 1960.
Neal, Austin E., *Canals, Cruises and Contentment*, nd [1921]
Owen, David E., *Water Byways*, 1973.
——, *Water Highways*, 1967.
——, *Water Rallies*, 1969.
Pilkington, Roger, *Thames Waters*, 1956.
Ransom, P.J.G., *Holiday Cruising in Ireland*, 1971.
Rolt, L.T.C., *Green and Silver*, 1949.
——, *Narrow Boat*, 1944.
Seymour, John, *Sailing Through England*, 1956.
——, *Voyage into England*, 1966.
Smith, Cyril H., *Through the Kennet and Avon Canal by Motor Boat in 1928*, 1929.
Thurston, E. Temple, *The 'Flower of Gloster'*, 1911.

Vine, P.A.L., *Pleasure Boating in the Victorian Era*, 1983.
Westall, George, *Inland Cruising on the Rivers and Canals of England and Wales*, 1908.

General works – a selection

Aickman, Robert, *The River Runs Uphill*, 1986.
Baldwin, Mark, *Canal Books*, 1985.
Baldwin, Mark and Burton, Anthony (eds), *Canals: A New Look*, 1984.
Bolton, David, *Race Against Time*, 1990.
Braithwaite, Lewis A., *Canals in Towns*, 1976.
Burton, Anthony and Pratt, Derek, *Canal*, 1976.
Cadbury, G. and Dobbs, S.P,. *Canals and Inland Waterways*, 1929.
Compton, Hugh and Carr-Gomm, Anthony, *The Military on English Waterways 1798–1844*, 1991.
De Mare, Eric, *The Canals of England*, 1950.
De Salis, H.R., *Bradshaw's Canals and Navigable Rivers of England and Wales*, 1904, 1918 and 1928 edns.
Denney, Martyn, *Historic Waterways Scenes: London & South-East England*, 1980.
Edwards, L.A., *Inland Waterways of Great Britain*, 6th edn 1986.
Fairbairn, W., *Remarks on Canal Navigation, Illustrative of the Advantages of the Use of Steam, as a Moving Power on Canals*, 1831.
Fulton, R. A., *Treatise on the Improvement of Canal Navigation*, 1796.
Gagg, John, *Canals in Camera*, 1970.
Hadfield, Charles, *Waterways Sights to See*, 1977.
Harris, Robert, *Canals and their Architecture* ,2nd edn 1980.
Holland, Stanley, *Canal Coins*, 1992.
Inland Waterways Association, *British Freight Waterways Today & Tomorrow*, 1980.
Mackersey, Ian, *Tom Rolt and the Cressy Years*, 1985.
McKnight, Hugh, *Canal and River Craft in Pictures*, 1969.
——, *The Shell Book of Inland Waterways*, 2nd edn 1981.
——, *Waterways Postcards, 1900–1930*, 1983.
Nettlefold, J.S., *Garden Cities and Canals*, 1914.
Paget-Tomlinson, E., *Britain's Canal & River Craft*, 1979.
Palmer, J.E., *British Canals: Problems and Possibilities*, 1910.
Pratt, Edwin A., *British Canals: is Their Resuscitation Practicable?*, 1906.
——, *Canals and Traders*, 1910.
Ransom, P.J.G., *Waterways Restored*, 1974.
——, *The Archaeology of Canals*, 1979.
Rolt, L.T.C., *Landscape with Machines*, 1971.
——, *Landscape with Canals*, 1977.
——, *The Inland Waterways of England*, 1950.
Russell, Ronald, (ed) *Walking Canals*, 1984.
Smith, Peter L., *A Pictorial History of Canal Craft*, 1979.
Squires, Roger W., *Canals Revived: the Story of the Waterways Restoration Movement*, 1979.

——, *The New Navvies,* 1983.
Tew, David, *Canal Inclines and Lifts,* 1984.
Vernon-Harcourt, L.F., *Rivers and Canals,* 2nd edn 1896.
Ware, Michael E., *A Canalside Camera, 1845–1930,* 1975.
——, *Historic Waterways Scenes: Britain's Lost Waterways: Vol 1: Inland Navigations,* 1979.
——, *Historic Waterways Scenes: Britain's Lost Waterways: Vol 2: Navigations to the sea,* 1979.
——, *Narrow Boats at Work* ,1980.
Weaver, C.P and C.R., *Steam on Canals,* 1982.

Index to the 'Canals of the British Isles' Series

This index notes the volume in the series that contains the principal historical account of each canal, river navigation or branch in the British Isles. Unlike those in earlier editions of *British Canals*, this list only includes those projected waterways that were authorized by Act of Parliament. However, apart from navigable drains, this attempts to list every branch and every name under which particular canals have been known.

Subsidiary but useful references also occur in other volumes covering neighbouring regions; for example the principal account of the Rochdale Canal is in *The Canals of North West England*, but there is much subsidiary information in *The Canals of Yorkshire and North East England.*

Abbreviations

B = branch
C = canal
R = river
Nav = navigation
pr = projected, authorized by Act of Parliament, but no work carried out
uf = unfinished and never opened for navigation

Key to the *Canals of the British Isles* series:

BC	Hadfield, Charles, *British Canals.*
CEE	Boyes, John and Russell, Ronald, *The Canals of Eastern England,* 1977.
CEM	Hadfield, Charles, *The Canals of the East Midlands,* 2nd edn, 1970.
CNI	McCutcheon, W.A., *The Canals of the North of Ireland,* 1965.
CNWE	Hadfield, Charles and Biddle, Gordon, *The Canals of North West England,* 1970.
CS	Lindsay, Jean, *The Canals of Scotland,* 1968.
CSI	Delany, V.T.H. and D.R., *The Canals of the South of Ireland,* 1966.
CSSEE	Hadfield, Charles, *The Canals of South and South East England,* 1969.
CSWB	Hadfield, Charles, *The Canals of South Wales and the Border,* 2nd edn, 1967.
CSWE	Hadfield, Charles, *The Canals of South West England,* 2nd edn, 1985.
CWM	Hadfield, Charles, *The Canals of the West Midlands,* 3rd edn, 1985.
CYNEE	Hadfield, Charles, *The Canals of Yorkshire and North-East England,* 1972–3.
WS	Hadfield, Charles and Norris, John, *Waterways to Stratford,* 2nd edn, 1968.

Cann Quarry C	CSWE
Cannock Extension C	CWM
Canterbury Nav & Sandwich Harbour pr	CSSEE
Carlingwark C	CS
Carlisle C	CNWE
Carron Cut	CS
Cassington Cut	CEM
Chard C	CSWE
Charnwood Forest B	CEM
Chelmer & Blackwater Nav	CEE
Chemical B	CWM
Chester C	CWM
Chesterfield C	CEM
Chet R	CEE
Chichester C	CSSEE
Chippenham B	CSSEE
Churchbridge B	CWM
Cilybebyll B	CSWB
Cinderford C	CSWB
Circular Line	CSI
Cirencester B	CSSEE
Clifton & Kearsley Coal Co's C	CNWE
Cnel Bach B	CSWB
Coalbrookdale B	CWM
Coalisland C	CNI
Cod Beck	CYNEE
Colne R	CEE
Compstall Nav	CNWE
Cong C	CSI
Coombe Hill C	CWM
Corbally B	CSI
Corrib, Lough	CSI
Cottenham Lode	CEE
Counter Wash Drain	CEE
Court Sart B	CSWB
Coventry C	CEM
Crayford Creek	CSSEE
Crier Cut	CYNEE
Crinan C	CS
Cromford C	CEM
Croydon C	CSSEE
Crumlin B	CSWB
Crymlyn & Red Jacket C	CSWB
Cuckmere R	CSSEE
Cumberland Arm	CEM
Cyfarthfa C	CSWB
Dane Nav pr	CNWE
Danks B	CWM
Darley Mills B	CEM
Dartford & Crayford Nav	CSSEE
Dartmouth B	CWM
Daw End B	CWM
Dearne & Dove C	CYNEE
Dee R	CWM
Derby C	CEM
Derwent (Derbyshire) R	CEM
Derwent (Yorks) Nav	CYNEE
Dewsbury Cut	CYNEE
Dick Brook	CWM
Digbeth B	CWM
Dingwall C	CS
Dixon B	CWM
Doctor's C	CSWB
Don (Dun) Nav	CYNEE
Donnington Wood C	CWM
Dorset & Somerset C uf	CSWE
Douglas Nav	CNWE
Downs Dock C	CSSEE
Dr Thomas's C	CSWB
Driffield Nav	CYNEE
Droitwich C	CWM
Droitwich Junc C	CWM
Druxton B	CSWE
Ducart's C	CNI
Duckett's C	CEM
Dudley C	CWM
Duke's Cut	CEM
Dulais B	CSWB
Dundyvan B	CS
Dunkirk B	CWM
Dutch R	CYNEE
Eardington Forge C	CWM
Eastwood Cut	CYNEE
Eden R	CNWE
Edenderry B	CSI
Edinburgh & Glasgow Union C	CS
Eglinton C	CSI
Ellesmere B	CWM
Ellesmere C	CWM
Ellesmere & Chester C	CWM
Elsecar B	CWM
Emmet's C	CYNEE
English & Bristol Channels Ship C pr	CSWE
Erewash C	CEM
Erne, Lough	CSI

Ivel R CEE
Ivelchester & Langport Nav uf CSWE

Jamestown C CSI
Jersey C CSWE

Kemmett's C CSSEE
Kennet R CSSEE
Kennet & Avon C CSSEE
Kensington C CEM
Ketley C CWM
Kidwelly & Llanelly C CSWB
Kilbagie C CS
Kilbeggan B CSI
Kildare C CSI
Kilgetty C uf CSWB
Kilkenny C uf CSI
Knostrop Cut CYNEE
Knottingley & Goole C CYNEE
Kyme Eau CEE
Kymer's C CSWB

Lady Lee B CEM
Lagan C/Nav CNI
Lake Lock-Bottom Boat C CYNEE
Lakenheath Lode CEE
Lancaster C CNWE
Langloan B CS
Lark R CEE
Latton B (North Wilts C) CSSEE
Lea (Lee) R CEE
Lea Wood B CEM
Leeds & Liverpool C CNWE
Leek B CWM
Leicester Nav CEM
Leicestershire & Northamptonshire Union C CEM
Leigh B CNWE
Leominster C CSWB
Leven C CYNEE
Liffey R uf CSI
Limehouse Cut CEE
Limerick-Killaloe C CSI
Linton Lock Nav CYNEE
Liskeard & Looe Union C CSWE
Lismore C CSI
Little Eaton B CEM
Little Ouse R CEE
Little Stour R CSSEE
Llangollen C CWM
Llanymynech B CWM
Llansamlet C CSWB
Llechryd Cut CSWB
Loch Morlich Cs CS
Lockington Nav CYNEE
Long Sandall Cut CYNEE
London & Cambridge Junc C pr CEE
Longcot B CSSEE
Longford B CSI
Longford Bridge B CNWE
Lord Hays B CWM
Lothing, Lake CEE
Lough Allen C CSI
Lough Corrib CSI
Lough Erne CSI
Lough Neagh CNI
Loughborough Nav CEM
Loughor R CSWB
Louth C CEE
Lower Avon (Warws) Nav WS, CWM
Lower Bann R CNI
Lower Douglas Nav CNWE
Lower Medway R CSSEE
Lugg R uf CSWB
Lydney C CSWB

Macclesfield C CWM
Mackworth's C CSWB
MacMurray's C CSSEE
Maesmarchog B CSWB
Maigue R CSI
Mallow-Lombardstown C CSI
Manchester, Bolton & Bury C CNWE
Manchester & Salford Junc C CNWE
Manchester Ship C CNWE
Manvers B CEM
Mardyke C CEE
Market Weighton C CYNEE
Medway (Lower) R CSSEE
Medway (Upper) R CSSEE
Medway & Thames C pr CSSEE
Melton Mowbray Nav CEM
Mersey & Irwell Nav CNWE
Mersey R CNWE
Methley Cut CYNEE
Mexborough Cut CYNEE
Middle Level Navs CEE
Middlewich B CWM
Milltown Feeder B CSI
Millwall C CEM

Rievaulx Abbey Cs	CYNEE
Ringsend B	CSI
Ripon C	CYNEE
Robinetts B	CEM
Rochdale B	CNWE
Rochdale C	CNWE
Roding R	CEE
Rolle C	CSWE
Romford C uf	CEE
Rother (Eastern) R	CSSEE
Rother (Western) R	CSSEE
Royal C	CSI
Royal Military C	CSSEE
Rufford B	CNWE
Runcorn & Latchford C	CNWE
Runcorn & Weston C	CNWE
Rushall C	CWM
St Columb C	CSWE
St Helens C	CNWE
St Nicholas Bay Harbour & Canterbury C pr	CSSEE
Salisbury & Southampton C	CSSEE
Saltney C	CWM
Salwarpe R	CWM
Sandhills B	CWM
Sankey Brook Nav	CNWE
Sankey Canal	CNWE
Scarriff R	CSI
Seaton Nav	CSSEE
Selby C	CYNEE
Severn R	CWM
Severn & Wye Rly & C	CSWB
Shannon R	CSI
Sharpness New Docks & Gloucester & Birmingham Nav	CWM
Sheffield C	CYNEE
Sheffield & South Yorkshire Nav	CYNEE
Shrewsbury C	CWM
Shropshire C	CWM
Shropshire Union C	CWM
Slaney R	CSI
Sleaford Nav	CEE
Slough B	CEM
Smith's C	CSWB
Sneyd B	CWM
Soar R	CEM
Soham Lode	CEE
Soho Loop	CWM
Somersetshire Coal C	CSSEE
South Forty Foot Drain	CEE
Southampton & Salisbury C	CSSEE
Springs B	CNWE
Stamford C	CEE
Stafford B	CWM
Staffs & Worcs C	CWM
Stainforth & Keadby C	CYNEE
Staniland's C	CYNEE
Stanley Dock B	CNWE
Stevenston C	CS
Stockport B (Ashton)	CNWE
Stockport B (Bridgewater) pr	CNWE
Stort R	CEE
Stour (Kent) R	CSSEE
Stour, Little (Kent) R	CSSEE
Stour (Suffolk) R	CEE
Stour (Worcs) R	CWM
Stourbridge C	CWM
Stourbridge Extension C	CWM
Stover C	CSWE
Strabane C	CNI
Stratford-upon-Avon C	CEM,WS
Stroudwater C	CSSEE
Suir R	CSI
Suffolk Broads	CEE
Surrey & Hampshire C	CSSEE
Surrey & Kent C	CSSEE
Sussex Ouse	CSSEE
Sutherland's, Duke of C	CWM
Swaffham Lode	CEE
Swale R	CYNEE
Swansea C	CSWB
Tamar Manure Nav	CSWE
Tame Valley C	CWM
Tattershall C	CEE
Tavistock C	CSWE
Taw R	CSWE
Tees R	CYNEE
Teign R	CSWE
Teme R	CWM
Tennant C	CSWB
Thames R	CSSEE
Thames & Medway C	CSSEE
Thames & Severn C	CSSEE
Thanet's, Lord, C	CNWE
Thatto Heath C	CNWE
Thorne & Hatfield Moors Peat Cs	CYNEE
Thorney R	CEE

Index